NEGOTIATING LOCAL KNOWLEDGE

Power and Identity in Development

EDITED BY
JOHAN POTTIER, ALAN BICKER AND PAUL SILLITOE

Pluto Press

LONDON • STERLING, VIRGINIA

First published 2003
by PLUTO PRESS
345 Archway Road, London N6 5AA
and 22883 Quicksilver Drive,
Sterling, VA 20166–2012, USA

www.plutobooks.com

British Library Cataloguing in Publication Data
A catalogue record for this book is available from
the British Library

ISBN 0 7453 2007 4 hardback
ISBN 0 7453 2006 6 paperback

Library of Congress Cataloging in Publication Data
Negotiating local knowledge : power and identity in development / edited
by Johan Pottier, Alan Bicker and Paul Sillitoe.
    p. cm. — (Anthropology, culture, and society)
  ISBN 0–7453–2007–4 (hardback) — ISBN 0–7453–2006–6 (pbk.)
  1. Indigenous peoples—Politics and government. 2. Political
anthropology. 3. Ethnophilosophy. I. Bicker, Alan. II. Sillitoe, Paul.
III. Pottier, Johan. IV. Series.
  GN380 .N44 2003
  306.2—dc21
                                                            2002156330

10   9   8   7   6   5   4   3   2   1

Designed and produced for Pluto Press by
Chase Publishing Services, Fortescue, Sidmouth EX10 9QG, England
Typeset from disk by Stanford DTP Services, Towcester
Printed in the European Union by
Antony Rowe Ltd, Chippenham and Eastbourne, England

CONTENTS

ACKNOWLEDGEMENTS

The organisation of a large event such as the Association of Social Anthropologists' conference in 2000 at the School of Oriental and African Studies, University of London, and the subsequent collection of papers into a volume like this one, depends on the support and assistance of numerous people. We wish to thank in particular Jennifer Law and her band of postgraduate volunteers from the MA Anthropology of Development programme (SOAS) for efficient conference administration; Suzanna Cassidy for generous and invaluable assistance with preparing the manuscript; and Hadija Pottier, Fifi Pottier and Rachelle Woolman for witty conversations (and loads of fun). We also applaud the popular bank that used lavish space and inspired graphics at Heathrow airport to remind all travellers: 'Never Underestimate the Importance of Local Knowledge' (summer 2002).

We dedicate this book to the memory of
Patrick Sikana
whose young life and career as an advocate of local knowledge
and rights was brutally cut short in a plane crash in Adbidjan

1 NEGOTIATING LOCAL KNOWLEDGE: AN INTRODUCTION

Johan Pottier

Two decades ago, social anthropology became interested in 'indigenous knowledge' as a possible antidote to the failures of externally driven, transfer-of-technology focused, top-down development (UNESCO-Nuffic 1999: 11; Warren 1998). Underpinned by some deeply rooted assumptions, for instance, that local knowledge was bounded, static, consensual, non-reflective and unscientific (Howes and Chambers 1979), the initial search for indigenous knowledge convinced both anthropologists and developers that it was legitimate to look for and extract local knowledge elements for use in science. If local knowledge had anything to offer, it was because science could make use of it. The presumed consensual character of local knowledge, moreover, resulted in the further assumption that local knowledge 'systems' applied uniformly over extensive regions and time zones. Concretely and positively, the 'discovery' of indigenous knowledge demanded that development practitioners be receptive to the technology, skills and accumulated knowledge of people everywhere (Brokensha, Warren and Werner 1980; Richards 1985). On the negative side, the enthusiasm for local knowledge data produced some exaggerated claims about its value. Thus in agricultural research, correcting the bias against local knowledge sometimes resulted in the erroneous view that peasant farmers were *collectively* rational, even super-rational, everywhere (Fairhead 1993).

But the neat distinction between science and local knowledge did not last. First, under scrutiny, local knowledge began to reveal itself as the multifarious, contestable product of an ever-evolving syncretistic process (Scoones and Thompson 1994; Mundy and Compton 1995; Sillitoe 1998). The unitary concept 'local knowledge' fragmented into a plurality of local knowledges. Second, science came to be viewed as less universal

1

and more particularistic than hitherto assumed (Agrawal 1995; Gardner and Lewis 1996). These new understandings prompted anthropologists to rethink the dichotomy. Increasingly, the blurring of this grand divide made researchers more conscious of the political economy of knowledge-for-development; that is, more aware of the risk of intellectual (and material) hegemony and more aware that a degree of local autonomy is required if sustained development is to emerge.

The post-modern challenge, however, also problematised the concept of hegemony: the exercise of power was complex business. At the Fourth Decennial Conference of the ASA (Association of Social Anthropologists of the Commonwealth), a short decade ago, there was consensus that 'the bounded' needed to be replaced by 'the relational' – and that this substitution, this moving away from ontological categories towards interwoven patterns, meant that from now on anthropologists would regard 'knowledge' as simultaneously local and global (Moore 1996). The conference called for a better appreciation of 'the complexities and techniques of *knowledge production* within and between societies, groups and regions' (1996: 14; emphasis added). Today, the intersection of power and knowledge remains fraught with uncertainty and contra-diction. While there is much to be said for a perspective that views transnational hegemonic power as too fragmented to shape local conditions uniformly (Long 1996; Arce and Long 1999), it is also clear that powerful processes of disempowerment *are* at work, most notoriously through the patenting of life forms (Shiva 1992; IDRC 1994; Pottier 1999). Processes of disempowerment beg the question whether the optimistic, relational approach to understanding hegemony can be sustained.

Set in the broad context of global change and planned development, this volume explores knowledge as embodied practice and addresses the negotiated character of knowledge production with reference to the knowledge interfaces (Long and Long 1992) between local communities (their practices and discourses) and external agents of change, who have their own practices and discourses. No clear-cut distinction between 'local community' and 'external agents' must be assumed, however. Contributors recognise that the production of knowledge, in both development and non-development contexts, is acutely political, because 'what is excluded and who is qualified to know involves acts of power' (Hobart 1993). Knowledge production, we maintain, is embedded in social and cultural processes imbued with aspects of power, authority and legitimation; the act of producing knowledge involves social struggle, conflict and negotiation. Detailed attention to knowledge interfaces allows us to study what happens when 'local knowledge' – which means different things in different places, and different things to people who share the same space – is translated for the purpose of national or international use. And, vice versa, the interface approach throws light on what happens when international policy discourses are invoked for use in specific local settings. There are implications here for anthropology's role in development. We argue that an empirically grounded understanding of how knowledge(s) is (are) produced through the mediation of unequal power relations and processes of translation is a prerequisite for any serious attempt to instigate dialogue and make *all* stakeholders benefit from development initiatives.

The volume's focus on how knowledge for development is negotiated through processes of translation demands that we reflect on the nature of what is loosely called 'local knowledge'. To enable appropriate reflection on how local knowledge is constructed, the volume contains some contributions that are not about development *per se*. This is particularly true of the early chapters by Marchand (Chapter 2) and Kaur (Chapter 3), where the emphasis is on demonstrating ethnographically that researchers need to be aware of the fact that 'local knowledge' may have properties that lie beyond language (Marchand) and even beyond the strictly local (Kaur). The latter are 'allowed in' (and transformed) through the mediation of established cultural parameters. Developers need to take heed of these important corrections to the common assumption that all manifestations of 'local knowledge' are strictly local and always accessible through verbal communication.

LOCAL KNOWLEDGE IN DEVELOPMENT

What do we mean by local knowledge in the context of development? When reviewing two landmark publications from the late 1980s, *Farmer First* (Chambers et al. 1989) and *Indigenous Knowledge Systems* (Warren et al. 1989), David Marsden outlined the views and expectations of the day:

The problems of rural development are no longer seen to reside in the 'traditional' cultures of under-developed people, but rather in the partial and biased understandings that have emanated from the unreflexive application of a western scientific rationality, and in the results of a rapacious and selfish capitalism that has exacerbated rather than reduced inequalities. Indeed, 'traditional cultures' are now seen as containing the bases for any effective development.

For all these reasons there is a heightened awareness of the central importance of indigenous knowledge systems in the construction of sustainable strategies for rural development. ... The 'blue-print' approach is giving way to a negotiated, situation-specific approach which demands a dialogue between the different parties to the interventions that are constructed in the name of development, and which recognises the important, often crucial, knowledge that the traditional recipients of development aid have to offer. (Marsden 1990: 267)

The present volume provides an update on the idea of a 'negotiated, situation-specific approach' to development situations. Is the demand for dialogue being met, who is participating and on whose terms? These are key questions. But the specific aim of this volume is to go beyond the over-simplistic 'us' and 'them' dichotomy, Western scientists versus local knowledge holders, in order to explore a number of local encounters in which knowledges (plural) are negotiated by a multitude of stakehold-ers. This specific aim invites us to unpack some of the boundedness in vogue in the late 1980s, in particular regarding the concept of 'traditional culture' and the implied assumption that there is consensus on what constitutes useful local knowledge. New questions beg. If there is dialogue, how is it structured? Whose representations are conveyed? Are there dialogues within Dialogue, knowledges within Knowledge? How exactly does power come in? Is dialogue necessarily about the search for and validation of local knowledge(s)? The focus of our collection concerns *local-level processes of knowledge negotiation*; processes that remain little documented and understood.

In offering ethnographies of development dialogue, we demonstrate that 'local knowledge' needs to be understood in the broadest of terms to encompass not only people's understandings of the social universes they inhabit, but also of their rights. As Sillitoe and Wilson (this volume, Chapter 11) put it in the context of mining in Papua New Guinea, 'when we talk about indigenous knowledge … we are referring largely to the need for a better understanding of, and accommodation to, people's knowledge of their rights to land, their tenure arrangements and their approach to payments such as compensation' (p. 244). In other words, the local knowledge debate is not limited to discussing seemingly bounded, technical expertise, of which it is sometimes said that it belongs to 'traditional culture'. Instead, over the past decade, a clear under-standing has emerged that knowledge cannot be separated from the social context in which it develops, and that any analysis of the concept must include an appreciation of the power relations that underpin it.

It is exceedingly recognised that what is important in studying local knowledge is not so much 'bodies of facts', but the issue of 'how, rather than what, things are known' (Gardner and Lewis 1996: 74). When it first emerged, this *how*-focused approach was tied to a critique of the 'Farmer First' movement. While the latter had provided a welcome corrective to the common assumption that traditional beliefs and practices were obstacles to progress, as Marsden's review indicates, the movement tended 'to simplify and essentialise local knowledge' (Gardner and Lewis 1996: 74) by assuming that, like scientific knowledge, it too could be understood as a 'system' (see Gatter 1993; Richards 1993; Scoones and Thompson 1994). Today, we know that this assumption is not necessarily true, not even in the case of modern science. The growing awareness that local knowledge does not exist in isolation but interacts in a variety of ways with the science and practices of development agencies, has resulted in a thorough questioning of its presumed boundedness. Local knowledge 'never stands still' (Sillitoe 1998: 230), it is 'dynamic and strategic' (Sikana 1994: 82), continually shaped and reshaped, thus giving rise to a plethora of diverse knowledges and practices. Consequently, we take care not to approach local knowledge as unquestioningly endogenous, but highlight how local people regularly experiment with exogenous elements to strengthen their own knowledge repertoires.[1] The incorporation of external/global elements in local knowledges receives much attention in this volume, for example, where Hindu religion meets nuclear science and politics (Kaur, Chapter 3), and where Welsh oil workers weave their active engagements with global corporate discourse into their own thoughts on local industry (Arce and Fisher, Chapter 4). In the latter case, the oil workers' dynamic under-standings of their work environment contrast sharply with the reductionist understanding held by transnational stakeholders. People's knowledge, in other words, is never exclusively local, but results from complex *negotiation practices* linked to knowledge interfaces. Similarly, Raminder Kaur documents that festival tableaux at the Mumbai festival (Maharashtra, India) reveal how local understandings of the nuclear debate are embedded in a web of intersecting discourses whose discursive elements are part of the larger narrative of the nation.

In the same sense that the binary endogenous/exogenous view of knowledge does not apply much to everyday reality, so we must let go of the misconception that science and local knowledge (or Rural People's Knowledge [RPK] in *Beyond Farmer First* jargon) would be diametrically opposed, with RPK being specific, context-bound and practical, and science objective and generalisable. In the mid-1990s, Scoones and Thompson argued convincingly that 'RPK and western agricultural science are both general *and* specific, theoretical *and* practical. Both are value-laden, context specific and influenced by social relations of power' (Scoones and Thompson 1994: 29–30). The image of two opposed knowledge 'systems' does not reflect the complex and often contradictory processes that structure development at the local level.

Moreover, we must be open to the suggestion that expressions of local knowledge may say more about the social relations in which they emerge

than about knowledge as such. Fairhead's research in Bwisha, eastern
Zaire (now DR Congo) has yielded a telling example, which he discusses
within the wider problematic of whether and how technical knowledge
is locally varied and disputed. From his fieldwork Fairhead recalls how a
woman and her husband discussed

> whether or not cassava cultivation in a fallow killed *Digitaria abysinica*. She
> claimed it could, which he denied. What they were really arguing about,
> however, and what made the discussion so impassioned, was whether or not the
> husband would allow his wife to cultivate cassava (a crop she would control) on
> their fallow. This example forces us to question a common assumption: that ITK
> [Indigenous Technical Knowledge] exists like a lost and untranslated technical
> manual authored by a particular 'culture', and published by the researcher who
> has acquired the script. ... If I had asked only men, I might have treated the
> statement 'cassava cannot suppress *Digitaria abysinica*' as a quotation from
> Bwisha's 'technical manual'. Asking men and women independently, I might
> have felt compelled to publish two (gender differentiated) 'manuals', relating
> each to their different experiences with cassava.
>
> ... what is interesting here is less that men think this, or women think that,
> but (a) that as an agro-ecological process 'suppression' is locally understood and
> probably underlies many practices; (b) that differences of opinion (in applying
> this principle) exist, and these differences may reflect different politico-economic
> experience as well as technical experience; and (c) that it is quite common to find
> political or gender disputes (e.g. over access to and control over resources) being
> argued in an ecological idiom. Thus the ... issue is not just 'to what extent is
> technical knowledge distributed in a community' but also 'how and to what
> extent is technical explanation locally varied and disputed?' and 'how are varied
> indigenous technical opinions socio-politically as well as technically
> constructed?' (Fairhead 1992: 4)

Another demonstration showing that technical knowledge is structured
through politico-economic experience, and thus open to contestation,
came to me during a PRA exercise on food security in Soroti, Uganda, in
1993. During this workshop, the first one in the region since the end of
the insurgency, a prominent local farmer volunteered a technical lesson
in how to grow millet successfully. Farmer Obi

> shared his thoughts on millet, saying that after he had lost his bulls during raids
> by Karimojong, he picked up the hoe and started digging. This he did mostly with
> the help of his wife and children, but *timing* was of the essence: 'My wisdom is
> that I start preparing my land in December, so that by the end of January I am
> already sowing millet. The seeds are left in the soil until the rains come. I also
> make the garden very clean before sowing. And, as soon as the rains come, I
> plant groundnuts in a different field when others are just starting their millet
> cultivation. Then, as soon as possible, I prepare a third garden for potatoes. This
> is the order in which I grow my crops. When you delay broadcasting millet until
> the rains have started, the germination will be poor.' ...

Hearing this, a [poor] woman farmer challenged him: 'The problem with early planting is that a lot of weeds sprout up, which is not the case when you delay until the rains start.' She implied that Mr Obi's method might be the best, but that farmers need *access to sufficient labour power* if they are to weed thoroughly. And most farmers in the workshop area simply do not command a sufficiently large labour pool. ... Food insecurity, [this farmer implied,] is best understood as a problem rooted in social inequalities that restrict access to labour. (Pottier 1997: 209; emphasis added)

Examples such as the above, and others can be added, make it imperative that development practitioners accept that one cannot discuss 'knowledge' without discussing the economic and political dimensions of its emergence and use. Power and control are central to the articulation of knowledge, and a multitude of actors needs to be considered. When this is done, it mostly follows that all talk of 'knowledge' becomes talk of 'knowledges'.

Besides demonstrating that 'local knowledge' is dynamic, diverse, sometimes contested or used euphemistically, and always socially and culturally embedded,[2] anthropologists have reflected on the issue of how knowledge is expressed and accessed. In particular, they have questioned whether language is a sufficient tool for accessing knowledge. Paul Richards, for example, has shown that indigenous knowledge among West African cultivators contains strong elements of improvisation, which include drumming as well as meeting contingencies through altering cropping patterns, and that this level of performed improvisation goes unnoted when 'scientific' agricultural experts assess farmer knowledge (Richards 1993). The thin line between verbally expressed knowledge, and performance and creativity is a focus for discussion in the chapter by Trevor Marchand (Chapter 2), who warns that those in pursuit of local knowledge are disadvantaged when they take language to be the principal means of knowledge transmission. In Sana'a, Yemen, where the formation of a moral subject constitutes the distinguishing hallmark of the relations between the master builder and the apprentice, language is an inadequate tool for understanding the transmission of knowledge skills. The content of the master builder's knowledge eludes any coherent verbalised articulation, largely because such expert knowledge is not objectified. Marchand's fieldwork experience as an apprentice builder prompts him to challenge the language-centred theories of knowledge transmission that have dominated the twentieth century. While the chapter is a sophisticated theoretical exploration of how knowledge must be approached as embodied practice, its insights into the acquisition and transmission of knowledge have important consequences for good practice in development.

Whatever form they take, articulations of local knowledge are always complex. Where language plays a key role in transmitting knowledge, which happens in the majority of chapters in this volume, local people's concepts and words are often marked, as Alex Argenti-Pillen writes (Chapter 9), by polysemy and ambiguity, qualities that have no place in the discourse of national elites involved in development or humanitarian assistance. The theme is a central preoccupation in this volume. Mary Rack (Chapter 8) observes a similar contrast in her research on temple renovation in West Hunan, China, where state representatives label complex practices at unregulated temples as backward superstition. Complex articulations of local knowledge are also discouraged in the context of development research in Uganda (Frankland, Chapter 13), in land-compensation claims in Papua New Guinea (Sillitoe and Wilson, Chapter 11), and in the land claims by Aboriginal groups in Queensland, Australia (Smith, Chapter 6). Analysing the procedures through which Mungkan Kaanju Aboriginees attempt to reclaim land, Ben Smith observes that the process revolves around the production of two opposed representations of knowledge, that is; an official legal representation which distinguishes between sites with which claimants are 'traditionally' affiliated and sites that are *merely* of 'historical' importance (and in which the former are prioritised over the latter), and an Aboriginal representation in which it is inappropriate that 'traditional' and (even brief) 'historical' associations should be separated.

The emphasis on power in the study of local knowledges inevitably means that questions must be asked about profit and compensation. In his overview paper 'Indigenous Knowledge and Applied Anthropology' (1998), Paul Sillitoe underscores that sensitivity to ethnocentrism must go beyond the exposure of the erroneous assumption held by some scientists that they can simply 'pluck information relating to their specialisms out of cultural context and treat it as independent technical facts' (Sillitoe 1998: 228). An awareness of the pitfalls of ethnocentrism, Sillitoe stresses, must include a response to the burning question of who will benefit. The establishment of partnerships founded on dialogue and participation – involving a range of stakeholders – may be much needed, but one still needs to ask: 'Empowering Whom through Participation?' While it is true that the business of incorporating local knowledge into development theory and practice hinges on the successful 'translation' of culturally embedded knowledges, which is a bridging exercise, it is equally true – and crucial if 'translation' is to succeed – that political agendas must be identified and understood. One central problem here is that development initiatives launched from the outside smack of paternalism (*we* have come to help *you* solve *your* problems), another is that such initiatives may be hijacked by local interest groups. Referring to the actor-oriented approach to the study of development, an approach spearheaded by Norman Long (1992, 2001), Sillitoe points out that

negotiations [between stakeholders] may be difficult not only because of diffi- culties in cross-cultural communication and understanding but also because of the inevitable political aspects (Long and Villareal 1994). Different interest groups may interpret research findings quite differently and manipulate them accordingly, attempting to use them to impose their views on others. (Sillitoe 1998: 232)

In this volume we go further still. Not only do local interest groups attempt to *interpret* research findings, but they are also actively involved in *generating* research data that acquire an aura of respectability through so-called participatory development practices. With every 'knowledge encounter' we ask: whose knowledge is privileged? Today, with the benefit of an actor-oriented approach to studying development, answers can never be easy or straightforward. Not only is there a plurality of knowledges to be grappled with – and this affects even the so-called rational, scientific knowledge of development – but we are also asking questions about the locus of power, questions that at times force us to abandon the idea of hegemonic domination.

Here again, the thinking within anthropology and sociology has become dynamic. It used to be different, less complicated. In the early days of 'Anthropology of Development', power used to be approached more in terms of hegemony.

HEGEMONY AND THE KNOWLEDGE-POWER REGIME

Contributions to the post-modern critique of development (Ferguson 1990; Escobar 1991, 1995; Hobart 1993) all stress that development can only be an instrument of domination, that is, an instrument for the production and reproduction of relations of social inequality. Development practice, they highlight, involves discourses and techniques that are integral to the exercise of power. Gardner and Lewis reflect on the legacy of the post-modern critique:

Development practice, [Escobar] argues, uses a specific corpus of techniques which organise a type of knowledge and a type of power. The expertise of development specialists transcends the social realities of the 'clients' of development, who are labelled and thus structured in particular ways ('women- headed households' / 'small farmers', etc.). Clients are thus controlled by development and can only manoeuvre within the limits set by it. As he puts it in *Encountering Development*, 'Development has achieved the status of a certainty in the social imaginary' (Escobar 1995: 5). (Gardner and Lewis 1996: 72)

Within the same framework, development policy is understood to be institutionally grounded activity. The post-modern interest in viewing development as a knowledge-power regime has led some anthropologists to argue that 'setting the limits' ultimately results in attributions of ignorance. From this perspective, 'the scientific and "rational" knowledge favoured by development constructs foreign "experts" as agents, and local people as passive and ignorant' (Gardner and Lewis 1996: 72). The gap, Hobart believes, is 'unbridgeable' (Hobart 1993: 16).

Despite its immensely valuable insights, the post-modern critique has itself come under fire for being overly preoccupied with discourse, with the language of construction, thus paying insufficient attention to development as a set of situated practices and relationships. Absent from the post-modern critique are refined questions about the locus of power, questions that have drawn the attention of *anthropologists with development experience*. The latter have challenged the assumption that development situations are necessarily marked by hegemony, disjuncture and an absolute incommensurability between so-called local and western scientific knowledge (Rew 1994; Gardner 1997).

Critics of the post-modern critique of development have been quick to point out that their own first-hand experiences of development *practice* reveal that there is little room for an argument structured around the 'growth of ignorance' paradigm. One problem with viewing development as aiming towards control and surveillance, development anthropologists stress, is that it is not always easy to determine the direction of power. Analyses of development in terms of hegemonic power fail to recognise, for instance, that a discourse of control can also be a discourse of entitlement through which 'recipients' press claims on the state or on international development agencies (Cooper and Packard 1997: 4). As Cooper and Packard put it: 'locating power does not show that it is determinant or that a particular discourse is not appropriable for other purposes' (1997: 3). Recipients of development attention, moreover, can also – sometimes, not always – impact on policy formulations. It is therefore difficult to feel confident about the notion of an absolute incommensurability separating development agencies' representations and the actualities of situated social practices (Hobart 1993: 16).

Using the positive experience of a development encounter in India in which 'locals' and 'outsider experts' resolved their differences and negotiated mutually acceptable outcomes, Alan Rew has forcefully challenged Hobart's ignorance/incommensurability thesis. Rew's ethnographic analysis of the negotiations he recorded (and took part in) in Rampura, a village in the process of relocation because of mining activity, made him reflect that the 'communication difficulties' of development practice look very different – that is, less a matter of forceful imposition – when they are understood

through direct analysis of the representations of development project protagonists rather than through conjecture. Although there were gaps and difficulty in communication at Rampura, there was also a tactical use of representational systems to aid negotiations. The end result was a *growth in knowledge and social innovation*, not ignorance and incommensurability. (Rew 1994: 292; emphasis added)

Rew's conclusion was based on the observation that villagers, engineers, bureaucrats and several anthropologists had successfully conducted 'long-drawn-out negotiations ... concerning the character and lay out of the new housing and the method of rebuilding individual houses' (Rew 1994: 285). The issue of house design, an issue as difficult to resolve as that of compensation, was ultimately resolved in a manner that met both the requirements of the Government of India (that is, the mining company agreed to adopt a 'site and service' approach) and the villagers' requirement 'for self-built farmsteads with space to lock up their animals, equipment and crops, while remaining adjacent to their *jati* co-members' (1994: 289).

In a different context, David Seddon (1993) reached a similar conclusion when working for an IFAD project in Mali, where one chief consultant was 'a Malian, a Touareg, a native of Kendal *cercle*, and a socio-linguist' (Seddon 1993: 99). This consultant's role and performance '[did] not square readily with Hobart's inclination to interpret development as a Manichean struggle of epistemologies between which communication is difficult if not impossible' (Grillo 1997: 24, commenting on Seddon 1993).

Equitable, complementary partnerships between scientists and local farmers are possible, as has recently been observed also in Siaya district, south-west Kenya. From here, Nelson Mango (2002) reports how farmers working impoverished soils have been attempting to de-link from the use of expensive technology and infrastructure, and to recover 'traditional' crops they used to grow. The search is on for 'the right maize seeds' to substitute for the hybrid maize that has dominated the landscape for some time. This search is accompanied by a strong interest in the use of *Tithonia diversifolia* (wild sunflower) as green biomass manure. Introduced into the region over a hundred years ago, as an ornamental shrub from Mexico, farmers now grow this shrub in hedges. They know that it produces

large quantities of biomass that can be incorporated directly into the soil as green manure or used as mulch. ... Farmers continuously apply this green manure during the growing period of the [maize] crop either by placing it along the rows of plants or by incorporating it into the soil.

   Tithonia was farmers' own discovery. (Mango 2002: 246)

Siaya farmers' determination to de-link from expensive technology (and thus achieve better household food security) is now supported by extension staff from the joint ICRAF/KEFRI/KARI programme based at Maseno station.[3] Researchers at Maseno station have conducted trials and have proved 'that *Tithonia* leaves contain 50% more phosphorus than legumes, and similar levels of nitrogen and potassium, even though *Tithonia* is not a nitrogen-fixing plant' (2002: 247). Scientists then contributed some of their own knowledge to that of the farmers: combining *Tithonia* biomass with rock phosphate on soils low in phosphorus effectively restores soil fertility. The technique of combining *Tithonia* biomass with rock phosphate is now increasingly popular on degraded soils. The senior research scientist at Maseno clarifies:

We obtain rock phosphate from Minjingu in Tanzania as it is not available in the local markets. Between 1996 and 1999, we have been providing it for free to farmers who offered their land for on-farm trials. The challenge is to create awareness on the benefits of rock phosphate for Western Kenya and to assure that it will be available from local traders. For sustainability, it requires normal processing, packaging and subsequently selling in the market regularly. (quoted in Mango 2002: 248)

Mango's appreciation of the positive co-operation between farmers and extension workers shows that dialogue can take place. He does not pretend that everything is perfect, for some development interventions in the area have indeed resulted in serious village-level power struggles (2002: 262–6), but the prospect of an empowering dialogue very clearly exists in the search for better soil fertility.

   David Lewis and colleagues (Lewis et al. 1993) also provide a compelling argument that shows how local knowledge – in this case, of aquaculture – can be harnessed in ways that effectively reduce poverty. Lewis starts from the observation that development planners and imple-menters lack knowledge about the social and economic conditions under which low-income fish-seed traders in Bangladesh operate, and that this knowledge gap implies that communities often receive few benefits from development programmes aimed at them. Faced with this everyday reality, he proposes that the knowledgeable but economically vulnerable fish-seed traders could be trained as extension workers. The advantage of an 'indigenised' extension-trader strategy would be that the approach could 'build upon local knowledge systems and transactions, utilise existing regular face-to-face contact with the client group in remote locations, keep down costs and follow the existing patterns of information demand and exchange' (1993: 193).

Ethnographic appreciations of the diversity and dynamic nature of development encounters invite us to take a closer look at the social and political construction of knowledge. As we shall see later, and as contributors to this volume also suggest, understanding how knowledge is constructed is hugely important because misreading local politics means misreading the potential for 'empowerment'. This misreading is a concern that should lie at the heart of the every debate on local knowledge.

While there is no shortage of evidence that positive partnerships can be forged, it remains imperative that social analysts consider the likelihood that even positive outcomes may still create or reinforce certain forms of inequality. The issue is taken up in Fairhead's reflections on his role as a 'cultural broker' positioned between CIAT's bean improvement programme in the Great Lakes Region, Central Africa, and local farmers (Fairhead 1993). Fairhead's brief was to record farming practices and local statements about these practices, and thus help improve the knowledge CIAT's plant pathologist in the region had of local farming. Although many aspects of local farming were meticulously detailed, such as those relating to crop health and failure, Fairhead ended up questioning his role as a knowledge broker. One particular frustration was that what he presented as local knowledge was far more empirical and dynamic than scientists understood.

In Bwisha, the dramatic and ceaseless changes in local agriculture and social organization over the last seventy years mean that each new generation of farmers faces new agricultural problems. Local knowledge is better envisaged as empirical and hypothetical. Nobody locally is in a position to say what is 'right' and what is 'wrong' and to turn a farmer's hypothesis into truth. Perhaps those who document ITK have taken up this role and have become 'arbitrators of truth' for this knowledge. But they (we) should recognize that local knowledge lies as much in its methods, in its lack of overbearing authority, and in its fluidity as in 'what is known'. It is living and dynamic, so in describing it one ought to be very careful not to see it as – or worse, turn it into – stone. (Fairhead 1993: 193)

Those who aspire to be 'knowledge brokers', Fairhead continues, should be more conscious of the fact that social distinctions (between men and women, for instance, or between ethnic groups) are often drawn in relation to knowledge. And this 'knowledge' may be more akin to myth. The point is that social differences (and distances) are created and maintained

through the ideological production of ...'myths of difference' and through related depictions of 'different knowledges'. These define what people can and should know, what they can, or should, or should not do, or have done. Although there is a concomitant ideology of complementarity between the groups, it is a com-plementarity within a hierarchy; complementarity within domination. I consider the representations of difference between researcher (science) and farmer (ITK) according to their knowledge as a similar mythology of difference in which com-plementarity (science-researcher and ITK-farmer) is created between the ideologically created entities, but in a hierarchical way (science-researcher > ITK-farmer). It leads us to think that the farmer complements the scientist, and not vice versa. (Fairhead 1993: 201)

Fairhead is not alone in making this kind of argument. In an important contribution to *Beyond Farmer First* (1994), Patrick Sikana argues that soil scientists are not interested in local perceptions of how topsoil properties tend to change over time. Instead, scientists 'invite' farmers to force their categories – categories that have so much practical value – into the technical framework used by soil surveyors. It is here that scientists need to rethink. To achieve real partnership between science and indigenous knowledge, Sikana contends, conventionally positivist scientists need to come to terms with the dynamic and strategic nature of farmers' knowledge and practices. Scientists need to prove to farmers that they are capable of synthesis, in the same way that farmers themselves have already proved how they can incorporate 'elements from outside' into their own knowledge system(s) (Sikana 1994: 82). The appropriation of local knowledge for use in science has been well documented (for example, Fujisaka 1992: 72; Mooney 1993; Pottier 1999: 168–87), but appropriation is not the same as achieving synthesis. To achieve synthesis, scientists need first to drop the (political) tendency to squeeze flexible farmer categories into more rigid scientific categories. They must begin by asking how useful Western scientific categories are in the quest for a better understanding of local knowledges and practices. There are signs, especially in Kenya, that scientists and their organisations are increasingly prepared to incorporate local per-spectives and knowledge (Verma 2001: 242–3). Scientists must sustain the effort and follow it up with (political) questions about whose knowledge counts. And here various levels of knowledge production need to be taken into account. For indeed, what is at stake is not just the dominance of scientific knowledge over local knowledges, the latter must also be understood and assessed in terms of the social hierarchies in which they have arisen.

The conclusion that partnerships, if achieved, are still achieved within relations of inequality and hierarchy, is one that contributors to this volume examine through their first-hand observations. They do so in relation to a number of development scenarios. While debates of 'local knowledge' tend to pertain mostly to the domains of natural resource management and health/medicine,[4] the chapters in this volume apply the concept to a wider range of development domains, including architecture, conflict and conflict prevention, cultural heritage and a number of NGO activities. Each time, debates about knowledge take place in settings controlled by gatekeepers conscious of the power of inter-cultural translation.

DEVELOPMENT INTERVENTION, ACTORS AND THE SOCIAL CONSTRUCTION OF KNOWLEDGE

Appreciating the dynamic (and at times contradictory) nature of development intervention implies that the positivist approach to knowledge needs to be dropped. Instead of seeing knowledge as unitary and systematised, we need an approach premised on different guiding principles, on notions such as

> *discontinuity* not linkage, and *transformation* not transfer of meaning. Knowledge [then] emerges as a product of the interaction and dialogue between specific actors. It is also multi-layered (there always exists a multiplicity of possible frames of meaning) and fragmentary and diffuse rather than unitary and systematized. Not only is it unlikely therefore that different parties (such as farmers, extensionists and researchers) would share the same priorities and parameters of knowledge, but one would also expect 'epistemic' communities (that is, those that share roughly the same sources and modes of knowledge) to be differentiated internally in terms of knowledge repertoires and application. (Long 1992: 274)

The positivist view that knowledge is unitary and systematised explains why modern scientists continue to regard science as superior to local bodies of knowledge, and why they believe that their superior knowledge can easily be transferred, indeed needs to be transferred, in order to replace 'backward' local knowledge. This conceptualisation does not prepare for the reality interventionists often face, which is a reality marked by intended *and unintended* consequences; outcomes shaped by 'the ongoing, interlocking, interplay, distantiation and mutual transformation of different actors' projects' (Long and van der Ploeg 1994: 81). To understand knowledge-in-development one needs to go beyond the simple, binary 'contrast between the perspectives of rural producers and those of bureaucrats' (and scientists) and grasp how knowledge, all knowledge, is imbued with a dynamic quality that stems from 'the ways that different knowledge processes interrelate, and thus reinforce and transform each other, across the rural development interface' (Arce, Villarreal and de Vries 1994: 156). It is best, therefore, to approach knowledge as 'essentially a social construction that results from a particular context and is being reshaped by the encounters and discontinuities that emerge at the points of intersection between actors' lifeworlds' (Long and Villarreal 1993: 160). This actor-oriented approach builds upon the awareness that development intervention

is never realized as a linear process, proceeding in an orderly fashion from 'correct' initial analysis through 'correct' decisions towards 'good' goals. It is often a messy business of decisions that have to be taken in difficult circumstances on the basis of inadequate knowledge, reactions, counter-reactions and compromises and it always constitutes a learning process for all involved. (Crehan and Von Oppen 1988: 114)

By taking an actor-oriented approach to development, Norman Long and colleagues have familiarised us with the idea of knowledgeable local actors whose projects interlock with or de-link from the intervention programmes run by national and international institutions. In doing so, the 'recipients' of development assistance often develop their own solutions by redesigning that which is on offer. The actor-oriented perspective on knowledge has made it possible for us to think in terms of knowledge interfaces, and how these are managed. The approach demands a focus on how 'Knowledge is generated and transformed not in abstract but in relation to the everyday contingencies and struggles that constitute social life' (Long 2001: 170). In this conceptualisation, knowledge 'is not given by simple institutional commitments or assumed sources of power and authority, but rather is an outcome of the inter-actions, negotiations, interfaces and accommodations that take place between different actors and their lifeworlds' (2001: 170).

The emphasis on agency has made Long and others react to the (in their view) misconception that so-called structural obstacles to local actors' creativity would emanate from an essentially rigid structure. Instead, they insist, we must regard structure as consisting primarily of a fluid – and thus transformable – set of properties. Long and van der Ploeg

object to ... the notion of structure as *explanans*. Such a notion of structure amounts to nothing more than a reification of what are considered to be 'central tendencies' and, as soon as heterogeneity is introduced in the analysis, this 'structural approach' withers away. ... In more substantive terms, structure can be characterized as an extremely fluid set of emergent properties, which, on the one hand, results from the interlocking and/or distantiation of various actors' projects, while on the other, it functions as an important point of reference for the further elaboration, negotiation and confrontation of actors' projects. (Long and van der Ploeg 1994: 81; see also Long 2001: 61–3)

Not everyone accepts this conceptualisation, as contributors to this volume testify, and the structure versus agency debate is likely to continue in lively fashion. For the time being, however, we do well to heed the advice of David Booth, who edited the volume in which the paper by Long and van der Ploeg appeared. Booth argued that 'the structure-agency issue remains a central topic for the future of social development research' (Booth 1994: 17).

In debating power and knowledge there is as yet no 'final word'. The tendency is still to go along with Michel Foucault's broad claim that 'the criteria of what constitutes knowledge, what is to be excluded and who is designated as qualified to know involves acts of power' (Foucault 1971). The role of power in the social construction of knowledge remains pervasive and often has a particular effect on knowledge encounters between people or groups differently placed in the social hierarchy. What we must not lose sight of, in other words, is that 'discourses of development are produced by those in power and often result (even if unintentionally) in reproducing power relations between areas of the world and between people' (Gardner and Lewis 1996: 154–5). The effect is well captured in the notion of 'hidden transcript', which James Scott (1990) has introduced

to describe how the exercise of power in nearly all public encounters between resource-rich and resource-poor (and between authority and subordinate) almost always drives a portion of the full social transcript – that is, people's opinions, beliefs, ideas and values – underground. The normal tendency will be for the subservient individual or group to reveal only that part of their full transcript to authorities in power-laden situations that is both safe and appropriate to reveal. The greater the disparity in power between two individuals or groups, the greater the proportion that is likely to be concealed. (Scoones and Thompson 1994: 27)

The 'hidden transcript' theme is central to Novellino's ethnographic portrayal of the knowledge encounters in which Pälawan Batak take part (this volume, Chapter 12).

KNOWLEDGE PRODUCTION AS NEGOTIATED TRANSLATION

In attempting to understand what local knowledge means in specific settings, analysts must turn their attention to the role local elites play – as gatekeepers – in making complex knowledge available to international audiences. In addition, they must recognise that, at a higher level, developers and policy-makers may themselves insist on reducing the complexity of 'local data' accessed by intermediaries. The theme of knowledge production *as negotiated translation*, the volume's most persistent theme, will be examined in the context of Aboriginal land claims (Smith); traumatic stress counselling in war-torn Sri Lanka (Argenti-Pillen); the operations of an international NGO in Bolivia and a transnational company in Wales, UK (Arce and Fisher); the building of a dam on the river Nile (Frankland); participatory development in Batak communities, The Philippines (Novellino); the international response to the conflict in Central Africa (Pottier); conservation in the Algarve, Portugal (Ramos et al.); and negotiation strategies between mining companies and local people in Papua New Guinea (Sillitoe and Wilson).

Contributors commonly report that polysemic local concepts (if not dropped altogether) frequently undergo significant simplification, or more correctly *disambiguation*, before they come to the attention of international development workers. In the counselling of war victims in Sri Lanka, for instance, where local-level translation is mediated by a national elite victorious in the civil war, some highly complex village-level concepts are watered down and then 'relegated unambiguously to the domain of spirit religion, possession and spirit worship' (Argenti-Pillen, this volume p. 199). The Colombo-based elite involved in this humanitarian aid effectively discards all village-level concepts that describe terror-related illnesses and their cures, because such concepts do not fit – and would endanger – their own professional and elite identity. In Uganda, Frankland observed a similar *meltdown of meaning* in the context of a dam project on the river Nile, at Bujagali, where a survey by the construction company had established that the majority of the local (and multi-ethnic) population attaches no importance to the Bujagali shrines and associated myths. The all too wide multi-ethnic sample, however, deflected attention from the ethnographic fact that Bujagali is a Basoga cultural site. The distortion meant that the complex Bujagali spirit world could be trivialised and reduced to the realm of the fantastic; there was no need to take local Basogo cosmology seriously. The meltdown of meaning was reinforced further by the company's recourse to a dubious ethnographic text in which it was claimed that only one clan, the Ntembe, had any real interest in the shrines.

The case studies by Argenti-Pillen and Frankland also reveal that the loss of complex cultural meanings is strongly encouraged by global policies and practices; respectively, the dominance of an international (that is, Anglo-American, and therefore indigenous) discourse on war trauma counselling, and the influence of the World Bank's guidelines on culture. World Bank guidelines, Frankland demonstrates, use a narrow framework in which complex cultural notions and practices are reduced to the more manageable idea of cultural property. Local religious knowledge and practice can thus be 'transmogrified into something that can be bought and sold, built up and then relocated' (Frankland, this volume, p. 312–13). In a similar vein, Sillitoe and Wilson report how the western mining companies that exploit resources on tribal land in Papua New Guinea promote hierarchies within Melanesian societies by forcing them to select individuals as 'representatives' through which to channel their negotiations. Local people and mining companies have come into violent conflict over issues relating to compensation, socio-economic change, land rights and environmental degradation, and there are urgent demands to pioneer innovative new strategies to deal with these problems. The authors contrast the mining companies' approach to negotiations with that of local communities, and investigate the prospects for advancing culturally appropriate methods further to empower local people in decision-making.

The theme of how global discourses are translated in specific cultural settings is also taken up in Kaur's chapter on how the rights and wrongs of nuclear armament are articulated at the Mumbai festival, where the dominant narrative which guides the translation is a religious discourse that sanctifies nuclear power. Identifying a further four politico-cultural narratives, Kaur concludes that the festival displays do not just represent aspects of nuclear knowledge, but re-present them wrapped in narratives that are indicative of, and feed back into, wider socio-cultural contexts. These re-presentations are effectively acts of disambiguation, albeit very creative ones.

Disambiguation also marks the scene Novellino describes. He reports on the nature of development communications involving Batak (Pälawan, Philippines) and national developers who promote conservation measures through participatory means, showing how communications are marked by intended and unintended miscommunication. Not only is local knowledge about the environment deliberately misrepresented (Batak withhold information; outsiders appropriate partial knowledge in order to dismiss it), but Batak also learn to their cost that *their* negotiation skills and rules are routinely misunderstood. For example, Batak silences observed during meetings are commonly mistaken for consent (and sometimes apathy). Such silences, Novellino explains, must be understood rather with reference to Batak ethics, including notions of 'fear', 'anger', 'individual will', 'withdrawal' and 'refusal'. But these notions appear too complex for outsiders to grasp and appreciate. Crucially, outsiders extract Batak knowledge about the environment via pre-set questionnaires that force Batak to respond in terms of restrictive options or outright alien categories. The result is that Batak are portrayed in the development literature as dependent on a single economic activity – the gathering of non-timber forest products (the presumed key to sustainable development) – while not a word is said about the hetero-geneous nature of their economy. This latter point suggests that translation occurs at *both* local and national/international levels.

The occurrence of 'double translation' is taken up also by Arce and Fisher, who comment on the use of anthropological data in policy documents, and by Smith, who shows that whatever biases occur locally (for instance, through the influence of urbanised Aborigines), land claims are ultimately presented in the western legal terms imposed by the Aboriginal Land Act 1991. From their no-win situation, claimant groups oblige by offering the kind of information that reinforces the reductionist form of tradition which white-Australian officials seem to need and desire. Likewise, Arce and Fisher argue that the NGO and the oil company for which they undertook consultancy research, categorised local people in the narrowest of terms (as 'credit beneficiaries' or as 'employees'), terms derived from international policy discourses that do not do justice to local people's rich engagements with global institutions. The problem became most obvious when the qualitative ethnographic reports Arce and Fisher had prepared were melted down into extremely short, manageable chunks of information that would not challenge the universal measuring of human experiences according to abstract units of knowledge. The consultancies thus acted as an affirmation of sound expert knowledge about 'other places'.

Disambiguation at international levels is also explored in the context of the United Nations' search for a solution to the crisis in eastern Congo-Zaire in 1996, a solution applauded by the international community as morally superior because it was *an African solution*. As Pottier analyses, however, the UN perspective on the crisis coincided with that formulated by the Government of Rwanda, led by the Rwandese Patriotic Front and composed mostly of an elite returned from the diaspora, and thus failed to connect with the very complexity of local politics and discourses in eastern Zaire itself (Chapter 10). Humiliated by its failure to halt the genocide in Rwanda in 1994, the UN Security Council made no attempt to contextualise and scrutinise the official Rwandan narrative. Disambiguation resulted, with serious consequences for the population of eastern Zaire (now DR Congo), which at the time I revised the chapter (July 2002) remained subjected to foreign occupation, human rights abuses and an extensive looting of its natural resource base. The events in eastern Zaire in 1996 illustrate the danger – a danger already well understood in debates on technology – that local knowledge is all too often treated as homogeneous, incontestable and applicable over vast areas.

Manuel Ramos et al. (Chapter 7) also focus on the 'meltdown of meaning', which occurs when a high-level authority with development responsibility, called the Park Authority, discovers that the ethnographic study it has commissioned challenges its own worldview and ambition. Here as well, fieldwork-based ethnographic data were sought and then sidelined to make way for whatever 'correct' version the Park Authority wished to promote. Commissioned to study the indigenous culture and knowledge of the Park's 'native population', the researchers ended up exposing authoritative misconceptions about 'the natives' and their role in Portugal's cultural heritage. Reinforcing the key argument that dominant policy-making institutions reduce local complexities to further their own worldviews and interests, Ramos et al. demonstrate how the Park Authority produces and reproduces a technical discourse in which fishing and shellfish collecting communities are portrayed as possessing an exotic culture at the root of (an imagined) Algarvian identity. In this exotic representation, which has urban roots that can be seen in literary texts, photography and film, the park's 'natives' are viewed as the privileged custodians of the lagoon and the oceanic eco-systems that lie beyond. It is this 'exotic culture' which the Park Authority had hoped the team of commissioned anthropologists would also discover, vindicate and reify. Once the ethnographic study completed, the Park Authority showed no interest in how its own re-presentation of a pristine Algarve culture was locally understood and critiqued.

While most contributors touch on the issue of how assisted development is locally critiqued, the theme is addressed most explicitly in the chapters on post-disaster assistance to Montserrat (Skinner, Chapter 5) and temple renovation in West Hunan, China (Rack, Chapter 8). On Montserrat, the indigenous critique, which amounts to a critique of the practices introduced by Britain's Department for International Development (DFID), is conveyed through cultural performances, especially popular theatre, poetry readings and calypso. Performances highlight that outsider knowledge about the island is generalised and insensitive to the local competencies that exist. The local population ('Monts'ratian born and bred'), the critique suggests, possesses the required expertise to turn disaster-related interventions into activities that, compared with DFID practice, will be more accountable, more equitable and more appropriate. As things stand on Montserrat, Britain's colonial government mentality prevails with little or no sign of DFID's commitment to social development. Although it is difficult to say whether the protesters are making any impact on DFID and Whitehall circles, readers will wonder, as does Skinner himself, whether the next generation of Social Development Advisers (SDAs) might not come from within the ranks of the island's expert performers. It may be premature to attempt an answer, yet it is certain that the performers' creativity can be seen 'as part of the general press for cultural, social and political self-determination, or for the recognition of local knowledge and expertise at the very least' (this volume, p. 109).

Rack's chapter on temple practices in West Hunan is another illustration of how modern development initiatives are locally critiqued, that is, criticised and accommodated. Rack proposes that we understand temple practices not as 'superstition', but as modern-day responses to a changing world marked by out-migration and (perceived) local dislocation. While local government applies the label 'superstition' to all activity in temples not registered with an approved religion, those who visit the temples and use their services are well aware, as are those who run the temples, that their 'local traditions' are far from a simple continuation with the past. As with the performances on Montserrat, the resurgence of 'superstitious' practices in West Hunan is best understood as part of an ongoing process by which forms of local knowledge engage with outside forces of change; a process that can also be read as a critique of planned development intervention. This was most clearly illustrated by the spirit medium at the government-controlled temple of the Celestial Kings, who, after government officials expropriated village land to meet urban expansion, announced that the deities had expressed their displeasure by moving out of the temple to a rock outside government control.

IS THERE STILL A ROLE FOR KNOWLEDGE BROKERS?

Requests for the inclusion of 'the poor' in policy debates are on the increase. Without the poor participating, the argument goes, there is no hope that sustainable development strategies can ever be achieved (Middleton et al. 2001). This conviction is exceedingly articulated within the World Bank and IMF (Robb 2002), and chimes well with Sillitoe's contention that the objective of research in local knowledge 'is to introduce a locally informed perspective into development, to challenge the assumption that development is something outsiders have a right to impose, and to promote an appreciation of indigenous power structures and know-how' (Sillitoe 2002: 9).[5] The proposition is self-evident to any anthropologist (2002: 2).

At the core of the challenge, however, lies the more difficult issue of what anthropologists should do when confronted with diametrically opposed representations of local knowledge. Should they get involved in advocacy as 'arbitrators of truth' or should they stick to documenting what goes on? Favouring the second position, Argenti-Pillen rejects the view that anthropologists should be 'knowledge brokers' or 'cultural brokers', the role of broker being politically untenable. Instead, she sees herself as providing a 'more distanced political analysis of the knowledge interface between [in this case] Western mental health specialists and Sri Lankan intellectuals' (this volume, p. 191). The position resembles that adopted by the Ramos team when it realised that the Park Authority had intended to use the commissioned research to promote a reified understanding of local culture. The team then turned to studying up, treating the political administration of the Algarve as part of the problem of managing Portugal's heritage. Ramos and his fellow researchers are today using a variety of means to promote a counter-narrative on development in Algarve.

In other instances, however, it is argued that the anthropologist is best engaged as a two-way knowledge/legal broker. The position is advocated in the chapters by Smith, and by Sillitoe and Wilson. Smith articulates the view with reference to Aboriginal land claims in Queensland, Australia, where opposed representations of indigenous knowledge clash head-on. Rather than fight the subjugation of complex Aboriginal knowledge and organisation or provide a 'more distant' analysis, Smith argues that the current era, despite its faults (read: disturbing disam-biguation), has 'introduced the possibility for Aboriginal people, after many years of radical disempowerment, to realise that they are able to assert more reciprocal relationships with government agencies and the "mainstream" on the basis of their own system of law and custom' (this volume, p. 142). In this kind of situation, the anthropologist's role is to assist in *negotiating compromise.* This is a position not unlike that taken up by Sillitoe and Wilson, who see 'a need to undertake research inde-pendently of [the mining] companies and yet in close association with them. At the same time, it is necessary to work closely with local communities without alienating companies' (this volume, p. 267). But there are limits to the involvement. Ultimately, 'we should not advocate outsiders sorting out [the relationship between local communities and the mines] because we believe that it is for local people to reach their own decisions about how to participate, but we think that companies might do more to make participation possible on local terms' (p. 268). I reached a similar conclusion in my own research on Rwanda: I could not legitimately speak on behalf of Rwandan people, but I did claim the right to speak to members of the so-called 'international community' (Pottier 2002: 5).

Which position works best – more distanced analysis of knowledge interfaces or an informed involvement in negotiations of compromise – may well depend on the circumstances researchers find themselves in. It is also to some extent a personal choice. What is indisputable, though, is that the position which favours direct involvement is not one that is necessarily naive when it comes to politics. Sillitoe and Wilson, and also Smith, are all clear that negotiating compromise requires sophisticated, in-depth analysis of how 'local' and 'global' power structures interpenetrate.

Opportunities for research on 'local knowledge' are on the increase. Over the past few years, the strongest request for policy change informed by local perspectives has come from the World Bank and IMF, who in the mid-1990s launched what they called Participatory Poverty Assessments (PPAs). Now conducted in over 60 countries, these PPAs are meant to influence the design and implementation of effective Poverty Reduction Strategy Papers, PRSPs (Robb 2002: xxv). The research politics of these assessments are fascinating, as is the analysis of how (and whether) they make for better poverty reduction strategies (see Whitehead and Lockwood 1999). What the WB/IMF envisages is that the poor will be 'empowered through bringing their analysis, priorities and voice into the decision-making process, thereby making the policy framework more relevant and responsive to their needs' (2002: 90). It is further anticipated that the participating countries will themselves drive and own their respective PRSPs, which will 'encourage accountability of governments to their own people and domestic constituencies rather than to external funders' (2002: 88). Likewise, it is envisaged that the poor too will become 'active participants, not just passive recipients' of policy directives, while 'donors [will] provide more predictable medium-term financial support for domestic budgets' (2002: 88). It requires little imagination to realise that there are rich opportunities here for anthro-pological debate.

The PPA approach has had its successes, mostly in the sense that a broader range of themes was broached, but rich empirical detail has not necessarily made policy agendas better attuned to the complexity of local situations. With reference to the Zambia PPA, for example, Whitehead and Lockwood argue that when 'moving backwards from the PPA volume (5), through volume 3 (on rural poverty), to the main report, volume 1, we witness a loss of many themes from the PPA' (1999: 540). The PPA, in other words, is an add-on and does not break the domination of 'analytical and policy agendas which are extraneous to the local situation' (1999: 540). Whitehead and Lockwood feel the same about the Uganda PPA. While they acknowledge that this PPA stands out because it was an adjunct to existing data and was used in the war zones where surveys could not be carried out, they do conclude that there is 'very little evidence that the results of the Uganda PPA in any way influenced ... policy discussion' (1999: 540). To Robb's question 'Can the poor influence policy?', which is the title of her book (2002), the answer is at best a half sceptical 'not yet'.

Despite the well-founded criticism of World Bank PPAs and their (limited) policy impact, it is also obvious that donors increasingly recognise, on paper if not always in practice, that 'true partnerships' do not exist in a political vacuum. A recent DFID paper on the role of economic and social research in the context of poverty elimination (DFID 2001), for instance, heeds the 'warning that consultation without due recognition of power and politics will lead to "voice without influence"' (DFID 2001: 44). Whatever their positions on academic analysis and advocacy, the contributions in this volume will ensure that 'power' stays firmly on the research agenda.

NOTES

1. 'Knowledge that enters a locality is not simply or straightforwardly inter-nalised but becomes transformed or – as Callon and Latour (1992) and Latour (1994) would argue – translated. A model that assumes linear knowledge production (outside a locality), dissemination (to a locality) and utilisation (in a locality) is misplaced. Both incoming knowledge as well as certain locally existing bodies of knowledge get transformed resulting in a broadening of knowledge' (Mango 2002: 14–15).
2. The same argument also applies to the knowledge of developers. As Gardner and Lewis argue, on the basis of their literature review, 'development plans are often far from rational, and relationships within development institutions are as hierarchical, unequal and culturally embedded as any of the societies usually studied by anthropologists. ... [The] paradigms within which developers work are as contextually contingent, culturally specific and contested as those of the special groups whom they target' (Gardner and Lewis 1996: 154–5).
3. ICRAF = International Centre for Research in Agroforestry; KARI = Kenya Agricultural Research Institute; KEFRI = Kenya Forestry Research Institute.
4. The link between social distance and representations of knowledge has also come to the fore in the promotion of primary health care practices. For example, Carl Kendall et al. (1984) report that a Honduras-based project aiming to control diarrheal disease through oral rehydration therapy (ORT) attempted to bring the concept of *empacho*, which is a folk conceptualisation, into its publicity. When this happened, there was strong official opposition: folk categories could not be used for the promotion of modern medicine. The authors recall that there was 'expressed resistance on the part of Ministry staff physicians to both the illness label "*empacho*" and the use of "purgative" in [the campaign] activities. *Empacho* was not considered a disease entity and physicians did not want the programme to appear to support purgative use' (Kendall et al. 1984: 257). The 'professional distance' between physician and layperson was not to be narrowed.
5. Sillitoe argues that it is difficult to draw lines between 'indigenous knowledge' and terms that can be used as alternatives: local knowledge, insider knowledge, people's science and folk knowledge, etc. (2002: 8; also Grenier 1998).

REFERENCES

Agrawal, Arjun (1995) 'Dismantling the Divide between Indigenous and Scientific Knowledge', *Development and Change*, 26: 413–39

Arce, Alberto and Norman Long (eds) (1999) *Anthropology, Development and Modernities: Exploring Discourses, Counter-Tendencies and Violence* (London: Routledge)

Arce, Alberto, Magdalena Villarreal and Pieter de Vries (1994) 'The Social Construction of Rural Development: Discourses, practices and power', in David Booth (ed.), *Rethinking Social Development: Theory, Research and Practice* (Burnt Hill and Harlow: Longman Scientific and Technical), pp. 152–71

Booth, David (1994) 'Rethinking Social Development: An overview', in David Booth (ed.), *Rethinking Social Development: Theory, Research and Practice* (Burnt Hill and Harlow: Longman Scientific and Technical), pp. 3–34

Brokensha, D., Warren, D. and Werner, O. (eds) (1980) *Indigenous Knowledge Systems and Development* (Maryland: University of America)

Callon, M. and B. Latour (1992) 'Don't Throw the Baby away with the Bath School! A reply to Collins and Yearley', in A. Pickering (ed.), *Science as Practice and Culture* (Chicago: University of Chicago Press), pp. 343–68

Chambers, R., A. Pacey and L.A. Thrupp (eds) (1989) *Farmer First: Farmer Innovation and Agricultural Research* (London: IT Publications)

Cooper, Frederick and Randall Packard (1997) 'Introduction', in F. Cooper and R. Packard (eds), *International Development and the Social Sciences: Essays on the History and Politics of Knowledge* (Berkeley: University of California Press), pp. 1–41

Crehan, Kate and Achim Von Oppen (1988) 'Understandings of "Development": An arena of struggle. The story of a development project in Zambia', *Sociologia Ruralis*, XXVIII (2/3): 113–45

Department for International Development (DFID) (2001) *Poverty Elimination: The Role of Economic and Social Research* (London: DFID)

Escobar, Arturo (1991) 'Anthropology and the Development Encounter: The making and marketing of development anthropology', *American Ethnologist*, 18 (4): 658–81

—— (1995) *Encountering Development: The Making and Unmaking of the Third World* (Princeton, NJ: Princeton University Press)

Fairhead, James (1992) Indigenous Technical Knowledge and Natural Resources Management in Sub-Saharan Africa: A critical review. Paper commissioned by the Social Science Council, New York

—— (1993) 'Representing Knowledge: The "new farmer" in research fashions', in J. Pottier (ed.), *Practising Development: Social Science Perspectives* (London: Routledge), pp. 187–204

Ferguson, James (1990) *The Anti-Politics Machine: 'Development', Depoliticisation and Bureaucratic Power in Lesotho* (Cambridge: Cambridge University Press)

Foucault, Michel (1971) 'The Order of Discourse', in R. Young (ed.), *Untying the Text: A Post-Structuralist Reader* (London: Routledge and Kegan Paul)

Fujisaka, Sam (1992) 'Farmer Knowledge and Sustainability in Rice-Farming Systems: Blending science and indigenous innovation', in Joyce Lewinger

Moock and Robert Rhoades (eds), *Diversity, Farmer Knowledge and Sustainability* (Ithaca and London: Cornell University Press), pp. 69–83

Gardner, Katy (1997) 'Mixed Messages: Contested "development" and the "plantation rehabilitation project"', in R.D. Grillo and R.L. Stirrat (eds), *Discourses of Development: Anthropological Perspectives* (Oxford: Berg), pp. 133–56.

Gardner, Katy and David Lewis (1996) *Anthropology, Development and the Post-Modern Challenge* (London: Pluto)

Gatter, Philip (1993) 'Anthropology in Farming Systems Research: A participant observer in Zambia', in J. Pottier (ed.), *Practising Development: Social Science Perspectives* (London: Routledge), pp. 153–86

Grenier, L. (1998) *Working With Indigenous Knowledge. A Guide for Researchers* (Ottawa: IDRC)

Grillo, R.D. (1997) 'Discourses of Development: The view from anthropology', in R.D. Grillo and R.L. Stirrat (eds), *Discourses of Development: Anthropological Perspectives* (Oxford: Berg)

Hobart, Mark (ed.) (1993) *An Anthropological Critique of Development: The Growth of Ignorance* (London: Routledge)

Howes, M. and R. Chambers (1979) 'Indigenous Technical Knowledge: Analysis, implications and issues', *IDS Bulletin*, 10 (2): 5–11

International Development Research Centre (1994) *People, Plants and Patents: The Impact of Intellectual Property on Trade, Plant Biodiversity, and Rural Society* (Ottawa: IDRC)

Kendall, Carl, D. Foote and R. Martorell (1984) 'Ethnomedicine and Oral Rehydration Therapy – A case study of ethnomedical investigation and program-planning', *Social Science and Medicine*, 19 (3): 253–60

Latour, Bruno (1994) 'On Technical Mediation – Philosophy, sociology, genealogy', *Common Knowledge*, 34: 29–64

Lewis, D.J. et al. (1993) 'Indigenising Extension: Farmers, fishseed traders and poverty-focused aquaculture in Bangladesh', *Development Policy Review*, 11: 185–94

Long, Norman (1992) 'Conclusion', in Norman Long and Ann Long (eds), *Battlefields of Knowledge: The Interlocking of Theory and Practice in Social Research and Development* (London: Routledge), pp. 268–77

—— (1996) 'Globalization and Localization: New challenges to rural research', in H. Moore (ed.), *The Future of Anthropological Knowledge* (London: Routledge), pp. 37–59

—— (2001) *Development Sociology: Actor Perspectives* (London: Routledge)

Long, Norman and Ann Long (eds) (1992) *Battlefields of Knowledge: The Interlocking of Theory and Practice in Social Research and Development* (London: Routledge)

Long, Norman and Magdalena Villarreal (1993) 'Exploring Development Interfaces: From knowledge transfer to transformation of meaning', in F.J. Schuurman (ed.), *Beyond The Impasse: New Directions in Development Theory* (London: Zed), pp. 1–34.

Long, Norman and Magdalena Villareal (1994) 'The Interweaving of Knowledge and Power in Development Interfaces', in Ian Scoones and John Thompson (eds), *Beyond Farmer First: Rural People's Knowledge, Agricultural Research and Extension Practice* (London: Intermediate Technology Publications), pp. 41–52

Long, Norman and Jan Douwe van der Ploeg (1994) 'Heterogeneity, Actor and Structure: Towards a reconstitution of the concept of structure', in David Booth (ed.), *Rethinking Social Development: Theory, Research and Practice* (Burnt Hill and Harlow: Longman Scientific and Technical), pp. 62–89

Mango, A.R. Nelson (2002) 'Husbanding the Land: Agrarian Development and Socio-technical Change in Luoland, Kenya'. PhD Thesis, Wageningen, University of Wageningen

Marsden, David (1990) 'Using Local Knowledge (review article)', *Community Development Journal*, 25 (3): 266–71

Middleton, Neil, Phil O'Keefe and Rob Visser (eds) (2001) *Negotiating Poverty: New Directions, Renewed Debate* (London: Pluto Press)

Mooney, Pat (1993) 'Exploiting Local Knowledge: International policy implications', in W. de Boef, K. Amanor and K. Wellard, with A. Bebbington (eds), *Cultivating Knowledge: Genetic Diversity, Farmer Experimentation and Crop Research* (London: Intermediate Technology Publications), pp. 172–8

Moore, Henrietta (1996) 'The Changing Nature of Anthropological Knowledge: An introduction', in H. Moore (ed.), *The Future of Anthropological Knowledge* (London: Routledge), pp. 1–15

Mundy, P. and J. Lin Compton (1995) 'Indigenous Communication and Indigenous Knowledge', in D.M. Warren, L.J. Slikkeveer and D. Brokensha (eds), *The Cultural Dimension of Development: Indigenous Knowledge Systems* (London: Intermediate Technology Publications)

Pottier, Johan (1997) 'Towards an Ethnography of Participatory Appraisal and Research', in R.D. Grillo and R.L. Stirrat (eds), *Discourses of Development: Anthropological Perspectives* (Oxford: Berg), pp. 203–28

—— (1999) *Anthropology of Food: The Social Dynamics of Food Security* (Cambridge: Polity Press)

—— (2002) *Re-Imagining Rwanda: Conflict, Survival and Disinformation in the late Twentieth Century* (Cambridge: Cambridge University Press)

Rew, Alan (1994) 'Social Standards and Social Thought', in C. Hann (ed.), *When History Accelerates: Essays on Rapid Social Change, Complexity and Creativity* (London: Athlone Press), pp. 276–99

Richards, Paul (1985) *Agricultural Revolution – Ecology and Food Production in West Africa* (London: Hutchinson)

—— (1993) 'Cultivation: Knowledge or performance?' in M. Hobart (ed.), *An Anthropological Critique of Development: The Growth of Ignorance* (London: Routledge), pp. 61–79

Robb, Caroline M. (2002) *Can the Poor Influence Policy? Participatory Poverty Assessments in the Developing World* (Washington: The World Bank and International Monetary Fund, second edition)

Scoones, Ian and John Thompson (1994) 'Knowledge, Power and Agriculture – towards a theoretical understanding', in I. Scoones and J. Thompson (eds), *Beyond Farmer First: Rural People's Knowledge, Agricultural Research and Extension Practice* (London: Intermediate Technology Publications), pp. 16–32

Scott, James (1990) *Domination and the Arts of Resistance: Hidden Transcripts* (New Haven, CT: Yale University Press)

Seddon, David (1993) 'Anthropology and Appraisal: The preparation of two IFAD pastoral development projects in Niger and Mali', in J. Pottier (ed.), *Practising Development: Social Science Perspectives* (London: Routledge), pp. 71–109

Shiva, Vandana (1992) 'The Seed and the Earth: Biotechnology and the colonisation of regeneration', *Development Dialogue*, (1/2): 151–68

Sikana, Patrick (1994) 'Indigenous Soil Characterization in Northern Zambia', in Ian Scoones and John Thompson (eds), *Beyond Farmer First: Rural People's Knowledge, Agricultural Research and Extension Practice* (London: Intermediate Technology Publications), pp. 80–2

Sillitoe, Paul (1998) 'The Development of Indigenous Knowledge: A new applied anthropology', *Current Anthropology*, 39 (2): 223–52

—— (2002) 'Participant Observation to Participatory Development: Making anthropology work', in P. Sillitoe, A. Bicker and J. Pottier (eds), *Participating in Development: Approaches to Indigenous Knowledge* (London: Routledge), pp. 1–23

UNESCO-Nuffic (1999) *Best Practices on Indigenous Knowledge* (Paris: UNESCO; The Hague: Nuffic)

Verma, Ritu (2001) *Gender, Land, and Livelihood in East Africa: Through Farmers' Eyes* (Ottawa: IDRC)

Warren, D. Michael (1998) 'Comment' on Sillitoe 1998, *Current Anthropology*, 39 (2): 244–5

Warren, D. Michael, Jan L. Slikkeveer and S. Oguntunji (eds) (1989) *Indigenous Knowledge Systems: Implications for Agriculture and International Development* (Iowa State University, Centre for Indigenous Knowledge in Agriculture and Rural Development: Studies in Technology and Social Change 11)

Whitehead, Ann and Matthew Lockwood (1999) 'Gendering Poverty: A review of six World Bank African Poverty Assessments', *Development and Change*, 30: 525–55

2 A POSSIBLE EXPLANATION FOR THE LACK OF EXPLANATION; OR, 'WHY THE MASTER BUILDER CAN'T EXPLAIN WHAT HE KNOWS': INTRODUCING INFORMATIONAL ATOMISM AGAINST A 'DEFINITIONAL' DEFINITION OF CONCEPTS[1]

Trevor H.J. Marchand

The assumed goal of anthropology is to learn about what members of (other) societies and cultures know about the world, the manner in which people come to know what they know, and the ways that they represent and communicate their knowledge. The primary aim of this chapter is to move towards a better understanding of the nature of knowledge – as something acquired, possessed and communicated – by introducing a theory of concepts.

In order to know about knowing, we must understand what knowing consists of, that is, what are the constituents of what we call knowledge or thought – and how do we, as humans, come to acquire them? As a basic premise, a representational theory of mind will be assumed throughout, according to which concepts are mental representations, and as such are understood to be the constituents of thoughts and beliefs (which comprise our knowledge and inform our actions-in-the-world). It is not my aim to develop a methodology whereby one might separate out and individually identify these constituents, but rather it is to move towards a closer approximation of what concepts are, and the manner by which they constitute knowledge. Following Fodor (1998), I will argue that concepts, though mental representations, do not acquire their content via an inferential role semantics or induction, nor do they have meanings in any definitional sense. The denial of inferential role semantics – which claims that the 'meaning' of concepts is derived inferentially via their relations to other concepts – has shattering implications for structuralist theory in general. Put simply, the constituent elements that comprise a (closed) system are *not* 'defined' in relation to each other, or for that matter in relation to *what they are not*. The claim that concepts are not definitions will be presented as a direct challenge to the nature of standard anthropological inquiry, and more specifically to how anthropologists learn about, interpret and represent indigenous systems of knowledge.

I will begin with a summary background of my cognitive research with traditional builders and their associated teaching–learning processes before proceeding with a theory of concepts. The chapter will conclude with a discussion of why a theory of concepts is important for anthropology and how it may eventuate in a more informed recognition of the limitations of verbal communication as an expression of knowledge. I explore here some of the core ideas presented by the philosopher Jerry Fodor, which will have foreseeable impact on the direction of my own research, and will oblige those of us with a serious interest in cognition to assess critically the foundational premises of our theories and working models. It should be noted that, because of the scope and originality of Fodor's theory (as well as the comprehensiveness of the attacks it makes on the doctrines central to nearly all current work in the cognitive sciences), I will deal only with the aspects most relevant to this chapter. This will require a somewhat lengthy recapitulation of several of Fodor's ideas in order to provide an adequate background to the specific questions I raise regarding the relation between anthropology and indigenous knowledge: namely, the challenge of accessing (expert) knowledge in a context largely devoid of verbal communication.

MASTER BUILDERS, TRADE KNOWLEDGE AND APPRENTICESHIP

In previous studies with traditional builders my work has been primarily concerned with the expert knowledge possessed by skilled craftsmen in Sana'a, Yemen (see Marchand 2000a, 2000b, 2000c, 2001). More specifically, and while working as a building labourer, I examined the manner in which trade knowledge is acquired, transmitted and controlled by a specialised team of mosque-minaret builders. The system of apprenticeship that they employed was recognised to be the principal means of regulating and transferring skills and expertise, as well as forming 'moral agents' who could be identified as competent, responsible 'authorities' within the socio-political system. My research sought to elucidate various cognitive and performative processes, which were typically fostered and exercised in the course of the builders' training. These included the labourer's obedience and regulated mind–body comportment, which was achieved through his subjection and subjecti-fication to the disciplinary apparatuses on the work site and within his living environment (that is, in cohabitation with his fellow workers); the apprentice's capacity to observe, practise and reproduce trade skills, which entail the mastery of spatial judgements, and which are cultivated through his privileged introduction to the act of 'making'; and the honing of the master builder's intentionality, which imbues and directs his co-ordination of the numerous aspects involved in the trade (including design, economics and resource management, client relations, and the capacity to conceptualise the project at various physical scales of production).

The position most coveted by the ambitious labourers was working high on top of the vertically extending walls of the minaret, at the side of the master builders. This position admitted the builder to participate more directly in the processes of 'making', and this normally included an introduction to, and a frequent engagement in, the carving of (and occasionally the setting of) the clay *ajurr* bricks. Jockeying for the position of apprentice entailed fierce competition amongst the young contenders, as well as a considerable amount of politically motivated favouritism on the part of the master builders in their selection. At this stage in the builder's career, a higher degree of understanding regarding the trade and their role within it was expected from them, and this understanding continued to evolve in tandem with their increased responsibilities and duties.

A characteristic feature of the apprenticeship system at all stages in the training process – beginning with the disciplining of the common labourer's performance to inculcating specialised skills and responsibil-ities in the higher-level apprentice – was the (nearly complete) absence of verbal communication. It was noted that few skill-related directives were issued by the teachers (whether masters or other builders of senior rank), and questioning from the novices was highly discouraged. The clear exception to this 'silent communication' was the plethora of verbal abuse (occasionally accompanied by blows) that was rained on the apprentices by their masters, and likewise passed down the chain of rank by the apprentices to the lowly labourers.

It was therefore deemed necessary to go beyond language in order to investigate the builders' expert knowledge and the issue of spatial cognition, and to adopt a modularity-of-mind approach to thinking about thinking. Jackendoff and Landau's highly influential study on the relation between language and spatial cognition (in Jackendoff 1992) served as a main source of inspiration to my project. They argue that there exists an evident correlation between the split in the expressive power of language, namely between the ability to describe the 'what' of an object versus the 'where' of an object, and the anatomical bifurcation for spatial representation in thought. In brief, they reason that this innate bifurcation in thought is evidenced in language by the rich and potentially infinite store of vocabulary to render object descriptions versus the relatively impoverished lexicon for expressing spatial relations between objects (namely prepositions).

My own study with Sana'ani traditional builders sought to expand Jackendoff and Landau's window onto human spatial cognition from one that was exclusively language-based to one that was performance-based and concentrated on the processes of making. It was thus necessary to develop an understanding of how 'thinking about building' (in terms of objects-as-entities and the spatial-relations-between-entities at varying scales of the composition) and 'performing building-related skills' interface in a dialogical fashion, each informing and modifying the content of the other. The recognition that theory and practice are mutually dependent in the production of systems of knowledge is not an original one. In challenge to Ryle (1949), Fodor notes that 'if it's not obvious that learning how requires hypothesis testing, it's also not obvious that it doesn't: in lots of cases it appears that how-learning itself depends on that-learning' (1998: 124–5). Though I fundamentally support this observation, I would also emphasise that that-learning must likewise be informed by how-learning in many cases, and that though there may be interface (but not translation) between the two, they represent essentially different forms of knowledge. This is an extremely important point, which I will take up later in the discussion of concepts.

Fodor does not specifically address what the constituents of skills are, except to suggest, in the context of arguing that skills are not concepts (thus not the constituents of beliefs), that skills cannot be the constituents of anything except other skills (1998: 125, n6). Clearly skills are not concepts according to the way in which he has defined concepts as mental particulars. I would argue, however, that like conceptual thought or 'knowing something about the world', performative skills are direct expressions (or embodiments) of knowledge and are thus necessarily constituted by concepts. To claim otherwise would effectively promote an acceptance of a mind–body dualism – whereby the body is manipulated by a rational mind and higher order of propositional thought – to which I am not willing to concede, and nor, do I suspect, is Fodor. Moreover, I am suggesting that the likelihood that performative knowledge (like that expressed by the Yemeni builder in his 'making') is not amenable to the same methods of analysis used to understand propositional statements made about the world through language because the constituents of performative knowledge (namely concepts) do not necessarily assemble in like manner. This is not to deny composition-ality, but rather, more basically, to call into question any (convenient and simplistic) analogies drawn between the compositionality of language and that of performance and action-in-the-world. In accord with Fodor's position, I am challenging the language-centric theses of knowledge that have dominated twentieth-century theory and am thereby contesting the notion that performative knowledge can, or should, be analysed syntactically and semantically.

In my case study, the builder's apprenticeship served to enhance his expert knowledge and judgement regarding space and assembly through the training, continual practice and inhabiting the processes of making, which largely defined his role and position. The labourer was typically initiated into the process of making with the carving of his first brick – whereby the brick represented the basic unit of construction – and from there the scale of making was gradually increased. As the traditional builder mastered the increasingly complex spatial relations inherent in the increasing scales of the assemblies he worked on, his conceptual understandings of their abstract spatial relations were gradually translated and simplified into known objects (that is, the brick; the carved brick of type A, B or C; the wall; the decorative relief brick pattern(s); the internal spiralling staircase; the stone base, the brick shaft, and the dome; the minaret-as-entity). Consequently, these objects could be manipulated in an incremental manner, both in his conceptual thought and physically with his hands and tools, which enabled the young builder to move between scales of varying magnitude – from the micro to the macro – over the course of the apprenticeship.

I have suggested elsewhere (Marchand 2001, 2000a) that the propensity to reconstrue spatial relations conceptually into known objects demonstrated an entropic process of cognition, which guided the builder's understanding of an object from one of abstract spatial relations towards a categorised description of the object-as-entity. This categorical way of thinking about component parts of the assembly served to create discrete building blocks of knowledge over which the mind of the builder exerted his power as 'maker', manipulating and reconfiguring relations between these objects of knowledge to conceptually construct new objects of knowledge. This process of manipulating conceptually constituted building blocks was in dialogic relation with the physical processes of making since, ultimately, the knowledge and the making were demonstrated to be one and the same. In other words, the builder's concepts assembled compositionally to produce a knowledge that was expressed through his linearly organised actions-in-the-world, and his engagement in this process served to produce increasingly complex understandings which in turn became manifest in skilled performances – and so on.

A second point raised by my studies of expert knowledge, and one related to the ensuing discussion of concepts in this chapter, is the question of personal knowledge acquired by the builders (in contrast to the technical knowledge gained about building). More specifically, this knowledge of the self may be defined in terms of a recognition, acceptance and active promotion of one's own status, obligations and responsibilities, and mode of conduct, both on and off the work site. Again, I have emphasised the non-verbal nature of this type of knowledge and its transmission, and have argued that the teaching/learning processes that characterise a traditional master–apprentice relation are complex and multidimensional. Consequently, they are not amenable to the type of formalised teaching methods imposed by institutional instruction. In discussion, several prominent western-trained architects promoted the idea of establishing officially operated trade schools to replace the authority of the competitive families of traditional builders in the city, and therefore, in theory, implement quality control and secure the survival of a 'Sana'ani style' over the long term. Their concerns for heritage reflected the growing conservation-minded attitudes of Sana'anis, bolstered by the inclusion of the city on the UNESCO list of World Heritage Sites in 1984.[2] I would argue, however, that trade schools, which would aim to revive or sustain traditional craft production and building techniques, might successfully train corps of craftspeople to reproduce accurately the material products in question, *but the traditional building trade, defined by its distinctive set of human relations and methods for transferring knowledge, cannot be easily replicated.* Ultimately, 'tradition' lies in the process and qualitative aspect of the human relations, not in the materiality of the object. It is the master–apprentice relation, and the formation of a moral subject, which constitute the distinguishing hallmark of the trade. This 'moral subject' is characterised by their capacity for creativity and innovation beyond mere mimesis, whereby the imaginative component in both their technical production and production of self is moderated by a disciplined reason informed by the established norms, procedures and practices of the trade.

In summary, the content of the master builder's knowledge eludes any (coherent) verbalised articulation largely as a consequence of the way in which his expertise is transferred, acquired and possessed by his apprentices. I have suggested that this knowledge is sedimented in the performance, the understanding and ultimately the intentions of the builder as these are correspondingly achieved via the disciplining (characteristic of the labourer's training), mimicry and practice (characteristic of the apprentice's engagement in making), and a hard-earned concentrated focus and ability to reflect holistically on the multiple aspects of the project(s) at hand. His knowledge is not an objectified one that can be acquired by mastering a formulaic recipe of procedures (*'ilm* in Arabic), but rather can be properly characterised in Arabic as *ma'arifa* – a deeply personal knowledge. This was not preserved in written accounts (though arguably the constitution of a moral agent in the trade is significantly informed by those virtues prescribed in the Qur'an and Hadith), and thus the distinctive educational processes had not been objectified as a public social fact. Therefore, the expert knowledge associated with the trade could not be reflected upon, discussed and disputed in either quantifiable or qualitative terms (that is, terms regarding specified duration, marked boundaries in the stages of training, exact procedures or content, etc.).

The common response offered by the *usta* (master builder), when queried about his knowledge, was that 'it's all in my head' (*'kull fi ra's'*). The simplicity (and suggested mysteriousness) of the claim was generally accepted by his public without further questioning, and was reproduced in their sustained understandings and beliefs about the 'innate qualities and powers' of master craftsmen. Precisely because the expert knowledge was not objectified, the traditional builder was not proficient at explaining how he knows, and arguably, to some extent, he was unwilling to explain. This unwillingness (though not the lack of proficiency at communicating his knowledge verbally) should be understood as goal-directed since the master builder was arguably fully cognisant of the power wielded by the ambiguity of his responses. The secrecy that shrouded the traditional builder's knowledge and performance from public scrutiny effectively served to mark the boundaries that defined the trade and sustained his privileged expert status within Sana'ani society. It is the incapacity, however, and not the issue of unwillingness, which I will consider in the following sections.

ON CONCEPTS

The subject of knowledge has been investigated quite comprehensively in my previous writings, where I explored the multiple mediums – social, cultural, political and cognitive – through which knowledge is defined, transferred and acquired within a framework of apprenticeship. In the remainder of this chapter I will specifically pursue the cognitive aspect of my research by exploring the issue of concepts and advancing a recent innovative theory that has emerged in the field of cognitive philosophy.

The key questions addressed here are the following: What are concepts, and how do we acquire them? And how might an understanding of concepts impact on an anthropological inquiry about the nature of knowledge? Because of the scale and complexity of this largely uncharted terrain, I will present only those aspects of the theory (and in brief) that relate directly to my main ethnographic concern: viz. why might the master builder be incapable of explaining what he knows? Evidently, my appropriation of the theory and its application to this issue remains experimental and elementary at this early stage, and will I hope invite comment and critique from both anthropologists and scholars in the cognitive sciences. Because the theory in question is primarily concerned with concepts (which are understood to be the constituents of thought, and not thought itself – in other words, we don't *think concepts*, we think *with* concepts), this chapter will not address the mechanics of thought, nor the particular neural operations behind concept acquisition. Rather, the aim is to define better what concepts are so that we might eventually develop a more plausible understanding of the nature of knowledge. Following Fodor's lead, my priority will be to render an account of concepts, rather than starting in the opposite direction to determine what the (cognitive) conditions for having a concept are (1998: 2–3), thereby avoiding the common pitfalls that Fodor enumerates throughout his book (see Fodor 1998).

A PRESENTATION OF THE THEORY

To date, my discussions on cognition have been primarily grounded in Fodor's modularity-of-mind thesis (1983) and much of the subsequent work by scholars in various fields who have applied and expanded the basic tenets of this theory in understanding domain specificity (for example, Sperber and Wilson 1986; Sperber 1994; Boyer 1996). I have also looked to Jackendoff's work on the 'architecture of the mind', and particularly his study with Landau on spatial cognition (see above). In order to shift the investigation from one centred on models of thought processing and domain specificity to one concerned with the basic constituents of thought, I have adopted Fodor's account of informational atomism.

Informational atomism is a proposal to replace the standard versions of a representational theory of mind (RTM) current in philosophy and in cognitive science. RTM, as Fodor points out, 'requires there to be infinitely many concepts that are complex and finitely many that are primitive ... [and also] requires concepts to have their content essentially'. The current versions also demand that 'most lexical concepts should not be primitive, and the content of concepts should be determined, at least *inter alia*, by their inferential-cum-causal relations to one another' (1998: 120). Fodor argues convincingly that 'lexical concepts do not in fact act as though they were internally structured by psychological or linguistic test ... [and] the question [of] *which* aspects of a concept's inferential role are the ones that determine the meaning appear to be hopeless' (1998: 120–1).

Fodor's doctrine is comprised of an informational part derived from informational semantics, and an atomistic part derived from conceptual atomism, for which he provides the following accounts:

informational semantics: 'content is constituted by some sort of nomic [law-like], mind-world relation. Correspondingly, having a concept (concept possession) is constituted, at least in part, by being in some sort of nomic, mind-world relation' (1998: 121). A theory of informational semantics 'denies that the grasp of any interconceptual relations is constitutive of concept possession'. (1998: 71)

conceptual atomism: 'most lexical concepts have no internal structure'. (1998: 121)

Informational atomism represents a serious challenge to the prevalent notion in anthropology (and all other disciplines that investigate epistemology) that a concept is 'knowing something', and that concepts have structured content: for example, that the concept BRICK is equivalent to its definitional sense, which may be stated as something like 'a block of clay hardened by drying in the sun or burning in a kiln, and used for building' (*Webster's Encyclopedic Unabridged Dictionary*, 1996). Based on this assumption, many of us, as anthropologists, proceed to ask our informants to explain what they know and how they come to know what they know in our attempts to grasp the essence behind indigenous forms of knowledge. Much ink has been spilled trying to decipher why 'twins are birds', and the like. Such a notion of concepts as definitional and structured (that is, constituted by other concepts) implies inferential role semantics and necessitates a small, finite base of primitive (and presumably innate) concepts upon which others are constituted. The (innate) primitives are often assumed to be those concepts that are acquired by us perceptually, and over which we have no conscious control in the way that they 'strike us'. For example, the concept RED is more or less automatically acquired perceptually from our encounters with red things or 'redness', and everyone generally agrees upon the fact that such concepts have no definitional sense beyond what they are (that is, RED means red). Appearance concepts like RED are not regarded as being metaphysically primitive, nor are they thought to contain some hidden natural essence (that is, like WATER = H_2O),[3] but, following Hume (1975), are thought to be acquired by the stimulation of an (intentionally specified) innate sensorium (Fodor 1998: 123). They are thus considered both innate and primitive.

By contrast, Fodor first contests a 'definitional' definition of concepts in favour of an atomistic one devoid of structure; viz. concepts are not internally structured by other concepts. In other words, concepts are not equivalent to their definitions, and our use of concepts in no way implies a structured, definitional content. Nor, for that matter, is it necessary that we possess (all of) the other concepts implied by the definition. For example, following on from the definition of brick suggested above, to possess the concept BRICK (that is, to be nomologically locked to BRICK), we need not necessarily possess some, or any, of the concepts associated with its definitional sense (that is, BLOCK, CLAY, HARDENED, SUN, KILN, TO USE, or BUILDING). Therefore, to entertain BRICK (to be in a mental state by virtue of a mental representation with the content BRICK) does not equate to entertaining its definition. The definition (as in the case of any definition) might be more appropriately understood as a thought about bricks (or anything else), and as only one of many possible thoughts that employ the concept. Also, it is important to note that mental representations/concepts are not images-in-the-mind's eye. To entertain a mental image of something is to be thinking about that thing in a particular way: viz. to be thinking in terms of visual or imagistic definitions that are constituted by a multitude of constituent concepts. In sum, the concept BRICK is merely a 'meaningless' constituent that carries information of the content 'brick' in brick thoughts. To inquire about what bricks mean is to inquire into thoughts about brick, and thoughts about bricks may be thought in a potentially infinite number of ways. Thus BRICK has no equivalent (structured) definition. In short, and in fact, there are no definitions for any concept, and *mutatis mutandis* concepts cannot be definitions.

Thoughts may (and do) enter into inferential relations with other thoughts (they are systematic and productive) and thoughts have meaning by virtue of expressing propositional attitudes – but concepts do not. Assuming that this is so, the concepts that we possess do *not* have the content that they do by virtue of being what they are not. More specifically, and according to the argument so far, concepts are not acquired inferentially, nor inductively. Therefore, the content of one's concept BRICK cannot be so due to any oppositional relations that it enters into within a closed system of knowledge about the things that one knows-in-the-world. In other words, to make reference to a popular analogy in structuralist thought, the pieces on the chessboard do not in fact acquire their content via their relations within a closed system of meaning. Structuralist theory, best exemplified in Lévi-Strauss's binary model of thinking (Lévi-Strauss 1966), requires a finite base of innate primitives from which more complex concepts may be inductively acquired (that is, concepts as definitions, and, in the case of Lévi-Strauss, premised on the supposed nature:culture dichotomy). Problematically for the structuralists, there is no popular consensus on what this innate primitive base consists of, or why we as humans should universally possess them. If innateness is denied, the circularity of this argument is blatantly apparent. And that is as it should be, because there are no innate concepts. If this is so, the Saussurean-based structuralist theory that has guided our thinking about cognition through much of the twentieth century (de Saussure 1960) has led us seriously astray. We have confused concepts with thoughts and knowledge, and mistakenly accepted cognitivist accounts (that is, inferential and inductive accounts) of concept acquisition.

The 'Standard Argument' (as coined by Fodor) against informational atomism contends that if most lexical concepts are not internally structured, and thus primitive (as required by informational atomism), they must not be subject to being learned. If concepts are unlearned, they are *ipso facto* innate. This argument begins with the assumption that learning a concept is necessarily an inductive process; 'specifically, that it requires devising and testing hypotheses about what the property is in virtue of which things fall under the concept' (Fodor 1998: 123). Support for an inductive account of concept acquisition (that is, concepts are learned) necessarily entails a cognitive account of concept possession (that is, that having a concept is knowing something). Therefore, according to the Standard Argument, one must be in possession of concepts (that is, already know something) in order to acquire (learn) additional concepts. Unless one accepts nativism (that is, the existence of a finite number of primitive concepts which are innate, and in terms of which other concepts are defined), the circularity of this argument is, once again, self-evident. Therefore, in summary, concepts cannot be learned. So then, how might informational atomism, which advocates that concepts are indeed primitive (that is, non-definitional), but denies innateness, account for concept acquisition?

Before proceeding with such an account, it might be summarised that:

[Informational Atomism] is explicitly non-cognitivist about concept possession; it says that having a concept is (not knowing something but) being in a certain nomic mind-world relation; specifically, it's being in that mind-world relation in virtue of which the concept has the content that it does ... Because it is non-cognitivist about concept possession, IA invites a correspondingly non-cognitivist account of how concepts are acquired. (Fodor 1998: 124)

In his ultimate metaphysical solution to the question of concept acquisition, Fodor, employing 'doorknobs' as a representative example of a mundane artefact-in-the-world, and one of which we may possess the concept DOORKNOB, ventures to make the very profound statement that:

Maybe what it is to be a doorknob isn't *evidenced* by the kind of experience that leads to acquiring the concept DOORKNOB; maybe what it is to be a doorknob is *constituted* by the kind of experience that leads to acquiring the concept DOORKNOB. (1998: 134)

In other words, though our sensorial perceptions play an important role in mediating our semantic access to mental representations (that is, doorknob sightings or touching doorknobs connect DOORKNOB tokenings), they do not constitute our having the concept. To suggest that they do (that is, that the artefact-in-the-world is evidenced by the kind of experience that leads to acquiring a concept of it) would necessitate that artefacts-in-the-world possess some innate use, or possess their *artefacthood* independently of, and *a priori*, our minds. Very importantly, this would also require that the cognitive mechanisms responsible for concept acquisition must be intentionally motivated, since the acquisition of concepts would be *of* meaningful-things-already-in-the-world, and thus may be regarded as being within the domain of psychological explanation rather than metaphysics. In sum, this suggests in the case of doorknobs, the necessity of a 'doorknob-dependence of mind'. A theory that sanctions a 'world-dependence of mind' requires a mind that is innately comprised of intentionally motivated cognitive mechanisms. Intentionally motivated cognitive mechanisms are necessarily content-full, and this brings us back full circle to a cognitivist theory of concept acquisition and the compromising predicament that one must possess *a priori* knowledge in order to acquire knowledge.

Rather, what Fodor is sensibly suggesting is the reverse: namely, that being a doorknob, or *doorknobhhood*, is mind-dependent. The property that a doorknob, or, for that matter, any other mundane artefact-in-the-world, expresses is constituted by the way that those things that have it strike us. And, 'if a property is constituted by the way that things that have it strike us ... then being locked to the property requires only that things that have it do reliably strike us that way' (1998: 142). It is important to note that the mind-dependence of such concepts such as DOORKNOB or BRICK in no way suggests that doorknobs and bricks are not real things-in-the-world, because, simply, 'doorknobs [and bricks] are constituted by their effects on our minds, and *our minds are in the world*' (1998: 149). Therefore, what it is to be a doorknob, for instance, as an artefact-in-the-world, is:

having the property to which minds like ours generalise from experience (as of) the properties by which the doorknob stereotype is constituted. *That's what the mind-dependence of doorknobhood consists in.* (1998: 140)[4]

The doorknob/DOORKNOB effect (that is, the acquisition of the concept DOORKNOB from doorknobs) is metaphysical, and thus there is absolutely no need to assume that DOORKNOB is learned inductively. What I mean is that concept acquisition is made possible by *a priori* (that is, necessary and universal) cognitive capacities and mechanisms, but not by the existence of some *a priori* content. Therefore, psychological approaches to concept acquisition and concepts can be ruled out since concept acquisition is not about *learning*, the operations of such a mechanism are not about *thinking*, and concepts themselves are not beliefs or thoughts. Fodor's version of informational atomism convincingly argues that concept acquisition is mind-dependent, and if, as stated earlier, having a concept, or concept possession, is taken to being nomologically locked to the property that the concept expresses, then 'the kind of nativism about DOORKNOB that an Informational Atomism has to put up with is perhaps not one of concepts but of mechanisms' (1998: 142). In other words, concept acquisition need not be intentionally specified, and concepts themselves may in turn be primitive without being innate. All that must be necessarily innate are the mechanisms for acquiring concepts, but, since this nomological locking is taken to be metaphysical rather than psychological, 'intentional vocabulary' is not required to explain it (1998: 143).

PERFORMATIVE KNOWLEDGE – OR, 'WHY THE MASTER BUILDER CAN'T EXPLAIN WHAT HE KNOWS'

The final section of this chapter presents me, as author, with a formidable challenge. The expert knowledge that I am referring to in the case of the master builder includes both the technical skills that he possesses for building and the personal skills that guide his (moral) conduct as a professional craftsman. Initially, I grappled with how, and to what extent, I might *discuss* the performative knowledge of the Sana'ani builders, which is of an essentially non-propositional form, and how I might *explain* what those builders themselves are not proficient at explaining. After much deliberation, I was forced to conclude that an attempt to discuss or explain their specific skill-related knowledge would be counterproductive. Like Bloch (1991), and Ryle (1949) before him, my admission was guided by a recognition that the *knowing that* and the *knowing how* are two different types of knowledge. Though these two forms of knowledge are not mutually exclusive of one another in that, in certainly many cases, much of our *knowing how* is surely informed by our *knowing that*, and *vice versa*, the 'communicative' interface between the two is necessarily one of interpretation and not translation. Jackendoff's theory of interface modules demonstrates to us that these behave as Fodorian modules, and additionally that only select features are communicated between one domain and the other, and these undergo transformations in the process. Therefore, the rendition of one form of knowledge by another is only ever partial. For example, my knowing how to carve a brick of type 'A', which I learned at the building site through mimicry and practice, is not entirely translatable into a propositionally constituted form of knowledge. Much of the practical experience that constitutes the knowing how eludes being 'fixed' by language, and is therefore filtered out in the descriptions. After reading my book on minaret builders (Marchand 2001) you may know all that there is to know about carving clay bricks in Sana'a, but that is no guarantee that (without prior practical experience) you can then pick up an adze and carve a brick. Moreover, the performance of a 'moral agent' that is recognised and aspired to by members of the profession, as well as by the Yemeni society at large, presents the task of anthropological 'explanation' with an even more slippery subject than the expression of technical building knowledge. Conclusively and ideally, any form of performative knowledge enjoins a performative demonstration.

The conventional genres for communicating academic research favour the medium of language – whether in writing or in oral presentations – which places considerable constraints on the type of knowledge we typically seek and the manner in which we convey it. The same sorts of constraints apply to the image-centric forms of scholarly presentation including (documentary) film and the use of multi-media: that is, how does one surmount the omnipresent obstacle of 'translating' knowledge systems, not simply culturally and linguistically, but between different modes of knowledge? This dilemma that we face as addicts of the written word and slaves to propositional thinking is perhaps more a product of the misguided tasks that we define for ourselves than anything else. For example, in my initial search for a way to *explain* the content of the builder's expert knowledge, I sought some truer essence behind the 'veneer' of his performative acts: 'How do you know that?' I asked. 'It's all in my head!' Aside from the metaphysical difficulties that I have outlined here, I would also contend that rendering a mimetic account of the *content* of the builder's (or anyone else's) knowledge is not, in fact, the most interesting task for a study of knowledge. What seems to me more appealing is an engagement with the *nature* of performative knowledge, or more specifically what constitutes it, and a movement towards an understanding of why it is that those who perform (often) cannot *explain* what they know.

It is perhaps mildly amusing that a major strand of Fodor's polemical argument in *Concepts* is that 'concepts don't mean' (viz. concepts do not equate to the definitions that are associated with their lexical terms), yet he manages to dedicate the entire book to *defining* what a concept is. On closer inspection, however, it is clear that Fodor, by seeking to understand what the constituents of thought are and how knowledge about the world might actually arise, is doing the more interesting philosophy – a philosophy of mind – rather than analytic philosophy. In a liberating passage in the concluding pages of his book, he himself states that:

It's natural ... to suppose that conceptual atomism means that there are no conceptual truths, hence that there are no analytic truths. And, if there are no analytic truths, I suppose that there are no such things as conceptual analyses ... If, there aren't any conceptual analyses, the moral isn't that we should stop doing philosophy, or even that we should start doing philosophy in some quite different way. The moral is just that we should stop saying that conceptual analysis is what philosophers do. (1998: 163)

This very much echoes the position within anthropology that I have been advocating in this chapter. The research issue of prime importance to an anthropological study of (performative) knowledge is not the analyses of the content of the (builder's) knowledge, but an engagement with how this knowledge is constituted.

Once again, I am proposing that we expand our notion of what knowledge is, and include the possession of skills within our analytical frameworks. Skilled performance as action-in-the-world is an expression of (sensori-motor) knowledge, and some limited comparison may be drawn with language as an expression of beliefs and ideas. Note that I am advocating a 'limited comparison', purposely leaving open the need for further investigation into the potentially more significant differences between the two forms of knowledge and their expressive mediums. Therefore, skills (as knowledge) must necessarily be constituted by concepts in the way that they are defined in Fodor's account of conceptual atomism. This means that, as concepts, they are primitive, but not innate, and their properties are constituted by the way that 'those things' that have them reliably strike minds like ours. The question arises as to what 'those things' are. Propositional knowledge is both organised by, and expressed with, language, and therefore the constituents (that is, the concepts) of propositional knowledge may be expressed as lexical items like those referred to by Fodor throughout his book: that is,

WATER, DOG, DOORKNOB, etc. Performative knowledge, on the other hand, is not a propositional form of knowledge, and therefore the constituents of this knowledge do not lend themselves to lexical itemisation. They cannot be objectified as 'those things' in the world that can be named. So then, how might they be discussed, or for that matter, 'thought about' or 'thought with' in language? The answer is simply that they cannot. They are exclusively 'thought with', or are the constituents of thought, in the realm of performance-based knowledge. And this is an important point. It tells us a great deal more about the nature (and more specifically, the limitations) of our minds than about the nature of concepts in particular. This also presents us, as researchers of knowledge accustomed to presenting our 'ideas' in writing, with a formidable hurdle.

Before addressing how we might possibly tackle this constraint, I will add that the concepts constituting performative or sensori-motor knowledge (that is, skills or intelligent practice) are not assembled in a language-like way. Although I would accept that they are assembled compositionally, I propose that sensori-motor-based knowledge does not share the grammatical principles or syntax rules that characterise propositional knowledge. If this were the case, one would map neatly onto the other and the builder could easily *explain* what he *does*. It must be considered that though we may be able to 'think about' and communicate descriptive accounts of (certain) performances that we engage in, the accounts rendered are the product of a very different domain of knowledge than the one they strive to represent. Each domain might be characterised by its distinctive (and innate) compositional rules that govern the assembly of concepts in the production of thought or knowledge; by the productivity and systematicity of this knowledge in producing further domain-specific knowledge; and by the means by which this knowledge is expressed.

A theory of interface modules (as mentioned above) is perhaps the most viable model for explaining how the two knowledge systems in question might 'communicate' with each other, and how, in this communication, only certain aspects or qualities of either form of knowledge are made available to the innate interpretive functions of the interface module. I see no reason to assume that all forms of knowledge are organised by some innate universal grammar in order for 'communication' to occur between them via these specialised interface modules. Presumably, if this were so, the procedures of 'translation' between them would be a relatively more straightforward one, much like translating between different spoken languages. My research with builders demonstrates that they are not. Though he does not address the issue of 'intelligent practice' in great detail, Fodor does note in support of this claim that 'there are many classes of performances in which intelligence is displayed, but the rules or criteria are not formulated ... [and] it is therefore possible for people to intelligently perform some sorts of operations when they are not yet able to consider any propositions enjoining how they should be performed' (1998: 163). Many linguists may lose interest at this point where the focus has shifted from language and propositional knowledge to the (possibly many) forms of human knowledge that are arguably not language-like. It might be appreciated, however, that a better (perhaps non-linguistically constituted) understanding of the nature of these other domains will serve to define better the boundaries and limitations of cognitive linguistic research, and lead to a more profound diversity of research approaches to human cognition and knowledge.

CONCLUSION

The proposal before us is that the constituent concepts of performative knowledge cannot be expressed or itemised by lexical terms, and that performative knowledge is most likely organised by principles of compositionality which differ from the innate grammar that is assumed to structure language and propositional thought. In effect, this is precisely why the master builder *cannot explain what he knows*. Any explanation offered must therefore be recognised to be what it is: an incomplete account that has been filtered in the interface between two domains of knowledge, and ultimately rendered in a domain distinct from its original form. Anthropology's traditional emphasis on verbal accounts and search for some hidden essence beneath the surface of many of the forms of knowledge that we study is, therefore, misdirected. If we continue in this vein, we will be forced to recognise that, in many instances, we are not in fact studying what we think we are studying, but are relying on an impoverished representation – namely, a propositional one – which can hardly account for the complexity of performance-based knowledge. Rather, the performer's knowledge as manifest in their practice and objectified in the world for public scrutiny must be considered as the direct subject of anthropological inquiry. This demands a recognition of the fact that the traditional builder's knowledge as a craftsman is a practised one, an habituated one, acquired over time and in conjunction with other forms of knowledge, most importantly learning to be a certain kind of person in the world, and that much of this has been achieved without verbal directives. Our engagement with this knowledge calls for good-old-fashioned fieldwork with an expanded critical notion of what 'intelligence' is and where we might seek to find it. Evidently, this engagement is characterised by participation, coupled with close observation and detailed description of the multifactorial factors that inform the production and reproduction of the expert knowledge *in situ*.

Instead of explaining (and interpreting) what intelligent action 'means', or 'reading it as text', it would surely be more productive to develop an anthropological understanding of the complexity of conditions and circumstances that give rise to it. As argued above, it may not be possible to itemise lexically many of the concepts that constitute sensori-motor knowledge in our written accounts, but this is probably not the important factor in understanding skilled knowledge like, for instance, that of the Sana'ani builder. What is arguably important is a recognition and understanding of how *different types* of knowledge are constituted, and how they are characterised. By implicating more complex understandings of knowledge in our studies, we can also render accounts of the manner in which different domains of knowledge inform and modify each other.

For example, continuing with builders and bricks, a young apprentice may be asked to carve a brick of type 'x' which has a specified geometry, and will be used as a component in the relief decoration on the façade of a given structure. Just as it was demonstrated that brick may exist as an atomistic concept (BRICK), which may enter as a constituent in thoughts about bricks, type 'x' bricks may exist as atomistic concepts ('X') and enter into thoughts about bricks of type 'x'. The young builder may *think about* 'x'-type bricks in a potentially infinite number of ways, but none of these ways of thinking about 'x's is equivalent to the concept 'X': concepts are non-definitional. Presumably, *thoughts about* bricks of type 'x' will be constituted by other concepts associated with such things as qualities, materials, colour, geometries and shapes, as well as potential uses (that is, in decorative assemblies). Importantly here, 'X' will also enter into thoughts about how to make or carve 'x'-type bricks. From the processes of *thinking about* to actually *making* in physical terms, it might be considered how the apprentice's engagement in making 'x's (that is, engagement in a sensori-motor form of knowledge recognised to be constituted by concepts) will in turn modify his 'thinking about' (that is, propositional knowledge) bricks of type 'x'. Based on my own experience as a builder on the minaret projects in Sana'a, I propose that it produces a simplification and clarification of one's initial *thoughts about* 'x' (though note that the concept 'X', as a definition-less primitive, necessarily remains unaltered). Like the other labourers on site, when initially confronted with my first opportunity to make/carve 'x's, I thought about 'x'-type bricks in a careful and methodical manner. Squatting with the brick held firmly in my left hand, and the adze in my right, I was absorbed in a heightened awareness of the material and geometrical properties of the brick and the spatial relations between the edges where cuts had to be made. My 'stream of consciousness' was dominated by an inner voice that monitored and guided the positioning of my body and my (initially clumsy) engagement in the act of carving with an adze. Repetitive engagements in carving transformed my *thinking about* 'x's (in relation to making) into an increasingly simplified economy of *performance* in relation to 'x's: gradually I was no longer engaged in mental calculation, nor was I intensely 'conscious' of either the brick or the actions that I performed upon it. The steps, procedures, geometries and spatial relations were progressively incorporated into a skilled, habituated practice. In other words, the initial theory, or *knowing that*, that (awkwardly) guided my first attempts at carving 'x's (in co-ordination with what my body already 'knew' in terms of positioning and performance) was succeeded by a skilled and efficient performance, or *knowing how*. Retrospectively, it was apparent that this *knowing how* had likewise modified my 'conscious' *thinking about* how to make 'x's, and that the two may be considered to be in dialectical relation with one another via an interface mechanism which selectively interprets information between them.

This account represents a merely preliminary (and simplified) consideration of the way in which we, as anthropologists, may engage more productively with knowledge, and more fruitfully investigate the complexities of human cognition. Arguably, the most important contribution that anthropology can make to a more comprehensive and cross-disciplinary study of human cognition and knowledge is in our ethnographic accounts. Ethnography not only serves to contextualise knowledge, but also bears the potential to instigate further questioning and critical examinations of the wide variety of ways in which individuals acquire and express knowledge. This necessitates, on our part, a broadening of the scope of our traditional analytic framework to include, at the very least, intelligent practice within the realm of knowledge. It also challenges us as anthropologists to develop more appropriate research methodologies above and beyond those constrained by their use of language and their search for 'meaning'. If the goal of our discipline is to learn about what members of societies and cultures know about the world, then we had better investigate how knowledge is constituted, under what conditions and in which contexts, and how systems of knowledge are produced and reproduced.

NOTES

1. An earlier version of this chapter was published in the *SOAS Working Papers in Linguistics*, volume 10. I would like to thank Professor Ruth Kempson and

Anna Portisch for their extremely valuable comments and criticisms on my earlier version. I have tried to address these in this present chapter, though I am still working through several of the more complex issues.

2. Rapid urban expansion throughout the country from the early 1970s onwards, with annual population growth rates of up to 10 per cent quoted by some sources (Unicef 1993: 22), led to speculations that the traditional building crafts would be eradicated by an onslaught of new building materials and technologies. In response, the General Conference of UNESCO at its 21st session in 1980 adopted a resolution to work out a plan of action for the preservation and restoration of Sana'a, and the city was later added to the roster of World Heritage Sites.

3. Fodor classifies water as a natural kind concept because it is 'a property which is not mind-dependent. It is not a property things have in virtue of their relations to minds, ours or any others' (1998: 150).

4. With regard to the issue of stereotypes, in addressing the question, 'why is it the concept X rather than the concept STEREOTYPIC X that one normally gets from experience with stereotypic Xs?', Fodor states that, 'If our minds are, in effect, functions from stereotypes to concepts, that is a fact *about us*. Indeed it is a *very deep* fact about us. My point in going on about this is to emphasise the untriviality of the consideration that we typically get a concept from instances that exemplify its stereotype' (1998: 130–40).

REFERENCES

Bloch, M. (1991) 'Language, Anthropology, and Cognitive Science', *Man*, 26: 183–98

Boyer, P. (1996) 'Cognitive Limits to Conceptual Reality', in J. Gumperz and S. Levinson (eds), *Rethinking Linguistic Relativity* (Cambridge: Cambridge University Press)

de Saussure, F. (1960) *Course in General Linguistics* (New York: McGraw-Hill)

Fodor, J.A. (1983) *The Modularity of Mind* (Cambridge, Mass.: MIT Press)

—— (1998) *Concepts: Where Cognitive Science Went Wrong* (Oxford: Clarendon Press)

Gumperz, J. and S. Levinson (eds) (1996) *Rethinking Linguistic Relativity* (Cambridge: Cambridge University Press)

Hirschfeld, L. and S. Gelman (eds) (1994) *Mapping the Mind* (Cambridge: Cambridge University Press)

Hume, D. (1975) '"Our Idea of Identity", "Of Personal Identity" and "Second Thoughts"', in J. Perry (ed.) *Personal Identity* (California: University of California Press)

Jackendoff, R. (1992) *Languages of the Mind: Essays on Mental Representations* (Cambridge, Mass.: MIT Press)

Jackendoff, R. and B. Landau (1992) 'Spatial Language and Spatial Cognition', in R. Jackendoff *Languages of the Mind: Essays on Mental Representations* (Cambridge, Mass.: MIT Press)

Lévi-Strauss, C. (1966) *The Savage Mind* (Chicago: University of Chicago Press)

Marchand, T.H.J. (2000a) 'Mastering Making and Mastering Space', *SOAS Working Papers in Linguistics*, 9: 359–72

—— (2000b) 'Walling Old Sana'a', in *Terra 2000: 8th International Conference of the Study and Conservation of Earthen Architecture* (London: James and James Scientific Publishers)

—— (2000c) 'The Lore of the Master Builder', in *'Traditional' Knowledge: Learning from Experience*, Traditional Dwellings and Settlements Working Paper Series (Berkeley: University of California Press)

—— (2001) *Minaret Building and Apprenticeship in Yemen* (London: Curzon)

Ryle, G. (1949) *The Concept of Mind* (Harmondsworth: Penguin)

Sperber, D. (1994) 'The Modularity of Thought and the Epidemiology of Representations', in L. Hirschfeld and S. Gelman (eds), *Mapping the Mind* (Cambridge: Cambridge University Press)

Sperber, D. and D. Wilson (1986) *Relevance: Communication and Cognition* (Oxford: Blackwell)

Unicef (1993) *The Situation of Children and Women in the Republic of Yemen 1992*. Unicef, Sana'a, Government of the Republic of Yemen (Amman, Jordan: al-Kutba Publishers)

3 EXPLOSIVE NARRATIVES: THE ARTICULATION OF 'NUCLEAR KNOWLEDGE' IN MUMBAI

Raminder Kaur

Starting in May 1998, India and Pakistan carried out a series of nuclear tests in an obsessive game of one-upmanship. Whereas ambiguity, if not secrecy altogether, was previously the order of the day, a new, unmitigated visibility of nuclear capability has emerged in these rival countries. Formerly both governments swore to the concept of 'recessed deterrence' vis-à-vis nuclear weapons; now both have switched to 'overt deterrence' (Deshingkar 1998: 1298). This is not to say that military and scientific knowledge has become totally transparent, but to observe that nuclear weapons have walked onto the South Asian stage of conflict drama. As Itty Abraham states, 'Secrecy marks the limits of public information, accountability, recognition, and knowledge and as such is a boundary producing mechanism' (Abraham 1997: 2137). Even though former secrets have been made public, undoubtedly a thick cloud of censorship hangs over the newly disclosed information. We could consider this vortex in terms of a tension between the *disclosure* and the *withholding* of information about nuclear matters: disclosure being imbricated in national pride associated with technological and military prowess; withholding being linked to vigilance about national security. It is the cusps of this tension that can be productively explored in the realm of public culture, where nuclear knowledge about nuclear power is creatively portrayed in relation to ethical and socio-political concerns.

A focus on nuclear armament raises key themes considering the question of knowledge. Most obviously, there is a need to consider the scientific rationality that underwrites the growth of the technology. The development of nuclear power in South Asia represents a particular case within the indigenisation of more 'global' arenas of knowledge, even though the 'global' here is circumscribed by those countries that stand

51

at the pinnacle of techno-scientific knowledge, namely the Nuclear Five – the United States, Britain, France, Russia and China.[1] The idea that these countries have the prerogative on scientific knowledge is, for better or worse, challenged by newer nuclear powers, India and Pakistan among them. Indigeneity from this perspective becomes part of a hegemonic project with manifold, sometimes contradictory, features: even though technological parts and information might have been brought in from outside India, the process nonetheless informs an indigenous, homespun rhetoric which argues that nuclear weapons were developed through national scientists and expertise. There are several Indian terms that semantically overlap with the notion of indigenous (Needham 1975), but the term that is most apposite for the nuclear topic is *Swadeshi* – a notion that has fuelled the development of nationalism since the early twentieth century.[2]

While India and Pakistan are globally perceived as 'developing', or as part of the 'Third World', they now have recourse to a sophisticated ammunition science that could cause inordinate damage. This is compounded with neo-Orientalist notions of rivalry and impulse – that they might just 'press the button' – as if to say that despite technological achievements, these countries' capacity for 'rational' management is still wanting. Thus nuclear knowledge is deemed alien to the Indian landscape, even though Indian nationalists see the development of nuclear technology as part of the *Swadeshi* discourse.

If the discourse of indigeneity informs contestatory regimes of knowledge to do with the nation and its place in the global ecumene, how are we to consider the views and opinions of other constituencies *within* the nation on the nuclear question? It appears that there is a need to investigate the fault-line between *indigeneity* and *locality*. Whereas, as with China, the former has entered into state discourse about the ownership of technology and power (Rack, this volume), the latter becomes the more operational concept for understanding the positionality of localised constituencies within the nation. By 'local', I take heed of Arjun Appadurai's notion of locality as 'a complex phenomenological quality, constituted by a series of links between the sense of social immediacy, the technologies of interactivity and the relativity of contexts' (Appadurai 1995: 204) – that is, 'local' is not a static entity, but always relational and contextual. The locality is, of course, traversed by translocal concerns to do with the nation-state and its position in the global ecumene; but it differs from the project of indigeneity in that it provides variegated perspectives that lie on a continuum between acquiescence with, and critique of, nation-state discourse. These local perspectives are *refractions*, not reflections, of the hegemonic view on nuclear armament as proposed by government representatives. This is not to assume that national discourse is homogeneous, for local opinions never cease to critique the hegemonic positioning of nuclear power within national rhetoric.

Evidently, the categories of local, national and international are per-spectival, and nuclear knowledge hinges on their shifting intersections. Beyond the arenas of politicians, activists and scientific experts, however, the question begs how the population at large comprehends the nuclear debate. An ethnography of nuclear knowledge is still absent from the literature, the focus being more on the 'hard lens approach' of political science, international relations and environmental studies. It is almost as if the subject is deemed marginal to the everyday worlds that people inhabit even though it has a fundamental effect on their sense of self, community and environment. The hiatus parallels the differences and, we can add, hierarchy between scientists and non-scientists in relation to agricultural knowledge (see Sillitoe 1998). This chapter considers the nuclear issue largely from the viewpoint of non-scientists *and* non-politicians, that is, from the more local perspectives of Mumbai residents who are just as affected by India's decision to enter the nuclear arms race as are nuclear experts and government representatives.

I consider how nuclear knowledge is consumed, rearticulated and re-presented to others. Whilst *representation* implies reflection that underwrites much of Eurocentric epistemology surrounding an abstract and neutral discourse called knowledge, *re-presentation* implies the refraction of knowledge transmission characterised by perpetuity as well as modification (Hollway 1984).[3] (The hyphen alludes to the fact that every practice or display of nuclear capability becomes itself a production, not a facsimile copy.) As this production is interwoven with other cultural narratives and not simply represented or merely translated (Hobart 1993), the knowledge becomes part of wider cultural processes that undermine its reification. These more diffuse narratives perform multifarious purposes of legitimation, celebration, interrogation, critique and also inform further praxis. In the case of India, popular conceptual-isations of nuclear knowledge are often intertwined with moral, religious, nationalist or *swaraj* (self-reliance or independent) discourses. In 1998, these debates were particularly conspicuous in festival displays during the Ganapati festival (*utsava*) in Mumbai, Maharashtra, which took place just three months after the first round of tests.

After a brief background note on the rise of nuclear visibility in Indian public culture, I shall consider how knowledge about nuclear issues filters into the popular imaginary, and how, in turn, it becomes the basis for other kinds of public dissemination of knowledge.[4]

THE NUCLEAR BACKDROP

In India, the increased visibility of nuclear power is exemplified by National Republic Day parades of Agni ballistic missile warheads. As elsewhere, public culture has a global fetish for scientific advancement as accreditation for full participation on the international political stage. Since independence, the command of science and technology – of which the nuclear issue is an integral part – has re-presented India's narrative of modernity (Abraham 1998). There seems to be urgency attached to making the Indian arsenal (both nuclear and conventional) part of a pageantry of power in order to make it seem more credible. The increase in visibility is consonant with, although not completely determined by, the rise of a politicised visual culture with masculinist overtones. This is particularly associated with the Hindutva (Hindu nationalism) brigade, whose project likens technology to toughness. The nuclear debate, however, has its supporters across the political spectrum.[5] Shiv Visvanathan describes the popular appeal of nuclear programmes amongst most political parties as 'an orgy of agreement ... Every political group wants to be implicated, get a lick of the nuclear ice-cream' (Visvanathan 1998). Recent reports have shown that successive prime ministers of India, with the exception of Morarji Desai, have supported the Indian weapons programme (cited in Deshingkar 1998: 1298). Indira Gandhi was one of the first to express an interest in nuclear developments with the first nuclear tests held in Pokhran in 1974.

As nuclear weapons are arguably the currency of international power, the tests signalled India and Pakistan's attempts at a new global positioning. Due to the West's subsequent backlash with economic sanctions, this could be argued to have only been partially successful. Nonetheless, the five declared nuclear states were given the message that other countries wanted admittance to their nuclear club. Debate between pro- and anti-nuclear weapons groups has been vehement in India since the 1998 nuclear tests. Anti-nuclear opponents point to the human and ecological disasters, the vast expenditure that could be siphoned towards the need for water, food, housing and welfare for the poor, and India's co-option into an unequal nuclear world in what effectively constitutes the US nuclear emporium (*Outlook*, 11 September 1998).[6] Critics also point to the hypocrisy and bias inherent in such treaties as the Comprehensive Test Ban Treaty (CTBT) and the Nuclear Non-Proliferation Treaty (NPT) (Deshingkar 1998: 1297). Their viewpoints have received sanction by the Indian state and fuelled their sense of righteousness. Pronuclearists point to the threat posed by the two neighbouring countries, particularly with Pakistan over the conflict in Kashmir, and China due to earlier border skirmishes in 1962.[7] Hindu chauvinists point to the need to protect India through the deterrent of nuclear weapons, since the subcontinent has for centuries been either threatened or invaded by foreigners. Nuclear strength is equated with a louder voice in global affairs. Despite opposition, the most lyrical being Arundhati Roy's much publicised essay, *The End of Imagination* (1998), and her frontline protests, the nuclear issue has attained hegemony, its novelty value seeping into popular consciousness.

Rather than seeing the debate simply in terms of a dichotomous relationship between pro- and anti-nuclearists, or treating nuclear knowledge as the reified entity it has become in mainstream media reporting, festival narratives demonstrate that nuclear power issues are embedded in a web of intersecting discourses, whose discursive elements are part of the larger narrative of the nation. Effectively they make the unknown familiar and lay the premises for the indigenisation of what might be considered alien knowledge.

In what follows, I outline five recurring themes from the displays. The selection is merely heuristic, for it is the intermingling of themes which underwrites the illustrious array of the festival tableaux.

The first and most conspicuous discourse is the intricate entanglement of nuclear power and religious ethos. Modern technology is sanctified by recourse to a religious discourse, to such an extent that it takes on a fetishistic quality (Abraham 1998: 20). Just as Mother India sanctifies new dam projects in the namesake film (Thomas 1990), so Ganapati is seen to bless the social issues placed in front of him – whether it is to do with the person, the family or the nation. Occasionally, nuclear weapons are discussed in light of well-known religious stories from the *Mahabharata*, for example, or gods are shown giving their blessings (*ashirvad*) to nuclear power for the national welfare. These narrative strategies enable the updating of an old tale and impart a moral message to modern innovations; modernity and morality become intricately entwined. When discussing the festival displays (below), I shall refer to this phenomenon as the sanctification discourse.

Linked to the above, the second discourse is the Gandhian ideal for peace, or *satyagraha* (truth-force or the theory of moral action). *Ahimsa* (non-violence) is an integral feature of Gandhian notions of *satyagraha*: as is well known, (Mahatma) Mohandas Karamchand Gandhi declared that 'Truth is the end; non-violence is the means.' However, despite differing perspectives, Gandhi's stress on spirituality is easily channelled into a Hindu spirituality characteristic of Hindutva ideologues. India's public profile as a nuclear country has allowed the *ahimsa*/non-violence discourse to be resurrected for a modern purpose, in what some critics consider a distortion of Gandhi's ideas (Bharucha 1998). This 'new era of *ahimsa*' (Bharucha 1998: 1295) is about 'weaponising', but with no intention of using the weapons, accompanied by rhetoric of the need to protect India and promote regional peace. In contemporary India, nuclear weapons are overwhelmingly seen as the most credible way of protecting the nation in hostile surroundings and a means with which to uphold issues to do with national security in a 'peaceful' manner.

This conjunction of military technology and the rhetoric of peace promotion has arisen out of 'the peculiar condition of atomic energy: at one and the same time a potentially peaceful technique as well as being a deliberate means of mass destruction' (Abraham 1997: 2145). But it has also to do with earlier tensions between modernity and tradition, where technological developments are most welcome if they are embedded in age-old ideas to do with spirituality and a sense of indigenous ethics, again indicating the harmonisation of rationality (science and modernity) and religiosity. Gandhian notions of *ahimsa* become an extension of the discourse of spirituality that lends modern progress – this time, in the form of nuclear weapons – credibility and acceptance.

The third discursive articulation has to do with the Nehruvian legacy of modernisation and national development. Even though Jawaharlal Nehru himself proposed steps towards nuclear disarmament, his support of modernisation and development has been conflated with the argument that nuclear power is beneficial for the development of India (Abraham 1998: 2). The glorification of nuclear weapons follows earlier precedents of celebrating the nation's military strengths and achievements, and more widely those of science, technology and industrialisation.[8] The development of nuclear bombs is equated here with technological progress, rather than with their potential for (environmental or economic) destruction. Science and technological progress has formed part of the official government drive since at least Nehru's administration following India's independence. Nehru regarded science as the new national religion, and large-scale industries as the temples of modern India (Pandey 1994: 50–1). The Nehruvian association of national religion and development has filtered into most party considerations, whether Congress or the Bharatiya Janata Party (BJP) or more left-wing parties. Gandhi, in turn, has emphasised the spiritual essence found in the cottage industries and rural idyll of India; they too are displayed in some *mandap* tableaux.[9]

The fourth discourse recalls India's historic struggle for freedom and independence. Nuclear weapons are utilised to continue the narrative that technology grants a degree of autonomy in the global ecumene, and re-presents a quest for regional supremacy to end India's vulnerability to neo-colonial yokes. The rhetoric of self-reliance recalls Gandhian notions of *swaraj* (self-reliance), but from very different premises. It is self-reliance not based on the nurturing of cottage industries but premised upon control of the outcome of modernisation programmes. The rhetoric recalls Gandhian notions of spirituality, fuelling Hindutva ideals for a religious ethos, but underpinned with masculinist pretension to ward off any suggestions that India is a 'soft state'.

The final interwoven discourse deals with the threat of the external Others, specifically China and Pakistan. The nuclear race, which began in 1998, was accelerated by the fear that neighbouring countries would avail themselves of military technology to harm India's interests. Previous wars, border skirmishes and the threat of invasion and infil-tration have provided grist to India's national mill. The notion of the Other sitting right outside the door is a constant reminder of the country's precarious geo-political position, and provides an extra boost to nuclear armament. But the Other is also a fickle category, prone to shifting alliances with friends and foes swiftly swapping place. The vigilant awareness which is called for as a result is further supplemented with a penumbra of other nations who oppose India's aspirations. The West, or perhaps more to the point, countries already in the nuclear club, particularly the US, have come under repeated attack as Indian politicians appeal for equanimity in the world of nuclear treaties. So, whereas with sworn enemies like Pakistan the desire is to expunge and control, in relation to other nuclear countries, the Indian government's desire is to mimic and attain a comparable international ranking.

Each of the festival tableaux detailed below presents a creative combination of the above discourses. They not only reproduce elements of the above, but 'reproduce' them. *Mandal* members, in their creation of tableaux, select, reject and recombine elements of the above discourses in an interactive and innovative way. In the process, they demonstrate a locally produced inflection on more national concerns. Of the five festival displays I concentrate on, one *mandal*, the Spring Mills Sarvajanik Ganeshotsava Mandal, demonstrates the explicit patronage of a politician from the parochial Hindutva Party, the Shiv Sena. It is one case where straightforward relations between nuclear power and Hindutva prowess and masculinity are shown. In other cases, however, this equation is not tenable; the displays are not simply about 'boys playing with their toys', even though this is what the stand-off between Pakistan and India over the number of nuclear tests led us to believe. Occasionally the reproduc-tion leads to some notable ambiguities. For instance, whilst it can be asserted that nuclear armament enables an equation between chauvinism and masculinist bravado, other narratives tend to present a more ambiguous picture, celebrating both technological prowess and the need for non-violence and social harmony. Similarly, the Nehruvian emphasis on science and state-led development programmes would seem to conflict with Gandhian resistance to the technical and scientific world associated with the West. However, as will be made evident, several contemporary nuclear narratives present a fusion of the two. They demonstrate a conjunction of both Nehruvian and Gandhian narratives, with their correlates of national progress (science, technology, industrialisation, masculinity) and non-violence (peace, femininity and what might be described as traditional values).[10] Narratives of spiritual harmony and peace rest alongside those celebrating science, technology and industry to each other's benefit. The fact that these displays are offered for sanctification by Ganapati is further testament to the need to marry new technology with Indian religious values. As is suggested by the blurred boundaries between Hinduism and Hindutva, critics arguing that gods are often used as 'pretexts for communal agendas' (Bharucha 1998: 1295) do not account for the full story.

EXPLOSIVE SCENES

The Ganapati festival is a major event in Maharashtra dedicated to the elephant-headed deity Ganapati (otherwise known as Ganesh, and predominately seen as the 'remover of obstacles' [Courtright 1985]). The festival provides a site for presenting a variety of narratives in illustrative shrine displays, sometimes accompanied with audio-taped narration. Many displays represent not only religious matters, but also historical narratives, as well as more topical subjects.[11] The public Ganapati festival as we know it today was started by Bal Gangadhar Tilak in the 1890s as a means to circumvent colonial laws prohibiting collective gatherings. By using the pretext of a religious festival, and the British reservations against interfering in the religious affairs of indigenous communities, Tilak was able to disseminate his political views to large audiences (Cashman 1975; Courtright 1985). Similarly, today's political uses of the festival represent dynamics of nationalism, with differing political motives and contexts (Kaur forthcoming). There are several Ganapati festival organisations (*mandal*) with Shiv Sena affiliations in contemporary Mumbai. The Shiv Sena is a regionalist party that since the 1980s has adopted the Hindutva mantle. Since 1995, it has been in alliance with the BJP, and heads the Maharashtra State Legislative Assembly. The affiliated festival organisations invariably re-present displays in the interest of party agendas, and in obeisance to its leader, Bal

Thackeray. The audio-taped narrations accompanying the displays assert a Maharashtrian-biased martial brotherhood, socio-political issues in favour of the party, and a call for action, effectively exemplifying political praxis sanctified by religion. This sits comfortably with the celebration of a modern, strong and nuclear India, and is most noteworthy with the Spring Mills Compound tableau considered below.

Space does not allow me to concentrate on the construction and financing of the *mandal*, or account for the tableaux' stylistic conventions.[12] These are the subject of detailed attention elsewhere (Kaur 1998; forthcoming). Suffice it to say that many of the men in the residence-based *mandal* are involved in the decision-making and construction of the displays along with professional artists contracted to produce items such as models, audio-taped recordings, and Ganapati *murti*.[13] Thus the *mandal* displays and narrative re-present a collective authorship. They channel the input of a number of people including the main artists and decision-makers along with the endorsement of local residents (of perhaps a building, compound or a street section) who contribute to the construction funds.

The first *mandal* display considered here, constructed by the Sarvar Vidya Sarvajanik Ganeshotsava Mandal, celebrates India's achievements where technological progress for the betterment of the people as a whole is equated with nuclear weapons. Vignettes of electricity pylons, dams, satellite dishes, fighter planes, the Agni missile, an astronaut, computers and farming technologies are represented (illustration 3.1). The accompanying Marathi audio-taped narration, which I translate, is as follows:

For 150 years, the British ruled India. On 15 August 1947, India became independent due to freedom fighters' self-sacrifice. Love and devotion towards the Motherland led to her freedom.

The states of India are very powerful – they have their own language, customs and lifestyles. But all of them were united in the freedom struggle. They all fought for freedom. After that there were several differences and divisions and some people were not loyal to the country. Due to this India has suffered a setback. Now it is the dream of every Indian that in the twenty-first century, India will be such a country: self-sufficient, independent and well developed.

The progress of the country in the economic field is very important as it makes for employment. The main thing is that unemployment should come to an end. We should concentrate on the agricultural economy. If there is proper farming, India will not need to import food from anywhere.

Second, we need to adhere to family planning, because we need to bring down the population of India. We should spread literacy. We should also take care of the environment. India can have cordial relations with our neighbours,

3.1. The Sarvar Vidya Sarvajanik Ganeshotsava Mandal display.

but it also needs to be protected if required. Development in science and electronics is important.

India's freedom has been gained through a long struggle. So we should try to keep unity from Kashmir to Kanya Kumari, from Gujarat to Bengal, and maintain its cultural harmony keeping it integrated and alive. India should be a country that is prosperous in science and industry. For this we are prepared to sacrifice everything for the development of the country.

The narrative does not explicitly mention nuclear issues, but as can be seen from the Agni missile replica in the display, it has conflated nuclear power with the discourse of national development. The display also hints at the need to protect India from its neighbours who could be potential enemies with a nuclear development programme. The discourse of independence is recalled as a lesson for contemporary times. Science, along with economic development, is held to be in the nation's interests, and for the people's good. This is all enveloped in a sanctification discourse as a prayer to Ganapati. Such tableaux on the benefits of modernisation programmes to the nation have been prevalent prior to 1998 as well. Displays such as those of dams, pylons, power stations, the Konkan railway, and the Indian astronaut, Rakesh Sharma, in space are common features in tableaux presenting the best of the nation's achievements. Nuclear weapons have provided an additional technology in displays to the glory of the nation. In this case, we can see that the display and narrative demonstrate an overwhelming acquiescence with a benign nationalism.

The second tableau was constructed by the Spring Mills Sarvajanik Ganeshotsava Mandal. The *mandal* was headed by the President, Kalidas Kolambkar, a Shiv Sena MLA (Member of Legislative Assembly). The tableau depicted a giant mountain (Mount Kailash), inside which was a Shiv temple (*mandir*) made to look like a rock-temple.[14] A scene of the Pokhran desert is created at the far end, with nuclear tests indicated by flashes of light, and with deities on a cloud (Brahma, Vishnu and Shiva) effectively blessing the tests (*ashirvad*) (illustration 3.2). Abraham's provocative observations are not too far from the truth:

Symbolically, the hyper-traditional met the hyper-modern in the shape of the atomic reactors, the most modern of objects so similar to the *lingams* found in countless Shiv temples across the country. (Abraham 1998: 10)

3.2. The Spring Mills Sarvajanik Ganeshotsava Mandal, I display.

Many respondents in Mumbai also likened the *lingam* to an atomic reactor, as this *mandal* stunningly evokes not only conceptual but also visual parallels.

The tableau is defiantly chauvinistic and aspires to present India as a member of the world nuclear club. The major nuclear countries – USA, Russia, France, Britain and China – are represented in all their glory with iconic representations of each country: the Statue of Liberty (illustration 3.3), Red Square, the Eiffel Tower, Tower Bridge and a Chinese pagoda with a dragon, respectively. These are placed on opposite sides to tableaux of the Indian parliament building, the Lok Sabha (the Indian parliament) and freedom fighters on the other side. The short narration runs like a tour guide, highlighting the features of the walk-through display:

> You are about to do *darshan*[15] of Ganapati. The sceneries around him show the contemporary situation of all the main countries of the world. We have had fifty years of independence and are celebrating the progress of our nation.

As one *mandal* member explained, 'The scene promotes self-dependency. Now we should be able to protect ourselves, otherwise other nuclear countries will rule over us.'

This tableau relies upon a combination of an elaborate sanctification discourse, alongside a recollection of India's independence struggle, and an allusion to other foreign nuclear powers. Not only is the display sanctified by virtue of being part of a Ganapati festival display, but also

3.3. The Spring Mills Sarvajanik Ganeshotsava Mandal, II display.

because other deities, too, are blessing the tests. On a parallel note, when shockwaves from the nuclear blasts lifted a mound of earth the size of a football field by several metres, one of the scientists is known to have said, 'I can now believe stories of Lord Krishna lifting a hill' (*India Today*, 22 June 1998). Pokhran, the site itself, is venerated as a significant scientific and quasi-sacred site. Its sacred nature has arisen due to the nuclear programme's affinity with the nation, already a mythicised entity. There is a recollection of India's freedom struggle against British colonialism with portraits of Bhagat Singh, Subhas Chandra Bose, Gandhi, Tilak and Nehru. The contemporary foreign powers recall the fight against colonialism, but they also represent an ideal position for India to aspire towards. However, there is an uncomfortable realisation that, despite the *mandal*'s claim to India's greatness, the Nuclear Five are reluctant to side with India's claims to nuclear armament. This is hinted at in the placing of the foreign countries' tableaux on the opposite side to the Indian displays. The absence of a display on Pakistan in the walk-through construction is also noteworthy. With the pomp and grandiosity surrounding this display, the mood is that of an assured, perhaps aggressive, nationalism.

The next festival organisation, the Khetvadi Sarvajanik Ganeshotsava Mandal, shows another recombination of the five main discursive elements. The display is narrated in the form of a conversation between a scientist/teacher standing in front of a replica of the Homi Bhabha Atomic Research Centre, and a female student (illustration 3.4). To the other side is a representation of a scene from the *Mahabharata* involving the characters of Arjun, Dronacharya (Arjun's teacher), Krishna and Ashvatthaman (who was also taught by Dronacharya, but on the rival side of the Kauravas). The Ganapati deity is not visible at the start of the show, being situated behind sliding doors. With slide projections, the scientist discusses various subject matters. The narration proceeds as follows:

Man: A person who is powerful should have weapons, but not misuse them. Take a tale from the Mahabharata. Dronacharya, guru of Arjun – whose son was Ashvatthaman – he uses a powerful weapon, the *brahmasastra*, to destroy the Pandavas. But if it strikes earth, it will destroy everyone. Krishna advises him not to use it, otherwise Brahma might have to create another earth. But Ashvatthaman says he only knows how to use it, not to stop it. Krishna changes the direction of it so as it does not destroy the world. It strikes somewhere else.

Krishna cursed Ashvatthaman's third eye. Whereas before it was a source of bright energy, now it'll be a source of pain, 'you will never be able to live or die in peace. That's because you tried to use something which is not in your power to use.'

Woman: If it [nuclear power] can be progressive, why is the whole world saying it's bad?

3.4. The Khetvadi Sarvajanik Ganeshotsava Mandal display.

Man: It can be very destructive, but our neighbours can take it upon them to destroy India. We have to be very careful. History itself is a witness that we have never attacked any country, nor made slaves. Our message has always been for peace. [*slides of Mahatma Gandhi are shown*]

We will use nuclear power for positive and peaceful purposes. Only a strong person can talk about peace. A weak person cannot talk about peace. Whatever we got is for our protection. We shall use it positively, such as creating power, developing radioactive isotopes to cure cancer, and innovations to replace farming seeds. We wish for peace all over the world.

[*Sliding doors open to reveal Ganapati*]

We pray to Ganapati to let there be peace in the world, and let the flag of India fly high.

In this tableau, nuclear power is legitimated with recourse to narratives of religious events from the *Mahabharata*, and India's nationalist history. The parable from the *Mahabharata* makes the point that nuclear power is not inherently evil; the main problem, rather, is that its controllers can be selfishly motivated. The insinuations are that Pakistan, which is likened to the unscrupulous Kauravas dynasty, is more liable to abuse nuclear power, because unlike India the country does not have a history of non-violence. The narrator claims that the Gandhian discourse of *ahimsa* (non-violence) is inherently Indian – despite the fact that both countries were carved out of the same landmass. The point is explicated when the scientist comments, 'Our message has always been for peace.' Nuclear power is justified with recourse to the fact that India is a worthy owner, as it has always pursued a peaceful path. It claims India needs to go nuclear, otherwise it will again become a dependent nation as in colonial times in view of the threat posed by India's neighbours. Even though this *mandal* offers an element of doubt as to nuclear weapons and their possible abuse, ultimately it is not anti-nuclear. The story from the *Mahabharata* represents a parable for modern times, asserting that nuclear power can be used for the nation's development by not only protecting India, but also providing other sources of fuel, and agricultural and medicinal benefits.

The fourth *mandal* considered here, the Mazgaon Dakshin Vibhag Sarvajanik Ganeshotsava Mandal, interrogates chauvinistic supporters who have not thought properly about the negative aspects of going nuclear. The tableau is presented in the form of a conflict between a peace-loving Mother India and her young upstart of a son discussing various aspects of the nation's history, present and future, illustrated by suitable vignettes that are lit up as the narration proceeds. The vignettes include a replica of Bill Clinton behind nuclear arms, skeletons and vultures representing the deaths from the Hiroshima and Nagasaki bombings in 1945, a large green[16] snake – a metaphor for British colonialism – and a creature eating away Kashmir, indicative of the conflicts in the region (illustration 3.5):

Son: Oh Mother, I have made you proud. The whole world recognises you as nuclear. They all know we are very powerful now.

Mother: OK, you have done this, but in my country people have made me proud by crowning me with peace. People like Mahatma Gandhi have been born from my womb. The ultimate truth of life is peace. Only peace can prevent the destruction of this country. So why are you moving to the wrong path?

Son: The century has come to an end. This dream of truth (*sukhasvapna*) has also come to an end. History will say that we have never attacked any other country. But Sikander, Babar, Ala'uddhin Khirji have all destroyed you. The British ruled over India for 150 years, and they took all the wealth from you. To get that freedom it is not that we have only got it by peace, but also by fighting as with Bhagat Singh, Chaphekar and Vasudev Phadke. The British are like a black snake (*kalasarpa*). These people did not leave just because of our peaceful conducts, but also due to our blood. Freedom fighters burned the black snake with their blood. Now it has left.

Pakistan is the first poisonous tree (*visha vruksha*) that the British left behind. From one side Pakistan, the other China – they were both attacking causing a storm. Pakistani terrorists have infiltrated your Indian boundaries and started spreading terrorism in India. They converted a heaven like Kashmir into a cemetery.

The message of peace that you were spreading could not save a great leader like Rajeev Gandhi. After we achieved independence, we have always been spreading peace and non-violence. That is why people have taken advantage of

3.5. The Mazgaon Dakshin Vibhag Sarvajanik Ganeshotsava Mandal display.

us and spoilt us with terrorism. Now we have created so many weapons that we can call all the shots. That is why whatever steps we have taken to become nuclear are right.

Mother: Forget it! Don't even bring such thoughts into your mind. Go back to history and see Japan. America dropped two nuclear bombs in Hiroshima and Nagasaki. Look at the state of them now. Generations and generations have suffered diseases due to the radiation. Even the land has become barren and dangerous. If everyone becomes nuclear, the entire planet will be made barren. I am the mother of a hundred crore[17] children. Even after so many children, if any one of them is destroyed, I will roam around like a mad woman.

Son: OK, I can understand your feelings, but today the world has changed. Non-violence and peace are the words of the weak. Someone comes and hits you on the cheek, and you put the other one forward – this is only part of the story. For if you become so powerful, then no one will dare to touch your cheek at all. That is the whole truth.

Make yourself so powerful that even god will have to come and ask you himself, 'Now tell me what is your request?' (*Kudhikor kar boland itna ki khudha khudh apne bande se puche, bol teri razakya hai?*)

So we made Pokhran our proving ground/destiny (*karmabhumi*). We didn't just blast one or two bombs. We blast five [models of five missiles go up in the air]. But what did the world say when we became nuclear?

India is a poor country. A poor country has become nuclear so they imposed more sanctions, because they consider India to have committed a big crime. They say India is not supposed to have done this. It is like telling a newly wedded couple about family planning straight after their ceremony.

The CIA are spending millions of rupees on satellites to capture activities around the world. That satellite could not even detect the nuclear tests in Pokhran. Yet they call themselves a First World country. For that information they had to come to our doors to understand how their satellites did not pick up the tests. We are now self-sufficient in nuclear power so don't even threaten us with your nuclear weapons.

Our hearts are full of patriotism. Let's see how much strength our opponents have. How to live with our neighbours peacefully? There are certain rules and we follow these, but you need to also follow these rules. We are in search of peace. Ahimsa is our motive. If you are going to threaten us, we are not going to sit back. Today we are united – *Jai javan, jai kisan* – victory to the soldier, victory to the farmer. Now it is *jai javan, jai kisan and jai vigyan* (victory to the scientist).

Mother: Humanity of mankind has been destroyed. It has been replaced by the devil. Ultimately man only requires 6½ square feet so why do they want the land of someone else? Because man has developed science so much – out of which he developed the nuclear bomb.

O Ganesh you created the universe and humans, but the same humans are trying to destroy the universe. The human being's wish is that the entire world shall dance under his feet. For that he is sitting around with the remote-control in his hand, and trying to destroy the world. But he doesn't understand he too will be destroyed. Ganesh you are the creator of destiny. If that is the destiny of mankind – self-destruction – then kindly destroy the lines of my forehead [the lines of the forehead are said to decide man's destiny]. You destroy those lines and let mankind be the messenger of peace and let him create an earth which is run by people progressive in nature. It is through man that the creator sees what you want in the world. So show him the right path; because you are the person who creates and can make others work towards creation.

Here, the narrative presents an intermingling of discourses to do with sanctification, national development, *ahimsa* (non-violence), independence and the threats posed by India's enemies with the infiltration of 'terrorists' within its borders. The two main characters in the tableau – mother and son – portray a splitting of the pro- and anti-lobbies on nuclear power, as well as representing the masculinist, or aggressive, and pacifist poles of the debate. The tableau reflects the ambivalence of the *mandal* members, ultimately preferring to circumvent the dilemma by offering it as a prayer to Ganapati. The *ahimsa* (non-violence) discourse is revealed in both its old and new forms: even though Mother India argues for peace as in the Gandhian sense, her son proffers the new versions of the *ahimsa* argument, asserting that nuclear power brings peace and stability to the area. The double-splitting is also apparent in the accounts of India's history: Mother India represents the more peaceful and selfless perspectives on Indian achievements in history, whilst the son presents the aggressive and masculinist view characteristic of the contemporary Hindutva brigade. *Jai vigyan* (Victory to the scientist) was in fact used after the tests (Deshingkar 1998: 1298). *Jai javan, jai kisan* (Victory to the soldier, victory to the farmer), probably from Lal Bahadur Shastri with reference to the 1965 and 1971 wars with Pakistan (Pinney 1992: 31), is now conjoined with 'Victory to the scientist'. Nuclear science is legitimated with recourse to concerns about both national security and the country's progressive development.

The display mocks the West, specifically the US, for its pretensions to be a promoter of world peace. The narration highlights its violence by recalling the horrors of nuclear warfare with the example of the bombing of Hiroshima and Nagasaki in 1945, and slights the US satellites' inability to detect the nuclear tests. Indeed, the media had reported that the military satellites which monitor infrared radiation could pick up Pakistan's Kahuta plant, but not India's dispersed plutonium reprocessing plants (*Frontline*, 11 September 1998). The overwhelming mood is one of critique of anti-national and 'outer-national' forces peppered by ambivalence between a peaceful, non-nuclear nationalism and that of an aggressive pro-nuclear nationalism.

The last tableau is by the Barvenagar and Akhil Bhatvadi Sarvajanik Ganeshotsava Mandal. The display presents both rural and urban issues. Vignettes of youth dabbling in drinks and drugs, scenes of rioting hordes, water systems and nuclear missiles with a dove of peace carrying a missile characterise one side of the display. On the other is a representation of Buddha sitting under a bodhi tree, tractors and dams, and farmers in the act of committing suicide due to there being no annual crop yields (illustration 3.6). Ganapati is not visible at the start of the show as the *murti* is situated behind sliding doors:

11 May, 1998 – the time: 3.45 pm in Rajasthan
There was a blast in Pokhran and the scientists were very happy. After 1974, this is claimed to be the second success. Lord Buddha is smiling. But what does this mean? Buddha is a god for peace. If he smiles, what does it mean?

Ultimately the blasts are an insult to the god of peace. The major (First World) countries have now put sanctions. This has affected the economy very badly. So the dove of peace is now moving towards the First World country. Now they are preaching peace. Indian peace messengers are trying to go to America and settle it. But the First World countries are thinking something else about India.

What is the situation in India? There is a lot of religious, caste and economic differences. On top of that sanctions have been imposed. If India's aim is to be a First World country, how can it achieve such a goal under such circumstances?

The road that India has adopted is self-destructive. When you see the situation of youth in India, Buddha laughs, but now that laugh is frightening, ominous. The youth are important to the development of any country. However youth are involved in drugs, so the country is weak.

3.6. The Barvenagar and Akhil Bhatvadi Sarvajanik
Ganeshotsava Mandal display.

Now India has become nuclear and this message has been spread all over the world. But there are so many uneducated people in India who don't even know the meaning of nuclear.

Even in this Indian economy that is largely based on agriculture, the farmers are in such vulnerable circumstance that if there is no crop farmers have ended up committing suicide. At moments like that you can understand why Buddha might be mocking. These are the harsh facts. Under such circumstances, even though India has become nuclear, is it possible that it can also become a superpower?

To give all people justice, we require alertness and awareness of what is really required. Everyone should be educated, literacy rates should rise, industry should develop, economy should progress. Just by making nuclear explosions and shaking the world, it's not going to solve internal problems. This is not the solution.

[*The doors open to reveal the Ganapati murti*]

So what is required? *Rashtriya nishta* – commitment to the nation that will develop the country with the strength of its youth (*yuvashakti*) and not nuclear bombs. Unity among the people will create a sense of integrity. Just like the seven lights of the rainbow, even though it's one ray of light.

Mankind has created such weapons that will destroy mankind itself so what's the use of it? What is required is peace. Ganapati with his hand on the *veena* is giving the message of peace to the world. He makes a promise not to use these nuclear weapons. We're praying to god to give us the strength to safeguard mankind and bring peace to the world. We want to be the major country in the world which promotes peace. We want to give the tricolour the status of peace promoter (*vishvashanti*).

This narration is the most critical of Indian policy, as it is of the world powers. The tableau represents a potent critique of the co-option of *ahimsa* arguments by contemporary political parties. It points to the economic disparities amongst the country's populace and the need to promote peace in other ways. The future development of the country rests largely upon the shoulders of India's youth, asserts the *mandal* narration. Thus the development discourse is more people-centred than in the previous tableaux. The narrative moves the threat of the external dangers to those that are trenchant within the country, such as illiteracy, drugs and sectarianism, and points out that these need to be rectified before India can claim to be a superpower. The code-word for success after the first three nuclear tests on 11 May 1998, 'The Buddha is smiling', is cleverly twisted to show the Buddha is 'mocking' as an ironic commentary on India's aspirations for nuclear might. Nonetheless, even though this *mandal* is critical of nuclear power, there is a reluctance to advocate the total dismantling of India's nuclear capacity. The message seems to be: now that it is here, there is nothing that can be done to reverse the trend, but the country can set an example by never using the nuclear weapons. As one member said, 'We want to explain to the West, that they [the weapons] are now here to promote peace.'

*   *   *

After the testing of the atom bomb in New Mexico on 16 July 1945, J. Robert Oppenheimer quoted verses from the *Bhagvad Gita* in which Krishna states: 'Now I have come as Death, the Destroyer of Worlds.' These prescient remarks have now been brought home to the land of their inspiration. Arundhati Roy (1998) adds further lyricism in *The End of Imagination*: 'From now on it is not dying we must fear, but living.' But nuclear armament has not spelled total death to the social imaginary; indeed in some cases it is the reverse. Activist resistance to nuclear armament, as opposed to critical engagements, is not as apparent amongst Ganapati festival organisers. Even though the festival organ-isations and their displays are distinct, they partake of similar discursive agendas, and position themselves within it with variations upon a theme. The tableaux do not just represent aspects of nuclear knowledge but re-present them embedded in several cultural narratives that are indicative of, as well as productive of, wider socio-cultural contexts. Per-spectives on the nation and its position in the globe are thus negotiated, that is, tinged by the creative thoughts of locally based community artists. Each *mandal* had a different inflection on the nuclear debate current in August 1998, some more oppositional than others. However, the narratives that have been highlighted above are less anti-nuclear to the point of advocating their total dismantlement than pro-nuclear so long as the weapons are considered for peace promotion.

The *mandal* members' reluctance to scorn nuclear power altogether arises out of, on the one hand, the rise of nationalism in times of liberalisation and rivalry with Pakistan, and on the other, the normalisation of discourses to do with science and technological progress for the national good. *Mandal* members largely support the view that 'science may not quite be ready to go out of the business of making weapons' (*India Today*, 31 August 1998). The displays demonstrate a tenuous hold on the intricacies of nuclear debates, policies and treaties. Moreover, nuclear power is harboured in historical and religious narratives, along with the resurrection of Gandhian notions to do with non-violence, and Nehruvian ideas of state-led development. The viewpoints mainly arise out of the need to keep vigilant yet peaceful relations between neighbouring countries, and a criticism of the hegemony and the hypocrisy of the Nuclear Five countries.

ACKNOWLEDGEMENTS

My sincere thanks go to the named Sarvajanik Ganeshotsava Mandal and their members for permitting me to record their tableaux, and Shomal Nasnolkar for help with Marathi translations. This chapter has been developed from my PhD, which was funded by the Economic and Social Research Council (award number R00429334179), SOAS, the Central Research Fund and a RAI/Sutasoma Award.

NOTES

1. India is one of three 'hold-out' countries to the NPT, which recognises five nuclear weapon countries. The other two 'hold-outs' are Pakistan and Israel.
2. See Abraham (1997, 1998) for a discussion on the rhetoric and actuality of *Swadeshi* nuclear technology.
3. Rather than invoke Foucault's totalising notions of discourse, I find Laclau and Mouffe's formulation more useful. Laclau and Mouffe refer to the differential terrain of hegemony but also point out the 'impossibility of any given discourse to implement a final suture' – describing it as the 'field of discursivity' (Laclau and Mouffe 1985: 111). This proposition enables an identification of how sets of discursive fields articulate in society, as well as an exploration of the power differentials between them.
4. There appear to be changes in mainstream public opinion since the initial tests, as was evident in the comparatively muted reception of the tests in April 1999. The tides of political currents since the 1998 tests are beyond the main scope of this chapter.

5. Nuclear technology follows in the wake of better known visual technologies which the Hindutva brigade have availed themselves of late, including audio-visual media, mobile video *rath* (chariots) (Pinney 1992: 3) and computer technology.

6. Such effects were greater on Pakistan than India. The Pakistan government was compelled to delve into reserve funds more than in the Indian case.

7. See Vanaik (1997: 2236) for a critical assessment of the possibility of strategic threats posed by China.

8. Indeed, 11 May 1988, the day of Buddha Purnima, was declared 'Technology Day', by the prime minister, Atal Behari Vajpayee, not 'Peace Day' as we might associate with Buddha himself.

9. Contrary to earlier representations of new technologies and the tensions between rural and urban ways of life, in India's cities technology is celebrated for reconciling modernity with traditional values. Thus, modernity need not be about greed and expansion, but can also be for the benefit of fellow citizens. Pinney discusses tensions between tradition and modernity as it applies to oleographs in Bhatisuda and Nagda. For urban metropolitan contexts, the tension between modernity and tradition is less apparent. Instead modernity is enframed by 'that older, purer order' (Pinney 1992: 19).

10. Qualifications such as Gandhian and Nehruvian are not always articulated amongst festival participants. However, to note the associations of varieties of nationalism is not to assume that they are necessarily in the minds of festival participants, for much of their arguments have been normalised as part of the nation's vocabulary. I use these terms as analytical tools with which to illustrate the convergence and gradual normalisation of such discourses.

11. Often, the *mandal* members would come together to construct the displays, even though the Ganapati *murti* and any other three-dimensional models would commonly be commissioned by a professional artist (*murtikar*).

12. Here I am interested in how the narratives are constructed and information publicly channelled. Within the limits of space, I focus on the content of the texts and displays, not so much on audience reception. In 1998 most spectators and festival participants generally felt they needed weapons to protect India from attack, and they needed peace. I focus on such questions at more length in my forthcoming book (2003) with Permanent Black, *Performative Politics and Cultures of Hinduism: Public Uses of Religion in Western India*.

13. *Murti* is the three-dimensional model of a god.

14. As the 'father' of Ganapati, Shiv is one of the three main gods in the Hindu pantheon, the others being Vishnu and Brahma.

15. *Darshan* is about 'seeing' the god, but also being seen by the god. See Eck (1985).

16. No one at the *mandal* could explain why the snake was painted green (as against the black snake in the narrative). Perhaps the artists had run out of black paint or thought a green snake looked more realistic.

17. *Crore* is a quantity of 100,000.

REFERENCES

Abraham, Itty (1997) 'Science and Secrecy in Making of Postcolonial State', *Economic and Political Weekly*, 16–23 August: 2136–45
—— (1998) *The Making of the Indian Atomic Bomb: Science, Secrecy and the Postcolonial State* (London: Zed Books)
Appadurai, Arjun (1995) 'The Production of Locality', in R. Fardon (ed.) *Counterworks: Managing the Diversity of Knowledge* (London: Routledge) pp. 204–25
Bharucha, Rustom (1998) 'Politicians' Grin, Not the Buddha's Smile', *Economic and Political Weekly*, 30 May: 1295–7
Cashman, Richard (1975) *The Myth of the 'Lokmanya': Tilak and Mass Politics in Maharashtra* (Berkeley: University of California Press)
Courtright, Paul B. (1985) *Ganesa: Lord of Obstacles, Lord of Beginnings* (New York: Oxford University Press)
Deshingkar, Giri (1998) 'Equating Technological Progress with Nuclear Bombs', *Economic and Political Weekly*, 30 May: 1297–8
Eck, Diane L. (1985) *Darsan: Seeing the Divine Image in India* (Chambersburg: Anima Books)
Hobart, Mark (ed.) (1993) *An Anthropological Critique of Development: The Growth of Ignorance* (London: Routledge)
Hollway, Wendy (1984) 'Gender Difference and the Production of Subjectivity', in J. Henriques et al. (eds) *Changing the Subject*, (London: Methuen), pp. 227–63
Kaur, Raminder (1998) 'Performative Politics: Artworks, festival praxis and nationalism with reference to the Ganapati Utsava in western India' (PhD, SOAS, University of London; and forthcoming with Oxford University Press)
—— (forthcoming) 'Remote-Control Influence and the Ganapati *Utsava* in Mumbai', in Lynn Thomas and Jacqueline Hirst (eds), *Creating the Future: The Use and Abuse of Indian Role Models Today* (Delhi: Oxford University Press)
Laclau, Ernesto and Chantal Mouffe (1985) *Hegemony and Socialist Strategy: Towards a Radical Democratic Politics* (London: Verso)
Needham, Rodney (1975) 'Polythetic Classification', *Man* 10(3): 349–76
Pandey, Gyan (1994) 'Nationalism, Communism, and the Struggle over History', in Mehdi Arslan and Janaki Rajan (eds), *Communalism in India: Challenge and Response* (Delhi: Monahar), pp. 51–9
Pinney, Christopher (1992) 'Moral Topophilia: The signification of landscape in Indian oleographs' (Department of Anthropology and Sociology, SOAS, University of London)
Roy, Arundhati (1998) 'The End of Imagination', reprinted in *Guardian*, 2 August
Seshan, T.N. and Sanjay Hazarika (1995) *The Degeneration of India* (New Delhi: Viking)
Sillitoe, Paul (1998) 'The Development of Indigenous Knowledge: A new applied anthropology', *Current Anthropology*, 39(2): 223–52
Srinivas, M.N. (1995) 'Gandhi's Religion', *Economic and Political Weekly*, 24 June: 1489–91
Thomas, Rosie (1990) 'Sanctity and Scandal in Mother India', *Quarterly Review of Film and Video*
Vanaik, Achin (1997) 'Three Misrepresentations', *Economic and Political Weekly*, 6 September: 2234–6
Visvanathan, Shiv (1998) 'Welcome to the Patriot Games', http:/www.desk.nl/~nettime/

4 KNOWLEDGE INTERFACES AND PRACTICES OF NEGOTIATION: CASES FROM A WOMEN'S GROUP IN BOLIVIA AND AN OIL REFINERY IN WALES

Alberto Arce and Eleanor Fisher

This chapter examines encounters between international institutions that frame their objectives through a global policy language, and people whose lives are the focus for change heralded by these institutions. It explores how a global policy language, which seeks consensus and equality, can be at odds with local understandings, conflict and intentions. This is done by examining two cases based on commissioned research undertaken by the authors as members of larger research teams.[1] The first piece of research focuses on the perceptions of women from a development group in Bolivia, which has received assistance from a European bilateral donor. The second focuses on the experiences of people confronted by the immanent closure of the oil refinery where they work. This oil refinery is located in Wales, but it is part of a transnational corporation.

Experiences that emerge in the narratives of women in Bolivia run counter to representations of women's empowerment promoted by the European bilateral donor. Likewise, experiences of oil refinery workers in Wales are hard to equate with images of corporate social responsibility generated by the transnational corporation. Although they have very different rationales, modes of operating and objectives, both the donor and the corporation use a global and encompassing policy language. This global policy language incorporates dominant cultural concerns, technical categories and politically correct semantics, and generates normative abstractions couched in neutral terms (Pottier 1999: 41; Arce 2000). Although these (eminently malleable) abstractions encompass only part of people's experiences, they act as powerful representational fields used to orient institutional action; they are part of an apparently rational expert communication process, and may be used to organise consultations between different stakeholders.

We would argue that the way people experience the representations and policy language introduced by global institutions may generate different interests among social actors. The mismatch raises a particularly important question: How do negotiation practices take place in situations where a global language treats people as equal in terms of power and knowledge, and where negotiations are oriented towards finding a consensus between different actors? Furthermore, what implications do negotiation practices have for the lives of the people affected? A focus on knowledge interfaces to explore negotiation practices between different social actors enables us to see how encounters between local people and representatives of global institutions can have a profound if somewhat unpredictable effect on people's lives.

By concentrating on actors' experiences that enter into practices of negotiation, we wish to comprehend the nature of contradictions and struggles that emerge from knowledge interfaces. Our analysis thus builds on the efforts of anthropologists to understand the significance of people's social practices, and their ability and capacity to socially construct and make sense of the world. Three aspects of knowledge as a process are explored. First, we show how people's knowledge may emerge as a counter-narrative to the knowledge incorporated within global policy language. Second, we consider the social discontinuities that are generated between the role that is attributed to local people by global institutions and the way in which people's agency is manifest in everyday struggles and contractions that are part of negotiation practices. Third, we briefly mention how the ethnographic data collected as part of each piece of commissioned research were reassembled to maintain an image of good development practice in Bolivia and of corporate social responsibility in Wales.

PRACTICES OF NEGOTIATION

A focus on knowledge has been an important means for social anthropology to understand different cultures and give expression to the world view of 'distant others'. This has contributed to a process of challenging stereotypes, assumptions and parochial views concerning the significance of knowledge in the organisation of social life. It has also formed part of a criticism of science in terms of its limited capacity to encompass other rationalities and representations of the world.

To place knowledge at the centre of analysis in practices of negotiation may help to bring out startling discrepancies of interest between global institutions and local social actors. These discrepancies rest on different knowledge frames, which emerge in the interpretations made by different actors. Negotiation practices arise when the global policy language emerges as a field in which different interpretations, intentions and activities are played out as actors seek to achieve different ends. In effect, a multiplicity of interests becomes located within a framework, which intersects across different understandings of a given situation. This emerges as a social background that policy-makers take for granted but, because the conflicts can generate unintended outcomes, it should not be conceived simply as a platform for identifying a common future for the parties interacting within the scope of the global policy language.

When development interventions were re-thought in the 1980s and 1990s, there occurred a re-evaluation of the role of local knowledge in rural development, which challenged the western paradigm of progress and modernisation as an effective vehicle for development (Chambers 1983; Richards 1985; Pottier 1993; Cernea 1996). Part of the challenge involved recognising that local knowledge is an important element within social change (Arce and Long 1994). This gave rise to a critical assessment of the methodologies used by experts, contributing to the promotion of participatory approaches to development. Coupled with an emphasis on the importance of indigenous knowledge, the development of participatory methodologies has highlighted the role social anthropology can play in analysing knowledge encounters between social actors (and their actions and feelings) present at the local level. One way to study these encounters is through the methodological notion of the interface.

The term interface conjures up an image of two surfaces coming into contact. However, it has been used more specifically in rural development to refer to 'a critical point of intersection or linkage between different social systems, fields or levels of social order where structural disconti- nuities, based upon differences of normative value and social interest, are most likely to be found' (Long 1989: 1–2). One can debate the relative merits of this definition, but what is useful is that it enables us to analyse the way different social actors negotiate their interests in processes of development or economic change. In this respect, the notion of interface helps us to give due importance to the dynamic and potentially conflictual nature of social encounters that draw on different knowledge frames and diverse understandings of actors' entitlements to power. Knowledge is part of the relations of power that exist between social actors and their position in society, generating confrontation as well as collaboration in situations of change. In these power relations, negotiation practices are important because they highlight the way different actors attempt to organise their livelihoods within specific institutional and social environments.

Here we can define negotiation practices as the capacity actors have to accept or reject value assertions and the normative aspects of a policy language. The ambivalent character of the relationship between everyday action, on the one hand, and the symbolic meanings contained within a policy language, on the other, can generate the space for actors to redirect the symbolic orientation of a given policy language. Thus, through a partial selection of some aspects of a symbolic policy language, actors may be able to legitimise their actions and provide these actions with locally situated meanings and aims. This process of legitimisation involves interpretation of the symbolic elements of a policy and serves to orient action in different directions away from the framework of shared understanding initially intended by a global institution. This leaves the global policy language as a frame of ambiguity in terms of the interests, relevance and identity of different actors.

In this context, negotiation takes place as an exercise in the accommodation of different objectives, which cannot be explained simply by reference to the normative aspects of the policy language, but also needs to encompass an understanding of actors' capacity to reinterpret the normative aspects of the policy language through their own understandings and everyday actions. It becomes important to recognise the accommodations different parties make in adapting the global policy language to their own ends, and in so doing, imbuing the symbolic orientation of the policy with different meanings and intentions.

Negotiation practices can be understood in at least two different ways. The first is a consensus view of negotiation, namely the idea that actors must confer with one another in order to reach an agreement or a compromise within a common framework of understanding. This conveys an image of people coming together around a negotiating table with a shared language, use of resources and policy aims in order to resolve their differences. The second view goes a step further: while it recognises that compromises can be made, it gives analytical significance to the contradictions and struggles that arise in everyday life. These contradictions and struggles emerge in practices of negotiation as diverse understandings within a global policy language, bringing disparities in power and resources to the fore.

In this chapter we follow actors' experiences in processes of negotiation by taking the second position on negotiation practices. This enables us to recognise that inequalities of power and resources are inherent within any negotiating situation. It also locates negotiation in relation to meanings that are given by existing social relations and knowledge, rejecting the idea that negotiation should simply be equated with purposive rational communication. In effect, negotiation forms a 'battlefield of knowledge' (Long and Long 1992) between different actors who attribute specific social meanings to particular situations, institutions, values and discourses.[2]

THE MULTIPLE DIMENSIONS OF INDIGENOUS KNOWLEDGE

A plethora of terms are used to refer to the knowledge people hold; they include 'local knowledge', 'traditional knowledge', 'indigenous knowledge', 'indigenous knowledge systems', 'indigenous technical knowledge' and 'rural people's knowledge'. Often these terms are converted into acronyms (IKS, ITK, etc.) in keeping with the transfiguration and encoding of expert linguistic symbols that, one assumes, accord with the technical and consultancy leanings of the different authors. Such variations in terminology reflect different research interests, theoretical stances and practical applications, as well as the influence of disciplines that have sought to appropriate indigenous knowledge issues (ecology, geography, anthropology, sociology, forestry, etc.). Nonetheless, participatory approaches to development have played a central role in placing indigenous knowledge at the forefront of development practice. From a participatory perspective, development should start from the position of an equal partnership between local people, development workers and researchers (see Chambers 1983; Farrington and Martin 1988). It follows that local people's understandings should be given equal merit alongside other sources of knowledge such as scientific understanding (Richards 1985; Chambers et al. 1989; Scoones and Thompson 1994). From this perspective, outsiders become catalysts to local development processes, being at most facilitators of discussion.

The emphasis on placing indigenous knowledge at the heart of development practice emerged as a critique of both the modernisation approach and of the inability of political economy to deal with political and technological issues at the local level. It sought to dislodge and make relative the position of expert knowledge as the engine of social transformation (Sillitoe 1998). But participatory thinking still provided an optimist's view of science as an equaliser between different actors, carrying an image of political neutrality. Perhaps because they drew on western notions of equity and democracy, the most populist veins of the participatory approach to indigenous knowledge failed to reflect on the issue of how local knowledge was 'used' in development. In particular, insufficient attention was paid to the difficulties associated with social inequality, contradiction and conflict, central elements affecting people's lives. In effect, there was a concentration on popularising science, and merging it with an understanding of certain indigenous skills, while disregarding the more conflictual aspects of everyday knowledge and the complexity of how people negotiate their livelihoods.

More recently, attempts have been made to incorporate a socially differentiated view of development, where factors such as gender, ethnicity, class, age and religion are highlighted as important to knowledge issues (Scoones and Thompson 1994). The way local knowledge is manipulated within participatory activities to express certain views to the exclusion of others has also been highlighted (Mosse 1995), as has the way project workers shape local knowledge (Arce 1993).

Another step in thinking about knowledge issues was the identification of the power held by scientific and technical experts in directing planned social change (Long and van der Ploeg 1989; Long 1990; Long and Long 1992). This line of analysis emphasised that expert knowledge generates systematic modes of ignorance out of the specialisation and inherent fragmentation of development expertise (Hobart 1993). What this position was unable to achieve, however, was an appreciation of how the experiences of diverse actors become part of a negotiation process interconnected with aspects of different modern projects of development (symbols, images of the future, values, practices, etc.). More recently, thinking has shifted towards a concern with the rebounding effect of knowledge in its diversity (see Parkin 1995). Unlike a structural interpretation of knowledge construction, which locates the relationship between people and experts as a purposive rational outcome of the interaction of culturally distinct knowledge categories or systems, Parkin emphasises the merging and 'relocation of the origins of beliefs and behaviour' (1995: 148). This merging process occurs as people engage in a 'counter-work', which involves the interplay of hegemonic and non-hegemonic discourses and values, irrespective of whether they emanate from global or local scenarios.

It has become increasingly apparent that locally situated actors have the capacity to reposition expert knowledge within the context of everyday life (see Leeuwis and Arkesteyn 1991). Hand in hand with this local capacity is a critical attitude towards what are interpreted by actors to be external features. People's everyday existence can be expressed in fusion, blending and counter-movements to expert knowledge. Counter to this position, the recent emphasis on the semiotic dimension of knowledge (see Latour 1993; 1994; Law 1994) could lead us to ignore an appreciation of the deeply political and contradictory nature of knowledge negotiations in development processes and socio-economic change (Golinski 1998: 37–43). Therefore, an understanding of negotiation practices has to deal with dynamic and globally generated features, and related conflict. This constitutes a background against which people incorporate and reorganise knowledge elements; negotiation is not simply a matter of maintaining the status quo but 'the re-assembling of the recursive properties of entities and the redrawing of boundaries in such a way that new social forms emerge out of existing ones' (Arce and Long 2000: 17).

A utilitarian representation of knowledge, in which indigenous knowledge is merely an expert's translation of people's everyday knowledge and skills, does not capture the political struggles of local people. Portraying knowledge as a local resource depoliticises it from the context in which social contradictions arise. Instead, we need to realise how multiple realities surrounding negotiation practices are socially and materially generated through people's experience.

GLOBAL INSTITUTIONS: TWO ILLUSTRATIONS

Examples from two pieces of commissioned research will now be used to explore processes of knowledge negotiation in people's lives and in their dealings with global institutions. Although the two studies were undertaken for different purposes and audiences by two very different organisations, one being a bilateral donor and the other a transnational corporation, there are parallels when we discuss the way change is heralded by these organisations, and people's subsequent responses. Each organisation is global in outlook and activities. In the case of the transnational corporation, its global reach is concerned with the maintenance of its rate of profitability within a highly competitive international market. In the case of the bilateral donor, its global reach is concerned with development assistance to alleviate poverty in different areas of the world. Both organisations use a normative language of equity, support and social responsibility as a platform to negotiate their interventions with actors at the local level. In the pursuit of their objectives, both organisations present themselves as defenders of western notions of equity and democracy, and as firm believers in consultation processes.

The two cases presented here complement each other by emphasising two aspects that need to be tackled when studying processes of negotiation. The first aspect is the outline of negotiation as a field of action and the different interpretations and interests of the parties concerned. This is mainly tackled in the Bolivian case. The other aspect is the importance of people's life experiences in their understanding of a global institutional language and how this has a rebounding effect on their assessment of how policies have consequences for their lives. This is mainly tackled in the case of the oil refinery in Wales.

INTERNATIONAL CO-OPERATION: A BOLIVIAN COMMUNITY

The first piece of commissioned research was conducted in three communities in Bolivia. A European bilateral donor who, at the time of the study, had been providing development assistance to Bolivia for ten years (late 1990s) commissioned the study as part of a larger evaluation. The terms of reference were to examine how people perceived development co-operation and establish whether the donor's policies had had an impact on their lives.

The bilateral donor promoted integrated development projects and provided funding for these projects to be run by local organisations. In the region where the research was carried out, a local NGO ran projects for the donor. The NGO, Procampesino, was supported by the Aiquile Regional Peasants Union, which promoted production and commercialisation projects as an integral part of social transformation through local empowerment. The bilateral donor framed its development policy in terms of a language of equality, sustainable development and participation as a means to facilitate the empowerment of local people. This was mediated by a local European co-operation expert, who helped the NGO to present a project to the donor in the appropriate language. This action managed to secure funding for the NGO to support micro-credit and communal shop projects at grassroots level.

The following example draws on the case of the NGO, Procampesino, and one community, Eloy, in the Aiquile Region. Eloy had been the locus for the implementation of NGO-run projects from the mid-1980s. In 1985, CARITAS, an international Catholic organisation, provided food to Eloy to improve child nutrition levels. A year later another Catholic NGO began to implement an irrigation project and a collective farm, with financial support from Spain. Neither project was in operation at the time of the study. In 1987, the latter NGO also began to implement a forestry nursery to boost reforestation on communal land. This project also failed because local people perceived their work to be unremunerated; only the nursery's caretaker appeared to benefit. At the end of 1989, a new rural development programme was started and led to the implementation of a number of projects over a five-year period. Several of these projects generated local conflict and were abandoned or discontinued as unsustainable. In 1990, Procampesino arrived with the mandate to implement a project supported by the European bilateral donor. Procampesino's project focused on micro-credit, which enabled it to give support to communal shops in the region surrounding Eloy. In Eloy itself, a shop had existed since 1985 but, because of social conflicts, it was not operating. Procampesino prompted interest in communal shops amongst female members of the community and two communal shops were established.

It is important to locate this project in the context of the NGO's political position. Procampesino had an ideology that promoted the local allocation of resources as a way for people to gain political awareness about their social position in Bolivian society. The allocation of resources through a small credit programme was part of a political strategy to guarantee the independence of local development from the Bolivian state and the promotion of political consciousness. This was part of the construction of a larger social movement intended to challenge and eventually negotiate development policies with the Bolivian state and the promotion of grassroots political consciousness. This political project was not the objective of the European bilateral donor and in this respect we can see the first step in a negotiation process that provided local political intentionality into the global policy language of the donor, generating in practice a counter-narrative that provided new local objectives and expectations to the project. The NGO managed to do this by agreeing with the donor on the perceived need to promote development through local empowerment. However, what was meant by local empowerment and how this was translated into practice were very different from the bilateral donor's understandings of local conditions.

In this context, Procampesino designed the micro-credit project and through their strategy bridged the objectives of the international development co-operation policies and their own political motives. One of the groups it started to work with was a women's group called 'Esperanza', which itself had its own understanding about what to achieve with the project. This understanding somehow was significantly different from that of Procampesino or the regional peasant union, which was another important party in this case. The interactions that followed the different orientations that each party attributed to the project constituted the field of negotiations to be analysed in the next section.

THE ESPERANZA WOMEN'S GROUP AND COMMUNAL SHOP

In 1990, a group of women who called themselves 'Esperanza' ('Hope') decided to reactivate a communal shop established in 1985 after being told informally by the local peasant union that the NGO Procampesino had 'a little bit of money' for this kind of investment. The women mobilised, obtained a loan of US$200 and used the money to buy household goods in bulk, which were subsequently brought to the community on a donkey. After the women had sold their first consignment of goods they contacted a man called Pablo who was one of the more important local traders of household goods. This action contravened bilateral aid guidelines, which stated that local merchants should not participate in the project, because given their social position they would benefit from the micro-credit instead of the intended bene-ficiaries. With the support of the NGO, the women negotiated an agreement with the trader. Pablo agreed to give the women household goods on credit and to transport these goods to the community in his truck. This arrangement worked so well that the women returned the loan of US$200 over a period of less than two years, and then borrowed a further loan of US$500, which, at the time of the study they were still trying to pay back. Now, a small number of women, based on their success, became the instigators of change within the community.

The history of the women can be traced back to the start of the communal shop. The group that started the shop initially had only 13 associates, linked across different generations and through ties of kinship and friendship. The women said they met every fortnight to give an account of financial expenditure and to discuss the many problems they confronted. Meetings normally lasted for a whole day, during which time they said that they told jokes, cooked together and exchanged important information regarding the organisation of communal religious cele-brations. Sometimes, they said, 'we shout at each other and sometimes we get angry with each other'. At the time of the research, the group was not only distributing household goods at lower prices than in the nearby commercial shops, but was delivering the commodities in the community. They also started to use their consumer-credit association to support one another socially. For instance, members agreed that when a woman dies, the women's credit-consumer association would buy her a coffin with money accumulated through the shop activities.

After two years, the shop had become strong enough economically to act as collateral to obtain agricultural credit for local producers (that is, the women's husbands). It was then that members of Esperanza came to be categorised as 'credit beneficiaries' by the Procampesino NGO. In practice, the way the women organised the communal shop meant that they successfully negotiated the institutional categorisation of 'credit beneficiary' to cover reciprocity relations and to create a social space to promote their own interests when negotiating with the NGO. This negotiation promoted their livelihood activities rather than their partici-pation in the regional peasant union or the NGO's political activities, as

Procampesino would have liked. Women's competence at running the communal shop was the outcome not of special properties peculiar to local or expert knowledge, but of a social composite of strategies and knowledge negotiations, such as their association with a local merchant, a relationship that clearly transgressed the bilateral donor's guidelines. In practice, these negotiations enabled the women's group to make sense of how they could succeed in their consumer-credit venture and in their negotiations with the NGO in order to achieve their aims and what was expected from them as 'credit beneficiaries'.

It is interesting to note that the women became involved in this project following the failure and unsustainable character of several other micro-credit projects targeted at male members of the community. The secretary of the women's group, Doña Felicidad Lopez, described how they accessed the credit to start the community shop:

There was a member of the regional peasant union that had a link with the NGO. Because Procampesino was active in the regional peasant union, it was this person who interceded on our behalf and the NGO provided us with the money. But after this it was our own responsibility to ensure that we paid parts of the loan back on time. In the beginning [1985], the association of women failed to mobilise resources because of internal divisions among ourselves. One section wanted to be part of the men's peasant union, the other wanted total independence because they argued it was impossible to develop in unity, constantly negotiating our interests with the men; usually we are not very good at making speeches in front of the men. Nowadays in the regional peasant organisation the number of women has been reduced to one and things are not going very well, because she is the only woman amongst hundreds of men ... we are not well represented in the regional peasant organisation.

In this narrative, knowledge and past experience of different interests are used to explain how the women's credit association became a partner of the NGO, Procampesino. It is interesting to recall different perspectives among women on how to address their relations with the powerful regional peasant union. Furthermore, the description of conflict and negotiation between men and women constituted the background to the women accessing the credit that started the community shop; it also presented their ability to negotiate in a situation that had a multiplicity of interests and no common framework for sharing understandings.

Doña Felicidad Lopez continued:

We don't have much relationship with political parties, but when they come they bring us T-shirts and footballs and sometimes they repair the road. All the people in the women's group are good friends and the direction of the chairmanship is rotated amongst the people who know how to read and write ...[only two]. The group does not want other women from the community to enter the group; we have invested so much work and time that the new people would benefit on our backs. The problem is they want to come but they never tell us directly whether they are going to work hard. We rotate the responsibility for selling the goods between ourselves, with some people responsible for up to five months, and then others take over. We also have special prices for associate members and another price for people who are not associated with us.

The fact that the women could not become more actively involved politically in the regional peasant union was in counter-distinction to their position as successful 'credit beneficiaries'. This shows us how actors negotiated different interests through their actions, attributing these actions with individual local meaning. This is significant if we remember that the European bilateral donor promoted empowerment as a key dimension of its policy on sustainable local development. Procampesino translated this into a strategy to encourage political engagement at the grassroots level, but the women's group Esperanza was blocked from this type of engagement by the male political leadership of the regional trade union. Instead, the women were oriented towards using their relationship with the NGO to achieve routine and mundane household consumption needs.

In the community of Eloy there is a geographical division between the women who live in the high and the low areas of the village. The women of Esperanza live in the low area and do not want certain others to join them. These others have themselves established a community shop. According to the accounts of the Esperanza group, there are good relations between the two groups, but they consider themselves separate and to some extent in competition. The groups have organised themselves according to different kinship and friendship relations; they have their own group identities and sense of belonging. The tensions between the two groups highlight tensions within the community, but at the same time ways of interacting and negotiating exist to control conflicts. As one woman explained: 'There are cases where one person organises other people in the community and then all the group buy one box of soap and then they share the benefits.'

SOCIAL DISCONTINUITIES AND NEGOTIATION PRACTICES

In Eloy, previous development interventions have taught community members that development usually means competitive relations and conflicts. One lesson was that to control conflicts people needed to appeal to kinship relations and feelings of friendship. In this respect, the history of the women's association can be traced back to an unsuccessful CARITAS programme in 1985. The programme, however, provided women with a network of contacts, which included several NGOs, the peasant regional trade union and traders in the local town, their husbands and other individuals in the community. At the same time, the women managed to negotiate resources, remaining independent from political parties and the political objectives of the peasant regional union, alliances that Procampesino actively tried to promote. Inter-generational ties, friendship and kinship also played a part in building the connections and creating the trust needed in tasks like selling goods and handling money.

Interestingly, the women's social position and their commercial success made them aware of the need to be better represented within the peasant regional union. However, their representation within the union was not recognised as politically important by the men or by the NGO. Perhaps, because the women's group had remained independent from the political objectives of the NGO and the peasant union, the perception was that women were a difficult group to control and could create problems in the men's world of regional politics. In spite of this, women were presented to the European bilateral donor financing the project as a showpiece of successful 'micro-credit beneficiaries' by the NGO.

This illustration highlights how important it is to look closely at people's negotiation practices. When common frameworks of under-standing are lacking, actors use these negotiation practices to build bridges to support their interests, often using a common global language (such as 'women's empowerment') but with very different meanings and intentions. This invites us to focus on everyday social life involving actor's strategies for working with one another and negotiating with other groups of people, including representatives of the European bilateral donor and of the development NGO.

Examining knowledge interfaces, such as those that arose between the bilateral donor and the NGO, on the one hand, and the NGO, the women's group and the regional peasant union, on the other, helps us to recognise people's social agency. How they engage and negotiate within the scope of the normative policy language of international development co-operation becomes a key issue. In this sense, the relatively successful experience of the micro-credit project can be easily abstracted by expert evaluators from the local situation; in the process, the diversity of meanings and intentions it embodied become ironed out in order to be relocated as a sign of development co-operation policy success in Europe. The idiom of women's empowerment became a negotiation bridge between the symbolic orientation of the development policy and the policy-makers' attribution of agency from their European office to these distant actors. However, the grassroots actors' aims, values and understandings were very different from those of representatives of the NGO and the bilateral donor who provided financial support to the project. It is at this point that the concept of negotiation practices can offer a window to approach the importance of people's experiences in bridging knowledge and social discontinuities, creating a heterogeneous reality that is the rebounding effect of knowledge in its social diversity of actors' interests.

CORPORATE SOCIAL RESPONSIBILITY: THE CLOSURE OF AN OIL REFINERY IN WALES

Our second example is based on applied research commissioned by a transnational oil company that had recently merged with another company and was undergoing a restructuring process (late 1990s). As part of this process, a decision was taken to close an oil refinery in Wales. The company commissioned the researchers to carry out a social and economic analysis of the refinery closure in order to know whether a socially responsible and cost-effective exit had been achieved. Here we draw illustrations from the section of the study concerned with qualitative social analysis (the larger study included a historical analysis, an economic impact assessment and a social impact assessment using quantitative as well as qualitative methods). The aim of this case is to show the importance of people's life experiences in assembling their own counter-narratives of 'corporate social irresponsibility'. In the following account, we shall refer to the oil refinery as 'the Oilworks' (a local name) and the transnational organisation as 'the Company'.

The Oilworks had been established in the 1920s when the company itself was newly formed. It had generated new employment and drawn people to the area. At its peak in the 1960s, the Oilworks employed 2,500 people (mainly men), but many others provided direct or indirect services or worked in construction. Residential concentration of the workforce, employment in a high wage industry and company support for local amenities contributed to a vibrant community. The oil refinery closed in the late 1990s; this was not, however, unexpected. The oil crisis in the Middle East in the early 1970s, together with an increased competitiveness within the industry, had focused attention on the need for tighter financial control. In keeping with an industry-wide trend, the early to mid-1980s had been a period of downsizing in which service trades (catering, security, bricklaying, plumbing, etc.) were farmed out to other companies, and 550 workers made redundant in 1985. A further 99 employees were made redundant in the early 1990s, at a time when the company was fighting to keep the refinery open. In the late 1990s, its closure was finally announced.

At the beginning of the study, representatives of the Company argued that the effect of closure on people connected to the refinery could be mitigated through a number of measures. These included: (i) assisting all staff to get a new job, if they wanted one; (ii) making suppliers aware of opportunities and providing them with support; (iii) alleviating effects of closure on the community and encouraging regeneration opportunities; and (iv) involving key stakeholders in planning, implementing and evaluating the closure process. This was framed in terms of a socially responsible exit from the site, in keeping with overall company policy commitments, which included meeting the concerns and needs of different stakeholder groups, involving 'mutual trust, dignity and respect' or 'fair treatment', as expressed by the Company.

When the Oilworks was thriving (prior to the mid-1970s) there was a sense that workers were part of a close-knit industrial community. People captured this by saying it was a 'family' industry: '[the local village] ...was built up because of the Oilworks. Virtually every household had a worker in it; sometimes 3–4 people under one roof.' In the past, workers who entered the Oilworks believed they had a job for life. Even in the late 1990s, a large number of employees born and bred in the area, had worked only at the refinery and could trace back three generations of family members who had worked there. 'My grandfather, father, uncles, aunt, you know, all worked there, even my mother during the war. She used to lag the pipes, came home all white, used to get called white mice those women ... [because of the asbestos].' Today, an older, retired generation (of men) portray the Oilworks as having offered people jobs and a prospect for the future: they express an enormous sense of loyalty to the company as it once was.

People employed at the Oilworks were based in the local community, many because they and their families had spent their lives there. This did not mean, however, that their experience and understanding of the 'oil world' were purely local in nature. This was expressed in the knowledge they held about people and countries in which the company had interests. Some of these distant people were trained at the Oilworks and a nearby technical college, and would stay in the local community, integrating to some degree. One informant recalled how a Nigerian visitor brought his family to a social evening in fancy dress, and how he and others had been very touched when they saw that the young daughter was dressed from head to toe in the Welsh flag. Company employees also travelled overseas. Another informant described how men skilled at working a particular type of pump in Scotland had migrated to work at the Oilworks in the early years when specialist knowledge and skills were in short supply. When later they or their sons moved to Abu Dhan, they became known as the 'Scottish Taffies'. Men also encountered raw products from different parts of the world.

Bench-B was originally intended for Palestine [oil] ... in 1948–9, it took 74,000 gallons an hour, 24 hours a day, that for two years. There was oil from Kuwait, Kiwana, Kucook, Agajari, and later Nigeria. They were all different types ... the Kuwaiti crude was stable crude oil, standard. Kuwaiti is light and sweet ... the specification for British oil is 4 per cent, it met the standards, but others are 2 per cent. All different, Nigerian crude has really low sulphur ...

Becoming intimately acquainted with different types of crude oil, men developed knowledge categories that made them masters of their craft.

At the Oilworks, the knowledge of their job provided men with the experience to devise practical ways to achieve the task at hand without necessarily following the safety regulations designed to avoid them hurting themselves. (As oil refineries are dangerous places to work in, numerous regulations and safety checks are linked to each operation.) 'The paraffin shed, the output was small but it took seven men ... the wax press ...the place was like a freezer. It was the most depressing place on earth, you wore special clothes, Brads, but we didn't wear the gloves, you got dermatitis if you wore gloves. Mind you, we very rarely lost time through the cold ...' Their experience made them weigh up risk against the practicalities of getting the job done and remaining in good health.

The people who held the knowledge accumulated during the operation of different plants on the site were confronted by the inevitability of closure of the refinery. The threat of closure generated a situation in which existing practices and social interests were challenged. We would argue that for the people concerned this experience cannot be understood adequately within a framework of abstract normative conceptions, such as the global language of socially responsible business, which the Company put forward by using terms such as 'mutual trust', 'respect' and 'fair treatment'.

Why the Oilworks had to close was a big issue with employees. Many made cases for keeping it open vis-à-vis other plants owned by the Company, for instance in France. Some argued that exiting from collective trade union bargaining in the early 1990s had been bad and had let them down, others that the senior management of the refinery were all of an age to receive a company pension (at 50) and therefore didn't care. 'We shut down not because the Oilworks was making a loss but because it was not making enough profit.' And, 'I feel a bit sore that the company have shut the Oilworks down because it got them out of a hole many, many times.' These were some of the arguments that were given. For these men the issue was not whether the process of closure was 'fair' in the terms of the corporate language. A characterisation of the closure process as 'fair' or 'equal' or involving 'mutual trust, dignity and respect' does not capture personal experiences, differences of opinion, unequal power relations or the conflicts that developed between different employees.

The closure in the late 1990s was a phased process, involving a three-year 'transitional operation'. In interviews, employees compared their experiences of the closure and their own situations with earlier downsizing. Several of them expressed that downsizing in the early 1990s was better handled than the redundancies made in the mid-1980s. One said that in the mid-1980s, 'it was horrendous, you got letters, there were men crying in the street'. Another described what it was like to learn about whether he had a job or not, and about how management decisions did not accord with his rationale about who should stay and who should go. 'In 1993 it was handled better ... you had to wait in a long line outside the office. You were called in one by one and told the decision. He asked you not to tell anyone but the whole shift was waiting outside. You knew who should stay and who should go, but it didn't work out that way.' Another described how at the time of the final closure announcement their wives had learned about the closure first, which had upset many people: 'there was more dignity about it, you learned about the closure in a meeting ... unfortunately it was leaked out via Teletext so many men's wives knew first ... and the press were waiting outside the gate, they always did when something was about to happen ... then when you learned about selection you didn't have a whole queue of men waiting.'

When employees were confronted by the imminent closure of the Oilworks, some were given assistance in coming to terms with the closure and applying for new jobs; this included counselling, skills assessment, CV writing, and training if needed. To initiate the counselling and job search process, company management brought in two successive employment agencies. The first was based outside the region and was chosen because it had carried out work for the company elsewhere. It began to assist employees following the closure announcement. However, it was found that although they were skilled in counselling, this was not matched by their capacity to identify suitable jobs because they did not have a local knowledge of different companies and informal relationships with personal managers in these companies, which could be drawn on. Subsequently, another company was brought in which had knowledge of the region and experience of assisting employees in the closure of oil refineries.

Most people interviewed were complimentary about the basic assistance offered by the employment agencies: 'She gave me good help with my CV' and 'You just have to say ... could you put in a CV for me on a particular job, so they are helpful in that respect.' When requested, assistance was also given to family members (not wives), although this depended on the discretion of human resource development personnel. Counselling came in for more negative comments: 'group counselling was a joke' and 'well the management get to hear'.

On announcement of the closure of the Oilworks, management needed to decide who would remain for the transitional phase and who would leave immediately. In interviews, employees compared this to the earlier process of selection when the company downsized in 1993. People perceived the 1993 selection to have been unfair due to personality conflicts, favouritism and anti-trade union sentiments, while the 1997/8 selections had seemed fair. 'In 1993 certain personalities dominated ... there was a petty vendetta ... ten people did the selection, five of whom you hadn't worked with for ten years.' Similarly, 'In 1998 it seemed the same information was used, but perhaps it was less personality based.' Other people argued that men who were active in the trade union were discriminated against. 'There are people who were experts in their jobs but they couldn't hold on to them, and then the people they moved in were far more incompetent.' There were other complaints too:

[In 1993] ... I was a supervisor and had to score people on 1–10 on such issues as punctuality. I had such a good team all the scores were around 98–99 per cent, but there were a lot of problems and complaints with the process. Now they have a review panel to assess people. That's much better.

It makes no sense when a man is transferred to the Bitumen plant because he needs training, he hasn't done the job before. The man is moving from another production unit, they use the selection criteria to transfer senior men from the boiler house, tank farm, other areas, even though they have never worked in the Bitumen plant.

What these accounts demonstrate is that the internal knowledge of the actors concerning how fair the selection process was and whether they had been treated with dignity and respect according to the language of corporate social responsibility, was mediated by the knowledge people held concerning internal conflict and divisions, favouritism, vendettas and anti-trade union sentiment. This led people to reassess critically and re-value fairness and social commitments within the company. This was expressed through personal stress and inter-personal tension, within both the workplace and the home.

There are animals on site and you get to know where they are. I was driving up by the reservoir and I hit this rabbit, it always came out at that place and normally I just avoided it, but I killed it, my mind was somewhere else.

His wife added

He was ever so upset, he's such a softy, then another time he missed the turning on the motorway, he's been driving there for years, it's not normal. We don't realise but the doctor took one look at me the other day and said, 'There's something wrong at home isn't there Mrs ...'

Catering staff working in the canteen gave a good example of the way workers were affected by the closure: 'The attitude of the men changed, they would take notice of little things and complain. It got so bad we took the issue to our boss but we were told to "grin and bear it" because the men were under stress. But we were under stress too. Life could have been made a lot easier for us if someone had told the men not to complain, but they just said keep smiling.'

One employee who had managed to transfer to a new job at another site owned by the company complained that there was a lack of support after the move: 'It was like being just another statistic to be moved on. I did my apprenticeship at [the Oilworks] ... and my dad was there but when I went up there as part of this new job it was like they didn't know me.'

In these accounts, we can see how important knowledge issues are for a more grounded interpretation of people's actions. This allows us to understand how awareness that the refinery would close and the impact it was having on individuals were expressed by people in different counter-narratives according to their experience of employment within the organisation and of the closure process. These experiences touched on social divisions and tension between different employees, of differences of opinion and also on individual insecurity and stress. When these features are taken into account it is very difficult to relate people's experiences to a normative understanding of corporate social responsibility.

As in the Bolivian case, this example shows how a lack of shared understanding between the management of the transnational corporation and employees at the refinery enhanced a diversity of conflictive situations at the local level. In the everyday conflicts that emerged, negotiation practices became important for building bridges between the experiences people had, and their way of representing these experiences, and the corporate language used by the corporation in which equality and fairness were emphasised. Thus, negotiation was part of local knowledge processes rebounding on the global policy language of corporate social responsibility, which shattered shared understandings about the need to close down the oil refinery.

CONTROLLING ETHNOGRAPHIES

It is interesting to reflect on how representatives of the European bilateral donor and those of the transnational oil company handled the research outputs. Unsurprisingly, given the practical nature of the applied research, knowledge issues, negotiation practices and conflict were not the explicit focus of analysis in either case. After the ethnographic data on people's perceptions in Bolivia were written up in the form of a long consultancy report, representatives of the European bilateral donor were at a loss to know how to handle the material. They decided that a summary would be made of the main points, in which tables of data were drawn, so information could be compared and contrasted. The data presented had a cartographic bias, influenced by the fact that these representatives of the donor were geographers by training. The information thus abstracted was then used to assess the general policy of the donor in Bolivia. This was presented in the form of a one-and-a-half-page report to parliament in the country of the bilateral donor, which primarily served to legitimise the good development practices of the bilateral donor and its support for local initiatives.

In the case of the social data on people associated with the oil refinery, a similar compression of the information took place. Much information on experiences, which comes into the realm of knowledge, remained unused from the start, while 'useful' data tended to be information that could be translated into a language of corporate social responsibility and integrated with quantitative findings without generating overall disparities. Workers' experiences could thus be evaluated against judgements such as fairness, mutual trust and responsibility. This involved a process of homogenising people's experiences, of underplaying conflict or differences of opinion, and of interpreting accounts according to the categories established by the transnational corporation. Once an initial 50-page social report had been written, the information was taken and integrated into the larger 299-page report. A 22-page summary was then compiled, and professionally produced, complete with glossy pictures. By this stage, the quantitative social statistics portraying a favourable view of the Company were dominant. Qualitative social information was largely reduced to illustrative quotations to 'flavour' the text alongside images of people achieving at the company, for example, playing rugby. In both cases, processes of abstraction of the ethnographic data occurred in which people's life experiences, knowledge and values were translated into abstract information to suit the perspectives of those who commissioned the reports.

In both illustrations, we see that the way people were categorised was restricted in accordance with the interests of the policy-makers or representatives of the private company. In fact, in neither case was diversity of experience, multiple voices or conflict incorporated into the final outputs. Our research, in contrast, revealed that people's agency and negotiation practices were much more complex than was represented by a global policy language, and than those funding the research wished to acknowledge.

CONCLUSION

In the two examples presented, we have focused on knowledge interfaces that were generated as part of struggles that challenged the interests, objectives and perspectives of policy-makers and company representatives, as they had been put forward in a global policy language. Knowledge was not a simple property of institutional or communal ownership; there was no all-encompassing and dominant knowledge. Rather, knowledge was the outcome of social relations and practices of negotiation in which a global policy language was brought into contact with actors' experiences and interests. The result of this was the rebounding of actors' knowledge in a diversity of interests, generating an understanding of the social process whose main characteristic was a lack of shared understanding that could negotiate a general consensus about the intentionality of the actions promoted by the global institutions.

The global policy language had been put into place in order to incorporate actors' practices, values, nostalgia and images of the future, in accordance with institutional objectives. However, people's knowledge engaged with the global language and ideas in ways not intended by the institutions. Through negotiation practices and knowledge encounters, people repositioned themselves vis-à-vis the global institutions. In the process, expert knowledge and objectives became re-inscribed, generating different interests between negotiating actors. In both cases, diverse interests generated conflicts and counter-narratives to the global policy language. The result was a set of practices of negotiation of a kind – in which people came to know how to interact with the global institutions and achieve certain ends or to criticise their lack of commitment to knowing people's way of life and experiences. This has led us to present a notion of negotiation that is very different from a concept of negotiation that presupposes the unfolding of a neutral practical rationality which 'glues' social action to a collective rational framework of shared understanding, and in so doing defines negotiation as a collective consensus. Negotiation practices as rational and driven by consensus present a view of 'life out there' as part and parcel of a functional knowledge system of global institutions. We believe this view of negotiation is a pervasive misrepresentation of actors' agency, but reinforces corporate images of global fairness.

The notion of negotiation as a concept to encompass the resolution of conflicts through social engineering of a shared way of life, seems to have little to contribute towards an understanding of the cases of a women's credit group in Bolivia, and oil refinery workers in Wales, and is even less useful in shedding any light on the connection between social events and people's local knowledge. Yet there is in our cases a significant continuity, such as in the cultural reaction against women from the regional peasant union, that blocked an improvement in women's political representation or in the oil workers understanding of the transnational company as a 'family industry'. In this sense, meanings, values, organisation and co-operation interact with different actors' interests and conflicts, generating the rebounding of knowledge as counter-narratives to global policy objectives. The problem of the relation between continuity and social discontinuity should be posed in terms of the possibility of increasing the features supposedly characteristic of negotiations, which are freedom of action and the creation of alternatives. Social action and alternatives are part of social life accommodations, which are not determined or controlled by the rational presuppositions required by a social engineering approach to achieve consensus. In this chapter we have shown that there are no objective aspects of life, which are independent from people's interpretation, attribution of meaning and actions.

To rethink the notion of negotiation we need to amplify actors' interpretative capacities through their capacity to act according to different life experiences. In this context, the local knowledge of social actors has an analogy with the experience of the global institutions. In this sense, the study of negotiations should keep the tension between global and local language, so as not to confuse the rhetoric of global policy language with local understanding, conflicts and interests appearing in the study of social processes.

NOTES

1. We would like to extend our thanks to Ian Barney, from the Centre for Development Studies, University of Wales Swansea, with whom research was jointly conducted with Fisher in Wales. We are also grateful to members of the research team in the Bolivian study. We would specially like to mention Professor Georg Frerks who made the commissioning of the study possible. The views represented here are solely those of the authors; they are responsible for any errors.

2.   See Arce (1993) for an early ethnographic analysis of negotiation practices
     and knowledge issues in relation to food policy implementation in Mexico.

REFERENCES

Arce, A. (1993) *Negotiating Agricultural Development: Entanglements of Bureaucrats
     and Rural Producers in Western Mexico*, Wageningen Studies in Sociology No.
     34 (Wageningen: Wageningen University Press)
—— (2000) 'Creating or Regulating Development: Representing modernities
     through language and discourse', in A. Arce and N. Long (eds), *Anthropology,
     Development and Modernities: Exploring Discourses, Counter-Tendencies and
     Violence* (London and New York: Routledge)
Arce, A. and N. Long (1994) 'Re-positioning Knowledge in the Study of Rural
     Development', in D. Symes and A.J.J. Jansen (eds), *Agricultural Restructuring
     and Rural Change in Europe* (The Netherlands: Wageningen Agricultural
     University)
—— (2000) 'Reconfigurating Modernity and Development from an Anthropo-
     logical Perspective', in A. Arce and N. Long (eds), *Anthropology, Development
     and Modernities: Exploring Discourses, Counter-Tendencies and Violence* (London
     and New York: Routledge)
Cernea, M. (1996) *Social Organization and Development Anthropology*, The 1995
     Malinowski Award Lecture, Environmental Sustainable Development and
     Monographs Series No. 6 (Washington, DC: The World Bank)
Chambers, R. (1983) *Rural Development: Putting the Last First* (Harlow: Longman
     Scientific & Technical)
Chambers, R., A. Pacey and L.A. Thrupp (eds) (1989) *Farmer First: Farmer
     Innovation and Agricultural Research* (London: Intermediate Technology Pub-
     lications)
Farrington, J. and A. Martin (1988) *Farmer Participation in Agricultural Research:
     A Review of Concepts and Practices*, Agricultural Administration Unit Occasional
     Paper No. 9 (London: IDI)
Golinski, J. (1998) *Making Natural Knowledge: Constructivism and the History of
     Science* (Cambridge: Cambridge University Press)
Hobart, M. (1993) 'Introduction: The growth of ignorance', in M. Hobart (ed.),
     An Anthropological Critique of Development: The Growth of Ignorance (London
     and New York: Routledge)
Latour, B. (1993) *We Have Never Been Modern* (Cambridge, Mass: Harvard
     University Press)
—— (1994) 'On Technical Mediations – Philosophy, sociology, genealogy', in
     Common Knowledge 34: 29–64
Law, J. (1994) *Ordering Modernity* (Oxford and Cambridge, Mass.: Blackwell)
Leeuwis, K. and M. Arkesteyn (1991) 'Planned Technology Development and
     Local Initiatives: Computer-supported enterprise – comparisons among Dutch
     horticulturists', *Sociologia Ruralis*, XXXI (2/3): 140–61
Long, N. (1989) 'Introduction', in N. Long (ed.), *Encounters at the Interface: A
     Perspective on Social Discontinuities in Rural Development*, Studies in Sociology
     No. 27 (Wageningen: Wageningen University Press)

—— (1990) 'From Paradigm Lost to Paradigm Regained: The case for an actor-oriented sociology of development', *European Review of Latin American and Caribbean Studies* 49, December: 3–24

Long, N. and A. Long (eds) (1992) *Battlefields of Knowledge: The Interlocking of Theory and Practice in Social Research and Development* (London and New York: Routledge)

Long, N. and J.D. van der Ploeg (1989) 'Demythologizing Planned Intervention: An actor perspective', *Sociologia Ruralis*, XXXIX (3/4): 226–49

Mosse, D. (1995) *Authority, Gender and Knowledge: Theoretical Reflections on the Practice of Participatory Rural Appraisal.* Unpublished mimeo, KRIBP Working Paper No. 2, KRIBHCO Indo-British Rainfed Farming Project (Swansea: Centre for Development Studies)

Parkin, D. (1995) 'Latticed Knowledge: Eradication and dispersal of the unpalatable in Islam, medicine and anthropological theory', in R. Fardon (ed.), *Counterwork: Managing the Diversity of Knowledge* (London and New York: Routledge)

Pottier, J. (ed.) (1993) *Practising Development: Social Science Perspectives* (London and New York: Routledge)

—— (1999) *Anthropology of Food: The Social Dynamics of Food Security* (Cambridge: Polity Press)

Richards, P. (1985) *Indigenous Agricultural Revolution: Ecology and Food Production in West Africa* (London: Hutchinson)

Scoones, I. and J. Thompson (eds) (1994) *Beyond Farmer First: Rural People's Knowledge, Agricultural Research and Extension Practice* (London: Intermediate Technology Publications)

Sillitoe, P. (1998) 'The Development of Indigenous Knowledge: A new applied anthropology', *Current Anthropology*, 39(2): 223–35

5 ANTI-SOCIAL 'SOCIAL DEVELOPMENT'? GOVERNMENTALITY, INDIGENOUSNESS AND THE DFID APPROACH ON MONTSERRAT

Jonathan Skinner

[*A DFID official in the UK is practising his golf in his office with a subordinate female beside him trying to get him to make some development decisions before a visit to Montserrat in the Caribbean via the neighbouring island of Antigua.*]
Official: ... The ferry. If we're late we can catch the 3:30 helicopter. They can drop you off on the way.
Subordinate: Sir. But the helicopter, sir. Don't you have to make a reservation?
Official: Reservation! What do you mean reservation? We're DFID dammit!

This extract from a sketch at the cultural show 'ASH: The Second Falling', performed by the drama group *Plenty Plenty Yac Ya Ya* on Montserrat in January 2000, summarises the feelings and perceptions held by many indigenous Montserratians towards the staff and strategies of the Department for International Development. Since July 1995, the island of Montserrat in the Eastern Caribbean has been in a state of emergency. For the last five years, there have been several increasing and decreasing phases of volcanic activity centred about Mount Chance on the Soufriere Hills mountain range in the southern centre of the island. Millions of cubic metres of pyroclastic flows have destroyed the capital city, Plymouth, and villages to the south. Villages in the centre of the island have been evacuated, leaving only a quarter of the original population on the island (3,000). It has killed 19 people, separated many families and resulted in many economic problems (see Patullo 2000; Possekel 1999; Skinner 1999). Islanders regularly tune to the national radio station for news from the local government and foreign scientists about the exclusion zone boundaries and entry times, earthquake frequencies and levels, evacuation drills, the occasional petrol rationing, shelter constructions and other development projects. Evacuated islanders maintain a virtual sense of identity and community – a 'virtual sociality' as I refer to it (Skinner undated) – on the Internet, if they can afford to. For islanders on-island, theirs is literally an everyday 'risk society' (Beck 1992) with a 'risk culture' (Giddens 1991: 3).

'Living with the unexpected' (Possekel 1999) is how another scholar describes life on Montserrat in her study of disaster recovery and sustainable development. Possekel's description of Montserrat as 'unexpected' fits with the island's present predicament, but is in sharp contrast with the island's quiet and traditional Caribbean and colonial history. A British colony since settlement in the seventeenth century, Montserrat went through the classic phases of the plantation society from slave labour to emancipation, but fell short of independence in the late 1960s when the first 'indigenous' leader, Chief Minister of Montserrat William Bramble, decided to reject Statehood in Association with Britain for economic reasons (Fergus 1994: 211–12). One might say, then, that Montserrat is a product of the British, the 'colonial state' (Comaroff 1998), which continues to dominate the historical past and present day of the dependent and formerly dependent territories. About these interstitial places and peoples, Comaroff has recently identified several characteristics:

postmodern notions of the workings of the colonial state ... include a broad range of disciplinary and regulatory practices, the object of which is twofold: to recast the experienced reality, the existential world, of the colonised *and* to re-present back to Europe its own modernist sense of self, thus to naturalise its world picture and the forms of knowledge legitimated therein. (1998: 322, original emphasis)

More specifically, 'colonial governmentality', with its 'rational administration', assumes control over the development of the native population, frequently employing the classic mechanisms of bureaucratisation, documentation, rationalisation and registration (Weber 1963 [1921]) to dispossess the indigenous (Comaroff 1998: 323–30). Montserrat's colonial history exemplifies these mechanisms even in the present day with, for example, new calls for land registration in the north of the island by a certain date after which land will become Crown property, though few can afford the surveyors' fees to substantiate local land knowledge for foreign planners. Development activities on the island are the result of 'white' colonial control by expatriates – 'professional expatriates' (see Skinner 1996b: 47ff.) such as His Excellency The Governor of Montserrat (a Foreign and Commonwealth Office diplomat on a brief tour of duty) and his army of elite Technical Co-operation Officers (TCOs) – who talk of Britain as 'home' and go on to think and shape the colony, whether Montserrat or old South Africa, into a 'proto-Euronation' (Comaroff 1998: 343).

This chapter is concerned with the perceptions of development amongst the indigenous of Montserrat and the indigenous of Britain.[1] It lends an ear to the salacious gossip and scandal of a small society (Gluckman 1963). Uncomfortable and challenging (Firth 1981), this technique brings to account the developers' 'Global Project' (Esteva and Prakash 1998) and their expert discourse (cf. Hobart 1993: 1; Gardner and Lewis 1996: 158). The suggestion is that DFID exists in Comaroff's Imperial guise and is, in this example, not dealing effectively with problems local to Montserrat. This is manifest in the problematic development programmes on Montserrat prior to the 1995 volcano crisis – 'a first world solution to a third world problem' (Skinner 1996b: 56) as they were characterised at the time. This update on development problems and critical indigenous perceptions shows that DFID continue to pursue their social development experiment *on* their 'island laboratory', rather than entertain or negotiate local knowledge *from* their 'island laboratory'.

'MONTS'RAT' KNOWLEDGE: LOCAL LORE VERSUS SOCIAL DEVELOPMENT MORES

Development policies and practices, it is widely acknowledged, frequently override local concerns with their international endeavours (Brokensha, Warren and Werner 1980; Hobart 1993; Dixon, Barr and Sillitoe 2000). Falling between the extremes of the Transfer-of-Technology model of the political Right, and the dependency, Marxist-informed models of the political Left (Sillitoe 1998), development fails by foisting inappropriate technologies upon the indigenous. This '*ying* and *yang* of development' (Sillitoe 1998: 214) rides roughshod over indigenous knowledge and identity, the sub-text of this critique of DFID social development work on Montserrat. For DFID, local knowledge comes from London. This is what ASH are playing to their indigenous crowd – foreign, anti-social development activities.

Development work has always been a contentious topic, empowering if given over to indigenous needs and integrated into local lore, but guilty of social engineering if imposed, bilateral and conditional (as is the case on Montserrat). Local lore we might define as bodies of tradition and knowledge on subjects held by particular groups – the predisposition towards distinctive farming strategies in Bangladesh as seen in the common-sense transition from crop production to fishing during the monsoon period (Sillitoe 2000: 4), for example. The disruption of such cultural patterns of activity can prove detrimental to food supplies as well as to one's sense of identity and belonging. Ideally, then, according to anthropologists keen to consider knowledge *in situ*, in its socio-cultural context, development projects should be socially and culturally aware, striking a balance between 'rational analysis and mystic intuition, scientific enquiry and local wisdom' (Sillitoe 2000: 17). In terms of development work on Montserrat, this might mean the TCO construction foreman's appreciation that the local work force is not 'lazy' and 'always on a go slow', but is rather pacing itself to be able to work through the long hot days, day after day.

Categories such as local knowledge and local lore, indigenous and locals, are, however, as contentious as development. As *affective* categories, the difference between knowledge and lore is semantic; both can be argued to be rational and effective approaches: Morrison et al. (1994, cited in Sillitoe 1998: 204) note from South Pacific studies that indigenous peoples have their own 'effective science' and resource-use practices. And, based around Japanese, Chinese and Maori scholarship, Clammer (2000: 2) has recently stated the case that knowledge may not be simply cognitive, but can be affective, corporeal, mystical and rooted in non-western experiences and non-Cartesian conceptions of nature. Similarly, the category 'indigenous' is bound up in notions of social identity, political aspirations and economic concerns; it is not simply a word for a people born to a place, but is more often than not used to convey the sense of a people from a place – natives, First Peoples. This might be clear-cut with the Indians of North America and the Aborigines of Australia, but in Transylvania it is an historical matter to be settled between Romanians and Hungarians, and in the Caribbean the notion of indigenousness is blurred due to the island's patchy and intermittent settlement patterns across the centuries from Carib to Arawak to European and imported – and subsequently freed – African slaves and indentured workers from the East.

Prior to the volcano crisis on Montserrat there was a great deal of ODA (Overseas Development Administration) work undertaken on the island, ranging from the construction of a new state-of-the-art hospital in the capital, to a new air-conditioned Government Headquarters nearby and general road upgrades to match. Much of this was in response to Hurricane Hugo, which devastated the island in September 1989, destroying over 98 per cent of all the housing on the island at a cost in excess of US$400 million (Possekel 1999: 78). This makes the island, and the development programmes there, an example of development mores clashing culturally with local lore. As we can predict, indigenous responses to the development programme at the time were often decidedly negative and the ODA intrusion unwelcome by many. As I mentioned above, international development prior to the volcano ignored many indigenous – here used as 'Monts'ratian' born and bred – worldviews (Skinner 1996b: 56): in more detail, the Government Head-quarters were colonial-styled to appeal to North American tourists' perceptions of British colonial buildings, and painted pink; the air conditioning system required all windows to be kept closed and the building was unusable if it broke down – repairs and expertise having to be flown in at the earliest convenience. Similar inappropriate designs were recounted to me about the Glendon hospital in Plymouth, indigenous stories told about extraneous expatriate activities, stories which – in their telling – included me in the tellers' camp and informed me of the resentment that they were being subordinated by others – though they had the necessary expertise and skills (Monts'ratian architects, Monts'ratian construction foremen, etc.) and, crucially, the local lore of the place.

Let me add, here, that there is a great deal of indigenous 'knowledge', not just about the suitability and appropriateness of the development on Montserrat, but also about life in Britain and the expatriates' position back home, much of it coming from the frequency of holiday and visiting movements back and forth between the metropole and periphery, the motherland and the dependency. The result is great awareness amongst Montserratians of their predicament and the circumstances of the development workers on their island: 'They come down here from their little semi in London with a contract in one hand and swimming trunks in the other,' one informant said during fieldwork in 1994/95. 'The development money goes from Barclays Bank in London to the Barclays Bank on Montserrat to pay the development workers' salaries, and back to their accounts in London again. We never see any of the money on Montserrat,' criticised another. Such indigenous knowledge and awareness have the ability to transform the sense of self and indigenous worldview (Bruner 1991), particularly when it is in reaction to DFID activities. A dialogue between grassroots Montserratians and onshore and offshore government organisations would make that reaction constructive and lasting – more than can be said for the past years of development work.

DFID is a new body created out of the ODA in 1997 when New Labour came to power in Britain.[2] Headed by a Secretary of State with Cabinet rank, and assisted by a Parliamentary Under-Secretary of State, DFID is 'responsible for managing Britain's programme of development assistance to poorer countries' (DFID undated a) with a budget of £2,144 million in 1996/97. The Department has a tense relationship with the Foreign and Commonwealth Office from where the ODA operated

(1970–97), and it has a terse relationship with the remaining British colonies, who maintain that they should be the first port of call for British aid money. Generally, Claire Short (1997), MP and Secretary of State for International Development, has articulated DFID's targets as social justice in the world, a need for basic human rights, sustainable development and an ethical foreign policy.

As DFID very clearly state (DFID undated b), their 'principal aim is to contribute to the elimination of poverty in poorer countries and to enable poor people to achieve sustained improvement in their living standards'. To facilitate this end, Short (DFID undated b) has established an internal advisory group within the Department to provide 'advice on the social policy and social protection dimensions of international development'. This Social Development Division gives advice on a range of social and economic topics from poverty analysis to labour rights, highlighting, in particular, 'the vulnerabilities of socially excluded groups such as children, youth and the aged, indigenous peoples and ethnic minorities, and people with disabilities' (DFID undated b). Broad in scope, their 'social development' 'refines development work by making it *more accountable, more equitable*, and *more appropriate*'. Within the Social Development Division there are approximately 50 development professionals – administrators and advisers with specialist knowledge. The Social Development Advisers (SDAs) apply their expertise to all DFID programmes, often through the Regional Departments in DFID. In other words, rather like the Governor of Montserrat, the SDAs are omnipresent and exercise great influence.

Social development is intended to remedy the failings, the inappropriateness, of the last four decades of development, to make British development work ostensibly more accountable, more equitable and more appropriate. We now have a Government Department concerned to put 'social systems and cultural values' at the base of DFID programmes in their aim to improve 'the capacity of civil society in the South' (DFID undated b). Thus, we might expect DFID strategies and practices to be less Eurocentric and bureaucratic, matching the expectations, desires and goals of the indigenous Montserratians.

Unfortunately, the proliferation of SDAs at DFID has not resulted in integrated – accountable, equitable and appropriate – development. SDAs are still not indigenous to the development recipient countries; SDAs frequently find themselves embroiled in a top-down bureaucratic institution seeking quantifiable outputs (Gardner and Lewis 1996: 131); and often their participatory rural appraisal techniques (as opposed to long-term anthropological engagements with the field) are used to co-opt the indigenous rather than amend the development project for the indigenous (Skinner 1996a: 25). There are examples of SDA work which has contributed beneficially to DFID work, but DFID's social development of Montserrat has not been apparent. This is, perhaps, due to Montserrat's continued colonial condition.

In this allegedly post-colonial and post-industrial era, local recipients of development – their indigenous knowledge and culture – are still assumed to be barriers to rational development (Crewe and Harrison 1998: 15). Since the eruption of Chances Peak in 1995, approximately two-thirds of Montserrat's population have migrated from the island, whilst 74 per cent of the remaining population have had to relocate to the north of the island, resulting in excess of 1,500 Montserratians allocated to 25 emergency shelters (tents, schools, hurricane shelters and churches) in the north of the island in 1997. When I arrived on Montserrat for Christmas 1999, I heard that there were still approximately 170 people living in shelters, some by choice, attracted to the rent- and electricity-free residences. In addition to the long-term use of temporary shelters, two villages have been built by DFID in the north of Montserrat at Lookout and Davy Hill, with some Jamaican and Caricom funding. Locals knew that the land at Lookout was too high for water pumping and too hard for properly sunk drains, but the development workers were the planners and surveyors; local construction workers and Caricom experts also knew that Australian pre-fabs would not be strong enough to withstand hurricanes, but their development say was left unheard; and local women suspected that their West Indian extended families would not fit into the European 2.2 family buildings, but the houses were built without their input (see also Skelton 1999).

The immediate development goals on Montserrat had been rehousing. Off Montserrat, rehousing was a similar issue presenting problems on a similar scale: some of the resettlement plans to assist the package of Montserratians overseas turned into paid vacations to the UK, others resulted in more returnees to Montserrat than departees (Hansard 1997: 1466). With a loss of insurance money, deprivation and colonial governmentality back home, and an uncertain status, identity and conditions in the motherland (no right of abode as British Dependent Territory Citizens, subsequently changed to a two-year – and now indefinite – permit of stay following extensive lobbying in the UK), Montserratians are truly caught between a rock and a hard place. They are left to argue and struggle and negotiate for their benefits and rights, a task that is harder to do on Montserrat than in the United Kingdom where there are several self-run refugee and migration organisations (in particular: a section of Refugee Action, the Montserrat Overseas People's Progressive Alliance, and the Montserrat Action Committee 1989).

Comaroff's 'rational administration' blueprint unfurled across 'DFID island' (a local characterisation) has resulted in local alienation and castigation of colonial development activities with their concern for high levels of appropriateness and accountability back home, but lack of concern for good management overseas (the *temporary* Government Headquarters cost nearly six times the initial budget, for example). Montserratians have failed to see the rational thought processes behind Britain's donation of £75 million in aid money, which was allocated but not spent until the evacuation zones had stabilised. 'Too little, too late' have been the coping strategies of DFID and Her Majesty's Government (HMG): to spend British taxpayers' money on a fluid situation would rate as bad accountability, yet 'waiting' until 19 Montserratians were killed by pyroclastic flow two years into the volcano crisis was insensitive politicking. These development activities and inactivities, this DFID *bacchanal* (disorder), resulted in political unrest (Chief Minister's public complaints to Whitehall and the British press about HMG), political agitation (calls for an independent Montserrat as a response to conspiracy theories that Montserrat was being deliberately 'wound down' by the British) and social disquiet (public riots on Montserrat in front of the Governor's House) (Hansard 1997: 1465).

Reacting to this troubled Montserrat climate, The International Development Committee (IDC) of the House of Commons commissioned the 'Montserrat – First Report' to explore 'apparent policy and administrative confusion in HMG' (IDC 1998a: v). They naturally focused upon DFID and DFID's social development approach. Despite the fact that there are two complementary and sometimes contradictory HMG aid channels in the Caribbean – DFID's British Development Division in the Caribbean (BDDC) and the Foreign and Commonwealth Office's Dependent Territories Regional Secretariat (DTRS) – the IDC focused their report upon DFID, who control the Montserrat social development programmes, as well as, one might say, indirectly, the Government of Montserrat.[3] On Montserrat, it is clear that the locally elected government is very accountable to DFID, whilst DFID is accountable to Whitehall – hardly an accountable, equitable and appropriate social development structure to facilitate or respond to Montserratian indigenous need.

INDIGENOUS CRITIQUE OF DEVELOPMENT

[T]here are so many players in this thing that it is very difficult to have authority over people who make the decisions or know the answers. (IDC 1998a: 15)

Such was the end of one of Claire Short's candid cross-examination answers to the IDC. Here, I am including the British as voices critiquing and commenting upon development on Montserrat, voices indigenous to Britain, indigenousness referring not just to those born and bred on Montserrat – to those who can say 'me navel string buried ya', 'me na bang watta cum ya' (I didn't travel across water to come here). Monts'ratians make use of this affective condition, considering themselves the indigenous of the island because they belong by blood – quite literally: 'Our parents and grandparents sweated and spilled blood on this island. This makes Monts'rat our island.' (Others become 'belongers' through residency and marriage, or close association with Monts'ratians.) This claim to an autochthonous identity comes both from kin ties and slavery roots, and is held along with an innate 'Africanness'. The slave descendant claim is more pervasive and powerful than colonial settlement history or invocation of Carib ancestry (see Young 1993: 43–4, on St Vincent). In Britain, indigenousness is seemingly more ecumenical, inclusive – understated because there has not been a recent tradition or history of control by external and alien forces, though Scottish/English indigenousness tensions are always fermenting. Indigenousness can be considered to be 'a relative term' like Evans-Pritchard's understandings of 'lineage' (1969: 195); it is a term with great political and strategic mileage, owned and invoked to legitimate and substantiate a claim, whether literally or metaphorically. In this section I would thus like to consider some critiques of DFID and their development work made by several indigenous groupings claiming expert knowledge of a locality: the motherland government; the governed of Montserrat; and a group of American expatriates on Montserrat who have bought into the locality and localness of Montserrat – the snowbirds.

THE MOTHERLAND GOVERNMENT

There has been a great deal of Parliamentary review, criticism and debate surrounding the Montserrat case, some of it unravelling a saga of DFID ineptitude beginning well before the volcano crisis. The Sixth IDC Report (1998b) developed the First Report's discovery that a UN scientific report into the state of Chances Peak (Wadge and Isaacs 1987) had been ignored and overlooked by both GOM and HMG authorities, despite summary comments stating that: '[t]he Soufriere Hills Volcano is active and will erupt again. It is a potential threat to many people that live in southern Montserrat' (Wadge and Isaacs 1987, cited in IDC 1998a: xiv). Two years after this report, Hurricane Hugo (1989) devastated Montserrat, giving rise to £16.8 million of redevelopment aid, most of which centred on Plymouth and the south of Montserrat and was subsequently destroyed as soon as it was completed. In other words, development aid between 1987 and 1995 had been *inappropriately* targeted at Plymouth and the south of the island – port jetty, hospital and government buildings in particular. In his accounting for the bureaucratic ignorance of this scientific report, former Governor Savage (IDC 1998a: 90) supposed that the Government of Montserrat's copies could have been blown into the sea by the hurricane!

In the light of some of these blunders and public political flak, HMG commissioned an official but objective assessment report in 1998, a seven-person team to spend one year investigating and reviewing 'HMG's preparations, organisation and delivery of emergency aid in response to the Montserrat crisis and identify findings and lessons learnt particularly with general application to aid responses to prolonged natural disasters' (Clay et al. 1999: 71). The Overseas Development Institute (ODI) in London investigated this Montserrat/London aid axis, characterising Montserrat a 'wait-and-see' disaster scenario (Clay et al. 1999: 3) divided into a 'waiting on the volcano' development response phase (September 1995–June 1997), and a 'moving from emergency to reconstruction' phase of subsequent infrastructural commitment and investment.

The ODI assessed the handling of the islanders' social assistance meted out by HMG and GOM, concluding that in terms of appropriateness, emergency actions were 'largely effective, but with much messy detail' (Clay et al. 1999: 5). Furthermore, whilst commending the general provision of infrastructure on Montserrat in the wake of Chances Peak eruptions (a new jetty, road works and new storage facilities), they made the following comment about the advantages to be had from using indigenous labour with their indigenous know-how (1999: 6): '[o]verall construction and adaptation using local materials, know-how and labour appear to have been more cost-effective than solutions based on the importation and assembly of pre-fabricated structures.' This can be read as a plea for appropriate development assistance, bottom-up social development which is determined by the local knowledge of indigenous islanders as opposed to the international credentials of the development workers – social development by the people rather than social development from the politicians.

Working as an anthropologist amongst the people of Montserrat, I am all too aware of the structure and utility of large-scale institutions, and their difficulty in dealing with small-scale, one-off situations, especially when they are caught without emergency contingency plans. My critical approach to DFID was extended to the ODI when I was recently invited to the ODI headquarters in London for a lunchtime workshop to share expertise and talk about their findings. There, I found out that the ODI had interviewed prominent Montserratians only on Montserrat rather than the 'Monts'rat neaga' (people) and that they had moderated their criticisms of HMG and GOM for diplomatic reasons. In addition to this, in the course of accounting for the reasoning behind the 'too little, too late' release of aid and relocation funding to the islanders, one ODI official articulated just how the colonial mind had been working:

put a frog into a pot of boiling water and it does something, it jumps out; put a frog into some cold water and slowly turn up the heat and the frog will do nothing and be boiled to death.

Perhaps playing with the image of the 'mountain chicken' (frog) stew cooked on Montserrat and thereby alluding to the Monts'rat population, the ODI social development sympathies for DFID become more than evident. Otherwise, this is another semi-indigenous critique of DFID, semi-indigenous in a bureaucratic sense of the term – caught in an off-guard moment.

THE GOVERNED OF MONTS'RAT

Throughout the volcano crisis on Montserrat, the governed people have continued with their traditional modes of expression, using calypso and soca, poetry and drama to give public audiences many examples of their talent for self-expression. Soca star and Montserratian calypsonian (known internationally for 'Hot – Hot – Hot'), Arrow has produced several albums featuring songs such as 'Ah just can't run away' (1995a) and 'Have a little faith' (1995b) and 'Montserrat Nice' (1998), celebrating Montserratian resilience to the volcano and imploring residents to stay on their island. Howard Fergus, Montserrat's national poet, university lecturer, Deputy Governor and Speaker in the local Parliament, is at the forefront of a new 'disaster literature' on the island with his production of anthologies (1995) and collections of poetry (1998). He, and others, use this medium to express themselves and make veiled criticisms in the newspapers of GOM and DFID, organisations which they both work for and with. 'Scientists Know' by Fergus (1995: 15, ll.14–19) is one well-known example:

> For a small island breed
> this volcano acting very
> independent. Doesn't want to heed
> technical advice from UWI
> or follow British protocol
> for aid. ...

Disaster tourism is the new way of attracting off-island money to Montserrat's shores. And in addition to the above examples, when on the island, tourists can purchase T-shirts created by local artists bearing words such as 'Now she puffs / But will she blow / Trust in the Lord / And pray it's No', postcard photographs of the eruptions are on sale with proceeds going to local photographers, and tourists can attend some of the many cultural shows on the island. The *Plenty Plenty Yac Ya Ya* performance mentioned at the start of this chapter was one such event, and took place in the Pelican Room of the Vue Pointe Hotel, an abandoned hotel straddling the Exclusion Zone border on the island between the Safe Zone and the Daytime Entry Zone (6 am to 6 pm), one in which performers and audience symbolically reasserted claims over buildings and identities lost to the volcano. Their show, ASH, was sanctioned and sponsored by the Government of Montserrat, many of whom were invited dignitaries; Ms Simba had been flown back to the island from Jamaica. Cumberbatch and Simba are known throughout the island for their lively shows, and the characters in this particular sketch, with its memorable ending, are almost as well known as the performers. Indeed, this sketch was much quoted to me during my return to Montserrat. It is, I believe, emblematic of the feelings and perceptions held by many indigenous Montserratians towards the staff and strategies of the Department for International Development. Surprisingly, the other sketches in the show were more about lampooning the Montserratian experience of migration than colonial/Montserratian/expatriate relations on the island. In sum, all of these activities can be seen as a part of the general press for cultural, social and political self-determination, or for the recognition of local knowledge and expertise at the very least.

The 1999/2000 Montserrat Festival highpoint is the Calypso competition, a time for 'social commentary' (Skinner 2001) and political expression. The crowned Calypso King of the competition was Cecil 'Cepeke' Lake, who won with the a song criticising the roads on the island ('Pot Holes'), and the song 'Pay Off', reputed to be about how subdued the Chief Minister's criticisms of HMG, and DFID in particular, had become since his 'co-option' onto their consultancy panels. Both songs caught and reflected the feelings of the masses, their dissatisfaction with HMG and GOM, their sense of indignation towards the iniquities and injustices of development work, and their concern for the large amounts of consultancy moneys depleting the overall development projects' effects, eating out of the pot. Such songs, however, are not the most effective means for challenging or changing British government development strategies and practices. The motherland government responds better to the agenda of Montserratian organisations in the UK than to her subjects overseas (whilst the Home Office supports Refugee Action's work with Montserratians in the UK, in August 1997, Claire Short infamously replied in public to the request for an increase in their relocation package made by Montserratians on Montserrat with the following: 'They say 10,000, double, treble, and then think of a number. It will be golden elephants next' [see Hibbs 1997]).

It is no small wonder, then, that there is a vehement indigenous critique on development, one that could be strengthened by closer co-operation and co-ordination with the snowbirds (see below). In addition to the above observations, development accountability on Montserrat is criticised as British 'accountants' column-checking' rather than a scru-tinising of costs, as bad accounting rather than good accountability. Development design, location and implementation have also been severely hampered by relying upon external expertise, a continuation of British colonial governmentality since original settlement on the island 300 years earlier. However, in the last few decades, Montserratians have gained their own expertise and certification in development work such as construction, design and surveying. Their technical know-how, coupled with their local knowledge of Montserrat, make them the ideal candidates for the social development of the island, though British bureaucracy dictates that they *cannot* be the beneficiaries of independent consultancy sterling. Certainly, there is the self-perception that Montser-ratians can do the consultancy work themselves, thereby allowing the money to enter the island's economic pool rather than the development business sump (in 1997/8, for example, £142,609 was spent in consultancy costs concerning airstrip siting viability which was known locally to be topographically unviable).[4] As one Montserratian put it, talking outside a local fisherman's bar:

[T]heir problem is accountability. It is not the spending of the money. If £75 million pounds is earmarked for Montserrat, £75 million pounds is going to be spent on Montserrat, £75 million must be accounted for right down to the last pence. ... But that's not accountability, because that's accounting for the money. ... We now are waiting for such and such and such and such. We're not asking you to spend more money. We're asking you to spend the money in a way that we feel is more feasible to our aesthetics, to our way of life, to our environment, to everything that is a benefit to establishing an infrastructure that will last into the future for us to help us to develop our country – not to put in place an infra-structure that is designed to fall apart in twelve years. That is utterly and totally ridiculous ... because then you're telling me that I have twelve years in which to catch myself, having lost everything I owned in the entire world.

One interesting consequence of this environmental and management crisis, the difficulty faced by on-island Montserratians to get their viewpoints across to the motherland, has been the furtherance of many on-island Montserratians' long-term goal of decolonisation and independence. Whereas the independence movement was set back several years by the destruction caused by Hurricane Hugo in 1989 and the accompanying shadow of direct rule from Britain (see IDC 1998a: xxx), the 1995-to-present volcano problems have shown Montserratians that the British are not such adept administrators and developers. The elderly population's affinity with the governing motherland has been tested and eroded, compounded by Montserrat now falling under a growing North American socio-cultural sphere of influence, many of the remaining young men on the island are feeling that they have to rely upon themselves and not the British; that they can do the necessary work themselves, respond better, more equitably and more appropriately but with less bureaucracy, and that it might even be in their best interests to do so. DFID and the British government's failure to negotiate and tap into the local knowledge resource on Montserrat, their failure adequately to expose themselves and their development plans and proposals out on the streets in consultation exercises, feedback sessions and explanation panels has further polarised an already segregated island community.

THE SNOWBIRDS

Perhaps the most vociferous criticism of DFID, as well as HMG, has come from a group of ungovernable expatriates, 'snowbird' residents retired to Montserrat or residential tourists escaping the North American or European winters, attracted to the island's colonial status and traditional political and social stability. Originally several hundred in number, living in 'white ghettos' on the island since the 1960s, the number of expatriates has now diminished to well under 100. Highly successful businessmen and lawyers, with high expectations that their money and opinions will be revered, this small group of predominantly North American snowbirds have become increasingly vociferous against GOM, HMG and DFID agreed evacuation boundaries.

Most snowbird residences happen to be clustered on either side of Belham Valley where their golf course used to run – now a pyroclastic flood plain of debris marking the evacuation line. Several properties south of the Belham river evacuation zone line jut out around a hill facing the sea, and are strongly perceived by the owners to be safe from the volcano's line of fire, as evinced by the pyroclastic flows well below them. Unfortunately for them, the authorities have cut off all water and electricity south of the river in a deliberate attempt to keep islanders to the north (both Monts'rat indigenous and self-styled snowbird indigenous). Not to be deterred by 'the British or the blacks', several of the elderly snowbird couples have refused to move or be relocated from their southern homes, establishing a siege mentality and invoking World War II memories: escape routes across the pyroclastic debris have been mapped, swimming pool water has been diverted to keep water systems running, generators have been brought in to power the residences, and fresh food and drinking water are sourced from sympathetic snowbirds north of the river. All this because these are their homes where they feel that they belong, where they have made their social and economic investments.

When I visited Montserrat, the 'South of Belham Committee' of snowbirds had recently paid the Governor a visit to protest and complain about the inequity involved in the drawing of the evacuation zone, one which – so they claimed – had more political and strategic reasoning behind it than scientific advice. Furthermore, it was unjust, so they argued, that DFID declare certain properties to the north of the zone to be 'at risk', to evacuate them and subsequently commandeer them for DFID personnel. Such activities gave rise to the snowbirds' entrenched position; one member of the Committee even printed off T-shirts illustrating the irrational colonial government mentality – a map of the island divided in two by the exclusion line, 'Exclusion Zone' in the south, 'Logic Free Zone' in the north. Commenting upon the entire act unfolding on the island, snowbird Krebs (Possekel 1999: 175), a native German who had settled on Montserrat, said: 'We have encountered a very interesting situation here, almost like a surrealistic theatre performance. Government and people are completely decoupled.' These snowbird, calypso and Parliamentary scenes, however, are by no means so sanctioned or polished as those from *Plenty Plenty Yac Ya Ya*, though in their own way they too are responding, reacting and dealing with the ridiculous and the sublime.

ANTHROPOLOGY, INDIGENOUSNESS AND THE KNOWLEDGE ECONOMY

Throughout this chapter, I have been somewhat ironic in my use of the 'indigenous' keyword, loosening the claim which Native Indians – First Peoples – have staked. Roots and origins are perhaps more debatable terms in the West Indies than in North America. Strictly speaking, there are no remaining indigenous on Montserrat; there are no First People pre-dating colonisation such as the Inuit (Eskimos) or North and South American Indians with their ancestral lands. On Montserrat, Monts'rat indigenousness is claimed through the sins and iniquities of slavery; and snowbird and development worker senses of belonging, identification with the lifestyle and relationships on the colony, come from their social and financial investments contributing to an affinity with the place. Indigenousness, then, can be posited as a rhetorical and sentimental term used for gain and advantage.

There are no truly autochthonous people on Montserrat; indeed, there are no truly autochthonous people anywhere: all are 'stakeholders' with individual and group techniques to employ to their advantage as the appropriateness of the Committee, Parliament or fisherman's bar allows. From such stakeholder divisions we have strategic notions of indige-nousness and exogenousness, of identity which impacts upon development knowledge and practices. At present, development workers bring specialist and technical knowledge to Montserrat, whilst the lay Montserratians exist as an untapped source of practical and everyday knowledge. Development on Montserrat, for all Claire Short's 'social' initiatives at DFID, continues to conform to the common pattern of pro-fessional dominance, one which lacks the modern management theories of flexibility, fluidity and responsiveness, and the modern development goal of sustainability (see Scoones and Thompson 1994).

I suggest that the regime of colonial governmentality, with its own – perhaps neo-colonial (*sic*) and dependency – agendas and issues of accountability back home, has led to the problems with accountability, equity and appropriateness of social development overseas. Long has been the call for an extension of anthropology into all spheres of public life (Wolf 1999 [1969]: 252), a golden opportunity for influencing bureaucracies, for 'studying up', for investigating 'the colonisers rather than the colonised, the culture of power rather than the culture of the powerless, the culture of affluence rather than the culture of poverty' (Nader 1999 [1969]: 289). These are calls for anthropologists to move beyond the false criticism that our discipline is an intension and extension of colonial practices, and to look to critiquing and scrutinising the 'power-elite strategies' which determine much of life in the Third World. *Whose Development? An Ethnography of Aid* (Crewe and Harrison 1998) is one such recent example of the enlightening contributions which 'the anthropology of development' can make to development studies and structures, practices and processes.

Elsewhere, in his article 'Indigenous Knowledge and Popular Spiritu-ality', Gerrit Huizer (1994) supposes that he is able to dichotomise the systems of knowledge which are used by the expert development workers and the local population. He does this in the interest of asking whether or not Westerners can truly come to understand indigenous knowledge systems such as the spiritual tie between people and land in Zimbabwe (1994: 74), or the participatory and inclusive approach to nature found in China (1994: 81), or the 'creative adaptation' practised by the Maya to colonial rule which came from their conceptions of survival as a collective enterprise between man, nature and the gods – linked and affirmed through the reciprocity of ritual sacrifice (1994: 80). Though I disagree with his Orientalism (a polarisation of the world into stereotypical categories such as West and non-West) and his sweeping generalisations, Huizer rightly returns our attention to the topic of *knowledge* – what Goody associates with the literate (a 'technology of the intellect'), as opposed to *wisdom* which is linked with the illiterate (cited in Richards 1985: 156) – which has the ability to keep certain people in power and government, and others out of power and government (Crick 1982: 303). As anthropologists, we view this commodity – knowledge – in the context of its historical and cultural construction, out of a mutually defining dialogic between self and other (1982: 308). This is demonstrated in one of Anthony Cohen's (1993) self-conscious essays about Whalsay, a Shetland fishing community, where he argues for 'the localisation of knowledge' (1993: 35), or rather *knowledges*, segmentary *à la* Evans-Pritchard, but not in the contrived and strategic fashion of Nuer alliances and allegiances. On Whalsay, Cohen found serial segmentation overlapping kin groups, neighbourhood groups and boat crews. Like identity, knowledge was a possession, one guarded by insiders when threatened by outsiders such as the British government trying to impose fishing quotas – an example of the difficulty involved in accepting extraneous knowledge (1993: 39).

On Montserrat, the knowledge situation is similar: to use Cohen's words, '[o]utsiders' knowledge of a locality is generalised and imputes to the members of the locality largely undifferentiated views. But by contrast, members' knowledge of their locality is highly particularised, and has a variety of competences' (Cohen 1993: 37). On Montserrat, extraneous controls are stronger than on Whalsay because of her colonial status and because of the urgency of the disaster development situation. On this island, the expatriate–belonger–tourist–Montserratian continuum is more 'clear-cut' than on Whalsay, due to the divisions along colour lines. There is an obvious tension between the development workers and their specialist knowledge, and that 'known' by the indigenous; as well as the development work desired by local Montserratians and GOM who, quite naturally, have a long-term perspective; and HMG and DFID who have immediate concerns and a projection into the future of scarcely twelve years for some projects (cf. Clay et al. 1999: 6). In 1980, Brokensha et al. (1980: 4) were arguing for indigenous knowledge to be included as a matter of course when development work is being planned. This argument may not be new, but it was thought to have become well received by the development community, as exemplified by the DFID social development initiatives and use of the Edinburgh Department of Social Anthropology as an Advice Resource Centre. Unfortunately, Short's social development work on Montserrat is perceived by the indigenous – in their gossip on the island and the scrutiny in London – to be more 'anti-social' than social. DFID have also recently ended their contract with Edinburgh. So, the traditional development knowledge economy would appear to be in a healthy state both on- and off-shore Britain.

CONCLUSION

As anthropologists, we work in the interstices of societies and social institutions, with them, between them and without them in the final instances of writing. Strategically, it is no wonder that after turning upon ourselves in academic debate, and turning in upon ourselves in semantic speculation, we next turn our focus upon the funding masters from whom we secure the tenure and continuity of our activities. As uncomfortable researchers, often bearing uncomfortable news, we are aware that our positioning is as axial as our positing. The old danger and threat of becoming inadvertently colonised by the colonising state, of working as professional informers, has not quite disappeared as anthropologists realise the ironic conundrum of state co-option: our expensive expertise lies in the purveyance of lay knowledge. Now, with the alleged tenets of social development at the heart of organisations such as DFID, the local indigenous knowledge which we make literate is in danger of becoming DFID's expert knowledge, making the anthropologist redundant. Unfortunately, or fortunately as the case may be, this is unlikely to happen because of the vested interests within and between competing institutions (HMG, GOM, FCO, DFID and ODI, in this chapter) and 'indigenous' stakeholders (His Excellency the Governor, a local fisherman and an artistic snowbird mentioned above). There will always be a place for the professional stranger, for the anthropologist as defender and broker – indeed, negotiator – of local knowledge.

By turning the colonisers as well as the snowbirds into indigenous peoples alongside perceived 'native' Montserratians, we gain interesting additions to the complex tapestry of rule, control, management and response over Montserrat. Indigenous SDAs on Montserrat (a grouping which could include snowbirds and cultural artists) would be more likely than the motherland consultants to raise the levels of accountability, equity and appropriateness of aid to the island, despite the criticism that they lack international objectivity and influence. To reach this level of enlightenment, the British government must first fully involve the governed of Monts'rat in the consideration and consultation, the planning and execution of development work from start to finish. This should be done with a view towards building up island resources and fostering local knowledge, in other words decreasing the well intentioned dependency development work with which the governed of Monts'rat currently live.

Montserratians have many sets of knowledge competences, they also have great resilience to natural disasters, and they have strong traditions of protest and representation through performance such as the calypso and popular drama (and poetry readings, see also Skinner 1997). In this chapter, I hope to have shown that local knowledge, 'indigenous' in all its connotations, is key to the future survival and success of Montserrat place and Monts'rat people. The case study sketches and scandalous comments about development, here, articulate perceptions of development on an island in a state of natural and social disaster – a state which is not being most effectively, accountably, equitably or appropri- ately alleviated by the mechanisms of the colonial state and its new social development approach. Might not the islanders' performers make the islanders' best representatives and advisers?

On Montserrat, *Plenty Plenty Yac Ya Ya* are *Zeitgeist* performers in an age of risk and uncertainty in Europe as well as the Caribbean Basin. They – like the anthropologist – tap into local social and cultural veins, mining aphoristic kernels of attitude, perception and value. As their title suggests, they – like the anthropologist – distil material from the lives and events around them, gathered predominantly through gossip and everyday interaction, interaction everyday with everyone. This is the key difference between social development advice from the street and from Possekel's (1999) distinguished focus group on Montserrat, or the ODI's three brief fact finding visits to the island to speak with 'British officials in Montserrat ... Government of Montserrat, some staff and rep- resentatives of civil society institutions concerned with the island as well as professional persons who have been involved with Montserrat' (Clay et al. 1999: iii). Despite the consultancy process, social development on Montserrat has not been social or practical. Even snowbirds such as Mr Krebs, and distinguished political figures such as Claire Short, admit that the eruption of Mount Chance could have been better negotiated – by the island's indigenous stakeholders, not the exogenous stakeholders, I conclude. So let me end this anthropological response to the Montserrat crisis with a move from a cultural show to a show of culture and contrasting governmentality, by contrasting the respective words of Mr

Savage (HE Governor of Montserrat during the initial volcanic eruptions) and Mr Patterson (Jamaican Prime Minister and Chairman of Caricom):

One of the problems during this crisis is I think this might have been the first time that development aid was to have been used on an emergency basis. (IDC 1998a: xx)

Britain's assistance to the island was an object lesson in how not to respond to a disaster. (Hansard 1997: 1466)

ACKNOWLEDGEMENTS

I am grateful to the University of St Andrews, The Carnegie Trust, the Royal Anthropological Institute and the University of Abertay Dundee for part-funding fieldwork periods to Montserrat (1994–5, 1999–2000); and I am grateful to the organisers and audience of the ASA 2000 conference for their constructive criticism, Paul Sillitoe and Johan Pottier in particular.

NOTES

1. See Patullo (2000) and Possekel (1999) for aid and development spending details, and Sives (1999), Mennear and Lancaster (1999) and Hansard (1998) for evacuee circumstances.
2. See Possekel (1999), IDC (1998a, 1998b) and Bose and Burnell (1991) for information on the troubled relationships between DFID/ODA and other Government Departments.
3. Budgetary aid is the shortfall between domestic revenue and the Government of Montserrat's expenditure, £12.1 million since 1995 (IDC 1998a: xvi), received from development aid amounts which are vetted by DFID.
4. Provisional DFID expenditure up until March 1998 (DFID undated c).

REFERENCES

Arrow (1995a) 'Ah Just Can't Run Away', soca song in Alphonsus 'Arrow' Cassell, *Arrow Phat* (Plymouth, Montserrat)
—— (1995b) 'Have a Little Faith', soca song in Alphonsus 'Arrow' Cassell, *Arrow Phat* (Plymouth, Montserrat)
—— (1998) 'Montserrat Nice', soca song in Alphonsus 'Arrow' Cassell, *Turbulence* (New York: Krystal Sounds Recording Studio)
Beck, U. (1992) *Risk Society – Towards a New Modernity* (London: Sage Publications)
Bose, A. and P. Burnell (eds) (1991) *Britain's Overseas Aid Since 1979: Between Idealism and Self-Interest* (Manchester: Manchester University Press)
Brokensha, D., D. Warren and O. Werner (1980) 'Introduction', in D. Brokensha, D. Warren and O. Werner (eds), *Indigenous Knowledge Systems and Development* (Washington: University Press of America Incorporated), pp. 1–8

Bruner, E. (1991) 'Transformation of Self in Tourism', *Annals of Tourism Research*, 18: 238–50.

Clammer, J. (2000) 'A Critique of "Cognitive" Development Anthropology', *Anthropology Today*, 16 (5): 1–3

Clay, E., C. Barrow, C. Benson, J. Dempster, P. Kokelaar, N. Pillai and J. Seaman (1999) *An Evaluation of HMG's Response to the Montserrat Volcanic Emergency – Volume 1*, Overseas Development Institute report for the Evaluation Department of DFID (London: DFID)

Cohen, A. (1993) 'Segmentary Knowledge: a Whalsay sketch', in M. Hobart (ed.), *An Anthropological Critique of Development: The Growth of Ignorance* (London: Routledge), pp. 31–42

Comaroff, J. (1998) 'Reflections on the Colonial State, in South Africa and Elsewhere: Factions, fragments, facts and fictions', *Social Identities*, 4 (3): 321–61

Crewe, E. and E. Harrison (1998) *Whose Development? An Ethnography of Aid* (London: Zed Books)

Crick, M. (1982) 'Anthropology of Knowledge', *Annual Review of Anthropology*, 11: 287–313

DFID (undated a) *Factsheet* (London: DFID)

—— (undated b) *Social Development* (London: DFID)

—— (undated c) 'DFID Expenditure in Response to Montserrat Volcanic Crisis: April 1995–March 1998' (London: DFID)

Dixon, P., J. Barr, and P. Sillitoe (2000) 'Actors and Rural Livelihoods: Integrating interdisciplinary research and local knowledge', in P. Sillitoe (ed.), *Indigenous Knowledge Development in Bangladesh* (London: Intermediate Technologies Publications Limited), pp. 159–75

Esteva, G. and M. Prakash (1998) *Grassroots Post-Modernism: Remaking the Soil of Cultures* (London: Zed Books)

Evans-Pritchard, E. (1969) *The Nuer: A Description of the Modes of Livelihood and Political Institutions of a Nilotic People* (Oxford: Oxford University Press)

Fergus, H. (1994) *Montserrat – History of a Caribbean Colony* (London: Macmillan Caribbean)

—— (1995) *Eruption: Ten volcano poems* (University of the West Indies, Montserrat: Montserrat Printery Limited)

—— (ed.) (1998) *Hope: Fiftieth Anniversay Poetry Anthology – Celebrating the University of the West Indies and Monterratian Hope during a Volcanic Crisis* (University of the West Indies, Montserrat: Montserrat Printery Limited)

Firth, R. (1981) 'Engagement and Detachment: Reflections on applying social anthropology to social affairs', *Human Organization*, 40 (3): 193–201

Gardner, K. and Lewis, D. (1996) *Anthropology, Development and the Post-modern Challenge* (London: Pluto Press)

Giddens, A. (1991) *Modernity and Self-Identity: Self and Society in the Late Modern Age* (Cambridge: Cambridge University Press)

Gluckman, M. (1963) 'Gossip and Scandal', *Current Anthropology*, 4 (3): 307–16

Hansard (1997) *Parliamentary Debates, House of Lords – Official Report*, 582 (58), 5 November, 1450–72 (London: The Stationery Office)

—— (1998) *Parliamentary Debates, House of Lords – Official Report*, 306 (122), 18 February, 1001–22 (London: The Stationery Office)

Hibbs, J. (1997) 'Short Calls for an End to Row over Aid for Volcano Island', *Daily Telegraph*, 25 August

Hobart, M. (1993) 'Introduction: The growth of ignorance?', in M. Hobart (ed.), *An Anthropological Critique of Development: The Growth of Ignorance* (London: Routledge), pp. 1–30

Huizer, G. (1994) 'Indigenous Knowledge and Popular Spirituality: A challenge to developmentalists', in J. Schuurman (ed.), *Current Issues in Development Studies: Global Aspects of Agency and Structure*, Volume 21, Nijmegen Studies In Development and Cultural Change (Saarbrücken: Verlag für Entwicklungspolitik Breitenbach GmbH), pp. 56–89

IDC (1998a) *Montserrat – First Report*, House of Commons (London: The Stationery Office)

—— (1998b) *Montserrat – Further Developments: Sixth Report*, House of Commons (London: The Stationery Office)

Mennear, B. and D. Lancaster (1999) 'Environmentally Forced Migration: Providing a culturally sensitive reception', *Anthropology in Action*, 6 (2): 16–28

Morrison, J., P. Geraghty and L. Crowl (1994) *Science of South Pacific Islands Peoples* (Suva, Fiji: The University of the South Pacific Institute of Pacific Studies)

Nader, L. (1999 [1969]) 'Up the Anthropologist – Perspectives gained from studying up', in D. Hymes (ed.), *Reinventing Anthropology* (Ann Arbor: The University of Michigan Press), pp. 284–311

Patullo, P. (2000) *Fire from the Mountain: The Story of the Montserrat Volcano* (London: Constable and Robinson)

Possekel, A. (1999) *Living with the Unexpected: Linking Disaster Recovery to Sustainable Development on Montserrat* (London: Springer-Verlag)

Richards, P. (1985) *Indigenous Agricultural Revolution* (London: Hutchinson)

Scoones, I. and J. Thompson (eds) (1994) *Beyond Farmer First: Rural People's Knowledge, Agricultural Research and Extension Practice* (London: Intermediate Technology Publications)

Short, C. (1997) *The Role and Functions of the Department for International Development* (London: DFID)

Sillitoe, P. (1998) 'What, Know Natives? Local knowledge in development', *Social Anthropology*, 6 (2): 203–20

—— (2000) 'Introduction: The state of indigenous knowledge in Bangladesh', in P. Sillitoe (ed.), *Indigenous Knowledge Development in Bangladesh: Present and Future* (London: Intermediate Technology Publications) pp. 3–20

Sives, A. (1999) 'Montserratian Relocation to Nottingham and Leicester', *Anthropology in Action*, 6 (2): 34–40

Skelton, T. (1999) 'Evacuation, Relocation and Migration: Montserratian women's experiences of the volcanic disaster', *Anthropology in Action*, 6 (2): 6–13

Skinner, J. (undated) 'Virtual sociality: newsgroup communication, culture and community from Montserrat and afar', unpublished manuscript

—— (1996a) 'Visions of Development: Haben oder sein', *Anthropology Today*, (12) 1: 24–5

—— (1996b) 'Conversing Montserrat: Perspectives and wordviews on development and dependence', *Arbeitsgemeinschaft Entwicklungsethnologie e. V.*, 2: 44–57

—— (1997) 'Impressions of Montserrat: A partial account of contesting realities on a British Dependent Territory', unpublished PhD thesis, St Andrews University, Scotland

—— (1999) 'Editorial – island migrations, migration cultures: The Montserrat case', *Anthropology in Action*, 6 (2): 1–5

—— (2000) 'The Eruption of Chances Peak, Montserrat, and the Narrative Containment of Risk', in P. Caplan (ed.), *Risk Revisited* (London: Pluto Press), pp. 156–83

—— (2001) 'Licence Revoked: When calypso goes too far', in B. Watson and J. Hendry (eds), *Indirection, Intention and Diplomacy* (London: Routledge), pp. 181–200

Wadge, G. and M. Isaacs (1987) *Volcanic Hazards from the Soufriere Hills Volcano, Montserrat West Indies* (Reading: Department of Geography, University of Reading)

Weber, M. (1963 [1921]) *Economy and Society* (Totowa, NJ: Bedminster Press)

Wolf, E. (1999 [1969]) 'American Anthropologists and American Society', in D. Hymes (ed.), *Reinventing Anthropology* (Ann Arbor: The University of Michigan Press), pp. 251–63

Young, V. (1993) *Becoming West Indian: Culture, Self, and Nation in St. Vincent* (London: Smithsonian Institution Press)

6 'ALL BEEN WASHED AWAY NOW': TRADITION, CHANGE AND INDIGENOUS KNOWLEDGE IN A QUEENSLAND ABORIGINAL LAND CLAIM

Benjamin Richard Smith

In this chapter I discuss the involvement of anthropologists, Aboriginal people and representative organisations in a land claim over a National Park in northern Queensland, Australia. Such claims, focusing on evidence presenting connections between an Aboriginal 'group' and the land claimed by them, depend on the production of particular representations of indigenous knowledge. In outlining this process, I attempt to show ways in which differing perceptions of what 'indigenous knowledge' is, or might be, often fail to articulate with each other, and the way such failure intensifies a separation between contemporary Aboriginal life and its representation – ethnographically, legally and politically.

'All been washed away now', 'We don't have our culture anymore', or 'you should have asked us long ago, it's thirty years too late' are frequent assertions by the Aboriginal people with whom I have worked as an academic anthropologist and as a consultant on indigenous land claims and development issues on Cape York Peninsula in northern Queensland over the past five years.[1] These statements in response to questions about Aboriginal knowledge of places and traditions present a superficial picture of a group of people whose way of life has been fundamentally compromised by colonial disruption.

Indeed, this is a view that has been put forward by anthropologists, amongst others, in the region since the 1930s. Lauriston Sharp (1938–39: 254, n2), who surveyed the Aboriginal tribes of the Peninsula in the early 1930s, reported the 'unsatisfactory nature' of much of the data he gathered, due in part 'to the demoralization of native life which has so swiftly followed the introduction of European and Oriental culture traits into so many parts of the region'. Whilst Sharp felt that some tribes were 'untouched by the lethal influences of civilization' he noted that 'elsewhere others are extinct and many have undergone foreign and inter-tribal acculturation' implying their lack of fitness as subjects for anthropological study.

Beyond the relatively informal setting of fieldwork I, like others, have elicited responses projecting similar images of acculturation from the Aboriginal people of the region in the taking of evidence during land claim processes.[2] Such responses present problems for the recognition of continuing customary title or recognisable Aboriginal traditions pertaining to claimed land under State and Federal legislation. In this chapter, examining one such claim under the Aboriginal Land Act (Queensland) 1991, I attempt to demonstrate that the situation pertaining to 'lost' culture is more complicated than such statements suggest and that particular understandings of 'tradition' and 'indigenous knowledge' held by both whites and Aborigines act to hinder the purposes and outcomes of land claims and frustrate the needs of Aboriginal claimants.

The Aboriginal Land Act was developed by Queensland's Labour Government under the premiership of Wayne Goss (Holden 1992) as a legislative mechanism for the granting of title over gazetted areas of land to Aboriginal people. Gazettal of this kind has typically either been of Unallocated State or Vacant Crown Land or National Parks. However, the Act is not as benevolent a piece of legislation as it may seem at first glance. Whilst a successful claim can provide freehold title to the claimed area, where an Aboriginal claim is successful over a National Park[3] the granted area must be leased back to the State in perpetuity, with no compensation or rent available to the Aboriginal titleholders.

Claims under the Act can be made on grounds of 'traditional affiliation', 'historical association'[4] or 'economic or cultural viability', although the latter has so far remained unutilised by Aboriginal people. In the majority of cases[5] claims have been made by claimant groups on both traditional and historical grounds. Applications of this kind are seen by the representative agencies administering the claims as giving 'two shots' at success, the 'historical' criteria encompassing those whom a tribunal might decide are unable to present sufficient evidence for a 'traditional' claim.

In the case of 'traditional affiliation', the Queensland Land Tribunal who hear Aboriginal Land Act claims must be satisfied that a 'group' of Aboriginal people have common connection with the land based on spiritual[6] and other associations with, rights in relation to, and responsibilities for, the land under Aboriginal tradition. (Aboriginal Land Act, section 53[1])

In the case of 'historical association', a 'group' of Aboriginal people must establish their claim by satisfying the Tribunal that

the group has an association with the land based on them or their ancestors having, for a substantial period, lived on or used –
(a) the land; or
(b) land in the district or region in which the land is located.
(Aboriginal Land Act, section 54[1])

However, in such cases, a claim may still be established

whether or not all or a majority of the members of a group have themselves lived on or used such land. (Aboriginal Land Act, section 54[2])

My first direct experience of the claim process under the Aboriginal Land Act came while I was working as an anthropological consultant for the Cape York Land Council, a representative organisation (now the Region's 'Native Title Representative Body') working on behalf of the Aboriginal people of Cape York Peninsula. In this claim, over the Mungkan Kaanju National Park,[7] it became apparent that despite the strategic convenience of these two claim options the two grounds for linking people and 'country'[8] were fundamentally inseparable. This was not simply because the claimants were able to assert their interests on both bases; rather, the two were mutually implicated in contemporary Aboriginal ties to land. And despite the legislative weight being placed on 'traditional affiliation' over 'historical association', it became apparent that for Aboriginal claimants 'traditional ties' were established within continuing historical associations with 'country'.

ABORIGINAL PEOPLE AND THE CLAIM AREA

For Aboriginal claimants, the Mungkan Kaanju National Park was an anomaly of recent origin.[9] They knew it better as Rokeby, a large pastoral station which had formed the background for, and been a constituent part of, their lives. For many of them Rokeby Station was also their 'home', the place where they had been born, raised, lived and worked. It was a place they were familiar with, felt comfortable in, a place that knew them.[10] Rokeby Station had existed for as long as people could remember, having been founded in 1884 by the Massey brothers, white pastoralists, and worked from that time by various owners and managers until the 1980s. At this point, in an era in which Queensland Aboriginal people confronted a conservative State Government on the emergent issue of Aboriginal land rights, John Koowarta, an Aboriginal man from the Archer River, but living at Aurukun on the west of Cape York Peninsula, sought control of the Archer Bend area. Supported by the Commonwealth Government, his actions were blocked by the State Parliament, which rapidly converted both Archer Bend and later the neighbouring Rokeby Station into National Parks without any Aboriginal consultation (Brennan 1992: 124–5; McKeown 1992: 3; Chase et al. 1998: 31). To great Aboriginal distress, the cattle on the former station were shot out and their former home and workplace became public property, managed by the Queensland Parks and Wildlife Service (QPWS), whilst they were stuck in the township of Coen, about 60 km away, or at former mission settlements elsewhere on the Peninsula.

The claimants in the Mungkan Kaanju claim came from three major sub-groups or 'tribes',[11] named after the languages with which they identified: Mungkan,[12] Ayapathu and Kaanju. As with the other people of Cape York, the Aboriginal claimants identified themselves in terms of these languages through the fundamental association of 'language' and 'country' established in a mythic 'Story-time' (elsewhere, 'Dreamtime') preceding the lives of Aboriginal people and their known forebears. Mungkan 'country' lies over a large western area of the Park, the Kaanju area over most of the eastern part, extending a few kilometres to the west of the Peninsula Development Road and the Ayapathu area over the south-eastern corner of the park area. Between these areas there appear to have been 'box-up' or 'company' areas (Smith 2001a) where groups associated with the different languages mixed and held shared interests.

Contemporary claimants developed their affiliation to 'country' through a lifetime's association with the Rokeby landscape. Many were born there, these births continuing earlier practices, including naming rituals and the ritual burial of afterbirth and establishing an affiliative link between a man or woman, their birthplace and specific kin who would play a prominent part in the child's development and identity.[13] These station births commonly occurred in the scrub surrounding the station's two major cattle centres: the Rokeby Homestead and the outstation (satellite cattle-camp) at New Yard (later known as Jabaroo), places that formed the base camps for the men and women working on the station and where cattle mustered from across the station were centralised for transport, initially by 'droving' across the Peninsula, and later for removal by road transport.

From the centres of Rokeby and Jabaroo, workers (predominantly male in later years) ranged across the surrounding landscape on horseback, mustering, branding and husbanding the station's cattle.

These musters typically lasted for days or weeks with the cattlemen camping across the property at established sites. Mustering routes, which covered the entire station area over the year, were relatively formalised and are remembered by all who worked on the station in earlier years. These men (and women in earlier years) combined cattle-work activities with previous forms of Aboriginal practice. Moving across the landscape they gained both professional experience as cattlemen and knowledge of places and practices from longer-running Aboriginal traditions through working and living alongside older people. As one Ayapathu man put it:

[w]ell, when we – you know like, when I left school, I worked as a – worked cattle, you know, like a stockman and that's what we been doing, you know, going out in the bush and mustering and all that and that's how we come to know that – these old people take us around and show us and sit down and talk to us. (Phillip Port, cited in Transcript Australia 1998: 78)

Whilst managing the property as cattle workers Aboriginal people simul- taneously husbanded their environment, 'caring for country', in part by conducting 'increase ceremonies' (Thomson 1933: 501–4, 513) to ensure the proliferation of indigenous species. Over time the two spheres of practice increasingly overlapped and syncretised. For example, management of the landscape by controlled burning, a long-running Aboriginal practice (Rose 1995; Langton 1998) was similarly employed as a core form of managing the cattle property.[14]

Male workers ranged across the station area, but women and children were more sedentary, living at the station or outstations or in the regional centre of Coen some 60 km away. This gendered difference in sedentisation increased over time. In the station's earliest days the forebears of the Aboriginal claimants had ranged across the area, hunting and gathering and working only occasionally at station homesteads in exchange for tobacco and rations. By the 1920s such arrangements had become increasingly formalised and younger people had moved from household tasks to cattle work. This generation, the oldest amongst the contemporary claimants, has memories of ranging across the landscape with their families, hunting, gathering and con- glomerating for ceremonial activity when they were children and learning cattle-work as teenagers (Chase et al. 1998; Land Tribunal (Queensland) 2001). Nonetheless both men and women from this generation maintained experiential ties with large areas of the station, camping and ranging over the area during 'holidays', and lay-off periods from cattle work (McGrath 1987; May 1994).

In later years, such 'holidays' decreased, and women became sedentised, first around homestead areas and later in Coen. A broader

Aboriginal population living on the station was demographically and numerically reduced to a smaller, mostly male Aboriginal workforce. In the early 1970s, with the introduction of award wages, Aboriginal labour proved economically unsustainable, resulting in a collapse in the region's cattle industry and radically reduced opportunities for Aboriginal employment. This led to the region's Aboriginal population shifting to Coen and the surrounding government settlements and the anomie and atopia[15] of a listless, town-based existence marked by unemployment, boredom and endemic drinking and violence.

This situation continued across the 1980s with Aboriginal feelings of disempowerment and helplessness compounded by governmental moves to block any shifts towards an Aboriginal self-determination that involved control of property or moves back to traditional 'country', including the suppression of the Koowarta case (Brennan 1992; McKeown 1992). Such moves demonstrated the determination of the Queensland State Government to refuse policies or programmes linking Aboriginal well-being with land or previous Aboriginal practice, instead pushing for solutions based on assimilation (Kidd 1997).

Throughout this period pressure increased on the Queensland State Government to recognise Aboriginal rights, including land rights, in part through the involvement of anthropologists with Aboriginal peoples across Cape York Peninsula. Funding and support for decentralisation and self-managed community development increased. Despite retarding factors, including Coen being a 'town' rather than an 'Aboriginal community',[16] a succession of Aboriginal Corporations were established there from the mid-1980s (Jolly 1997; Smith 2000a). Simultaneously, the Queensland Government enacted land rights legislation, the Aboriginal Land Act (Queensland) 1991, apparently in order to alleviate the threat of the Mabo case[17] and claims to Native Title, which were finally enshrined in Federal legislation two years later (Brennan 1992: 135). Unlike the Commonwealth's Native Title Act 1993, Queensland's Aboriginal Land Act 1991 grants land to Aboriginal people, rather than (partially) recognising the continuing existence and relevance of Aboriginal native title – where certain forms of non-Aboriginal land tenure exist and with a series of limitations through the recognition of coexistent non-Aboriginal interests – since the arrival of whites in Australia and the foundation of the nation.

The passing of the Aboriginal Land Act (Queensland) 1991 and the establishment of the regional Cape York Land Council and the local Coen Regional Aboriginal Corporation heralded a number of developments regarding Rokeby 'country'. The Lawrence family, a Mungkan-affiliating group living in Coen, established a seasonal outstation or bush camp on their 'country'. Simultaneously, they revived the push for indigenous control of both the Rokeby and Archer Bend areas, in conjunction with David Martin an anthropologist and former Queensland Government employee. This push had previously faltered with the deaths of John Koowarta and Charlie Kepple, another Mungkan man holding 'country' on the Archer River, a few years before. A claim was lodged by the Cape York Land Council on behalf of Mungkan people who asserted interests in the Rokeby area. Shortly afterwards, a second Aboriginal claim was registered privately over the eastern segment of Rokeby by a Kaanju woman, including an area of overlap with the Mungkan people's claim.

THE PRODUCTION OF THE CLAIMANT GROUP

As outlined above, the claimant group for the Mungkan Kaanju National Park was eventually composed of members of the Mungkan, Ayapathu and Kaanju sub-groups, who affiliated with 'country' in the area of the former Rokeby pastoral lease. Despite this tripartite tribal identity amongst the claimants, in asserting 'traditional affiliation' and 'historical association' under the Aboriginal Land Act (Queensland) 1991, they were required to demonstrate a common identity as a 'group' with 'common connection to' and/or 'association with' the claimed area(s).

This requirement was the cause of some concern for the employees of the Cape York Land Council in presenting the claim, in particular for the in-house anthropologist and the two lawyers working on the claim. As such it also became a focal problem for the consultant anthropologists, including myself, who were primarily concerned with establishing the ethnographic arguments to substantiate the claim during the course of the tribunal hearing.[18] There was a second, linked concern over the areas in which the three sub-groups held rights and interests according to local Aboriginal law and tradition. A particular worry here was that overlapping assertions of territorial interest would develop into public disagreement during the process of the tribunal hearing, undermining necessary evidence of shared group identity.

With the simultaneous registration of two overlapping claims on behalf of Mungkan and Kaanju people, the emergence of a vocal Ayapathu-identifying sub-group and concern about inter-group territorial conflict, the Cape York Land Council organised a meeting of Mungkan, Kaanju and Ayapathu people asserting interests in the Rokeby, Lochinvar USL and Archer Bend areas at Coen[19] in July 1996. The meeting set out to establish how the Land Council administered claim should best be run. As is typical of such meetings the majority of public[20] speaking was by the (mostly white) employees of the Cape York

Land Council and the consultant anthropologists, explaining the current state of the claims and the problems they sought to address as representatives of the Aboriginal claimants. In addition, the anthropologists, all of whom had conducted substantial periods of fieldwork with the groups that they were representing,[21] outlined their understanding of the linguistic and group affiliation of different areas across the region and raised the possibility of a triangular 'box-up' or 'company' area at the intersection of the three 'tribal' blocks associated with the sub-groups.

The Aboriginal audience of this presentation listened and made occasional interjections, limited by the characteristic discomfort or 'shame' (see Harkins 1990; Arthur 1996: 107) that characterises local Aboriginal reactions to public speaking and the white cultural form of the meeting. The most vocal members of the Aboriginal group, again typical of such meetings, were 'diaspora' people (see Rigsby 1995; Smith 2000b), Aboriginal people whose families had been removed from the region, usually through earlier government intervention, to other less remote settlements to the south. Diaspora people tend to be more comfortable dealing with the format of meetings and more confrontational towards the typically non-Aboriginal employees of representative organisations.

The behaviour of diaspora people at the meeting gives an apparent example of the 'oppositional culture' seen as providing a foundation for indigenous identities in urban Australia (see Keen 1999: 4; also Cowlishaw 1988; 1994). However, using Keen's terms, I would suggest that in this case 'oppositional culture' links both a reaction to 'external social and economic conditions' and 'a continuity from the past'. Although the two are opposed in Keen's analysis, the latter continuity itself partly expresses a sense of insecurity and 'culture loss', developed through the disruptions of colonial impact, through external aggression directed towards non-Aborigines.[22] As such it is no surprise that anthropologists, who are typically white, in asserting their knowledge and experience of indigenous knowledge in the form of 'Aboriginal tradition' are subject to particular confrontation by diaspora people who attempt to regain '*control over the production of knowledge of one's own cultural and political identity*' (Keen 1999: 5, emphasis added. Keen uses the phrase in the context of 'cultural revitalisation' movements).

The relationships between diaspora and local[23] Aboriginal groups tend to be more ambiguous and revolve around diaspora people's hopes of gaining greater knowledge about 'country' and family connections. Such hopes are often asserted too aggressively from a local perspective and local people also tend to be defensive towards people they do not or choose not to recognise as legitimately connected to '*country*'. Resulting tensions are often characterised by a degree of bad feeling, but relationships and goodwill tend to develop during the course of claim processes. However, diaspora people initially tend to be regarded with suspicion by Aboriginal families who had remained living on the Peninsula, partly due to their perceived lack of knowledge about '*country*', and partly due to their being 'strangers', people whose relations of kinship and sociality with the local Aboriginal families were less established than those between the latter families (Smith 2000b).

The diaspora/local distinction was of some import to the Coen meeting. The overlapping claim, lodged in reply to the one taken up by the Cape York Land Council, had been taken up by a diaspora woman about whom other members of her tribe felt some discomfort as a result of her actions in a previous land claim. The general feeling about this woman amongst senior local members of her 'tribe' was that she did not fully comprehend the finer distinctions operating between members of that tribe in relation to affiliation to 'country', and her understanding of 'where people come in for country' (that is, hold specific interests in land) was felt to be problematic.[24]

After those running the meeting had talked for some time, and after some informal discussions between white representatives and prominent Aboriginal men and women during breaks, it was agreed, following a suggestion by the Land Council employees and anthropologists, that the former group would leave the room allowing the Aboriginal claimants to discuss the problems amongst themselves. They were to inform the white representatives and consultants of decisions or of the need for further delay in due course.

After some time, the white representatives re-joined the meeting and were informed that:

- All current claims should be withdrawn, and three new claims would be lodged over Archer Bend National Park, the Mungkan Kaanju National Park and the Lochinvar USL block involving all relevant claimants as a single group for each claim.
- That the Mungkan Kaanju National Park land claim would cover the whole area of the National Park and would involve Mungkan, Kaanju and Ayapathu people in a united claimant group.[25] Discussions over territorial boundaries were not a matter for public airing and where these existed they would be resolved beyond the claim process between Aboriginal people.
- That a letter would be written to the (absent) woman who had lodged the overlapping claim, asking her to withdraw her privately lodged claim and inviting her to join the new Mungkan Kaanju National Park claimant group.

The latter decision was made possible partly as a result of the bad feeling that had ensued between local and diaspora members of her tribe in a previous claim, which many diaspora people felt was hindering their desire to re-establish ties with and better knowledge of their traditional land and kin. Both discussion and decision on this matter were undoubtedly facilitated by this woman's absence from the meeting despite a typical regional emphasis on the need for the presence of all interested parties in any discussion over land.

In general, it is apparent that a degree of artifice is involved in the outcomes of this kind of meeting, and that 'instructions' secured from indigenous claimants are, to a greater or lesser extent, produced through the active intervention of non-Aboriginal advisers and representatives. Such artifice is partly a result of the representational simplification of people and place relationships that characterises land claims (Maddock 1989: 158), but it is clear that it also occurs through the necessity of meeting the requirements of land claim legislation. Probable best-fit models are developed both by anthropologists and Land Council employees in more informal discussions with claimants days or weeks before the meeting itself. In fact, this process mirrors Aboriginal styles of discussion and negotiation, which demand time and appropriate contexts for agreements and dissent to be worked through. It also provides some impetus to a process, that is, the progression of a land claim, about which most local Aboriginal people feel isolated and uncertain to a greater or lesser degree.

Nonetheless, despite the suitability of some measures undertaken and apparent Aboriginal consent, there are grounds for questions about the control and shaping of outcomes in this process. Again, typically for local Aboriginal styles of negotiation, decisions are commonly made in agreement to or acquiescence about asserted models. In many 'Aboriginal' meetings the fact of agreement between parties is a more pressing priority than personally favoured options (Myers 1986: 270–6). This applies at least equally to ideas presented by 'sympathetic' and use-valued non-Aboriginal participants as it does to those originating from other Aboriginal people (Smith 2000a). This process is further compounded by a common inability amongst non-Aboriginal partici-pants to comprehend often subtle indicators of Aboriginal dissatisfaction. This is a fact noted by many Aboriginal people, who commonly say of whites that they *'can't listen'* (Berndt and Berndt 1998: 341; Tamisari 1998: 256).

It is clear that such meetings and the less formal discussions that surround them consist of the active production of claimant groups and assertions of indigenous interests, involving participation by employees of representative organisations and anthropologists as much as the indigenous claimants themselves. Moreover, it appears that the forms of 'group' and 'indigenous knowledge' contained in the representations of a land claim are at least partly produced through the articulation of indigenous knowledge and practice with the process of making a land claim, rather than simply reflecting indigenous relationships to 'country' and other indigenous people. Claim groups and claim books[26] are artefacts of practical utility as much as they are representations of ethnographic veracity. As a result, distinctions can be drawn between resulting models of land tenure and Aboriginal social organisation that are developed and asserted by anthropologists and lawyers in claims processes and local indigenous knowledge practice. This situation is further complicated when Aboriginal people undermine both representation and indigenous connections to 'country' through asserting their 'loss of culture'.

ABORIGINAL ASSERTIONS OF INTEREST

As Keen (1999) notes, the land claim process involves tribunals and courts,[27] typically with the assistance of anthropologists, interpreting and assessing the indigenous knowledge, law and custom that link Aboriginal people to 'country'.[28] But those seeking to elicit such affiliations to 'country' in the central Cape York region commonly encounter a paradox. Many among the region's Aboriginal population express an interest in and a continuing affiliation to the regional landscape, typically framing this, both in 'Aboriginal English' and 'Standard English' (see Arthur 1996; Rigsby 1998b) in terms of ownership. Most often, this is described in terms of 'traditional owners', drawing on the terminology of land rights legislation from the Northern Territory that has developed over the past thirty or more years. The use of such terminology by Aboriginal people marks the regional incorporation of land claims within the body of indigenous knowledge and practice. Yet there are simultaneous self-assertions of loss of Aboriginal culture that apparently undermine Aboriginal assertions of traditional connection with 'country'. Such expressions of loss centre on several key areas, notably language, knowledge about 'Stories' and 'Story-places', knowledge of ritual practice and knowledge of kinship ties between families. Underpinning all of these are ideas of what tradition is – or ought to be – and the ways in which non-Aboriginal culture recognises it.

1. Knowledge of Language

Linguistic knowledge varies immensely within the Mungkan Kaanju National Park claimant group. For the Coen people who formed the core of the Rokeby claimant group, 'language'[29] was for the most part infrequently used in day-to-day life. The exception was an extended Mungkan family group, whose ties to Aurukun (a west coast settlement where Wik-Mungkan is the lingua franca) and their peripherality to Coen social life enforced their continuing use of Wik-Mungkan in their domestic life in Coen (Smith 2000a). For the most part, the language of day-to-day communication was Aboriginal English, which, although it draws the majority of its lexical items from English, uses many other items, notably kinship terms, from non-English Aboriginal language varieties and which often contains grammatical structures more similar to these languages than to English.[30]

Though many older people were able to remember, and amongst Mungkan people converse with ease in their 'own language', younger people said that they 'can't speak language', although most claimed that they could 'hear' it (that is, understand the basics) when 'language' was spoken. One of the claimant languages, Ayapathu, had no living speakers remaining in the Coen region (cf. Smith 2001a). Nonetheless, as elsewhere in Australia (Merlan 1981; Rumsey 1989; 1993), 'language' continues to play an important role in defining Aboriginal identities and land interests within local Aboriginal society. Those unable to speak their language continued to own that language as part of their affiliation to areas of 'country' in the region. In this way even those unable to understand their language still speak of themselves as Mungkan, Ayapathu or Kaanju people.

2. Knowledge about 'Stories' and 'Story-places'

Unlike much of Australia, knowledge of ancestral activities in central and eastern Cape York Peninsula did not typically take the form of long 'Dreaming tracks' linking areas across a vast landscape (Chase 1980: 149). Nonetheless, a complex knowledge of ancestral actions provides a key feature of traditional landscape knowledge and part of the body of knowledge constituting traditional affiliation to 'country'.

Many contemporary people bemoan the 'loss' of such knowledge. Certainly, few can relate detailed accounts of the appearance of such places through ancestral action. It is not certain, however, that such knowledge was ever existent for many such places. In many cases, 'language names' have been 'lost', one site for example, a Red Kangaroo

Story Place, being referred to as 'Kangaroo Story' or 'that Kangaroo place'. However, over time spent conducting fieldwork in the region, it became apparent that most men and women in the region in their thirties and above, the age of full adulthood as well as the age above which contemporary Coen people would have worked in the cattle industry, have a good knowledge of the locations and importance of many such places, including prescriptions and prohibitions about behaviour there. Whilst direct questions about these places may provoke embarrassment, a fact not separable from restrictions on discussing such matters (see below) or the cultural inappropriateness of direct interrogative questioning, they remain part of the Aboriginal landscape of the region and people's constructions of Aboriginal ownership of and affiliation to 'country'.

3. Knowledge of Ritual Practice

A linked sphere of traditional or indigenous knowledge to that concerning 'Stories' and 'Story-places' is that of ritual practice. Despite evidence of continuing ritual performance in the region up to the early 1970s (Bruce Rigsby, personal communication), contemporary Aboriginal people, for the most part, do not remember songs, paint styles and dances associated with the grand traditions of regional ritual practice. Nor do they conduct elaborate 'increase ceremonies', and only rarely stage performances of the secular dance styles (*'malkiri'*) that were a mainstay of large gatherings up to the early 1970s (Chase 1972).

Despite this decline in performance of ritual, the loss has been less total than may initially appear to be the case. In 1933 Donald Thomson, an anthropologist working in the region, described the relatively minimal form of local 'increase' practice (Thomson 1933: 503). Working with contemporary Aboriginal groups it is apparent that similar descriptions could apply to their behaviour at some 'Story-places', where people 'wake 'im up' to ensure success in hunting. Similarly, rituals of calling out to spirits when visiting '*country*', where knowledgeable people 'baptise' visitors with local water and underarm sweat ('*give* smell') to ensure their safety from supernatural agencies, demonstrate continuing traditional practice amongst the Aboriginal people of the region. Whilst the grand local traditions of initiation ritual ('*Bora*') may have lapsed, everyday rituals remain of fundamental importance to the Aboriginal population.

4. Knowledge of Kinship Ties

Part of the presentation of an Aboriginal Land Act (Queensland) 1991 claim to the Queensland Land Tribunal involves the submission of detailed genealogies for the claimant group. In the Mungkan Kaanju National Park claim, as with other claims under the Act with which I am familiar, this involved the production of separate genealogies, indicating affinal or descent links with other families, for a series of local and diaspora claimant families. These genealogies tend to follow a generic construction portraying all known cognatic descendants of an apical ancestor (see Rigsby 1999b).

The development of these genealogies involved a combination of contemporary genealogical research with claimant families and other people of the region, use of field notes from earlier anthropological research (where available) and archival materials (for example, police or mission records). In the case of the Ayapathu genealogies the latter resources were limited and the bulk of the information was drawn from contemporary genealogical work with claimants. Ayapathu claimants expressed considerable concern about the depth and accuracy of genealogical information and suggested that, in earlier times, much more detailed and lengthy genealogies could have been produced.

I am inclined to treat such suggestions with caution. Available evidence suggests genealogical knowledge in the Coen region, as elsewhere in Australia (Neate 1995: 526), has tended to be limited to two or three generations preceding the oldest living informants. The historical depth of genealogical information available for the Mungkan and Kaanju groups in the claim came almost exclusively from information recorded by whites from now-deceased older generations and was, in fact, paid little heed by contemporary people to whom it was made available. What played and still plays a role in local genealogical reckoning is the attribution of classificatory kinship relations between people. The detailed classificatory system used by Coen people to record genealogical relationships amongst themselves is similar to that of the Iban of Borneo, who, as Freeman (1958) notes,

make no attempt to preserve lengthy genealogies ... The Iban, in their bilateral society, are much more interested in the spread or scatter of relationships, where – in the absence of exact genealogical knowledge – they are guided by their classificatory system of kinship. (Freeman 1958: 52, n20)

The Coen system almost certainly draws upon forgotten ties of ancestry and marriage in previous generations, but their importance is in the continuing structuration of relatedness between contemporaries.[31] Although younger people may be losing some of the finer distinctions of traditional kinship nomenclature (Smith 2000a), contemporary Aboriginal life in the Coen region continues to bear a marked emphasis on particularities of kinship relations, obligations and proscriptions, all of which are a core part of the Aboriginal 'rules' or 'law' that form a key aspect of – and foundation for – local indigenous knowledge.

It is not coincidental that Aboriginal notions of culture loss focus on these areas. All of the categories outlined are emphasised as key components of Aboriginal traditions both within anthropology, by representative organisations and by tribunals dealing with land claims (Rose 1996). Similar factors, highlighted by anthropological criticism based 'in a strong culture-loss view'[32] (Keen 1999: 2) have led to the failure of at least one major Native Title claim (Yorta Yorta) in Victoria and New South Wales (the decision in this claim is currently under appeal). Even (perhaps particularly) where outside agents are sympathetic to Aboriginal interests, this prioritisation of traditionality plays a role in Aboriginal perceptions of the necessary evidence they will need to present to non-Aboriginal people. Despite cases in which anthropologists have attempted to portray Aboriginal traditions as ongoing and changing – as was the case in the Mungkan Kaanju claim (cf. Chase et al. 1998) – or underline the continuities of 'culture traits' (Keen 1999: 2) in different forms, an emphasis on language, 'Stories', ritual and kinship continues as central to representation of indigenous knowledge by all involved parties.

For instance, the classical anthropological model of ownership of discrete estates, including defined tracts of land, by clans constituted through patrilineal descent continues to govern much of the anthropological representation of local Aboriginal systems of land tenure. This model is founded in the work of Radcliffe-Brown (1931). However, as Maddock (1989) indicates, land claims have also been instrumental in shifting both legal and anthropological conceptions of local descent groups away from patrilineality and towards ambilineal or cognatic models.

Sutton (1999) has recently emphasised – in part using data from the adjoining Wik region of western Cape York – an anthropological tendency to accentuate systemic fluidity in territorial organisation which has accompanied this cognatic shift and which has ignored a continuing core of patrifiliality (or, as Sutton insists, patrilineality) in contemporary north Australian Aboriginal social organisation. Nonetheless, despite Sutton's objections, the Rokeby evidence shows that an account centring on the concept of clan/estate organisation would fail to deal satisfactorily with the situations of many local families, not to mention the affiliation of diaspora interests. On the west of the Peninsula, historical experience may have been such that the system has successfully strained within limits that are recognisably patrilineal. In the neighbouring Coen/Rokeby region such an argument is more difficult to sustain.

This is not to suggest that Aboriginal affiliation to Rokeby 'country' is simply 'fluid'. Rather, a series of longer-running (and cross-cutting – see Smith 2000a) facets of filiation to 'country' have been emphasised in compensating for colonial disruption of Aboriginal practice. One of the most important has been the interplay between lower and higher-level groupings in relations to 'country'. As Merlan (1997) has shown, this interplay may be a longer-running aspect of an 'epistemic openness' within Aboriginal land tenure generally unacknowledged by anthropological models. Here there are commonly differences

> between those of us who expect or hope for systematicity in Aborigines' relationships to country (and anthropologists may here keep company with developers, government agencies and others), as opposed to the kinds of formulations to which Aboriginal people give expression from lived experience. (Merlan 1997: 11)

Certainly in the case of Rokeby and across the Coen region in general (Smith 2000a), more widely defined groups, including the Ayapathu 'language-named tribe' have given evidence, supported by other Aboriginal people from the region, of their joint interests in 'country'. Similar openness can be found in the case of an antecedent of a contemporary Mungkan family who moved upriver from his own patriclan *'country'* to the west to establish himself as 'king' of 'country' stretching along the Archer River between the Archer Bend and Rokeby areas (Chase et al. 1998: 66). Tellingly for Sutton's analysis, this man and his children's succession to control of this *'country'* would almost certainly be refused legitimacy amongst the contemporary Aurukun-living people of the more westerly Wik area from which he migrated (David Martin, personal communication),[33] but is seen as legitimate and proper amongst Coen people and within the Mungkan Kaanju National Park claimant group more generally.

In the case of the Mungkan Kaanju claimants, and in the region more generally, anthropology – at least as constrained within the requirements of legislated land claim processes – has found it difficult to address the historicised traditionality of Aboriginal lives. The Aboriginal Land Act (1991), with its separation of 'traditional affiliation' and 'historical association' fundamentally separates tradition and change, even though the separation has, to some extent been supplementarily addressed in claim hearings. The Land Tribunal report on the Lakefield National Park claim, for example, notes that

> [i]t seems to be generally accepted that no Aboriginal community or group retains complete and unchanged the body of traditions ... held by their ancestors ... [and] ... [t]he transmission of Aboriginal tradition may take a number of forms,

themselves subject to change ... some groups have augmented the practice of orally passing the culture from generation to generation by means of recording those stories and family histories in writing and paintings, and on photographs, film, videotape and audiotape. (Land Tribunal (Queensland) 1995: 67)

Nonetheless, a separation between 'traditional' and 'historical' was apparent when, during the preparation of the claim, Aboriginal claimants took myself and other anthropologists across the Rokeby area to identify a series of 'sites' of significance to them. The kinds of places that were seen by Land Council employees as possessing the greatest evidentiary value were those of 'traditional' importance. These places, including 'Story-places', resource centres (for example, fresh water lagoons for water and fishing, ochre quarries for ceremonial paint), traditional camping places, initiation grounds, burial and birth places, were to be compiled in a 'site register' to provide evidence for and a reference in understanding later oral evidence about claimant connections to the Rokeby area within Aboriginal tradition.

However, in discussing the Aboriginal landscape that constitutes Rokeby for Aboriginal claimants, people were equally – if not more – keen to draw attention to other places in the National Park. These included station homesteads and buildings, cattle yards, 'dinner camps' where breaks were taken whilst mustering, and bush camps used during mustering trips. Whilst these were seen by Land Council employees as 'fleshing out' the claimants' personal histories in the Rokeby area and providing evidence for the 'fall-back position' of a claim on the grounds of 'historical association', it is apparent that they were as important a part of the Aboriginal landscape as 'traditional sites' were for the Aboriginal claimants. In fact such places often co-occur. At Nobby Creek, a portion of the Coen River used for fishing and where 'traditional' ritualised behaviour had to be observed, there were also three yards used across the station's history by Aboriginal cattlemen. 'Historical' sites were also embedded within 'traditional' Aboriginal orientations to place. At the former Rokeby Homestead (now the Park's Ranger Station) a senior claimant touched and cried for cattle yards that he had not seen for many years, behaviour regarded as more typical at the spirit-imbued sites of the 'traditional' landscape such as 'Story-places' or 'Bora grounds'. Such behaviour again illustrates what Martin (in Chase et al. 1998: 56–7) has called, the 'syncretic interpenetration' of station and traditional life apparent in contemporary Aboriginal affiliation to the Rokeby area.

From indigenous perspectives, the inappropriate nature of the separation of 'traditional' and 'historical' is also highlighted by the personnel who would become grantees of the claim area if such a grant was made on 'historical' grounds. In this case, the 'group' would – under the terms of the Aboriginal Land Act (Queensland) 1991 – include all those with historical associations, however brief, with the station area. In fact, a claimant group so constituted would be regarded as immensely dissatisfactory to the key Mungkan Kaanju claimants[34] as it would include people considered to have 'no say' or 'no right' in the Rokeby area. Rather than being simply historical, claimant histories are interwoven with relations with other 'proper' Rokeby people, experience of place and '*country*' and underlying membership of a regional block constituted by shared regional-linguistic identity and familiarity. Similarly, despite such a shared regional identity (in part reproduced and strengthened through the claim process), interests in one part of the National Park would not constitute rights in the whole of the Rokeby area from indigenous viewpoints. This reveals the partial artifice of the shared 'group' identity asserted in the claim and lodged on the claimants' behalf, the claimants, in consultation with lawyers and anthropologists having decided to leave internal differences of indigenous tenure outside the constitution of the claim, allowing their resolution within indigenous politico-economic process should the recommendation of a grant be forthcoming.[35] A history of association with an area, within contemporary indigenous life, is both fundamental to yet simultaneously inseparable from ongoing 'traditional' forms of indigenous knowledge through which indigenous rights and interests are understood.

Given this situation, why do difficulties of representation and notions of loss of Aboriginal culture arise from Aboriginal people themselves? The answer, I believe, lies in a complex interplay of notions of tradition within the 'inter-ethnic field' (Smith 2000a), 'mimetic' practices (Merlan 1998) or the 'space of recognition' (Mantziaris and Martin 2000) that run through and beyond land claims in remote Aboriginal Australia. Claim processes, despite their intended purpose of restoring both a degree of social justice and allowing for the recognition of Aboriginal culture and knowledge (Rose 1996), remain firmly under white control in their constitution and enactment. This is epitomised for the Aboriginal people of the Coen region by the fact that 'we have to prove our right to them' by giving evidence in land claims, a fact that causes grave offence to many. Such offence is firmly embedded within Aboriginal conceptualisations of ownership of 'country', where the control of information lies with owners and visitors should concur to local authority rather than assume a position of authority when on another's land.[36]

The hegemonic relationships encapsulating and enacted within the Mungkan Kaanju National Park claim often reinforced Aboriginal experiences and expectations of relationships with whites. In particular, where information was offered about affiliation to 'country' which con-tradicted white lines of reasoning it often appeared to confirm the notion that whites 'can't listen' as such approaches were continued in an un-reconstructed manner. The nature of such communication, particularly where there is a degree of sympathy from whites, presents a situation where a tactical confirmation of white world-views is seen as a strategic necessity. To put it simply, if you want to get your 'country' back, then you have to work within the rules set by those who hold power. Whites are perceived as needing and desiring images of a particular form of tradition or indigenous knowledge in order to authorise the return of control of 'country' to Aborigines. As one senior Aboriginal man said to another, who had never given tribunal evidence before, 'you got to tell them about your sites'. Commonly, as a result, it is typically such information that Aboriginal people seek to put forward in land claims.

These expectations of 'traditional' evidence are likewise enshrined in the beneficial legislation of the Aboriginal Land Act 1991, and reproduced through the agency of Land Council employees, who seek to draw evidence – both from anthropologists and claimants – that meets the requirements of the Act rather than a nuanced ethnographic portrayal of contemporary indigenous knowledge and territoriality (see Maddock 1989: 170). In the Mungkan Kaanju National Park claim, Cape York Land Council lawyers worked from a checklist of the criteria necessary to fulfil the grounds for a successful claim when eliciting evidence. This – in turn – separated and privileged a 'traditional' over a 'historical' presentation of connections. Other aspects of knowledge and organisation may likewise have been distorted; in asserting the unity of a single claimant group a superficially true but unelaborated picture of the complexities of local organisation was presented in evidence.[37]

Such a portrayal may have served the immediate needs of claimants, but raises the question of whose interests, in the long run, are served by partial and limited evidentiary representations – which become a matter of public record – in a situation where Aboriginal society and culture are engaged in a complex process of transformation and continuity. Moreover this process is one within which land claims play a constituent part. Such claims have become more than a simple matter of granting or confirming land title to Aboriginal groups; they are also a process of reorganising land-focused relationships within and between indigenous and non-indigenous cultures (see also Rose 1996; Merlan 1998; Smith 2001b). To do so through a misplaced understanding of Aboriginal relations to 'country' and Aboriginal tradition is more than a matter of bad faith on the part of those representing claimants. It also structures future inter-ethnic engagements – both within legislative processes and more generally within Australian society – on fundamentally problematic premises.

It is such inter-ethnic engagement, I believe, that is the basis of Aboriginal representations of culture loss. Such representations are embedded in a long-running colonial history of self-understanding in which Aboriginal concepts of indigenous knowledge have been reproduced and transformed through engagement with non-indigenous Australia. Through this process Aboriginal people in the Coen region have to a greater or lesser degree internalised non-Aboriginal under-standings of tradition and authenticity. Whilst there are reasons for not producing evidence about sensitive topics, for example, 'Story-places', Aboriginal people also feel great anxiety based in notions of their lack of knowledge about these matters in comparison to that held by their 'old people'. Aboriginal people in the Mungkan Kaanju National Park claim noted that they felt compelled to discuss knowledge normally undisclosed to outsiders. They were keen to maintain control over what information they chose to 'open up' for the purposes of the land claim through legal restrictions. Nonetheless, they simultaneously revealed their insecurity about what they felt was their limited knowledge of such matters, which they clearly saw as falling below both outsiders' and their own expecta-tions of what qualified as proper 'traditional knowledge'.

Queensland life is replete with ideas about what 'real' Aboriginal people are like, reproduced in conversation, on television and radio and in schools and political discourse and government policy (Eckermann 1988: 31). These ideas contrast images of 'authentic' Aboriginal life, of language, ceremony and Dreamings – characterised by the 'traditional' Aboriginal population of the Northern Territory – with the 'accultur-ated' black population of rural Queensland towns. At a local level these images have formed a core theme in relationships between local whites and Aboriginal people, feeding back into indigenous notions of Aborigi-nality and tradition. The colonial history of the region has disrupted – although not displaced – local Aboriginal practice and knowledge, whilst simultaneously excluding Aboriginal people from full involvement in 'mainstream' Australian life. In the current era of land rights this leaves people desperate to re-assert their connections with 'country' whilst simultaneously uncertain and uncomfortable about their social and cultural future.

In this way originally alien but increasingly internalised notions of Aboriginal tradition and authenticity have driven a wedge between a compelling sense of inalienable connection to (and ownership of) 'country' – the basis for Aboriginal aspirations of post-colonial recovery and development – and Aboriginal understandings about how such connections should be constituted. When an Aboriginal person gives evidence about their discomfort that 'we have lost our language', or that land is 'coming back thirty years too late', that 'we don't really have our culture anymore' or that local Aboriginal traditions have been 'all washed away now', they are not simply overwhelmed by the contradiction between what constitutes their affiliation to land and what non-Aborigines expect to constitute such a connection. Utilising concepts resulting from a history of change and continuity, in which Aboriginal knowledge and practice have become embedded within a hegemonic relationship with non-Aboriginal culture and transformed through the resulting interactions, Aboriginal people in the Coen region are also agonised by their own uncertainty of the validity of their existence and future, however inseparably they feel these are bound to their 'country'.

PERCEPTIONS AND OUTCOMES

This uncertainty was apparent in other aspects of the claimants' assertions – or lack thereof – of control over the claim area. The 'traditional owners' of the claim area made strong assertions of their rights over 'country' in the Mungkan Kaanju National Park, and contested the assertions of other Aboriginal people, notably initial assertions by diaspora people, seen to be 'stepping over our boundary'. However, the willingness of claimants to contest non-Aboriginal control over the claim area was far less pronounced. One illustration of this came when, during one of the Tribunal's visits to 'country' in the National Park with claimants, a QPWS Ranger burnt nearby areas as part of the National Park's management regime. This burning was undertaken without consulting the claimants and was the source of considerable anger amongst them. However, rather than being voiced as an infringement of their control of the area as 'traditional owners', this anger was vocalised in terms of danger presented given the proximity of the fire to the area where the Tribunal was hearing evidence.

This lack of vocalisation of traditional ownership is interesting as, within the local Aboriginal population, the right to burn 'country' is considered to rest with those owning the area under Aboriginal Law.[38] I believe that for many Aboriginal people in the region, particularly older men and women, the history of relationships with non-Aborigines and government agencies has been such that it would be considered at best useless to vocalise rights based in ownership of 'country' to them. Whilst such ownership continues as a lived reality and as a basis for social action between Aboriginal people, lived experience and received understanding have engendered it as meaningless in dealings with whites. This has led to a situation in which many Aboriginal people do not appear to consider Aboriginal Law to be relevant in engaging non-Aboriginal agencies despite the sense of injustice that they feel about actions undertaken by these agencies remaining embedded within it.

Does this demonstrate a situation where Aboriginal Law has 'all been washed away' by the appearance of non-Aboriginal law and practice? I would suggest not. Rather, the current era has introduced the possibility for Aboriginal people, after many years of radical disempowerment, to realise that they are able to assert more reciprocal relationships with government agencies and the 'mainstream' on the basis of their own system of law and custom.[39] However, the repercussions of this fact will take some time to get used to. The confidence and understanding necessary to engage in satisfactory negotiations with outsiders about 'country' are still emergent in the case of the Mungkan Kaanju National Park but other examples in the region demonstrate that full emergence is likely (see Smith 2000a).

In fact, in the 'native title era' (Fingleton and Finlayson 1995) it is increasingly necessary for non-Aboriginal stakeholders to recognise the title which 'traditional owners' in the region maintain over their 'country', despite the fact that these 'traditional owners' remain uncertain of the assertion of such title *vis-à-vis* whites. Further, despite the Native Title Act (Commonwealth) 1993's provisions to determine extinguishment of Aboriginal title in the 'space of recognition' it creates between 'mainstream' Australian and Aboriginal law (see Mantziaris and Martin 2000), it is clear that Aboriginal law and custom pertaining to land may continue both where such extinguishment may be determined, or where no Native Title claim has been registered. In such circumstances, to declare Aboriginal title void is to ride roughshod over it, a further act of dispossession likely to be felt as illegitimate and to further impact on social and personal well-being amongst Aboriginal people. The situation calls instead for the careful clarification and development of the underlying fact of Aboriginal ownership by sympathetic agencies such as the Cape York Land Council, both within and beyond the provisions of legislation, in order to facilitate outcomes regarding 'country' that create the ground for sustainable coexistence between Aboriginal and non-Aboriginal Australians.

Within such a process, outsiders representing Aboriginal interests have a particular responsibility to 'listen' with the full sense of the Aboriginal term's emphasis on understanding (see Tamisari 1998: 256). At points during the claim process – notably in the negotiations with QPWS that stemmed from the claim – even supposedly sympathetic whites failed to 'listen' in this way. For at least some claimants, in particular many older local people, the potential outcomes of the process were seen at least as acceptable. Senior Aboriginal men and women appeared willing to accept an outcome wherein they would be able to establish and maintain permanent outstation infrastructure in the Mungkan Kaanju National Park, access to the area and control over important places which they felt should be restricted to outside visitors. However, the stance taken by some non-Aboriginal representatives – that full freehold title was the only right and desirable outcome for traditional owners – did not appear to match the views of senior claimants.

It may be that Aboriginal acceptance of more limited outcomes was based in an inter-ethnic political situation in which claimants felt isolated from and uncertain of the process. However, it was clear that many Aboriginal people were prepared to accept outcomes that facilitated their immediate and ongoing access to the area rather than a scenario that might result in protracted legal processes during which claimants' rights in the Mungkan Kaanju National Park area remained uncertain. On the other hand, negotiations with QPWS, facilitated by the Cape York Land Council, which managed to produce an agreement that the Joint Board of Management (which would be developed as a result of a successful claim) would include a majority of Aboriginal claimants met with con-siderable satisfaction amongst senior local claimants.

Again there are grounds here for questions about the control and shaping of outcomes. To presume that Aboriginal people are not prepared to compromise on an absolute form of ownership over a claimed area, however sympathetically motivated such presumptions might be, is to displace them from control over their own '*business*'. Not only has Aboriginal culture not 'all been washed away', but this culture also remains capable of acting as the basis for change, development and compromise. To deny this fact and to presume a fundamental, unchanging and uncompromising form to Aboriginal viewpoints is to act on a basis that removes Aboriginal people from their place in con-temporary social and political life in central Cape York Peninsula. In fact, my previous experience – in this region as elsewhere – shows that Aboriginal people are both able and prepared to negotiate compromises within claims processes, albeit through support and information provided by sympathetic agencies from beyond the local Aboriginal population.

Unfortunately – and ironically, given the background of the Mungkan Kaanju National Park claim (notably the Koowarta case) – the continuing experience of the Aboriginal people of central Cape York Peninsula was that despite the supposed acknowledgement of their traditional ownership within the claim process, dispossession continued as a result of State and Federal Government actions. For many claimants the Mungkan Kaanju National Park claim and its likely outcomes reinforced previous perceptions of the relationship between Aboriginal people and the Australian nation-state. Perhaps for this reason, many claimants were half-hearted about the land claim process. Given that, rather than ownership of their 'country' in any meaningful sense, the likely outcome of a successful claim would be an arrangement where there was no choice but to hand back Mungkan Kaanju 'country' for continuing use as a National Park, this is understandable. More so when the lack of freehold land as a basis for Aboriginal social and economic development is taken into account. Thus, whilst I concur with Rose (1996) that there is much to be gained beyond forms of title to land by Aboriginal people within claims processes (see also similar observations by Justice Maurice and Sutton cited in Rigsby 1999b: 6), I feel that the negative aspects of the claim process for indigenous people were keenly felt and dominated the proceedings for many. These feelings were compounded by the contemporaneous backlash against and restrictive amendments to the Commonwealth's Native Title Act 1993, focusing on the Wik Native Title claim area, which adjoins the Mungkan Kaanju National Park. These amendments provided further evidence for the region's Aboriginal population that land rights were granted and removed under the absolute control of politicians. Land claims seemed to offer little certainty of any kind for Aboriginal people, whether land rights were framed in terms of 'tradition', 'history' or continuing, historicised ownership under Aboriginal law.

INDIGENOUS KNOWLEDGE AND ANTHROPOLOGICAL PRACTICE – SOME CONCLUSIONS

In the space of this chapter it has not been possible to give the complex issues contained in Aboriginal land claims the thorough analysis they deserve. Rather, I hope I have provided some insights into the ways in which land claims hinge on understandings of indigenous knowledge and legislative requirements that produce accounts and actions detached – to a lesser or greater degree – from contemporary Aboriginal practice and understandings and which instead emphasise externally authorised and formalised notions of tradition. This is most striking in Aboriginal statements of culture loss that, unless addressed through careful analysis, threaten both to undermine indigenous interests in land and non-indigenous understandings of Aboriginal life.

In my experience, anthropologists remain in a unique position to address this situation. Whether as academics or as advocates we are neither compromised in the broader scheme of things by the necessity of adherence to legalistic frameworks, nor by a lack of sufficient knowledge. Perhaps most importantly of all, despite the history of our concepts, we are not bound to a notion of tradition or culture as removed from experience or as unchanging and essential. The importance of this fact has become all too apparent to those of us working as consultants in Aboriginal Australian land claims. Here our application of the discipline as experts and advocates in legal and development arenas has privileged us with an understanding, developed 'at the coal face', of how both 'fourth world peoples' and the societies by which they are encapsulated are increasingly inter-penetrating and transforming, in part through an engagement with each others' knowledge.

Criticisms of academic knowledge as ungrounded through a lack of practical application are familiar, for example in economics, where theories have demonstrated how they can fall drastically short when applied. We should not presume that our experience of grassroots life through fieldwork makes us immune from similar misapplications. Underscoring the debate, in Australia, of whether anthropology can combine objectivity with advocacy is a growing realisation of the increased sophistication of both practice and theory gained through this engagement. This is contrary to the views of Radcliffe-Brown and others who believe that

the demand on social anthropologists to spend too much of their time on practical problems would inevitably reduce the amount of work that can be given to the development of the theoretical side of the science. (Radcliffe-Brown, cited in Maddock 1989:170)

Such opinions are based in a world-view that, like Sharp's (1939), sees anthropology's subject matter and responsibilities as removed from any inter-ethnic engagement. A more sophisticated understanding of continually developing societies and cultures leaves us in a unique position to intervene through reconstituting the forms of inter-ethnic action, among which the practice of anthropology has always numbered.

In Australia – as elsewhere – the examples discussed above are not limited in their relevance to land claims and territorial matters. Wherever indigenous populations are marginalised by mainstream social, cultural and economic life they are presented with particular difficulties in engaging with state and other non-indigenous agencies. The field of 'development' is clearly one where this problem is endemic. Just as the distinction of 'tradition' from 'history', and 'continuity' from 'change' provides the fundamental framework of non-indigenous engagement with Aboriginal life even when non-Aboriginal agents are sympathetic, so too do the problems that result demonstrate themselves in development practice. Implicit white privileging of traditionality, constituted in terms of a reified Aboriginal past, have underscored countless problems in development projects in central Cape York Peninsula. To refuse to engage with changing Aboriginal understandings and practice is to impose our own notions of Aboriginality on indigenous groups, whose ability to represent and determine their own aspirations we should recognise and support.

In a world in which understandings of tradition – whose history is undoubtedly shared with previous anthropological accounts – are increasingly unsuitable to understanding the historicised traditionality of Aboriginal experience, anthropology has both the ability and obligation to change, develop and disseminate its own understandings. Nonetheless, we need also to recognise as many Aboriginal people do that the sources of continuing Aboriginal dispossession cannot be addressed simply through the adjustment of our approaches to indigenous knowledge. Recognition is important, but it is the level of policy that remains the most powerful – and the most removed – force impacting on Aboriginal communities. Beyond the academy, we also have an obligation to engage with government and its continuing impact on the lives of those we write about.

NOTES

1. The research on which the chapter is based took place mostly in and around Coen, Far North Queensland in 1996–99, and was supported by a Study Abroad Studentship from the Leverhulme Trust, a Research Grant from the Australian Institute of Aboriginal and Torres Strait Islander Studies, the Emslie Horniman Fund of the Royal Anthropological Institute and the University of London Research Fund. This chapter also draws on my work as a consultant on the Mungkan Kaanju National Park land claim for the Cape York Land Council between 1996 and 1999 on behalf of Aboriginal claimants, and benefits from numerous discussions with colleagues and clients, notably Peter Blackwood, Athol Chase, Louise Goodchild, Victor Lawrence, Tig Pocock, Phillip Port and Bruce Rigsby. It has benefited from the comments of Bruce Rigsby, Nadja Mack, Bob Layton and participants of the ASA 2000 conference. The work of David Martin has had a particular influence on the ideas developed here. In writing this chapter I am indebted to the Aboriginal people living in the Coen region and elsewhere for their willingness to share their knowledge with me and their patience with my more than occasional lack of understanding. The final responsibility for what is written here rests with me.

2. Aboriginal people across Australia are currently able to make claims for their traditional land, and in some cases land with which they have historical associations, under a range of State, Territory and Federal

legislation. The first such legislation was the Northern Territory's Aboriginal Land Rights Act 1976. As noted below, it was not until the last decade that similar legislation was enacted in Queensland.

3. The majority of land gazetted has been within National Park areas.

4. The inclusion of grounds for claim through 'historical association' appear to have been introduced to respond to the situation and land needs of 'historical' or 'diaspora' people, who form a substantial component of many Aboriginal settlements across Queensland (see Trigger 1983; Rigsby 1995; Smith 2000b).

5. One exception was the Flinders Islands/Cape Melville claim, where an initial claim on both grounds was revised to remove the historical claim to ensure that the claimant group was not divided by the Tribunal into 'traditional' and 'historical' people, the claimants feeling that the whole group should receive any grant of land on a 'traditional' basis (Rigsby 1999b: 3). In the Simpson Desert Land Claim, where the claimants submitted the claim on both grounds, the expert historian acting for the claimants recommended that the claim only be submitted on historical grounds. The claimants again wanted to be granted land on a traditional basis. However, the sitting Land Tribunal decided that a grant should be made on a 'historical' basis but not on 'traditional' grounds (Rigsby 1999a: 8).

6. It is noteworthy that the term 'spiritual' is basically undefined by the Act.

7. This claim was part of a jointly run claim over three areas, the former Rokeby National Park, the (now jointly managed) Archer Bend National Park to the west and a small area of Unallocated State Land known as the Lochinvar Mineral Lease, which sat in the south-eastern corner of the former Rokeby lease. In this chapter I include the Lochinvar block along with the former Rokeby area in my discussion although the Lochinvar block was claimed only by a sub-set of the Mungkan Kaanju claimant group (that is, the Ayapathu 'language-named tribe'). The claim over the Archer Bend area, on which I did little direct work, is excluded from the discussion here unless otherwise noted. However, the claimant group to this area had a degree of overlap with the Mungkan Kaanju National Park and Archer Bend was an important part of the work and life histories of many Mungkan Kaanju National Park claimants. The report of the Queensland Land Tribunal on the claim has recently been published (Land Tribunal (Queensland) 2001), and recommends the grant of title to the land in all three areas to the claimants on the basis of traditional affiliation.

8. 'Country' is a common term in 'Aboriginal English' for tracts of land embedded in an Aboriginal conceptualisation of the landscape, incorporating dimensions ranging from property and cosmology. The term, which has now entered the 'Australianist' literature (for example, Sutton 1995) is useful in its explicit interweaving of these dimensions, reflecting indigenous perspectives. As Rigsby (1992: 354, n3) notes, '... "Country" is the usual translation of one of the primary senses of a form that has lexeme equivalents in all the languages of the [Princess Charlotte Bay] region; e.g. Umpila [and Kaanju] ngaatyi, [Eastern] Ayapathu ngarrku, Umbindhamu 'aakurru, Umbuygamu eara, Lamalama ari..."Camp", "home", "ground" and "(period of) time" are other senses of this lexeme ...'. It is paralleled by

the Wik-Mungkan term *aak* (cf. Kilham et al. 1986) and the western Ayapathu term *agu* and Pakanh term *aaku* which Hamilton glosses respectively as 'land' and 'land, ground, earth, place, camp' (Hamilton 1997a: 1, 1997b: 2). Elsewhere (Smith, forthcoming) I discuss the fact that this lexeme's combination of places for habitation and belonging, ground or tracts of land *and* periods of time is strongly suggestive of the inseparability of place from 'temporalised' or 'historically embedded' personal existence in local indigenous tradition. The term '*country*' and others which appear in this chapter in single inverted commas are those used in the region's Aboriginal languages, including local Aboriginal English (see Arthur 1996). Bruce Rigsby (personal communication) has revised the spellings of the language terms cited above since writing his original (1992) article. The spellings cited here are the corrected ones.

9. Similarly, for most of them, Archer Bend was an area of 'country' that they had 'worked' from Rokeby and 'New Yard' or 'Jabaroo', the station's main outstation camp.

10. See below and elsewhere (for example, Rose 1992) on Aboriginal attributions of agency to place and Hunn (1991) for a comparable account of indigenous American animism. As Bruce Rigsby (personal communication) notes, places from a Cape York Aboriginal perspective are humanised, and are themselves social actors with all of the consciousness, motivation and agency of human persons.

11. See Smith (2001a) for a discussion of the term 'tribe' in the Aboriginal English of the central Cape York region.

12. 'Mungkan' people speak and own a series of languages associated with central and western Cape York Peninsula. These were amalgamated as 'Mungkan' or 'Mungkan-side' languages (and associated people) in the claim (see Chase et al. 1998, and in particular, Martin 1998). They are better known in current literature as members of the 'Wik' peoples. In the claim area, the predominant Wik languages associated with 'country' included Wik-Iyeny or Mungkanhu and Wik Ompom or M'biwom. Inland Ayapathu people are similarly members of the Wik claimant group under the Native Title Act (Commonwealth) 1993.

13. David Martin (personal communication) notes that a fundamental connection between person and place is established in Mungkan understandings through the coming into being and first awareness of space, time and existence in a particular location. Birthplace is regionally important across central and eastern Cape York Peninsula in establishing connection to and rights in '*country*' (Smith 2000a).

14. See Martin in Chase et al. (1998) and Smith (2001b) for more on what Martin has called the 'syncretic interpenetration' of cattle-work and indigenous knowledge and practice.

15. I follow Casey (1993: xi) in my use of these terms, which refer to the malaise and collapse of norms and values (anomie) linked to radical displacement (atopia).

16. Coen had a core minority of white families who owned town and cattle businesses, and who dominated decisions made about the area by the regional Shire Council and State Government.

17. A case brought by Eddie Koiki Mabo and other Torres Strait Islanders insisting that their traditional rights in land should be recognised. The final success of the Mabo No. 2 case in the Australian High Court led directly to the Native Title Act (Commonwealth) 1993.

18. Claims under the Aboriginal Land Act (Queensland), where they do not simply involve the transfer of land necessitate a hearing by sitting members of the Land Tribunal, where evidence is taken which forms the basis for the recommendation for grant of the land to the claimants or otherwise.

19. The major township of the central Cape York Peninsula region and home to many of the claimants.

20. See Smith (2000a) on the distinction between 'public' and 'semi-public' speaking surrounding meetings in the Coen region. 'Semi-public' speaking tends to occur in the background of meetings, in smaller kin-oriented groups away from the main meeting place, and where reservations and complaints are voiced in a way that would be inappropriate and productive of social division if voiced in front of the wider 'public' realm of large meetings.

21. I was the least experienced, and had worked and lived in the Coen region for six months before this meeting. The other anthropologists had twenty or more years experience working in the region.

22. 'Diaspora' people, who often perceive their connections as being denied by 'local' Aboriginal people, may direct similar aggression towards these people (Smith 2000b). In my experience, 'recognition' of traditional identity and rights – both by other Aboriginal groups and by non-Aboriginal people and agencies – is a key concern of more urban Aboriginal people across North Queensland and elsewhere.

23. I use the term 'local' to label those Aboriginal people, and families, that have remained on, or in the region of their traditional 'country', living alongside other similar groups and thus maintaining a system of locally-oriented territoriality, in which indigenous knowledge about *country* and ownership has remained embedded. See Smith (2000b) for further discussion of local (and diaspora) people in the central Cape York Peninsula region.

24. Such distinctions of interests in land between members of a 'language-named tribe' (Rigsby 1995) are typically transformations of earlier systems based around the corporate ownership of tracts of land by patrilineally- or patrifilially-recruited 'clans' (Sutton 1998, 1999; Smith 2000a). Such transformations may or may not have also led to the generation of conjoint '*tribal*' rights in land between members of the language-named tribe (see Smith 2001a for a discussion of one such case). Where such conjoint rights occur they may vary considerably in degree and kind.

25. As noted above, this was true for the Mungkan Kaanju National Park itself. The Archer Bend area featured a differently constituted Mungkan claimant group, and the Lochinvar USL area was claimed only by Ayapathu people.

26. Reports prepared by land councils and consultant anthropologists to present evidence of Aboriginal connections to areas claimed under State and Federal legislation. In Native Title claims (that is, claims under the Native Title Act (Commonwealth) 1993), these are increasingly referred to as 'connection reports'.

27. For example, the Land Tribunal (Queensland) in the case of the Aboriginal Land Act (Queensland) 1991 and the Federal Court and the National Native Title Tribunal in the case of the Native Title Act (Commonwealth) 1993.

28. In the following sections I have not detailed the process of such claims, which involve both formal tribunal hearings and 'site visits' with Aboriginal claimants to 'country' in the claim area. Similar processes are described more extensively elsewhere (for example, Rose 1996; Merlan 1995, 1998; Rigsby 1999b).

29. Coen people use the word 'language', in local Aboriginal English, to denote non-English based indigenous language varieties. By extension, I have also seen it used to denote other people's languages, for example, Mexican Spanish. The heart of this distinction between '*language*' and English is the perceived connection of 'language' to 'country', itself denoting the connection of people affiliated to that language to their own 'country' (see Smith 2000a).

30. As Keen (1999: 3) notes, similar continuities of 'culture-traits' – in kinship and spiritual belief as well in linguistic forms – have been well documented in the less remote (and more culturally 'disrupted') communities in southern Australia. See also Arthur (1996: 7).

31. I draw the concept of structuration from the work of Anthony Giddens (see Giddens 1984; Smith 2000a).

32. This criticism was contained in reports by the anthropologists Ron Brunton and Kenneth Maddock (see Keen 1999: 2; 1999: 5, n7).

33. The Wik area is one of the two through which Sutton (1999) illustrates his criticisms of 'fluidity' approaches in contemporary Aboriginal Australian ethnography.

34. I am indebted to David Martin for bringing this to my attention.

35. One reason for this decision is that separate claims within a block of land such as the Mungkan Kaanju National Park would, if the hearing proved successful, mean that internal boundaries would be surveyed. Given the ambiguous and potentially controversial nature of 'box-up' or 'company' areas of overlapping interest, the 'one mob' (single claimant group) approach to the claim was felt to be preferable by both representative organisations and indigenous claimants.

36. See also Merlan (1995) on the effects of this aspect of Aboriginal culture on land claim hearings.

37. In fact the Tribunal, in making their recommendation to the Minister, have commented upon their understanding of the importance of the sub-groups within the larger claimant groups for the Rokeby and Archer Bend areas and made their recommendations for grant on this basis (see Land Tribunal (Queensland) 2001).

38. It is of note that claimants expected their consultation in burning regimes as a core aspect of any future management plan following the claim.

39. Such realisations are, in my view, inseparable from the Mabo No. 2 case and the resulting Commonwealth legislation (the Native Title Act (Commonwealth) 1993).

REFERENCES

Arthur, J.M. (1996) *Aboriginal English: A Cultural Study* (Melbourne: Oxford University Press)

Berndt, R.M. and C.H. Berndt (1998) *The World of the First Australians. Aboriginal Traditional Life: Past and Present* (Canberra: Aboriginal Studies Press)

Brennan, F. (1992) *Land Rights, Queensland Style: The Struggle for Aboriginal Self-Management* (St. Lucia: University of Queensland Press)

Casey, E.S. (1993) *Getting Back Into Place: Toward a Renewed Understanding of the Place-World* (Bloomington and Indianapolis: Indiana University Press)

Chase, A. (1972) *Coen Races: An Aboriginal Meeting Time*. Unpublished Report to Australian Institute of Aboriginal Studies (Canberra: AIATSIS)

—— (1980) 'Which Way Now? Tradition, continuity and change in a North Queensland Aboriginal community'. Unpublished PhD Thesis, Department of Anthropology and Sociology, University of Queensland

Chase, A., B. Rigsby, D. Martin, B. Smith and P. Blackwood (1998) *Mungkan, Ayapathu and Kaanju Peoples' Land Claims to Mungkan Kaanju National Park and Lochinvar Mineral Field*. Unpublished Claim Book (Cairns: Cape York Land Council)

Cowlishaw, G.K. (1994/1988) 'The Materials for Identity Construction', in J. Beckett (ed.), *Past and Present: The Construction of Aboriginality* (Canberra: Aboriginal Studies Press)

Eckermann, A-K. (1988) 'Culture Vacuum or Cultural Vitality?', *Australian Aboriginal Studies* (1)

Fingleton, J. and J. Finlayson (eds) (1995) *Anthropology in the Native Title Era: Proceedings of a Workshop* (Canberra: Aboriginal Studies Press)

Freeman, D. (1958) 'The Family System of the Iban of Borneo', in J. Goody (ed.), *Cambridge Papers in Social Anthropology No.1: The Development Cycle in Domestic Groups* (Cambridge: Cambridge University Press)

Giddens, A. (1984) *The Constitution of Society: Outline of the Theory of Structuration* (London: University of California Press)

Hamilton, P. (1997a) *Ayapathu Wordlist*, http://www.geocities.com/~capeyork/ayapathu.htm

—— (1997b) *Pakanh Alphabetical Search Index*, http://www.geocities.com/Athens/Delphi/2970/pakalpha.htm

Harkins, J. (1990) 'Shame and Shyness in the Aboriginal Classroom: A case for practical semantics', *Australian Journal of Linguistics*, 10(2)

Holden, A. (1992) 'Easy Justice: The performance of the Goss Labor Government on Aboriginal and Islander issues', *Social Alternatives*, 11(2)

Hunn, E.S. (1991) *Nch'I-Wana, the Big River: Mid-Columbia Indians and Their Land* (Washington: University of Washington Press)

Jolly, L. (1997) 'Hearth and Country: The Bases of Women's Power in an Aboriginal Community on Cape York Peninsula'. Unpublished PhD Thesis, Department of Anthropology and Sociology, University of Queensland

Keen, I. (1999) *Cultural Continuity and Native Title Claims*. Native Title Unit Issues Paper No. 28 (Canberra: Native Title Research Unit)

Kidd, R. (1997) *The Way We Civilize: Aboriginal Affairs – The Untold Story* (St. Lucia: University of Queensland Press)

Kilham, C., M. Pamulkan, J. Pootchemunka and T. Wolmby (1986) *Dictionary and Source Book of the Wik-Mungkan Language* (Darwin: Summer Institute of Linguistics)

Land Tribunal (Queensland) (1995) *Aboriginal Land Claim to Lakefield National Park*. Report of the Land Tribunal established under the Aboriginal Land Act 1991 to the Hon. The Minister for Natural Resources (Brisbane: Goprint)

—— (Queensland) (2001) *Aboriginal Land Claims to the Mungkan Kandju National Park and Unallocated State Land near Lochinvar Pastoral Holding*. Report of the Land Tribunal established under the Aboriginal Land Act 1991 to the Hon. The Minister for Natural Resources and Mines (Brisbane: Goprint)

Langton, M. (1998) *Burning Questions: Emerging Environmental Issues for Indigenous Peoples in Northern Australia* (Darwin: Centre for Indigenous Natural and Cultural Resource Management, Northern Territory University)

Maddock, K. (1989) 'Involved Anthropologists', in E.N. Wilmsen (ed.), *We Are Here: Politics of Aboriginal Land Tenure* (London: University of California Press)

Mantziaris, C. and D.F. Martin (2000) *Native Title Corporations: A Legal and Anthropological Analysis* (Sydney: The Federation Press)

Martin, D. (1998) 'Mungkan Claimant Groups', in A. Chase, B. Rigsby, D. Martin, B. Smith and P. Blackwood (1998) *Mungkan, Ayapathu and Kaanju Peoples' Land Claims to Mungkan Kaanju National Park and Lochinvar Mineral Field*, unpublished Claim Book (Cairns: Cape York Land Council)

May, D. (1994) *Aboriginal Labour and the Cattle Industry: Queensland from White Settlement to the Present* (Cambridge: Cambridge University Press)

McGrath, A. (1987) *Born in the Cattle* (Sydney: Allen and Unwin)

McKeown, F. (1992) 'The Old Paternalism: Queensland Land Rights from a Northern Territory perspective', *Australian Aboriginal Studies* (1)

Merlan, F. (1981) 'Land, Language and Social Identity in Aboriginal Australia', *Mankind* 13(2)

—— (1995) 'The Regimentation of Customary Practice: From Northern Territory Land Claims to Mabo', *The Australian Journal of Anthropology* 6:1 & 2

—— (1997) 'Fighting over Country: Four commonplaces', in D.E. Smith and J. Finlayson (eds.), *Fighting over Country: Anthropological Perspectives*. CAEPR Research Monograph No.12 (Canberra: Centre for Aboriginal Economic Policy Research)

—— (1998) *Caging the Rainbow: Places, Politics, and Aborigines in a North Australian Town* (Hawaii: University of Hawaii)

Myers, F. (1986) *Pintupi Country, Pintupi Self: Sentiment, Place, and Politics Among Western Desert Aborigines* (Oxford: University of California Press)

Neate, G. (1995) 'Determining Native Title Claims – Learning from experience in Queensland and the Northern Territory', *Australian Law Journal*, 69, July

—— (1999) *Mapping Landscapes of the Mind: A Cadastral Conundrum in the Native Title Era*. Paper delivered to the UN/FIG Workshop, Bathurst, NSW, 18 October and International Conference on Land Tenure and Cadastral Infrastructure for Sustainable Development, Melbourne, Victoria, 26 October

Pearson, N. (1996) 'The Concept of Native Title at Common Law', in G. Yunupingu (ed.), *Our Land is Our Life: Land Rights Past, Present and Future* (St. Lucia: University of Queensland Press)

Queensland Government (1991) *Aboriginal Land Act: Reprint No. 3* (Brisbane: Government Publications Service)

Radcliffe-Brown, A.R. (1931) *The Social Organization of Australian Tribes*. Oceania Monograph No.1 (Sydney: University of Sydney)

Rigsby, B. (1992) 'The Languages of the Princess Charlotte Bay Region', in T. Dutton, M. Ross and D. Tryon (eds), *The Language Game: Papers in Memory of Donald C. Laycock* (Canberra: Research School of Pacific and Asian Studies, Australian National University)

—— (1995) 'Tribes, Diaspora People and the Vitality of Law and Custom: Some comments', in J. Fingleton and J. Finlayson (eds), *Anthropology in the Native Title Era: Proceedings of a Workshop* (Canberra: Aboriginal Studies Press)

—— (1998a) 'Aboriginal People, Spirituality and the Traditional Ownership of Land'. Draft MS to be published in the *International Journal of Social Economics* 26 (7–9) (Festschrift for Professor C.A. Tisdell series)

—— (1998b) 'Arthur, J.M. Aboriginal English: A cultural study'. Review article. *Journal of the Royal Anthropological Institute*, 4(4): 824–5

—— (1999a) 'The Traditional vs. Historical Distinction'. Unpublished MS

—— (1999b) 'The Lakefield National Park Land Claim (D829)'. Unpublished MS

Rose, D.B. (1992) *Dingo Makes Us Human: Life and Land in an Australian Aboriginal Culture* (Cambridge: Cambridge University Press)

—— (ed.) (1995) *Country in Flames: Proceedings of the 1994 Symposium on Biodiversity and Fire in North Australia* (Canberra/Darwin: Biodiversity Unit/North Australia Research Unit)

—— (1996) 'Histories and Rituals: Land claims in the territory', in B. Attwood (ed.), *In the Age of Mabo: History, Aborigines and Australia* (St Leonards: Allen and Unwin)

Rumsey, A. (1989) 'Language Groups in Australian Aboriginal Land Claims', *Anthropological Forum* 6(1)

—— (1993) 'Language and Territoriality in Aboriginal Australia', in M. Walsh and C. Yallop (eds), *Language and Culture in Aboriginal Australia* (Canberra: Aboriginal Studies Press)

Sharp, L. (1938–39) 'Tribes and Totemism in North-East Australia (Part One)', *Oceania* 9(3): 254–75

Smith, B.R. (2000a) 'Between Places: Aboriginal Decentralisation, Mobility and Territoriality in the Region of Coen, Cape York Peninsula (Queensland, Australia)'. PhD Thesis, Department of Anthropology, London School of Economics and Political Science

—— (2000b) *Local and Diaspora Connections to Country and Kin in Central Cape York Peninsula*. Native Title Research Unit Issues Paper 2(6) (Canberra: Native Title Research Unit, Australian Institute of Aboriginal and Torres Strait Islander Studies)

—— (2001a) 'The Ayapathu People of Cape York Peninsula: A Case of Tribal Resurgence?', *Aboriginal History*, 24

—— (2001b) 'Wither "Certainty"? Coexistence, Change and the Repercussions of Native Title in Central Cape York Peninsula'. Paper given at Twentieth Natural Environmental Law Conference, 'Land and Sea: Our Shared Environment' (joint session with NTRB Legal Network's Second Annual

Conference, 'The Past and Future of Land Rights and Native Title'), Townsville, 30–31 August

——— 'Changing Places, Shifting Centres: Place and Existence in Contemporary Cape York Peninsula'. Unpublished draft MS

Sutton, P. (1995) *Country: Aboriginal Boundaries and Land Ownership in Australia*. Aboriginal History Monograph No.3 (Canberra: Australian National University)

——— (1998) *Native Title and the Descent of Rights* (Perth: National Native Title Tribunal)

——— (1999) '"The System as it Was Straining to Become"?: Fluidity, Stability and Aboriginal Country Groups', in H. Bek, B. Rigsby and J. Finlayson (eds), *Kinship, Genealogies and Groups in the Native Title Era* (Canberra: CAEPR)

Tamisari, F. (1998) 'Body, Vision and Movement: In the footprints of the ancestors'. *Oceania* 68

Thomson, D.F. (1933) 'The Hero Cult, Initiation and Totemism on Cape York', *Journal of the Royal Anthropological Institute*, 63: 453–537

Transcript Australia (1998) *Transcript of Proceedings in the Matter of Aboriginal Land Claim to Mungkan Kaanju National Park: Claimant Evidence*. Draft, 27 July

Trigger, D.S. (1983) 'Land Rights Legislation in Queensland: The issue of historical association', in N. Peterson and M. Langton (eds), *Aborigines, Land and Land Rights* (Canberra: Australian Institute of Aboriginal Studies)

7   MANAGING NATURAL RESOURCES IN EASTERN ALGARVE, PORTUGAL: AN ASSESSMENT OF THE POLICY USES OF LOCAL KNOWLEDGE(S)

Manuel João Ramos, António Medeiros, Pedro Sena, Gonçalo Praça

WHEN ECOLOGY IS NOT AN ISSUE

In Portugal, the first ecologically-minded NGOs and associations were somewhat marginal forms that sprang from the political fever of the 1974 revolution. In many respects, it was Portugal's integration as a full member of the European Community (now European Union) that eventually led to the creation of a Secretary of State for the Environment. In other words, political issues deriving from human impact on the environment were initially fuelled not by popular concern but by administrative pressures from European institutions, which resulted in forms of imitative behaviour within Portugal's major political parties (strongly influenced by the political programmes of other European parties). Since then, the ecological debate has steadily gained in importance, if only because it easily lends itself to rhetorical manipulation in regional and national politics.

The creation of a number of 'Natural Parks' in the early 1980s, however, resulted from a marriage between the hastened import of European ecological ideologies and the remnants of the pre-revolutionary government's environmental policies, which had implemented some embryonic 'Nature Reserves' since the 1940s. Today, 'National Parks' are governed by an autonomous official institute called *Instituto Conservação da Natureza* (ICN, Institute for the Preservation of Nature), which inherited the functions and territories of the *Serviço de Parques e Florestas* (SPF, Park and Forestry Conservation Commission). But the role and organisational model of these 'Natural Parks', and of the ICN as a whole, are presently under scrutiny due to an upsurge in popular ecological awareness.

PARADISE AND LOSS

The present chapter considers the problematic survival of one 'Natural Park' in the coastal area of the Algarve, the southernmost region of Portugal. The focus is on the manipulative uses of the notion of 'traditional knowledge' as pertaining to the Algarve's fishing and shellfish-gathering communities. Under scrutiny are the social consequences, at the local level, of a fragile balance between the artificial state-imposed introduction of environmental concerns, the socially and environmentally damaging impact of the tourist industry, and the general embrace of developmentalist policies by social players in the area.

In the face of widespread indifference to environmental issues, it is the Portuguese state that has become the supposed driving force in the implementation of preservationist ideologies. The state, however, can also be a major obstacle, as our team found when studying the administrative functions and political competence within the Natural Park of Ria Formosa (*Parque Natural da Ria Formosa*, PNRF), the institution in charge of the coastal lagoon system in eastern Algarve. Our team was struck by the fact that the most damaging 'developments' were the direct responsibility of the national administration: on the marshes of the lagoon are located the international airport of Faro; a deep-water international seaport; depots of artillery ammunition; and a naval base. This contradictory situation must be understood as resulting from an apparently paradoxical flux of discourses. Indeed, when trying to reconcile the precariousness of the lagoon ecosystem with its own policy decisions, the Park's Directorate regularly confronts juxtaposed administrative powers (municipalities, various regional delegations of the central government) and socio-economic interests (unions, industrialist associations, private investors, contractors, etc.). Although the Park is shielded by a wide range of legal instruments, its Directorate finds it very difficult – and frequently impossible – to implement eco-friendly policies within the protected area.

Facing irreconcilable priorities and pressures, and unable to enforce the law in sensitive areas of the territory under his jurisdiction, the director of the PNRF resigned from his post in December 1999. By then it was known that the head offices of both the ICN and the Ministry for the Environment had overruled some of the director's decisions aiming to forbid the construction of new hotels and marinas inside the Park. These urbanising projects were deemed very disruptive to the environmental integrity of the marshes and lagoon by both the Park's technical staff and by regional and national NGOs (Amaral 2000: 12–17). The director's resignation caused a crisis of legitimacy, and his protests were publicly aired in the local and national press. *O Independente* wrote:

> The present situation of the Ria Formosa Natural Park is absurd. Its director claimed in a local newspaper, some weeks ago, that he 'must have been crazy' and 'out of [his] mind' when accepting the responsibility of directing the Park. He stressed that 'there are no [political] conditions whatsoever to help solve a series of problems in the Park. (Pinheiro 1999)

Besides the hotel industry's successful lobbying against certain Park rulings, the national government also licensed the plans by a state department, the *Instituto Portuário do Sul* (IPS, or Harbour Authority of Algarve), for the construction of 1,950 new moorings in new marinas, and some 3,000 beds in new seaside hotels.[1] The fact that these environmentally damaging initiatives could be planned and approved, revealed that ambiguous administrative policies continued to erode the authority of the Park's Directorate. Particularly problematic was that the territorial boundaries with which the Harbour Authority and the Park Authority exerted their jurisdiction had never been clearly established.

Despite the director's resignation, many locals welcomed the new projects. They share the hoteliers' and local councils' view that building tourist infrastructure is good for progress; they also hope to grab a slice or even a crumb of the financial bonanza which, they hope, will generate more employment, greater social and professional mobility, and more foreign currency. Seemingly successful developments already exist. One example is the Cabanas de Tavira, where a large tourist infrastructure was built in the 1970s and 1980s (*Pedras de Rainha*, *Almargem*, *Pero Gil* and *Golden Club*). Here, as in most seaside areas in Algarve, tourism is perceived as a valuable commodity, that is, linked directly to increased land and estate value, novel ideas in urbanisation, greater commercial activity and more job alternatives to fishing and agriculture. The majority of the population here thinks little of controlled forms of tourism.

WHAT ARE ANTHROPOLOGISTS FOR?

In 1998, one year before the director's resignation, the Park's Directorate proposed that a research project in anthropology be developed. Its chief aim would be the ethnographic study of the fishing communities inside the Park and under the Directorate's jurisdiction. Following a series of informal discussions between ICN and a Lisbon-based Department of Anthropology (at ISCTE, the *Instituto Superior de Ciências do Trabalho e da*

Empresa), a research project was launched under the name of 'Social Management of the Natural Resources in South-eastern Algarve'. A team from CEAS (*Centro de Estudos de Antropologia Social*) formally started research in March 1999. Financed by the ICN, the project was to run over two years and would involve five researchers, which was unusually large for a programme in Portuguese Anthropology. The team was granted full institutional support, free access to all PNRF archives and co-ownership of the research results.

The first and foremost research goal, according to the signed agreement, was to collect and organise data about the Park's maritime and coastal human settlements (Moreira 1987; Diegues 1995). The research was to cover not only villages where fishermen and shellfish-gatherers lived, but also at least one of the most important fishing towns in Portugal. The contents of an initial non-official working text, which the team co-ordinators presented to the Park, itemised the following objectives:

- a social and economic profile of the fishing and shellfish-gathering settlements;
- study of the traditional techniques for fishing and shellfish production and gathering;
- description of the means and equipment used in the pursuit of these activities;
- inquiry into the indigenous knowledge of the sea and the lagoon;
- study of local oral traditions.

The final text of the Agreement clarified how the Park authority perceived the goals of the research; it conveyed a different meaning to the agenda initially suggested by the anthropologists who were to co-ordinate the project:

We thus consider it important to develop a pioneering study that may help understand the cultural specifications of each settlement, as well as the problems of social identity that affect them. This study is intended to identify cases demanding urgent social intervention, and to bring together the stakeholders that share the common territory [of the Ria Formosa lagoon], with a view to managing integrated forms of development. These should pay equal attention to the preservation of traditional fishing and shellfish production activities, and to environmentally-minded tourism in a protected area.[2]

In the final text of the Agreement, the Park Authority stressed it wished to use anthropological knowledge in order to intervene in the management of human and natural resources. The Agreement thus endorsed the collaboration of academic researchers, normally guided by an independent status and self-declared scientific standards, with a state organism dependent both on national and regional levels of policy-making and managing a high-profile public campaign for environmental awareness. This train of events, culminating in the Agreement, reveals how the capacity of Portuguese ethnography and, more generally, anthropology, is commonly subject to misconceptions and clichés. As anthropologists, we were regarded as legitimately having the final word on issues like 'popular culture', 'authenticity' and 'national identity'. The agreed proposal also suggested that the anthropologists' work could offer an important contribution to the development of an environmentalist discourse. This idea, too, was based on a common-sensical and stereotyped understanding of what 'ethnographic inquiry' is and does. It was assumed that research rapidly directs anthropologists toward the identification and study of 'fishing villages', villages which conformed to the romantic vision expressed in the myth that non-industrialised cultures are environmentally benign (Milton 1986).

Importantly, too, the Park Authority was immersed in a logic of multi-lateral political and legal confrontations. The obvious potential for tension, now that the research team was poised to undertake applied anthropology, resulted in the above-mentioned clarification by the Park Authority. The call for applied research, however, also brought about the possibility, and indeed urgency, of a second level of inquiry, which the scientific co-ordinators at the ICN proposed in a report drafted before the signing of the Agreement (Branco et al. 1998). This second level of inquiry enlarged the scope of the study by suggesting it include all the social players involved in the management of the Park's natural resources. This broader scope directed the researchers' attention to the Park's officials and the policies for which they are responsible.

Using data gathered at both levels, the present chapter reflects upon the various kinds of knowledge produced and reproduced in the Ria Formosa, and uses to which such knowledge can be put. First, we present the empirical knowledge accumulated by the local communities inhabiting the settlements – a knowledge that has 'domestic' use, and which the team of anthropologists, by force of the Agreement, needed to collect and systematise. Next, we argue that the Park Authority also produces and reproduces particular forms of technical and scientific knowledge about the area under its jurisdiction. The resulting discourse shapes the Park Authority's relations with the inhabitants of the Ria Formosa, and with other social actors – the municipalities, the regional delegations of the central administration, the tourism industrialists and the non-governmental organisations. This is our second theme. Finally, the presence of the researchers themselves requires attention. Early on in the research, it became obvious how important it was for the development of the research constantly to take into account how Park officials and technicians, as well as the area's residents, related to and coped with the presence and objectives of the anthropologists. The weighing up of the implications of the team's work in this complex context would become an insurmountable issue. The team soon realised that the best way to guarantee a scientific standard for its research and freedom of discourse was to somewhat shift the focus of the study to the '*Parque Natural da Ria Formosa*' institution itself, and to guarantee the right to assess, and independently divulge, the information gathered both in the field (in the settlements and at the Park's administrative centre) and in several public and reserved archives.

A NATURAL ENVIRONMENT

The Natural Park of Ria Formosa covers an area of 18,400 ha along the coastal line of five municipalities (Loulé, Faro, Olhão, Tavira and Vila Real de Santo António), that belong to the District of Faro. The physical territory of the Ria Formosa extends over a 60 km stretch of coastal lagoon, characterised by marshes, moors, a barrier island chain comprising five small islands and two peninsulas, and a series of tidal areas, islets and channels. This territory is an ecosystem partially inhabited by human settlements and surrounded by various urban conglomerations. The PNRF, created by decree in 1987, was legally superimposed on a previously declared 'Nature Reserve'. As mentioned above, these successive classifications of the Ria Formosa reflect the introduction, in Portugal in the 1970s, of ecological ideologies calling for the preservation of the natural environment. With time, these ideologies have produced an increasingly powerful rhetoric (Guerra 1989).[3]

Recognised by various international conventions and organisations (the International Conservation Network, Natura 2000 Network, Ramsar Convention, Special Bird Protection Area, etc.), the ecological importance of the Ria Formosa lies mainly in the biological richness of its fauna and flora. An important number of local and migrant bird species nest in the lagoon, which is also a nursery for a large number of important fish species. The Park also serves as a major reproductive area for shellfish (mainly clams [*Ruditapes decussata*] and oysters [*Crassostrea* sp.]) both in the wild on natural banks and shores, and in licensed nurseries in the lagoon's tidal areas. These reproductive activities are important to the local economy.

Like shellfish production, traditional fishing continues as a key source of local income. Fishing is mainly coastal, local and marked by the use of multiple techniques, among which electronic detection (sonar) and positioning (GPS) systems are increasingly important. Although the fishing fleet is relatively large, motorised boats remain small in size, using minimal equipment but a wide range of capture techniques (Cavaco 1976, vol. 1; Costa and Franca 1982).[4] The fleet operates within the 200-mile limit of the Exclusive Economic Zones of Portugal, Spain and Morocco (Leal 1990), and keeps mostly to the coast. In more distant as in recent times, fishing has led to the creation and development of fishermen's settlements (temporary and permanent, legal and illegal; Serrão 1990), not only on mainland shores, but also on the islands and peninsulas round the lagoon.

The tourist industry in the district of Faro (Algarve) has been growing since the 1960s, and is one of the region's major sources of income. The ongoing national importance of this activity must not be overlooked, since the Portuguese economy depends largely on the tertiary sector (Barreto 1996). Every year, many national and foreign (mainly European) tourists visit the southern coast of Algarve, especially during the summer season.[5] During this period, the need for accommodation and complementary activities (food, leisure, transport) reaches well beyond the centres and resorts surrounding the Park, and into the Park's small popular settlements. Naturally benefiting from the Algarve's almost continuous stretch of sandy beaches, the tourist industry has boomed over the past 30 years, and has come to seasonally condition life in every community. Tourism also influences governmental policies, regional politics, the power games of the private investors and, consequently, the Park's ambiguous and shaky balance between its directives and its policy implementations.

IN SEARCH OF THE NATIVE

Although the Park's islands and peninsulas have suffered extensive illegal occupation and building in recent years, both by the fishing communities and (in most cases) by outsiders wishing to cash in on the holiday boom, there is as yet no coherent policy line of relationship between the Park authority and other local actors. Park officials have adopted a mixture of attitudes, sometimes stopping or curtailing illegal occupation, sometimes tolerating it, sometimes drawing public attention to the preservation policies of the protected lagoon area. The practice of building on the shifting sands of islands at risk (Pilkey et al. 1989) has seriously aggravated the conflict of interests between holidaymakers, local communities, municipalities and Park staff. After an initial period in which many illegal houses and shacks were forcibly pulled down on the order of the Park officials and the Secretary of State, an approach widely criticised, a new approach was attempted. This approach attempted to win local communities over to the Park Authority's perspective, which stressed the (seemingly desperate) need of preservation of the lagoon. A regulatory document of the PNRF stated clearly that local community members had the 'historical right' to occupy the islands and islets, as long as they demonstrated that their main professional activity was either fishing or shellfish-gathering. The document simultaneously recognised and conditioned their presence in the Ria Formosa area (Raposo 1986). When we initiated our research, the team immediately became aware of the Park Directorate's desire to enforce its perspective on who could legitimately live on the islands and peninsulas. The fishermen and shellfish-gatherers had this right, the tourists did not. For the Directorate, its desire to lay down the law had been the starting point for creating a detailed but unsystematic database of settlements near the Park's administrative centre. The initiative later developed into a formal Agreement of collaboration with our research team. 'Local knowledge' had become a resource.

More recently, at a scientific meeting, the ex-director of the PNRF had explicitly endorsed the rather dubious claim that local knowledge must be seen as a 'resource'. Within his vision, the 'sustainable' use of Nature was to be 'rediscovered' (by 'us') through the management and regulation – or rather 'promotion' – not only of the environment but also of indigenous knowledge and practices, which we, as anthropologists, were expected to reveal. The ex-director declared:

The Ria Formosa was classified as a Natural Park in 1987. The aims of this designation include: 1) promotion of the adequate use of the natural resources, 2) promotion of the cultural, social and economic development of the resident population, based on traditional activities, and 3) regulation of recreational activities in accordance with the natural and cultural resources. In order to conciliate human use of the territory (there are people living on the protected area – we are talking about a Natural Park, not an Integral Reserve), and the economic activities taking place there, a rational land management is required to allow the sustainable use of natural resources. Because preserving and protecting Nature doesn't mean (it cannot mean) 'not touching', 'not using'. For millennia this complex barrier-island system has provided the livelihood of countless generations of men who knew how to use it and shape it without risking its productivity and biodiversity. Can we, human beings at the dawn of the 3rd millennium, rediscover the sustainability of nature? (Fonseca 1999)

The assumption that present-day fishermen and shellfish-gatherers are the direct heirs of an ancestral indigenous population, and now the 'guardians' of the lagoon's natural resources, is a social representation which strongly influenced the course of the research. In a nutshell, the assumption became a topic of discussion in its own right.

The acknowledged reason why the Park Authority had decided to approach a university research team from Lisbon to produce an authoritative discourse on the Park's local population originated in growing scepticism regarding the feasibility of a strictly local response (that is, by Park officials or local social scientists) to the multiple developmentalist visions held by investors, the municipalities and the regional delegations representing the central administration (Campos 1999; Wells and Brandon 1995). The Park Authority believed that only outsiders could produce systematic, multi-layered scientific knowledge about the inhabitants of the lagoon, their 'traditional knowledge' and vision on how to manage a fragile natural environment. This belief underpinned the establishment of the above-mentioned Agreement. It must be stressed though that the Park Authority wished to fill in the knowledge gap as part of a larger discursive and political strategy, which aimed to reinforce its authority and improve its public image through better social practices. The promoter of the research ultimately hoped to obtain a larger power base than that conferred by the central administration (always dependent on shifting political contexts and agendas).

The Park Authority's managing policy was shrouded in ambiguity. On the one hand, the Authority wanted to empower local communities (cf. Cheater 1999) through suggesting they participate in the preservation of their own cultural and natural heritage. On the other, Park officials also believed that the same people were carelessly destroying that heritage by adopting exogenous, 'non-traditional' ways of life. In two letters written to the President of the *Região de Turismo do Algarve* (RTA, the Tourist Board of Algarve),[6] the Park's director reacted against the stereotyped vision of idyllic 'fishing communities', a vision favoured by the RTA when promoting tourism in the Algarve. He countered the stereotype with the idea that local traditions had been systematically destroyed, and that the present community was therefore uncharacteristic:

The great majority of houses to be found 'everywhere on the islands' is (unfortunately) neither 'typical' nor does it 'belong to fishermen'; apart from a few fishermen's houses, Praia de Faro is a holiday resort ... Santa Luzia was once 'picturesque'; today it is just another uncharacteristic village, and the rare hints of an authentic individuality reside in the (less and less picturesque) boats and fishing equipment lying on the lagoon banks. (Letter 1, March 1998)

Only on the island of Culatra and in a small fraction of the Praia de Faro ... do we actually find fishermen's houses. The other villages are composed of holiday-makers' houses. Furthermore, the fact that a house is inhabited by a fisherman and his family doesn't necessarily imply that it is a 'fisherman's typical house'. ... The houses of the villages on the barrier islands are uncharacteristic, chaotic, built with low-quality materials ... In Santa Luzia, we find the same: hollow brick, concrete, tiles, aluminium doors and windows, and a proliferation of sheds have obliterated all signs of the traditional architecture of the Algarve. This phenomenon is not exclusive to the Ria Formosa lagoon, but is happening everywhere in the coastal areas of the country ... The 'typicality' of Santa Luzia – if there is such a thing there – is limited to the fishing activities of that village. (Letter 2, May 1998)

Moreover, most constructions are illegal deriving from a judicial fact: access to the coastal stretch, as in the whole of the country, is public (that is, the land is owned and managed by the state) and managed for the common good. Nevertheless, some portions of the Park territory have benefited from a special legal regime, because they were alienated from the central administration as public heritage to be managed by local councils and other state organisms, which acquired them with the obvious goal of making profit from tourism (Praia de Faro, in 1956; island of Tavira, in 1966; islands of Armona and Farol, since the 1960s).

Praia de Faro village (an urban holiday resort and, simultaneously, the settlement of dozens of fishing and shellfish-gathering families) lies in the Ancão Peninsula and is subjected to strong coastal erosion (Simões 1984; Pilkey et al. 1989; Sousa 1999), which the Park Directorate tries to control by demolishing clandestine constructions and increasing political pressure through a range of legal dispositions. Frequently, the only way to preserve the thin dune line of the peninsula[7] and the threatened lagoon system has been to demolish the more endangered and endangering houses (in 1984, 1987 and 1991). The arguments and actions, however, apply only to the fishermen's houses on the margins of the village, because the holidaymakers' houses are under the juris-diction and responsibility of Faro Council, which favours construction over demolition. Consequently, it has not been possible, until now at least, to regulate the site through detailed urban planning.

The demolition of illegal houses, which brings with it the need to rehouse those evicted, is unpopular and expensive, causes social unrest and has damaged the public image of the Park Authority. In response, the Directorate tries to promote alternatives by transforming the modus vivendi of the social groups concerned with traditional fishing and shellfish-gathering. The intention is to promote eco-tourism and turn the groups concerned into living 'objects' (in the sense of museum pieces) who must preserve 'their tradition'. The Park Authority now views these groups as belonging to a 'community of memory'. The authority assumes that 'people agree that they do ... share some kind of cultural heritage, and [that] they talk about that heritage in ways that celebrate what is good or beautiful in it but criticise what is not' (Handler and Gable 1997: 235).

By requesting a series of ethnographic reports on the daily life of the populations settled inside the Park, the Directorate is opening the door for new developments in the discursive manipulation of tropes such as 'traditionalism' and 'authenticity' (Handler 1988). The continuous reference to traditional images of coastal Algarve before tourism took off confirms that Park officials do indeed imagine the place and its people as a set of community-based practices now remembered with nostalgia. (It is these new developments, and their practical consequences, which justified our research focus on the Park Authority itself.) Most of the images popular with the Park Authority originate in urban and literate circles, where they are divulged in texts, photos and films that depict a golden past with motifs such as (extinct) tuna fishing tackles, ichthyic bonanzas both at sea and in the lagoon, ancient environment-friendly fishing techniques, unpolluted sandy beaches and beautifully adorned wooden boats.[8] Among these 'cultural assets', one is particularly valued in preservationist discourse: the traditional fishing techniques (see also Letter 1 above). Because they are considered less predatory than the modern ways, these techniques are thought to stand for and guarantee an empirically proven, sustained and balanced exploration of maritime and lagoon resources. Assuming that the tourist industry will continue, and assuming that the government will maintain the Park's legal status of preservation area, one can easily envisage a future 'thematic' natural park which harbours a minimum of hotel and beach infrastructure and museum-like urban settlements in which the population takes responsibility as the privileged 'guardian' over the lagoon and the ocean's eco-systems; a respected role in accord with the current priorities of environmentalists (Wade 1999; see also Handler and Gable 1997). Within this framework, the Ordination Plan of the Parque Natural da Ria Formosa (see Raposo 1986) foresees the eviction of people deemed excessive to the endangered islands and peninsulas, and their subsequent relocation elsewhere in the Park.

Were they to go forward, these resettlement plans would affect mainly the socially and economically under-privileged, especially those groups without any prospect of finding immediate alternative housing, for example, those possessing only an illegal house on the sandy islands (see above). According to these plans, the fishing and shellfish-gathering communities are supposed to recreate a reified past in which they keep to the use of angling lines for fishing, take care of shellfish nurseries and live in 'fishermen's houses'. The fishing communities in the Ria Formosa are assumed to possess an exotic culture at the root of an Algarvian regional identity. At work here are the same ideological presuppositions that have, for more than a century, fed the urban representation of a Portuguese national identity which takes 'peasant culture' as its major reference. Other means of securing a livelihood will not be accepted. The Detailed Plan for the Praia de Faro (Plano de Pormenor da Praia de Faro; see above) even proposes to replace the existing brick, cement and plank houses with wooden shacks on stilts that imitate the extinct building style found in some coastal localities in central-northern Portugal. The Ria Formosa is by no means the only case, but is part of a more generalised international trend that has gradually become authoritative in the processes of inventing 'natives'.

CONCLUSION – FINISHING LINES

We have presented the PNRF as a collective and, to some degree, autonomous institution. Its ideological lines of action condition both the daily management of the Park and the implementation of longer-term social policies. Unfortunately, the degree of visibility and protagonism which the Park's Directorate lends to the marginalised social groups under its jurisdiction do not translate into concrete forms of empowerment. Empowerment, rather, reverts to the Park Authority itself, for the PNRF has become the *de facto* guardian of the natural resources of the Ria Formosa. In many respects, the fishermen and shellfish-gatherers have become imaginary categories within an official discourse of environmental protection and preservation, while the Park officials, whose discourses can be read almost as the ritual enactment of a prescribed role, have become technical specialists who work in an environment where political, financial and economic interests, public and private, are immensely strong.

There is some possibility, though, that the Park may disappear under the exceedingly unbearable pressures of the tourist industry and the rapid urbanisation of a coast still receiving migrant populations. These migrants come not only from the mountainous areas of the Algarve, but also from other Portuguese regions and indeed other European countries (namely the United Kingdom, Germany and The Netherlands). The Park may also disappear because of what geological and geo-maritime studies (ordered by the Park) have described as the annihilation of the lagoon system itself; a destruction triggered by the changing pattern and density of the sand line along Portugal's south coast.

For their part, the 'natives' of the Park show little interest in the proposals and the promise of 'empowerment'. Their expectations rather are overshadowed by doubts regarding the PNRF's capacity to deliver, and by a congenial suspicion that the institution's discourses and promised actions lack conviction. They seem aware that it is not they who destroy the lagoon's balance, even if they are ignorant (or pretend to be so) of the fact that they too play some small part through domestic pollution, the exhaustion of the lagoon's nursing fish population and by building on the islands. For the 'native' populations, the most visible forms of ecological pollution – created by the presence of great numbers of tourists, or caused by industrial and naval accidents – are proof that local administrations are corrupt and scientific authorities negligent. 'Pollution' is frequently discussed within the community, in interviews with the media, and in talking to social workers and social scientists. The 'native' rhetoric used in the public expression of concern masks and absolves the polluting and the depredating effect of the (legal and illegal) fishing and shellfish-gathering activities in the lagoon and open sea. 'We fishermen don't pollute or spoil the lagoon, it's the tourists who are responsible, and also the government who lets them, and the specialists who ignore all this.' The 'natives' also complain that the Park guards fine them when using illegal fishing techniques, while everyone else (the 'non-natives') seems allowed to abuse nature.

It is possible that a slow transformation in this state of affairs will occur via a growing regional civic sensitivity to environmental questions, in dialectic relation to the political weight that these questions are gaining in national political discourses. To this day, however, what is more noticeable is the perverse framework in which such discourses are expressed; the rhetorical claims about the need for sustained development with an environmental focus greatly disguise the *de facto* and unjustified depredation of the Ria Formosa environment. This is the general context in which scientists and environmentalists practise the 'virtues' of discursive self-empowerment; they lean on fishing and shellfish-gathering communities whom they endow with an imagined 'native' or 'indigenous' knowledge.

NOTES

1. *Expresso*, weekly national newspaper, 18 December 1999.
2. Minute of the Cooperation Protocol between the ISCTE and ICN, Clause 1, 1999.
3. See *Conservação da Natureza*, 1982, Lisboa: Serviço de Estudos do Ambiente.
4. For an overview of the Portuguese fishing fleet, see Moreira (1987); Leal (1990); Brito (1994).
5. See *Estatísticas do Turismo*, 1997, Lisboa: INE.

6. Letters sent to the President of the RTA in response to the article 'As ilhas formosas' (*Região Sul*, 25 March 1998), about the 'natural and cultural heritage' of the PNRF.
7. See Lopes and Cabeleira (1994).
8. See Cavaco (1992); Santos (1989) (local history textbooks supported by the PNRF).

REFERENCES

Amaral, Rosa (2000) 'Arraial Ferreira Neto: História de un atentado patrimonial', *Pedra & Cal*, 12–17 September

Associação dos Arquitectos Portugueses (1988) *Arquitectura Popular em Portugal*, 3º vol, 3ª edição, Lisboa

Barreto, António (1996) *Situação Social em Portugal, 1960–1995* (Lisboa: ICS)

Branco, Carlos M., Leonor Martins and Pedro Sena (1998) *Gestão Social dos Recursos Ambientais: as populações piscatórias e viveiristas do sotavento algarvio – averiguação preliminar*, ISCTE and CEAS (unpublished)

Brito, Raquel Soeiro de (dir.) (1994) *Portugal. Perfil geográfico* (Lisboa: Referência/Editorial Estampa)

Campos, Joaquín Rodríguez (1999) 'También se puede inventar la naturaleza? El poder del lenguaje de la cultura posmoderna', *Etnográfica* (Lisboa) 1 (3): 49–70

Castelo-Branco, Fernando (1968) 'Subsídios para o estudo das construções de materiais vegetais do litoral português – III', in *Mensário das Casas do Povo* (Lisboa) XXIII, 265: 14–15

—— (1969) 'Palheiros na Ria de Faro', in *Folclore* (Santarém) 1 (1): 25–6

Cavaco, Carminda (1976) *O Algarve Oriental. As vilas, o campo, o mar*, 2 vols (Faro: Gabinete do Planeamento da Região do Algarve)

Cavaco, Hugo (1992) *Espécies piscícolas dos mares e rios do Algarve nos finais do século* XVIII (Portugal: Comissão de Coordenação da Região do Algarve/Parque Natural da Ria Formosa)

Cheater, Angela (ed.) (1999) *The Anthropology of Power: Empowerment and Disempowerment in Changing Structures* (London and New York: Routledge)

Conservação da Natureza ([1980] 1982) (Lisboa: Serviço de Estudos do Ambiente)

Costa, Fernando Correia da and Franca, Mª de Lurdes Paes da (1982) *Pesca Artesanal na Costa Algarvia – subsídio para o conhecimento do seu estado actual*, Publicações Avulsas, 1 (Lisboa: INIP)

Diegues, Antonio C.S. (1995) *Povos e Mares* (São Paulo: NUPAUB)

Fonseca, L.C. da (1999) *Management and Conservation of a Coastal Lagoonal Environment: The Ria Formosa Natural Park*. Paper presented at the International Conference on Sustainable Management of Coastal Ecosystems. Oporto, 3–5 November

Guerra, Carlos (1989) O Turismo pelos recursos naturais e culturais e não à sua custa. In *Congresso de Áreas Protegidas*, Fundação Calouste Gulbenkian, Lisboa, 4–8 Dezembro 1989, SEARN, SNPRCN

Handler, Richard (1988) *Nationalism and the Politics of Culture in Quebec* (Madison: University of Wisconsin Press)

Handler, R. and E. Gable (1997) *The New History in an Old Museum: Creating the Past at Colonial Williamsburg* (Durham, NC and London: Duke University Press)

Leal, Manuel Cardoso (1990) *Transformação de Produtos de Pesca* (Lisboa: Banco Fomento Exterior)

Lecoq, Nuno (1996) 'Ria Formosa: um património da humanidade a preservar', in *Algarve Litoral*, 3, Dezembro: 4–5

Mendes, Maria Clara (1986) *Ria Formosa: população e território* (Lisboa: CCRA)

Milton, Kay (1986) *Environmentalism and Cultural Theory: Exploring the Role of Anthropology in Environmental Discourse* (London and New York: Routledge)

Moreira, Carlos Diogo (1987) *Populações Marítimas em Portugal* (Lisboa: Instituto Superior de Ciências Sociais e Politicas)

Oliveira, Ernesto Veiga de, Fernando Galhano and Benjamin Pereira (1994) *Construções Primitivas em Portugal* (Lisboa: Publicações D Quixote, 3rd edition)

Pilkey, O.H. Jr, W.J. Neal, J.H. Monteiro and J.M.A. Dias (1989) 'Ilhas Barreira do Algarve: Um sistema sem planície costeira em Portugal', *Journal of Coastal Research* (Charlottesville, Virginia) 5 (2): 236–61

Pinheiro, Zélia (1999) O Último Verão da Ria Formosa, *O Independente*, 2 July

Raposo, Hugo (ed.) (1986) *Plano de Ordenamento do Parque Natural da Ria Formosa* (Lisbon: SNPRCN/Divisão de Ordenamento e Projectos)

Santos, Luís Felipe (1989) *Pesca do Atum no Algarve* (Loulé: PNRF)

Silva, Baldaque da (1891) *Estado Actual das Pescas em Portugal* (Lisboa: Imprensa Nacional)

Simões, Pedro (1984) 'Ecologia das Cinturas de Vegetação da Ilha de Faro' in *3º Congresso sobre o Algarve – Textos e Comunicações*, Vol 1, Racal Clube: 523–6

Skalník, Peter (1999) 'Authority Versus Power: a view from social anthropology', in A. Cheater (ed.), *The Anthropology of Power* (London and New York: Routledge)

Sousa, David Silva e (1999) 'Erosão Costeira. O mar enrola na areia ...', *Fórum Abiente*, Janeiro, 59, Lisboa: 32–40

Wade, Peter (1999) 'The Guardians of Power: biodiversity and multiculturality in Colombia', in A. Cheater (ed.), *The Anthropology of Power* (London and New York: Routledge)

Wells, Michael and Katrina Brandon ([1992] 1995) *People and Parks: Linking Protected Area Management with Local Communities* (Washington: The World Bank/WWW/USAid)

'Ria Formosa' (1998), in *Vida Mundial*, 4, Maio, Lisboa: 30–6

Statistical Support

Gafeira, Celeste (1995) *Parque Natural da Ria Formosa: População activa 1981–1991*. SNPRCN, Divisão de Ordenamento e Avaliação de Áreas Protegidas

Estatísticas do Turismo (1997) (Lisboa: Institute Nacional de Estatísticas)

Pescas em Portugal / Portuguese Fisheries 1986–1996, INE, DGPA, 1998

Regional Land Management Plans

Parque Natural da Ria Formosa: Estudo sócio-económico das populações piscatória e viveirista da Ria Formosa (1998). Unpublished PNRF text

Raposo, Hugo (ed.) (1986) *Plano de Ordenamento do Parque Natural da Ria Formosa*, SNPRCN, Divisão de Ordenamento e Projectos

Vão – Arquitectos Associados, Lda (1988) *Plano de Pormenor da Praia de Faro – Estudo Base*, SNPRCN, Olhão

Vão – Arquitectos Associados, Lda (1993) *Plano de Pormenor da Praia de Faro*, Vol. 1, SNPRCN

Lopes, José L.M.A. and H.M.J. Cabeleira (1994) *Relatório das Demolições*, PNRF

Plano de Pormenor de Urbanização, Ordenamento e Reconversão da Ilha de Faro e Núcleos dispersos da Zona do Aeroporto – memória descritiva, (undated), PNRF

Dictionaries and Encyclopaedias

Serrão, Joel (dir.) (1990) *Dicionário de História de Portugal*, Vols I, IV, V and VI, Porto: Figueirinhas

Portugal Moderno. *Enciclopédia Temática – Agricultura e Pescas* (1991). Lisboa, Porto: 165–87, 215–18

8 INTERFACES OF KNOWLEDGE: THE REVIVAL OF TEMPLES IN WEST HUNAN, CHINA

Mary Rack

Throughout China, the economic changes following the reforms of the early 1980s have been accompanied by the rebuilding of temples destroyed during the Cultural Revolution. In this chapter, I consider forms of knowledge inherent in the activities that take place at these temples in West Hunan. I suggest that temple activities are not so much a return to a previous tradition, countering the disruption caused by China's involvement with modernity, as a form of constantly recreated local knowledge which is highly relevant to China's continuing economic and social changes.

West Hunan is an area where experiences of modernity are characterised by temporary out-migration and a perceived breakdown of social order. When writing of temple practices as forms of 'indigenous' or 'local' knowledge, I am concerned with both the knowledge of those who have rebuilt the temples and the knowledge attributed to the deities themselves, though the two are closely related. While this theme is a departure from topics more commonly considered under the rubric of indigenous knowledge, such as agricultural and technical knowledge, forms of knowledge inherent in Chinese temple activity are nonetheless related to development. In China's official discourses of development, temple activities are designated an important role, that of an impediment to progress. Among devotees, on the other hand, they are regarded as a means of dealing with the effects of economic change.

The terms 'indigenous' and 'local' knowledge imply a discontinuity with other forms of knowledge, such as state, official or scientific knowledge.[1] This implicit dichotomy highlights the power differentials that exist in development situations (Sillitoe 1998: 223; Arce and Fisher 2000: 3), but has recently been shown to be based on an over-simplifi-

171

cation in the sense that scientific knowledge is also a kind of local knowledge. Scientific knowledge, like local knowledge, is 'the multifarious outcome of ever-evolving syncretic processes' rather than a monolithic entity (Pottier 2000: 1). As a result, attention has shifted away from the apparent dichotomy between indigenous and scientific knowledge to a process by which

different discourses, values and practices associated with the notions of 'modernity' and 'tradition' intersect and are intertwined in the everyday encounters and experiences of people from diverse socio-cultural backgrounds. (Arce and Long 2000: 2–3)

Interfaces of knowledge are not necessarily found between official and local, or hegemonic and non-hegemonic forms. Rather, the process is seen as a continuing, seamless rebounding between many different forms of knowledge (Parkin 1995: 144; Arce and Long 2000: 24). Differentials in access to power remain (and the friction which results is still central), but they are not discussed in terms of simple oppositions. Arce and Fisher write of 'interfaces' that are 'dynamic and potentially conflictive ... social encounters between actors with diverse entitlements to power' (Arce and Fisher 2000: 1–2).

Knowledge concerning temple deities in West Hunan can be appropriately understood in terms of interfaces. Rather than being indigenous cultural forms, reappearing to challenge an atheistic Chinese state, they emerge from an interaction with modernity and with official discourses on progress and superstition. Often rebuilt on the basis of memory, today's revived temples represent not a return to a continuous tradition, but a flexible means of dealing with modernity, even to the point of expressing conflict. In writing about temple practices in West Hunan, however, I still find it meaningful to use (and investigate) the notion of 'official' and 'local' forms of knowledge, since these terms are prevalent in official discourses. More specifically, official discourses of development routinely constitute local knowledge as ignorant and represent it as an impediment to progress and modernisation (see Hobart 1993; also Novellino, this volume). I therefore begin my observations by considering the way in which official discourses attempt to portray activities at temples as 'superstition' (*mixin*), 'backwardness' (*luohou*) and as cultural relics of the past. I then consider the impact of this portrayal on 'local' knowledge itself, and will conclude that official discourses of superstition and progress, while not hegemonic, have a clear and perhaps unexpected influence. They reinforce the notion, among the inhabitants of West Hunan, that specifically 'local' forms of knowledge can and do exist.

DISCOURSES OF DEVELOPMENT IN CHINA

Before considering the ethnographic material I collected in and around the city of Jishou, the prefectural capital of West Hunan, between 1994 and 1996,[2] I present a brief discussion of development in China, suggesting that, despite a rhetoric of openness to indigenous forms of knowledge, official discourses have tended to construct other forms of knowledge as ignorance. This is particularly relevant to West Hunan. A mountainous area poorly served by public transport, West Hunan has long been considered *luohou* (backward)[3] and, in the Maoist period, was the recipient of a considerable amount of government investment. It still receives government funding, in part because it is now classified as the West Hunan Miao and Tujia Minority Autonomous Prefecture, but the area has not kept pace with the rapid economic development of the coastal areas. Its main exports are tobacco and rice spirits (*baijiu*), and rice spirits factories have been established in the urban centres. Levels of employment, however, are relatively low and, as in other poor areas of China, there is a considerable amount of temporary out-migration.

Between the 1950s and 1970s, writers on development often held up China's development policy as a successful alternative to the western capitalist model (for example, Potter and Potter 1990: 315). An important aspect of this policy was its claim to include forms of indigenous knowledge (Croll 1993: 161f.). With hindsight these claims appear less convincing, for the system in which 'development' took place was a hierarchical one. In the 1960s and 1970s all economic activity took place in collectives (in rural areas) and work units (in urban areas). These comprised the lowest of a hierarchy of social levels through which the directives of the Communist Party were passed and interpreted by local cadres. Croll writes that although some attention was given to the knowledge of peasants, 'in practice "outside" knowledge became increasingly privileged' with cadres becoming the agents of change (1993: 165, 167). In some cases this resulted in cadres imposing policies which the cultivators themselves regarded as inappropriate (see, for example, Chandler 1992: 214). Nonetheless, during 1949–79, many parts of China benefited from the introduction of education and improved infrastructure such as roads and irrigation systems. The Party channelled resources towards poorer areas such as West Hunan, where Party cadres arrived to settle permanently. Until the 1970s, Party cadres represented their economic and development policies in terms of the moral authority of the Communist Party.

The reforms that followed Deng Xiaoping's ascent to power, however, led to radical changes; the Party's role in guiding economic development became less directive. Communes were replaced by the 'responsibility system', in which land is allocated to individual households, who then become responsible for its cultivation. Relaxation of the laws concerning residency meant that many people were freed to work in rural industries known as township-village enterprises (TVEs). These changes have now resulted in a blurring of the once clear distinction between Party and 'people', since many enterprise initiatives are closely involved with Party and government organisations. The weakening of state provision has also led to a shortfall in educational and health provision for the poor. As a result, because of the perceived breakdown in social order, rural and older urban poor have become critical of local government and frequently express nostalgia for the past. These changes have made it harder for government officials in West Hunan, and elsewhere, to take a moral stance over questions of economic policy. Instead, they attempt to maintain a position of moral authority by taking a stance on religious and ritual activities, condemning in particular what they regard as superstition.

The contrast between superstition (*mixin*) and progress (*fazhan*) is not new in China. As a pejorative description of certain beliefs and ritual practices, the term 'superstition' came to China, via Japan, in the late nineteenth century, together with a number of western social scientific terms (Feuchtwang and Wang 1991). In both countries 'progress' was associated with the rise of nation-building projects (the Meiji reforms in Japan and the Republican movement in China) and the wish to make a break with a perceived feudal past. A policy on superstition was implemented with the establishment of the Chinese Republic in 1919 as part of the new Republic's modernising ethos (Duara 1995). This and the subsequent campaigns against 'superstition' by the Communist Party also had the effect of separating these practices off as discontinuous with other forms of belief, classified by another new term, 'religion' (*zhongjiao*), which did not carry the same negative connotations. As Anagnost writes, 'out of these practices is constructed an "otherness" against which the Party can exercise its legitimating activism' (1994: 231). Throughout the twentieth century, China's literate elites have contrasted 'superstition' with their own vision of a modern and progressive state.

The harshest campaigns against superstition took place during the Cultural Revolution, when all forms of religion were defined as superstitious; and many temples were converted into secular buildings or destroyed. Since 1980, however, it has again become permissible to take part in religion (*zhongjiao*), especially in the widespread, text-based traditions of Buddhism, Daoism, Islam and Christianity, and local governments issue guidelines on how places of worship are to be organised. Nonetheless, while belief in institutional religion is permitted among the general public, it is strongly discouraged among party cadres and students. Religious expressions, such as the funerals organised by Daoists, are not permitted in educational work-units. Employees of these and other state-run work-units are encouraged to regard religious sites as places for leisure activities (cf. Feuchtwang and Wang 1991). In many cases local government organises temples directly and these are tourist attractions as well as places of worship.

Official policy still makes a strong contrast between 'institutionalised religions which are normally recognised officially as "systematised (*xitonghua*) and well-organised" and the more negative category of "superstition" (*mixin*)' (Feuchtwang and Wang 1991: 260). The latter pertains to the building of village temples, spirit possession, drawing lots to predict the future and praying for children. Activities that fall outside the recognised institutional religions may be positively presented on national media if they are treated as historical reconstructions, but if they appear to be 'a living thing in the present' they are likely to be ignored or discouraged (Yang 1996: 95, 97). Like many areas considered 'backward', West Hunan is regarded both by those who live there, and by others, as a place that is particularly superstitious.

Campaigns against superstition, though sporadic, continue to be harsh and receive wide publicity. Active steps against temple activities are usually taken only when they are associated with crime, such as cheating people out of money or discouraging people from seeking medical help (cf. Feuchtwang 1989), but the subsequent destruction of temples on the orders of local Party officials is regularly seen in newspapers and on television. In addition to the criticism that they are backward (*luohou*), superstitious practices are also criticised for threatening public order. It is the latter which appears to be of particular concern in the recent banning of Falun Gong.[4]

It appears then that discourses of development in China have involved the labelling of ritual practices as ignorant, very much in the way that Hobart discusses when he writes of local knowledges being 'devalued or ignored' (Hobart 1993: 10). This labelling is part and parcel of the broader agenda of presenting China as a progressive modern nation under the leadership of the Communist Party. Official discourse has set up the appearance of a series of oppositions in which many practices are characterised as belonging to a feudal past (in contrast to a modern, progressive present), and as disordered and threatening (in contrast to the order and stability brought by the Communist Party). In the absence of a clear lead by the Communist Party on economic development, these contrasts have been promoted all the more in the area of ritual practice.

As I will discuss in the following section, however, the construction and promotion of the notion of 'backwardness' has failed in several respects. Despite formal opposition, the revived temples continue to appeal as repositories of highly relevant forms of knowledge.

FLEXIBLE RECREATIONS: THE BUDDHIST TEMPLE AT SHIZIAN AND THE TEMPLE OF THE CELESTIAL KINGS

Participation in 'superstitious' activities such as consulting mediums and drawing lots to predict the future are officially discouraged and negatively portrayed in the local media. Communist Party members, including the retired cadres sent to West Hunan to develop the area in the 1950s and 1960s, endorse this view; temple practices, they claim, are relics of the past, evidence of the backwardness of the area and of the need for a better educated population. It follows that temple activities must be regulated; that is, they must either be registered with one of the approved institutional religions or classified as relics of an ancient, non-Han culture. If temples are not registered, they risk being demolished by the Public Security Bureau. In this section I consider two temples, recently rebuilt, where so-called superstitious activities persist. Despite their official portrayal as forms of ignorant superstition or compliant forms of religion, these temples, I wish to argue, have been rebuilt not only 'from memory' but also on the basis of current needs.

The Buddhist temple at Shizian, situated in a village just a few kilometres outside Jishou, is the first of the two temples discussed. As a Buddhist temple, that is, one that could be classified as part of an institutional religion, it was registered with the United Front Department[5] in Jishou. The temple had been rebuilt by the villagers of Shizian on the basis of the memories of an old nun and the villagers themselves, who contributed materials and labour. They received no government funding. Like other temples in the area, Shizian had been rebuilt on the foundations of a previous structure. The pre-Cultural Revolution temple had been very beautiful, but was hidden from the road by a grove of old trees so that passers-by knew of its presence only from the sound of bells. During the Cultural Revolution, the temple was destroyed and the images of the deities thrown down a cliff into the river. Today, the temple is in full view. The trees have been cut down and the temple, rebuilt from breeze blocks and smaller than before, stands atop a rocky bank overlooking the river. As is common in the area, it is surrounded by mountains. There are also several shrines to honour guardian spirits and the Earth God, and some new trees have been planted. The old Buddhist nun and her sister take care of the temple during the day and tend its vegetable patches, but at night they sleep in the village below.

In contravention of official guidelines, this temple includes heterodox elements in the form of non-Buddhist deities. They are a Daoist goddess of childbirth and the Daoist god Yu Huang Da Di (The Jade Emperor) and his wife. There are also some painted rocks on the altar.[6] The nun who acts as the temple's custodian has distanced herself from these non-Buddhist elements and from many of the smaller deities by saying that she was not responsible for their presence; it was the local people who had brought them. In conversation she also revealed other divergences between government regulations and local practice. When I showed her some photographs I had taken of the temple, she said at once that had she been there she would have stopped me taking them. In one photograph, the heads of the deities were covered with a red cloth, which the local government did not permit.[7] She said that she did not put the red cloths on their heads, but that people had come up from the village and put them there. The local government perception of what the temple should contain did not agree with local perceptions.

A similar tension existed at the largest temple in the area, housing three military deities known as the Celestial Kings (*Tian Wang*). This temple is situated in the village of Yaxi, on the outskirts of Jishou. The deities, neither Buddhist nor Daoist, are believed to be heroic figures who once lived in West Hunan. They are dressed as imperial officials and are usually shown with imposing, even fearsome faces. Like other Chinese military deities, they 'sit augustly, with their legs apart and hands on their knees, gazing majestically out at their suppliants' (see Weller 1994: 52). The eldest brother is usually shown with a white face, the second with a red face and the third with a black face. The story of their lives, as told in the Jishou area, states that they once killed 7,000 people who were threatening the area.[8]

Falling outside what is considered institutional religion, over the past 50 years worship of the Celestial Kings has been subject to more intense official disapproval than has worship at Buddhist temples. Like other Chinese temples it suffered most during the anti-superstition campaigns of the 1950s and 1960s. The original temple building was closed in the 1950s and the images of the deities were destroyed by PLA soldiers. The temple building itself was allowed to remain as a storehouse, but was later destroyed during the 1960s Cultural Revolution. A *baijiu* (rice spirits) factory was then built on part of the site. During the early 1980s, however, a small version of the temple built by local people was reopened there. Based on the memories of old people, it was crudely built of rocks, but people brought small benches from their own homes to furnish it.

Later, the temple was destroyed by the members of the Public Security Bureau, and rebuilt again, a process repeated several times until the early 1990s. By this time the temple was allowed to stand. This structure was still standing in 1995–96, though the whole site was dominated by the walls of the (now famous) local rice spirits factory; it had the look of an unfinished building site.

While local government officials regard the temple practices as 'backward' and manifestations of ignorance, local worshippers do not view them in this light. They know that they are not blindly following 'tradition'. Nor do the temples simply attempt to recreate a kind of authentic past. While there are clear references to the past in the memories of the old people, and also in the dress of the deities, temple visitors know of the discontinuities with pre-Revolutionary times. For instance, before 1949 visitors did not draw lots at Shizian temple to predict the future; instead it was a place for reciting sutras and worshipping the Buddhist pantheon. As I shall now discuss, the revived temples embody a form of flexible recreation in which contemporary conditions are more relevant than continuity with the past. My observations and interviews have led me to disagree with writers who argue that unauthorised temple activities constitute a turning back to the past. Yang, for example, writes that temple rebuilding, together with the revival of lineage in Wenzhou, Fujian, constitutes a 'revitalisation of tradition' which 'knitted together local community relationships ... and enhanced local cultural, economic and political autonomy from the state' (Yang 1996: 109–10). This implies that there has been *a conscious return to tradition as an alternative to the uncertainties of modernity*. To apply this approach to West Hunan would be to underestimate the extent to which activities at temples are an interaction with modernity.

DRAWING LOTS: DEALING WITH MODERNITY

The central event of most visits to a temple in West Hunan is the drawing of lots. This is also a major source of income for temple custodians. Lots are drawn in order to make a request of the deities or to ask the likely outcome of a proposed action. Some visitors draw lots in a spirit of fun, but for many it is an attempt to resolve serious questions over decisions affecting an uncertain future. Officially, drawing lots constitutes a superstitious activity (Feuchtwang 1989), even though it is widely practised.

Visitors may begin by lighting incense and laying food and alcohol in front of the deities. After kowtowing to the deities, they kneel before them shaking a bamboo container with bamboo spills. They then choose one of the spills, usually the one sticking out furthest. Each spill has two numbers carved on it, references to quotations in a handbook. Before consulting the book, the custodian throws two divination blocks down in front of the altar and, according to the way they fall, will know whether the deity approves this choice of spill. The relevant quotation in the handbook is then interpreted in order to gain insight into one's circumstances and how they will unfold. The procedure is closely linked to the imperial past, the wooden spills echoing the bamboo sticks on which imperial magistrates gave out their orders (Ahern 1981) but, as we shall now see, it is also closely concerned with responding to present-day experiences.

I illustrate this with the example of a day trip by students from Jishou University, where I worked as an English teacher, to Shizian temple. We began by collecting firewood and cooking a picnic by the side of a river at the foot of the cliff where the temple stands. After lunch, some of the students stayed behind to play cards while I joined the others in climbing the hill to the temple, passing the shrines to earth gods and guardian spirits on the way. The students were talking about having their fortunes told and, though almost all of them said they were just doing it for fun, they seemed quite excited. At the temple, one of the students greeted the nun, who acted as a custodian there, and told her that we would like to draw lots. Each student had to donate a small amount of money and kneel down in front of the altar. The nun then gave him or her a bamboo jar holding bamboo spills and rang a bell to attract the attention of the Buddha. I was told that I would go to the south and make lots of money, an appropriate prediction in an area where so many people move to Guangzhou to look for temporary work. Then a student who used the English name 'Ada' with her foreign teachers went to draw lots. She was a cheerful and unsophisticated young woman from a peasant family. Each time she drew the spill the nun threw the divining blocks down and said '*bu xing*' (it won't do), though this had not happened in any of the previous cases. When she did pick a spill which, according to the divination blocks, was right for her, it indicated that she would have problems with her marriage, that she might have trouble finding a husband or she might separate from him later. Hearing this, Ada looked pale and shaken. She explained that she had had her fortune told before, and drawn exactly the same spill. The nun said reassuringly that everything would be all right if she prayed to Guanyin[9] and offered her money, but Ada seemed uncertain what to do. She went and sat with some of her friends and didn't say much except to repeat several times that she hadn't believed in these things before, but now she was beginning to. For a week or two after this she seemed subdued in class, but soon returned to her usual liveliness. Back at the university I never asked her whether she had prayed to

Guanyin, since I suspected she would not want to discuss it, but I noticed how sometime later she wore more feminine clothes and was, apparently, trying to modify her loud voice.

Ada may have raised the question of her future love-life out of a real concern, a worry about making the transition from peasant girl to educated woman, or it may have been just to amuse herself, for 'something to do'. But it was clear that the experience had raised some important matters for her, despite the light-hearted manner in which it had been undertaken. Drawing lots, for many, is a response to their experience of modernity. This is reflected in the fact that people often draw lots when they are thinking of leaving West Hunan to look for work, to ask if their luck will be good or not. Others come when the Public Security Bureau has failed them. One visitor to Shizian drew lots after his wife had disappeared in an effort to find out if she was dead or had been kidnapped; another (at the temple of the Celestial Kings) asked the deities to kill members of the clan that had driven him out of his village.

Although the procedure makes reference to the past, it is not useful to see the practice of drawing lots as a return to tradition. Drawing lots is often a way of finding a context to express current dilemmas, and, if appropriate, to decide on a course of action; it is 'a standardisation and an externalisation of an uncertainty' (Feuchtwang 1989: 15). Thus, the reappearance of temple activities is not just a continuation of the structures of the old order, but a *flexible re-creation* of them in ways appropriate to current economic situations. As Anagnost puts it, 'local traditions are retrievable through the "post-modern arts of memory" that reinvent them, as much as reconstruct them, in the context of contemporary concerns' (Anagnost 1994: 245). China's rebuilt temples thus respond to a situation also noted for urban Malaysia, where forms 'acquire new meanings and speak to new experiences in changing arenas of social relationships' (Ong 1988: 32).

Presenting such activities as aspects of a backward past, as the official campaigns against superstition do, fails to take into account their relevance to the present. Furthermore, to divide practices into modern or progressive, and superstitious or backward, underestimates the extent to which the two interpenetrate. Rather than being authorities on the past, the deities can be seen as highly knowledgeable about aspects of modernity. Temple activities must therefore be understood as 'localised modernities' or experiences which inter-relate 'aspects of both modernity and tradition' (Arce and Long 2000: 3, 15); they are part of *an ongoing process by which forms of local knowledge respond to change*. This fits with Hansen's argument that temple deities, previously appealed to for control over the elements, performed a similar (adjusted) role in the Southern

Song dynasty (1127–1276). Following the rise of marketing systems, the deities were attributed new forms of knowledge. Hansen writes:

They [the deities] demonstrated sophisticated commercial talents ... Familiar with price variations among different markets, they advised their followers where to trade. One deity was even able to manipulate national demand ... to make an enormous profit. (Hansen 1990: 10)

But drawing lots also indicates an interface between 'local' and state views of religious practice. Including a visit to a temple in a class trip was not controversial, since people, especially those in work-units, are encouraged to regard temples as places of leisure. However, the interest of the educated person is not always as secular as it appears since many have an ambivalent attitude towards religion. As Ada's experience indicates, drawing lots blurs any easy distinctions between visiting temples as a secular leisure activity and as a means of consulting the 'superstitious' knowledge which is believed to reside with the deities.

CONFLICT AND RESISTANCE

In contrast to the temple at Shizian, where there was more accommodation than conflict, the Celestial Kings was a site where open confrontation occurred. This had first arisen when the site was appropriated by local government as a cultural relic, transformed, and visitors were required to buy tickets. At the time I began my fieldwork, the temple was run by the villagers of Yaxi.[10] In the course of a year, however, it was replaced by a more imposing building housing larger deities, organised by local government. Although few Chinese tourists and hardly any foreign tourists visited the Jishou area, the temple of the Celestial Kings was transformed from a flexible recreation of the past to a local government-run initiative, which charged visitors. Proceeds from ticket sales went to the local government. The resentment this caused echoed a wider dissatisfaction over government land appropriation in the area. The land at Yaxi was particularly in demand since it comprised much of the flat ground on the outskirts of Jishou; it was therefore a site of urban expansion. Yaxi had already lost land to the new campus of Jishou University, to a new road and to the rice spirits (*baijiu*) factory. Though the people from whom this land had been taken were given financial compensation, the expropriation was resented since, Yaxi people said, 'it is our land'.

It is indicative that the Celestial Kings themselves were believed to have openly criticised the local government's policy over land. A spirit medium claimed they had told her that the building of the new road and the rice spirits factory had upset the *fengshui* of the area. In the past, it was said, Yaxi used to produce great people, but today the village was doing poorly and *fengshui* was the cause of this. The belief that the deities could express themselves brought a temporary resolution to the problem when they told the medium they had left the temple and moved to some rocks on a nearby hillside. This resulted in large numbers of people bringing offerings to these rocks rather than the figures of the deities installed by local government and a crude temple being built there. Some time later this was destroyed by the local Public Security Bureau.[11]

Once again, forms of local (spiritual) knowledge emerge as shifting and contingent;[12] temple recreations are concerned with the present rather than the past. Ironically, the official temple building, set on the original temple site and run as a cultural relic, bore far more resemblance to the pre-Revolutionary temple than did the makeshift temple at the rocks to which people turned for answers to their questions.

Events at the temple also draw attention to wider issues of power and conflict. People connected with the temple have different degrees of access to power. In this regard, local government officials are able to influence events either through characterising them as 'superstitious' or by forcefully imposing official guidelines. Certain groups, such as students and Party members, may thus feel they should avoid temples or treat them as places of secular leisure activity. Local government can also influence the form that temple buildings take because, eventually, they can physically demolish temple buildings that flout official guidelines. This normally results in a certain amount of accommodation between official policies and the wishes of those who run and visit the temple. For example, officials may tolerate the drawing of lots as a secular activity, or they may allow 'superstitious' activities to persist as long as the temple is registered as a 'cultural relic' of the past. On other occasions, though, there is tension and conflict, as for example when villagers bring deities to Shizian which are not permitted in Buddhist temples or when worshippers refuse to visit the newly built temple of the Celestial Kings.

The need to avoid the assumption of a straightforward dichotomy opposing 'the indigenous' and 'the modern' makes me reluctant to describe the situation found at the temples in terms of resistance. Resistance concerns events where confrontation has the capacity, eventually, to bring about a change in power relations. Despite the fact that the subject has been broadened out from a consideration of armed uprisings to forms of everyday resistance, the concept of resistance still assumes either that the actions taken are intended to weaken positions of power (Scott 1986) or that, although this is not the intention, this will eventually be the outcome. In either case it is difficult to prove that particular actions are 'everyday forms of resistance' rather than a means of dealing with the everyday without there being implications for the distribution of power (cf. Ortner 1995; Adas 1986). As Keesing (1992) and Comaroff and Comaroff (1991) point out, there is a problem with employing a term such as resistance when it is not used by the people to whom this resistance is attributed. In this case, there is a danger that the study of resistance reflects the concerns of scholars rather than those carrying out the activities (cf. Maddox 1997). The activities I have described in this chapter deal with here-and-now issues of everyday life, with the concerns of a particular village, rather than with an intention to change the overall balance of power.

REWORKING THE LOCAL

In this chapter, local knowledge has been shown to be something contingent and flexible, constantly recreated to deal with everyday life (see Arce and Long 2000: 3). Specifically, I have discussed temple activities in terms of interfaces of knowledge in the context of modernity rather than as traditional or indigenous practices, which have returned to confront the state. Within this situation, 'local knowledge' draws on state forms and discourses and indeed draws authority from them. This echoes what Kaplan and Kelly have written on the history of Fiji: 'It is tempting but wrong to picture colonial social formations as confrontations between a "whole social process" belonging to the colonizers, and a fragmented, superseded "whole social process" belonging to the colonized', since the colonised also make use of the 'tools in the politics past and present of the colonizers' (Kaplan and Kelly 1994: 144). Within the framework of the current study, the interaction between the official discourse and that of temple visitors resulted in the latter making use of the 'tools' of the dominant group.

Like Yang (1996) I was at first surprised to hear people talk of temples and temple practices as 'superstition' (*mixin*). The temple of the Celestial Kings was commonly described as such by the women from Yaxi village who worked there. The subject usually arose when they welcomed new visitors to the temple; it was therefore one of the first things I learned. This information was often accompanied by the explanation that temple practices were local (*bendi*) and that it was ordinary people (*laobaixing*; lit. 'old hundred surnames') who had donated the money to rebuild the temple. The Yaxi temple, I was repeatedly told, was not like the famous temples in Changsha or Shaolinshan, since the money for it had not come from the state (*guojia*).[13] As at Shizian, a contrast was made between the temple and state-supported temples elsewhere; far from being pejorative, the temple's status as 'superstition' was a matter of pride. Contact with official policy on 'superstitious' practices has reinforced the view that they are specifically local (*bendi*) and of the *laobaixing*. 'Superstitious' practices are rarely shown on television or in school textbooks and, when they are, they come with what Anagnost describes as 'thin description'. They are 'emptied of any value except for the purpose of negating them' (Anagnost 1994), that is, they are shown as the antithesis of the modern and progressive. Temples to military deities can be found in many parts of China, but many West Hunan people are unaware of this.[14]

Furthermore, the implication of the word *bendi* is not just that it is peculiar to a particular area of China, but also that it is particular to the population, the *laobaixing*, rather than to the elite. In imperial times the temple of the Celestial Kings, like those of other military deities, was attended by elites and commoners alike. As recently as Republican times, the temple was attended by officials[15] who dismounted from their horses at a particular stone before passing the temple. If they did not do this, it was believed the deities would show their displeasure by causing a gale to blow. Local officials also had a part to play in arranging temple festivals. Before the festival, a custodian from the temple would go from house to house collecting money from everyone, rich and poor. Those who did not have money could give rice or corn. This ensured a link between the temple and a China-wide, literate elite culture.

Today, as I have mentioned, current policy dissuades government officials from participating in religious activities at the temple of the Celestial Kings. Cadres may visit the temple, but they do not discuss this in the workplace. Festivals are arranged by the villagers of Yaxi, thereby intensifying the identification of the temple with the local and the *laobaixing*. A similar situation is found at Buddhist temples such as Shizian. With the destruction of written texts and the lack of literate monks and nuns, links with a wider, institutional tradition are weak. Here too, the mixture of deities, like other 'superstitious' activities, is perceived by the people as a uniquely local tradition, even though these deities are found in many parts of China.[16] The encounter with official discourses has led to an increased conviction, among the participants, that these practices are specifically 'local'.

In this chapter I have described a sense of locality which is expressed in opposition to local government. In particular, I have shown that, rather than existing as part of an ongoing fixed dichotomy, reminiscent of a great-and-little tradition, the opposition has arisen from ongoing interactions related to modernity and the experience of the state. Moreover, I have argued that the state discourses, as experienced through political study and the media, may be locally reappropriated in unexpected ways.

NOTES

1. A number of other terms are used around debates on indigenous knowledge (Sillitoe 1998: x; Arce and Fisher 2000). I use the term local knowledge, rather than indigenous knowledge, to avoid the idea of a primordial form of knowledge in opposition to modernity and the state.
2. This research was made possible through an ESRC studentship.
3. This term was used, not just by visitors to the region, but also by rural and urban inhabitants.
4. Falun Gong is a spiritual group, which draws on elements of Buddhism and Daoism and on exercises from the Qi Gong tradition. The organisation is considered particularly threatening because members recognise and follow a spiritual leader not recognised by the Chinese government. Banned in 1999, it was branded a 'heretical organisation'. In West Hunan as elsewhere it drew followers largely from an urban, educated population.
5. Throughout China, the United Front Department is responsible for situations that pose a potential threat to the comprehensiveness of Communist Party rule. The department also deals with people with connections with Taiwan and the relatively powerless minor political parties such as the Democratic Party (*Minzhu dang*), which is effectively subordinate to the Communist Party.
6. The worship of rocks and stones in China is also mentioned by Jordan (1972: 43) and Graham (1961: 177f.).
7. Red cloths are commonly hung above the altars of temples, including Buddhist temples. I did not ascertain why using them to cover the deity's heads was not permitted in this case.
8. Though to my knowledge the Celestial Kings are not found elsewhere, some of their attributes are shared with deities from other parts of China. There are accounts of other meat-eating deities in China and Taiwan, who are known by titles which imply a kingly or heroic status, some of whom are also found in groups of three (Diamond 1969: 85f.; Seaman 1978: 109; Katz 1987, 1995; Dean 1993: 101–2). Many are reputed to be able to suppress plagues and exorcise spirits, capabilities not, to my knowledge, particularly attributed to the Celestial Kings.
9. Guanyin is the Chinese form of the Bodhisattva Avalokiteshwara. Shown always in the form of a woman she embodies merciful and compassionate qualities.
10. Villagers had argued that it was an example of minority culture, though this was not how they themselves viewed it, and as a result local government had allowed the temple to remain.
11. See Rack (2002) for further discussion of issues of resistance at the temple of the Celestial Kings.
12. After this incident, worshippers at other temples were heard to say that their temples were also built on the site of rocks.

13. In Changsha, as in most Chinese cities, a number of temples have been renovated and opened as tourist sites. The Shaolin temple, in Henan, is one of the most famous in China.

14. This process is not new. Johnson (1985) writes of Late Imperial China, elite culture may permeate popular culture through writing, but communication between different areas of local culture is more problematic. The policy on superstition continues and reinforces the connection made between the heterodox and the local (*bendi*).

15. In some ways, West Hunan was run as an independent warlord enclave during the Republican period.

16. See, for example, Jordan (1972: 27). In fact, although both temples were frequently described to me as 'local', people did not often distinguish between Buddhist and military deities.

REFERENCES

Adas, M. (1986) 'From Footdragging to Flight: The evasive history of peasant avoidance protest in South and South-East Asia', in J.C. Scott and B.J. Tria Kerkvliet (eds), *Everyday Forms of Peasant Resistance In South-East Asia*. Journal of Peasant Studies, Special Issue 13(2): 64–86

Ahern, E. (1981) *Chinese Ritual and Politics* (Cambridge: Cambridge University Press)

Anagnost, A.S. (1994) 'The Politics of Ritual Displacement', in L. Kendall, C.F. Keyes and H. Hardacre (eds), *Asian Visions of Authority: Religion and the Modern States of East and Southeast Asia* (Honolulu: University of Hawaii Press), pp. 254–321

Arce, A. and E. Fisher (2000) 'Encountering the Pseudopodia Nature of Knowledge: Illustrations from Bolivia and the United Kingdom'. Paper given at the ASA conference Participating in Development: Approaches to Indigenous Knowledge, SOAS, London, 2–4 April

Arce, A and N. Long (2000) 'Reconfiguring Modernity and Development from an Anthropological Perspective', in A. Arce and N. Long (eds), *Anthropology, Development and Modernities: Exploring Discourses, Counter-tendencies and Violence* (London: Routledge), pp. 1–31

Chandler, R. (1992) 'Ecological Knowledge in a Traditional Agroforest Management System Among Peasants in China', PhD Thesis, University of Washington

Comaroff, J. and J. Comaroff (1991) *Of Revelation and Revolution: Christianity, Colonialism, and Consciousness in South Africa, 1* (Chicago: University of Chicago Press)

Croll, E. (1993) 'The Negotiation of Knowledge and Ignorance in China's Development Strategy', in M. Hobart (ed.), *An Anthropological Critique of Development: The Growth of Ignorance* (London: Routledge), pp. 161–78

Dean, K. (1993) *Taoist Ritual and Popular Cults in Southeast China* (Princeton, NJ: Princeton University Press)

Diamond, N. (1969) *Kun Shen, a Taiwanese Village* (New York: Holt, Rinehart & Winston)

Duara, P. (1995) *Rescuing History from the Nation: Questioning Narratives of Modern China* (Chicago: University of Chicago Press)

Feuchtwang, S. (1989) 'The Problem of "Superstition" in the People's Republic of China', in G. Benavides and M.W. Daly (eds), *Religion and Political Power* (Albany, NY: State University of New York Press), pp. 43–68

Feuchtwang, S. and Wang Mingming (1991) 'The Politics of Culture or a Contest of Histories: Representations of Chinese popular religion', *Dialectical Anthropology* 16: 251–72

Graham, D.C. (1961) *Folk Religion in Southwest China* (Washington: Smithsonian Miscellaneous Collections), Vol. 142: 2

Hansen, V. (1990) *Changing Gods in Medieval China 1127–1276* (Princeton, NJ: Princeton University Press)

Hobart, M. (1993) 'Introduction: The Growth of Ignorance', in Hobart, M. (ed.), *An Anthropological Critique of Development: The Growth of Ignorance* (London: Routledge), pp. 1–42

Johnson, D. (1985) 'Communication, Class and Consciousness in Late Imperial China', in D. Johnson, A.J. Nathan and E.S. Rawski (eds), *Popular Culture in Late Imperial China* (Berkeley: University of California Press), pp. 34–75

Jordan, D.K. (1972) *Gods, Ghosts and Ancestors: Folk Religion in a Taiwanese Village* (Berkeley: University of California Press)

Kaplan, M. and J.D. Kelly (1994) 'Rethinking Resistance: Dialogics of "Disaffection" in Colonial Fiji', *American Ethnologist* 21(1): 123–51

Katz, P.R. (1987) 'Demons or Deities? – The *Wangye* of Taiwan', *Asian Folklore Studies* 46: 197–215

—— (1995) *Demon Hordes and Burning Boats: The Cult of Marshal Wen in Late Imperial China* (Albany, NY: State University of New York Press)

Keesing, R. (1992) *Custom and Confrontation: The Kwaio Struggle for Cultural Autonomy* (Chicago: The University of Chicago Press)

Maddox, R. (1997) 'Bombs, Bikinis, and the Popes of Rock 'n' Roll: Reflections on Resistance, the Play of Subordinations, and Liberalism in Andalusia and Academia, 1983–1995', in A. Gupta and J. Ferguson (eds), *Culture, Power Place: Explorations in Critical Anthropology* (Durham, NC and London: Duke University Press), pp. 277–90

Ong, A. (1988) 'The Production of Possession: Spirits and Multinational Corporation in Malaysia', *American Ethnologist* 15: 28–42

Ortner, S. (1995) 'Resistance and the Problem of Ethnographic Refusal', *Comparative Studies of Society and History* 2: 173–93

Parkin, D. (1995) 'Latticed Knowledge: Eradication and dispersal of the unpalatable in Islam, medicine and anthropological theory', in R. Fardon (ed.), *Counterworks: Managing the Diversity of Knowledge* (London: Routledge), pp. 143–63

Potter, S. and J. Potter (1990) *China's Peasants: The Anthropology of a Revolution* (Cambridge: Cambridge University Press)

Pottier, J. (2000) 'Modern Information Warfare Versus Empirical Knowledge: Framing 'the Crisis' in Eastern Zaire'. Paper given at the ASA conference, Participating in Development: Approaches to Indigenous Knowledge, SOAS, London, 2–4 April

Rack, M. (2002) 'The Mu Yi Festival: Contesting Interpretations of a Territorial Temple Cult', in A. Hansson et al. (eds), *The Chinese at Play: Festivals, Games and Leisure* (London: Kegan Paul), pp. 55–68

Scott, J.C. (1986) 'Everyday Forms of Peasant Resistance', in J.C. Scott and B.J. Tria Kerkvliet (eds), *Everyday Forms of Peasant Resistance In South-East Asia,* Journal of Peasant Studies Special Issue 13(2): 5–35

Seaman, G. (1978) *Temple Organisation in a Chinese Village* (Taipei: The Orient Cultural Service)

Sillitoe, P. (1998) 'The Development of Indigenous Knowledge: A new applied anthropology', *Current Anthropology* 39(2): 223–52

Weller, R.P. (1994) *Resistance, Chaos and Control in China: Taiping Rebels, Taiwanese Ghosts and Tiananmen* (London: Macmillan)

Yang, M. (1996) 'Tradition, Travelling Anthropology and the Discourse of Modernity in China', in H. Moore (ed.), *The Future of Anthropological Knowledge* (London: Routledge), pp. 93–114

9 THE GLOBAL FLOW OF KNOWLEDGE ON WAR TRAUMA: THE ROLE OF THE 'CINNAMON GARDEN CULTURE' IN SRI LANKA

Alex Argenti-Pillen

I observed that the conflicts and tensions of today's world are affecting the mental health of millions of people. To cope with this situation – which is fully important, if not as immediate, as the need for food, medical care, and shelter – it is necessary that our vision be broadened ... The book 'International Responses to Traumatic Stress' is a major contribution to our future agenda ... [it] demonstrates the need to focus specifically on questions of traumatic stress, an area too often neglected ... Securing mental health for the people of the world must be one of the foremost objectives of the United Nations in its second half century. (Boutros Boutros-Ghali, Former Secretary General of the United Nations, 1996)

Indeed, that there is humane and effective care for a number of mental health problems is important news that needs to reach many more people in low-income societies ... *Progress* will be made when the world community openly acknowledges them as problems, develops a *blueprint* for addressing them, and works together in a focused and coordinated way to implement that blueprint. (Jimmy and Rosalind Carter, in Desjarlais et al.1995: viii, emphasis added)

For many members of international humanitarian non-governmental and governmental organisations a 'war trauma pandemic' is threatening to destabilise the current world order. Professionals within humanitarian organisations often depict large sections of the populations in war-torn societies as suffering from Post-Traumatic Stress Disorder, a condition that predisposes people to further violent upheaval and ongoing cycles of violence. Such western professionals do not, however, depict the impending catastrophic disintegration of any form of 'normal' social and political life as resulting from ever bolder forms of global capitalism and 'state terrorism' (Sluka 2000) or the crimes of multinational corporations and intelligence services such as MOSAD, the CIA or MI5. Instead, humanitarian discourses present the future of war-torn societies as threatened by the traumatised or mentally ill survivors themselves (Summerfield 1996). Humanitarian aid for war-torn societies now invariably includes trauma counselling programmes. Euro-American mental health professionals have thus become active in Rwanda, Bosnia and Sri Lanka – in the high-profile conflict zones of a global world.

In this chapter I experiment with a slightly ironical use of the terms 'local', 'indigenous' and 'global'. I refer to the professionals working in international political and humanitarian organisations as 'indigenous' to make the point that government officials, politicians and NGO personnel who play a role on the 'global' stage often remain 'locals' nonetheless, partly by virtue of being monolingual. This particular view of locality is inspired by a Wittgensteinian philosophy in which the limits of our language constitute the limits of our world. Within this perspective the western monoglot never effectively transcends his or her locale. While vast sums of money are available for Euro-American neo-colonial expansion and interventions, western nations carefully maintain a sense of 'locality' or bounded world because of a relative lack of financial investment in language training for western government officials and diplomats. Euro-American global expansion can thus be conceptualised as a sum of multiple, monolingual localities: the insular world of diplomatic missions and business districts of capital cities world-wide, where a predominantly monolingual, Anglophone (or Francophone) minority lives and is 'localised'. The more general question I wish to address concerns how these multiple, monolingual communities interact with the multilingual, multicultural world beyond their own exclusivist networks and how these Euro-American networks appropriate outside forms of knowledge in culture-specific, modernist ways. I argue below that western mental health professionals working for humanitarian aid organisations readily blend into this 'local' culture, and use it as a base to diffuse western knowledge on war trauma.

In this chapter I illustrate this argument by providing a case study of the flow of knowledge on war trauma to a rural community in southern Sri Lanka. As in many parts of the world, over the last decade a boom has occurred within the non-governmental mental health services. In Sri Lanka, international organisations (for example, UNHCR, UNICEF) and NGOs (Oxfam, SCF, International Rehabilitation Council for Torture Victims) regularly organise workshops on war trauma and invite international trauma specialists (often members of the International Society for Traumatic Stress Studies) to give lectures in the capital Colombo. A decade later there are more mental health NGOs[1] in Sri Lanka than psychiatrists (about 30) or psychologists (about 10). Most of the national mental health NGOs are based in central Colombo, in the vicinity of the Cinnamon Gardens. I therefore chose to call the cultural context of foreign mental health experts and the Colombo-based mental health NGOs[2] the 'Cinnamon Garden culture'. Sri Lankan humanitarian aid workers live their professional lives within the Cinnamon Garden culture and translate the humanitarian discourse on trauma into Sinhalese. I intend here to explore the nature of the translation process that occurs.

My approach has in many ways been inspired by the tradition of 'ethnographies for development' and 'total project ethnographies' oriented towards more humane forms of development (Pottier 1993b: 32), but at the same time it departs from them in two significant ways. First, I did not carry out 'development-oriented indigenous knowledge research' (Sillitoe 1998: 229) nor did I play a role in facilitating meaningful communication between western scientists and members of the rural community in Southern Sri Lanka. In other words, I did not position myself between Sinhala Buddhist villagers on the one hand, and development workers or agencies on the other. I did, however, position myself at a 'knowledge interface' (Arce and Long 1992: 214); a place where two epistemic communities meet; the community of western mental health professionals and the community of Sri Lankan intellectuals working for national mental health NGOs. Even within this knowledge interface situation, I did not play the role of a 'knowledge broker' (Sillitoe 1998: 231–2), 'cultural broker' (Pottier 1993a: 3) or cultural facilitator. As the ethnography in this chapter shows, such a position would have been politically untenable, and I thus opted for a relatively more distanced political analysis[3] of the knowledge interface between western mental health specialists and Sri Lankan intellectuals.

Second, I did not use my multidisciplinary background as both a medical doctor and anthropologist in the ways advocated by indigenous knowledge researchers (for example, Sillitoe 1998).[4] I certainly did not use my medical background to try to better understand the Cinnamon Garden culture or the healing practices in a rural community in southern Sri Lanka. I must admit, though, that this project would most probably not have been possible without a multidisciplinary background. Within the Cinnamon Garden culture the status associated with medical or scientific knowledge was the hard currency needed to gain initial access. As a doctoral student in anthropology it would have been much more difficult to be introduced to the mental health and humanitarian elite in Colombo, if not impossible. In other words, my multidisciplinary background provided me with the scientific identity I needed to begin a study amongst the Sri Lankan elite. In this sense, the mere status of a scientist proved to be a more crucial research tool than the possession of scientific knowledge as such.

Apart from extended fieldwork amongst Sinhalese Buddhist villagers in the rural south of Sri Lanka, I gathered data at conferences and workshops organised by members of the Sri Lankan national mental health NGOs, recorded conversations amongst NGO workers and conducted interviews with Sri Lankan mental health professionals. I also analysed information leaflets produced by Sri Lankan mental health NGOs. In this chapter I focus on a very small range of this total reality; the translation of the English terminology used to speak about war trauma and rehabilitation. For the sake of brevity, I refrain from providing an extended case study (see, for example, Arce and Long 1992) of the activities of a Sri Lankan mental health NGO. Nor do I provide an ethnographic analysis of the internal functioning of such an organisation or an in-depth ethnography of the Sri Lankan humanitarian elite. Rather, I present an analysis of the translation process itself; the way in which the discourse on war trauma is conveyed into Sinhalese within the context of the elite Cinnamon Garden culture.

VICTORS AS TRANSLATORS

In 1971, and again in 1987, Sinhalese left-wing activists (the Janatha Vimukthi Peramuna movement, hereafter JVP) organised an insurgency that resulted in a large-scale civil war in Sri Lanka.[5] It is estimated that during the civil war of the late 1980s about 30,000 people disappeared across the island (Amnesty International 1993). People were abducted and summarily killed by both the JVP and the Special Task Force (the STF), a counter-insurgency special commando unit trained by the government to combat the JVP. In 1971 the vanguard of the revolutionary movement came from the rural educated youth[6] who had gone through higher education but were nevertheless unemployed. They were essentially 'village boys', who had attended rural, Sinhala-medium schools, then had gone on to university and now lived amongst the landless peasantry. Their lack of knowledge of English meant they could not become 'science students' at university level, and were forced to study the human sciences that are taught in Sinhala. While their education made it more difficult to follow the footsteps of their parents and take up traditional occupations (Alles 1990: 254, 341), they acutely realised that, despite their education, they had no access to the close-knit, English-speaking ruling elite in Colombo – a legacy of the colonial administration – who effectively monopolise the job market. Bilingual science students who came from relatively privileged backgrounds, were/are a source of envy amongst the underprivileged students of the human science departments. As a result of the stark social polarisation of the education system, the human science departments, where between others sociology, anthropology and Buddhist studies are taught, are traditionally seen by the ruling elites as hotspots of JVP activity and schools for young insurgents.[7]

The JVP aspired/aspires to eradicate social evils such as bribery, nepotism and political patronage by offering to the people themselves moral authority based on a Marxist ideology. The initial programme of the JVP promoted the establishment of people's militias and people's courts (Alles 1990: 338). Youths had the authority to punish the corrupt, the thugs and alcoholics within a system of summary justice (Alles 1990: 319). The final aim of the JVP was to gain 'state' power, to overthrow the government and to install a Marxist political organisation: a politburo headed by the movement's leader Wijeweera, a central committee and district, town and village committees. To date the JVP has not been eradicated, and it has been predicted that, in view of its widespread network at the grassroots level, sporadic outbursts of violence from pockets of JVP supporters are bound to continue for a long time (Alles 1990: 304). The majority of the people killed by the state counter-insurgency forces repressing the JVP include local-level activists, national leaders or innocent bystanders. However, hard-core cadres at the regional level remain in position (Perera 1996: 47), and the future of the JVP depends on their capacity to mobilise popular support.

There is growing evidence that the counter-insurgency violence perpetrated during the late 1980s was particularly fierce in remote areas, in communities located at a distance from the main roads, especially in villages along district and divisional boundaries (Argenti-Pillen 2003). My analysis of the pattern of distribution of insurgency and counter-insurgency violence in a rural community in southern Sri Lanka has revealed that the excess of violence in remote areas could not be explained as related to traditional forms of hatred and family feuding within 'more traditional', remote communities. The similarities between the pattern of distribution of violence in the community I studied and the distribution of extreme violence resulting from techniques of community destabilisation and global counter-insurgency warfare in other neo-colonial or Cold War-type conflicts are, however, remarkable (Argenti-Pillen 2003). Moreover, hearings organised by the Commissions of Inquiry into the atrocities of the civil war of the late 1980s revealed CIA and/or MOSAD involvement in counter-insurgency training for the Sri Lankan Special Task Force;[8] the commandos responsible for many of the disappearances.

With international support the bilingual, English-speaking elite maintained their power by brutally repressing an insurgency pitted against their privileged access to resources and state power. The rural educated youth who had undergone their education in Sinhala today largely remain excluded from positions of power within the post-colonial nation-state. To date a struggle persists between professionals educated in English and others educated in Sinhala. Moreover the majority of the 'traumatised population' (the target group for the national mental health NGOs) – the people in rural, often remote areas who were especially vulnerable to insurgency and counter-insurgency violence – speak only Sinhala. During the civil war, rural youth educated monolingually in Sinhala challenged the supremacy of the bilingual members of the post-colonial state, but lost the war. The western monoglots of the international humanitarian community, faced with a communication/translation problem, now ironically turn to bilingual members of the Sri Lankan political elite, the *victors* of the civil war, when attempting to make their rehabilitation programmes for war trauma victims understandable to the *victims* of the atrocities. Members of the community of victors have thus become translators for foreign benefactors who intend to help victims of war.

WORD-FOR-WORD TRANSLATION INTO COLOMBO-STYLE SINHALA

Sri Lankan intellectuals are actively involved in the translation of the discourse on trauma propagated by the international humanitarian community. Notions such as 'Post-Traumatic Stress' or 'counselling for victims of torture' need to be conveyed into Sinhalese before they can be used to train rural mental health workers who work in former war zones. In some ways Sri Lankan intellectuals have taken up the role of ethnographers of the international humanitarian community. As they try to make the discourse on war trauma intelligible for the wider public in Sri Lanka, they are involved in the cultural translation of the scientific concepts of western indigenes. One of the many differences of this *reverse*[9] ethnography is that the Sri Lankan elite's command of English is of a very high standard when compared to the linguistic competence and command of the fieldwork language by average western ethnographers. Minute distinctions in the meaning of English words give rise to a myriad of distinctive Sinhalese translations and the debate regarding the choice of such translations is very lively.

A first, cursory analysis of the material I gathered suggests that the terminology of the trauma paradigm undergoes a word-for-word translation into Colombo-style Sinhala (see Table 9.1). Colombo-style

Sinhalese approximates 'high' Sinhala; the language spoken by the most educated elites who frequently borrow words from written Sinhala and the Buddhist scriptures. 'High' Sinhala also includes Sinhalese words that have previously been used to talk about western science and technology. The translators of the discourse on war trauma thus make frequent use of words that belong to the linguistic repertoire of Sri Lankan intellectuals. This extremely rich language, which is able to provide seemingly endless lists of words to translate a single English term lends itself particularly well to the translation of the discourse on war trauma. The Sinhalese discourse on war trauma mainly draws words and concepts from two 'semantic fields' (Daniel 1993), orthodox Buddhism and the western hard sciences. I would thus qualify the discourse on trauma as translated into Sinhala by Colombo-based elites as a conglomerate of concepts borrowed from orthodox Buddhist scriptures as well as Sinhalese words which have previously been used to teach physics or bio-sciences.

Table 9.1   Examples of high Sinhala words used in the spoken language of NGO elites in Colombo[10]

Bhauta chikitsaka pratikāra	Physiotherapy
Vurtiya chikitsaka pratikāra	Occupational therapy
Mitrakārakayin	Befrienders
Shetra niladharin	Field officers
Punuruttāpanaya	Rehabilitation
Chittavegaya	Emotion/ emotional disturbances
Visheshagna upadeshakavarun	Specialist counsellors
Mānushika pidāva	Mental trauma
Vatāvaranaya	A condition, in ordinary Sinhala one would use *tatvaya*
Hängim	Feelings
Katuka amihiri atdakimak	Trauma
Situvili	Thoughts
Sannivedanaya/ antarpudgali sannivedanaya	Communication/ interpersonal communication
Rahasya bhāvaya	Confidentiality, privacy, secrecy
Pratikāra abhyāsa	Healing exercises
Upadeshanaya/ upadeshakavaraya	Counselling, counsellor
Paudgalika drusttikonayak	Personal point of view, perspective
Dayāva	Pity
Manovidyātmaka kriyāvaliyak	A psychological process
Manovidyā pratikāra abhyāsa krama	Psychological techniques
Avavāda	Advice
Pratikārayak	Cure

I present some examples below (see Tables 9.2 and 9.3). The translations I provide are mere glosses and serve the purpose only of portraying an initial image of the issues at stake for the non-Sinhalese reader. In other words, I do not intend to participate in the debate on the translation of the discourse on trauma, and the translations of the Sinhalese terminology into English are mere working hypotheses.

Table 9.2   Words borrowed from the semantic field of the Sinhala translation of western hard sciences

Ātatiyak/ mānasika āatiyak	Stress/ mental stress – stress, tension in physics
Parāvartanaya	(counsellor as) a mirror – mirror, reflection in physics
Ekasvara karanavā	To be tuned into the point of view of the patient – to tune waves in physics (also used to describe the tuning of western musical instruments)
Kampanaya	Mental shock – wave, vibration, contraction – physics and medical science
Āropanaya	Conditioning – re-experiencing and avoidance behaviour of people suffering from PTSD – used in physics to describe e.g. static electricity and magnetism
Kriyākāritvaya	Mechanism e.g. of a motor or a heart, used to describe the psychological mechanism/mechanics of counselling
Kriyāvaliyak	Continuous process – used in biology or physics – used to describe counselling as an ongoing process

Table 9.3   Words borrowed from the semantic field of orthodox Buddhist philosophy and scriptures

Pidāva/ hinsā pidā karanavā	Stress/ to trouble, to harm
Svatiya	State of mind
Svatiya venas kam/vima	A change in the state of mind/ trauma
Chaitatika prashna	Emotional problems
Kalakirima	Despair, depression
Praguna	Expert

Much as western ethnographers use and abuse the language of western religions and philosophies to convey previously unknown world-views (see de Sardan 1992 and next section), so Sri Lankan intellectuals use language pertaining to the domain of Buddhist philosophy to translate the discourse on war trauma. For example, one information leaflet produced by a national mental health NGO describes an *upade-shakavaraya* (counsellor) as follows: the *upadeshakavaraya* will show you the path to drive the vehicle of life. In this case, the further description and Buddhist imagery associated with the translated word remains within the semantic field of Buddhist philosophy.[11] Other translations into Sinhalese are unsatisfactory and the ethnographic descriptions that accompany them to make them understandable to the Sinhalese public potentially make them lose some of their original meaning. This happens, for example, with '*hängim*' ('feelings'). Sinhalese intellectuals redefined the Sinhalese notion of *hängim* within a western, non-Buddhist, non-Ayurvedic world-view. I quote from an information leaflet on mental health distributed by a national mental health NGO:

Hängim are certain states of being that happen because of what we sense through the heart (*Hängim yanu hadavata* (scientific word for heart) *āshritava apata danena ektara tavayan ve*). Thoughts are not feelings. Thoughts are like sentences in language that move through our brain (*Situvili yanu hängim nove. Situvili, molaya tula yam bāshavakin ädena vākya ve*). According to these thought patterns, the shape and nature of the *hängim* are decided, as a shadow is made according to the shape of an object, and water takes the shape of a vessel ... Certain thoughts should be looked at in a scientific way (*adāla situvili vidyātmaka yatartavadi kirima*).

In some other cases the cultural gap is so vast that members of the Cinnamon Garden culture or the Colombo-based humanitarian elite have to make innovative use of the Sinhalese language (see Table 9.4). Words such as *klamataya* or *sahakampanaya* do not yet belong to Colombo-style Sinhala and are gradually making their entry into the cultural world of the humanitarian elite. In some instances the language spoken by the humanitarian elite, especially by people who only recently have become members of this elite, is more complex and 'advanced' than Colombo-style Sinhalese itself. This is at times achieved by innovative language use and at other times by the appropriation of Sinhalese words used to teach western hard sciences in Sinhala-medium secondary schools. This phenomenon of overcompensation, in which a language is used that is still more complex and diverse than the language used by the traditional Colombo-based political elite, allows people to build up the status of a professional and aspire to become a member of the elite. At the same time, however, this strategy reveals a person's upward social mobility and parvenu status.

None of the words mentioned in Tables 9.1–9.4 are used by members of rural communities who speak 'village', colloquial Sinhala and who have an equally rich – but distinct – repertoire of words and concepts to talk about violence and its effects. The Sinhalese discourse on war trauma constructed within the Cinnamon Garden culture thus needs to go through another translation process before it can be understood by members of rural Sinhala Buddhist communities, the main target group for many of the humanitarian interventions. The international humanitarian community is thus faced with an additional translation problem that often remains hidden for monolingual indigenes of the international community of professionals.

Table 9.4   Creative language use

Klamataya	Stress
Sahakampanaya	Empathy
Anuvegiya bhāvaya	Empathy
Saha anubhutika bhāvaya	Empathy

THE MODERNIST APPROPRIATION OF THE DISCURSIVE FORMATIONS OF SINHALA BUDDHIST RURAL COMMUNITIES

The concepts and words people from rural communities use to talk about violence and its effects contrast starkly with those of the Colombo elites because of their ambiguity and polysemic character. A young man from *Udahenagama*, a rural community in southern Sri Lanka where I conducted most of my fieldwork, described the atrocities committed by the Special Task Force in a style typical of this polysemy:

I don't remember very well, I wasn't very conscious in those days ... I only regained consciousness at three o'clock in the morning when almost half the [healing] ritual had been performed. During the ritual I was in a trance state (*āvesa*), they made me dance ... It is said that I did nonsensical things (*vikāra*), it is said that I didn't move, I just stayed in one place and I did odd things (*anang manang*) ... It was during the civil war, people had been killed that night, I had closed my shop, and I was coming home on my bicycle, they [the army] were burning and burning [His wife clarifies: They were burning a heap of cadavers], I had been on my bicycle, but I must have left it there, I had somehow come back home but it was as if I couldn't make sense (*vikāren vage*), I had come home without being conscious of it, I reached the house, entered and fell down... That was the first time I was ever terrified ...

Within the standard translations used by anthropologists, *āvesa* is translated as trance or spirit possession, *vikāra* and *anang manang* as the speech of the possessed 'speaking in tongues'. In this narrative, however, these terms could equally be translated as the confused, nonsensical speech and disorientation of the terrified. In fact, terms such as *āvesa* or *vikāra* are ambiguous and often refer both to affliction by spirits and affliction by cruel human beings. I have argued (Argenti-Pillen 2003) that within everyday conversation this ambiguity is crucial for the maintenance of long-term relations between perpetrators of violence and their victims in a small-scale rural setting.

Another example of the polysemic nature of local words is the word *dishtiya*, which is used along a sliding scale to refer to the gaze of the evil spirits of the Sinhala Buddhist pantheon (*Suniyam*, *Mahasohona*, *Kalu Kumāra* or *Riri Yaksha*), the gaze of abusive husbands or wartime criminals (see Argenti-Pillen 2003). The ambiguity thus evoked by victims' and survivors' use of this term is difficult to convey in English. Perpetrators typically choose to assert that their victims suffer from an evil spirit, while the victim might use the same terminology to refer to the perpetrator in an ambiguous manner. Most commonly, local concepts go through a process of disambiguation when translated into English and are relegated unambiguously to the domain of spirit religion, possession and spirit worship. This implies that anthropologists have unwittingly been involved in the occultation of the Sinhala terminology of suffering by providing standard translations and uni-dimensional religious interpretations of multi-layered village Sinhala concepts.[12]

De Sardan (1992) has identified the translation tools and translation procedures used by anthropologists as 'the crux of the problem' (1992: 13, 14). Differences become exacerbated and an 'overdrama-tised', 'exoticised' and 'occultised' picture (15) is created by the anthropologist in a quest that has more to do with protecting the sense of identity of a much criticised discipline than with genuine inquiry (5). He argues that what anthropologists have commonly approached as 'African magico-religious notions' 'do not have a great deal in common with current Western concepts of "religion" (matters of faith, of conversion, of dogma) nor with current Western perceptions of "magic" (matters of the occult, out of the ordinary)'. Kapferer (1997) likewise describes what has commonly been referred to as 'sorcery' and 'anti-sorcery practices' in southern Sri Lanka as mundane; arguing these practices objectify the very real experience of relations of power and domination amongst human beings which are anything but 'mystical'. Much like the contemporary practices of the Sri Lankan ethnographers of western humanitarian discourses, the translation practices of western anthropologists involve mobilising familiar religious concepts, which belong to the cultural context of Euro-American modernity, to describe an unfamiliar world. An additional problem is that essentially ambiguous notions lose their ambiguity in the translation process.

The cultivation of ambiguity within rural, Sinhala Buddhist war-torn communities goes beyond the use of ambiguous words, however, and poses additional problems for cross-cultural communication. I quote a young woman from *Udahenagama* to provide an example of such an ambiguous discourse:

Before, when that 'Mātin elder brother' was alive. He was the father of 'Sita', the one who killed herself by drinking poison. He was a good *worker!* (*eya hari harivāda karā*). It was him who did *things like that. Things* like the ones that destroy families. When I think how *those things* occur less frequently now I am very happy. Those have *bad things* in *them.* Now when we think about the *things* that happened to our family, it is impossible not to accept that there is truth in those *things.* My father did not believe in *those.* He did not allow us to do *anything*, because of that our family was destroyed. As time went on the *troubles* (*karadara*) were not finished. [my emphasis]

This family history, which takes the form of a lament, reveals in turn how sorcery, an enemy and the disappearance of family members are typically represented. The sorcery-spells of 'Mātin elder brother' – a close neighbour and arch-enemy – led to the illness and death of a teenage child as well as the disappearance of the head of the family. To a western observer it might seem surprising that all this has really been expressed in this apparently inchoate lament. This surprise parallels my confusion and disorientation as I discovered the ambiguity of everyday discourse in *Udahenagama*. First of all survivors frequently resort to the use of euphemisms (see the above-mentioned example: *vāda*, 'work' used to describe a sorcerer, and *karadara*, 'trouble' to refer to disappearances). Second, referential pronouns and phrases are used to build up the vague and ambiguous quality of arguments about misfortune, illness and violence. For example, what do 'those', 'things like that' and 'anything' in the example above refer to? Apparent lack of any referential intro-duction, and clear-cut reference tracking mechanisms makes it hard for an outsider to be able to identify the referent.

This is the linguistic context into which humanitarian trauma counselling services are introduced. In the aftermath of the civil war, victims and perpetrators continue to live together in crowded neigh-bourhoods. A weak post-colonial state and its largely insufficient judicial apparatus have failed to extract war criminals from the communities they recently terrorised. The discursive creation of ambiguity and uncertainty impedes collective action against such perpetrators from being taken. Perpetrators often remain individual people's enemies and the ambiguous and uncertain nature of the rumours that are spread about such perpetrators discourages collective and decisive actions from being taken against them. At the same time such ambiguous discourses and cautious ways of talking about suffering allow victims to continue to live in the vicinity of their enemies. The uncertainty created by such ambiguous ways of talking about violence allows victims and perpetrators to live in close proximity to one another. The number of internally displaced people has thus been kept to a minimum. Ambiguous discourses about war and violence allow many wartime criminals to continue to live within their own communities, but at the same time play a positive role in helping to reduce the suffering and social problems that come along with internal displacement (see Argenti-Pillen 2003).

The ambiguous terminology used within rural Sinhala Buddhist communities to talk about violence loses its ambiguity when subjected to a *modernist* form of translation: translation practices that are specific to the cultural context of Euro-American modernity. Moreover, generally ambiguous styles to talk about violence that do not depend upon ambiguous words as such also get lost (or disambiguated) in the translation process. The way in which a predominantly Anglophone international humanitarian elite deals with one aspect of the outside world (the rural communities in southern Sri Lanka) is commonly dominated by a culture-specific, modernist appropriation of the discursive formations of rural, Sinhala Buddhist communities. Some words (for example, *dishtiya, āvesa, anang manang*) go through a process of reductionistic disambiguation when translated into English and other aspects of non-Anglophone discursive astuteness are routinely ignored.

THE VIOLENCE OF CARE: MODERNITY, MONOLINGUALISM AND RELIGIOUS EXTREMISM

The above-mentioned standard translations are the tools by means of which bilingual members of the Sri Lankan elite assist foreign humanitarian aid workers. Anglophone interlocutors are thus informed about 'entranced devil dancers', 'exorcists', 'black magic' or 'possessed priestesses'; while village concepts that describe terror-related illnesses and their cures are not used to translate the discourse on war trauma. Such words are carefully and systematically avoided because they would endanger the professional and elite identity of the Sri Lankan humanitarian aid worker.[13] Moreover, within the Cinnamon Garden circles, the anthropologist is expected to use standard anthropological translations of village concepts (such as possession and exorcism), which thus take on objectifying and pejorative overtones. Meanwhile the anthropologist's use of low-status, colloquial, village Sinhala terminology (for example, *'bhuta dosha', 'yakā vage minissu', 'eduro', 'anang manang'* or *'dishtiya karanavā'*) gives rise to considerable hilarity, embarrassment and even censure. Members of the humanitarian elite sometimes pretend not to know what such low-status words mean. If the anthropologist opts out of the dominant translation practices of the Sri Lankan elite, it becomes difficult to maintain a professional identity necessary to continue her/his work. Within the Cinnamon Garden cultural context the use of low-status concepts and a close adherence to the way in which low-status people use such words is simply at odds with the status of a professional, let alone a foreign professional. By virtue of using stigmatised, low-status concepts, western ethnographers face problems of credibility within the semi-westernised, middle-class Cinnamon Garden culture.

Hypothetically speaking, the use of village Sinhala and vernacular idioms would enable NGO personnel to make themselves readily understandable to large sections of the population. While it would be naive to assume that this would improve the efficacy of the intervention programmes (see Hobart 1993: 20) the use of village Sinhala would allow rural survivors to understand which problems mental health NGOs are addressing and why the mental health NGOs are offering them their services. Some village concepts about fear, terror, violence and their effects in fact have certain meanings in common with concepts used within the trauma paradigm. The use of such words by the Cinnamon Garden elites and NGO personnel would virtually have the effect of a shortcut within the global flow of knowledge on war trauma. The discursive distance between members of the international humanitarian community and the rural populations they serve could thus be bridged by an immediate translation of English into village Sinhala. The establishment of such a linguistic shortcut is the sine qua non of any form of dialogue or participatory project development. The discourse on war trauma is however translated into the above-described Colombo-style Sinhala that is subsequently used to educate and train rural health care workers who take up the position of trainees. The linguistic helplessness of the western monoglots employed by international humanitarian agencies precludes them from taking an active role in this translation process and makes of them passive bystanders in a struggle for power waged by the Colombo elites who purport to serve as their facilitators.

The dominance revealed in the translation practices of the middle-class elite needs to be understood within the context of the conflict between orthodox, state-sponsored Buddhism and the heterodox, syncretic religious practices of Sinhala Buddhist villagers. The urban elite emphasise their role in preserving the sanctity and religious purity of the holy (*Sri*) Buddhist nation in counter-distinction to the rural, heterodox practices of worship and performance that syncretically include aspects of Hindu, Buddhist and 'animist' practices. This orthodox Buddhist nationalism of the political elite has taken genocidal proportions against the Hindu, Tamil minority of the country and has been paralleled by state-led violence against non-elite, non-orthodox Sinhala Buddhist citizens during the JVP insurgencies in 1971 and 1987–90. The prominent role of the orthodox Buddhist clergy in the state's erstwhile refusal (1983–2002) to undertake political negotiations with the Tamil Tigers reveals the close link between the Buddhist clergy and the state (also see Holt 1998). The religious extremism of the political elite goes hand in hand with an intolerance vis-à-vis heterodox Sinhala Buddhist practices, which are dismissed by means of the modernist discourse on superstition, ignorance[14] and backwardness ('*dushkara palāta*').

It thus comes as no surprise that the nuanced terminology used to talk about and negotiate violence and its effects within rural Sinhala Buddhist communities is shunned by the elites and that Colombo style Sinhala is used to translate the humanitarian discourse on war trauma into Sinhalese. By means of training manuals and training programmes for rural mental health workers, the rural 'traumatised' populations are offered a discourse on suffering which is imbued with the values of the orthodox Buddhist elite and 'Buddhist fundamentalism' (Bartholomeusz and De Silva 1998). Words that typically belong to orthodox Buddhist doctrine feature prominently within the Sinhalese discourse on 'trauma' and post-war rehabilitation, and the hegemony of the elite finds a new medium through which to propagate itself: the 'mental health' of its citizens. Moreover, the spectre of a nation plagued by the swarming mass of a mentally ill/traumatised rural and urban proletariat effectively crystallises Colombo middle-class anxieties regarding the majority they exclude from power.

During my interviews with members of national mental health NGOs, it transpired that the discourse on the importance of providing services at the 'grass-roots' level and organising trauma counselling services for people in 'remote' areas is central to the self-presentation of Sri Lankan NGO personnel. The discourse on war trauma as articulated by Sri Lankan nationalist politicians reveals a similar preoccupation. I quote from a speech by the Minister of Health and Indigenous Medicine, delivered during the 'National Mental Health Week' in October 1997:

With the National Mental Health Task Force, of which I am the Chairman, we are preparing to do everything for the mental health needs of our society ... a National Action Plan which will be implemented nation-wide. In the mental health sector there are the personal frustrations, the personal contact with the patient and the community that cannot purely be done by paid professionals and the paid staff of the government. It is there that the volunteers of the NGOs are really important. The NGOs, the non-profit making organisations, they are to *serve* the people, they have the mental capacity and ability to *support* the people, to *talk* about their problems and to thus *implement mental stability, mental courage and strength*, we are very happy that the NGOs are prepared to do that *but* I have

– I will tell you what – the [foreign] NGOs who work with the people without understanding the cultural, religious background of our country, without understanding the language, but I noted some of the NGOs, some are very good, most of the NGOs, they write very good reports in English and present them at international symposiums, but these symposium discussions do not bring us more results, indeed some are very good for the purpose of finding funding sometimes and also for foreign institutions to come, but *our* main objective is to reach the man in the village, to go into the *difficult areas in the country* and find what their problems are, go and ask questions about what are the problems of the mentally ill, find what their problems are, teach them, *do some counselling there*, so that is what is correct, so therefore I would like the NGOs to have a reorientation programme for you all NGOs because otherwise all the effort which will be put into this action plan programme will not bear very good results ... We first have to educate the people employed in high levels within the government, then we must wake up the people who do not belong to the government, after that we must let that knowledge spread in villages, across the whole country in all its corners, we must spread this knowledge like a hug, an embrace, this wakening up must be spread to towns and across villages, therefore we must have a successful plan. [original emphasis][15]

Nationalist politicians make sure that the discourse on war trauma goes through the appropriate process of cross-cultural translation. The minister quoted above does not mince his words: this nationalist 'hug' or 'embrace' of the whole country in all its corners is to be facilitated by the expertise and especially the funding which go along with the international humanitarian discourse on war trauma; a discourse which the Colombo elites have effectively subsumed to their hegemonic project. It is not hyperbolic to conclude that the international humanitarian community's linguistic helplessness and concomitant lack of participation in this highly politicised translation process leads them inadvertently[16] to sponsor the nationwide spread of religious extremism and intolerance.

CONCLUSION: WESTERN MONOGLOTS AND THEIR INDIGENOUS FORMS OF RESISTANCE

Most studies on 'creolisation' (Hannerz 1987) or culture-specific appropriations of outside influences presuppose a partly multilingual community that reaches out towards a global world by learning other languages. This chapter takes into account the problems that a predominantly monolingual, trans-local community faces in dealing with an increasingly uninhabitable and hostile environment in war-torn societies world-wide. Large resource-rich territories have become inaccessible and unsafe for western intelligence personnel, humanitarian aid workers and academic researchers alike. Within many of the humanitarian discourses, supposedly hostile, violence-prone populations are described as traumatised. While western countries (those with ethical foreign policies included) avoid measures that would damage the trade in military hardware, other types of interventions allow for the maintenance of a presence on the ground.[17] Within the array of such 'intervention packages' the implementation of counselling services for war trauma victims proves to be the most elusive and unintelligible for survivors from other cultures.

In contradistinction to the provision of food, medical care or shelter for war-torn communities, the organisation of counselling services for war trauma victims does not offer immediate, palpable benefits for the communities involved. The humanitarian discourse on war trauma's main message is that the organisation of mental health care services for traumatised populations will interrupt chronic cycle of violence by treating traumatised individuals. The effects of such interventions cannot, however, be immediately observed and the humanitarian community thus greatly depends on the correct transmission of its message to the targeted war-torn communities.

The world-wide implementation of mental health projects on the basis of the trauma paradigm is however becoming an increasingly controversial issue (see Bracken et al. 1995; Summerfield 1996, 1999; Young 1996; Argenti-Pillen 2000). The question of the cross-cultural applicability of the notion of Post Traumatic Stress Disorder (PTSD) has been addressed repeatedly within the context of the mental health profession. Two main strategies have emerged. The first consists of the design of culture-specific PTSD questionnaires designed to be used for the diagnosis of traumatic stress amongst non-western refugee populations (i.e. Mollica et al. 1987; Kroll et al. 1989; Westermeyer et al. 1989; Eisenbruch 1990, 1991, 1992; Boehnlein and Kinzie 1992; Mollica 1992; Hinton et al. 1993; Demartino et al. 1994). A second strategy questions the relevance of the trauma discourse across cultures and is more politically engaged (for example, Bracken et al. 1995; Summerfield 1996, 1999). In informal contexts this second strategy has been referred to as the 'anti-trauma movement'. As its name implies, this anti-trauma discourse involves a radical questioning of the consequences of the implementation of psychosocial projects based on the trauma-paradigm world-wide:

Those serious about the issues of torture and atrocity need to address them within a rigorous human rights framework, not merely confined to comfortable humanitarian responses which see survivors as victims needing individual medical or psychological help ... Western governments seem to have used the humanitarian effort as a shield to hide their own mixed motives over serious engagement with the political players and issues ... and to avoid 'difficult' questions ... Too frequently these [difficult questions] relate to the values of the Western-led world order, in which geopolitical and business considerations far outweigh issues of basic rights and justice. (Summerfield 1996: 32)

Humanitarian practices based on the trauma paradigm are castigated by the anti-trauma discourse as disempowering survivors. In Summerfield's critical account the war victim, an aggrieved party in a political struggle becomes a patient or consumer of the services of foreign experts and is taught to present distress in a 'modernised' way (as trauma or PTSD), while 'indigenous' or 'local' healers or health workers are made to feel ill-equipped, or become 'supervised' by NGOs and their donors (1996: 17).

In my interpretation, one of the major contributions of the anti-trauma movement is its questioning of the underlying assumption of the trauma discourse that links ongoing cycles of violence with 'PTSD epidemics' (for example, ISTSS 1996: A43). Predictions about future conflicts and wars world-wide are often based on estimations of 'untreated' or 'unresolved' trauma (Summerfield 1996: 22). Post-trauma morbidity, chronic PTSD, problems with the modulation of aggression and violent behaviour are depicted as the main contributing factors to group processes leading to further violent upheavals (for example, ISTSS 1996: A84). The role of indignation and outrage resulting from ongoing injustice or the assault on culture and ethnicity by nation-states are thereby left out of the picture. Meanwhile, the effects on potentially violent individuals of the disruption and destruction of the *social* (instead of mental) fabric such as the family or the community are made to fade into the background.

Euro-American professionals who operate within the trauma paradigm do not depict post-war realities as situations where the majority of people adapt well, while a minority withdraw from the social world, commit suicide or develop serious mental illness. Western humanitarians construct post-war realities as situations were the *majority* are at risk of developing PTSD, resulting in continuing cycles of violence. The anti-trauma movement challenges the way war is treated as a mental health emergency by international humanitarian agencies and trauma work has become the latest 'fashion' of western donors (Summerfield 1996: 11), who organise large financial transactions to war-torn societies for the implementation of counselling programmes for victims of war trauma.

In this chapter I have added a critical argument to these existing critiques of the global flow of knowledge on war trauma by describing the role of the Sri Lankan intellectual elite in the translation of the international humanitarian discourse on war trauma. I did not, however, use the categories of local, modern and global in the same way as the above-mentioned critics of the humanitarian discourse on trauma do. In Summerfield's terms 'indigenous' survivors are taught to present their distress in a 'modernised' way (1996: 17), as trauma or PTSD. Within the Sri Lankan context, however, both the term 'indigenous' to describe survivors from rural communities as well as the unspecified term 'modern' to refer to the Sinhalese translation of the humanitarian discourse on war trauma of Anglophone humanitarians are problematic.

I inverted the conventional representations of local, indigenous and global. To speak of the Sinhala Buddhist members of rural communities as 'indigenous locals' implies they submit to a hegemonic representation[18] that firmly ensconces them within the worldview of western imperialism. I have conceptualised the notions of 'local' and 'global' along a continuum and used the criterion of openness towards other cultural forms as a measuring instrument of global citizenship. While I realise an ethnographic text is not a place to use ironical language I teasingly referred to the western humanitarian aid workers and mental health professionals based in Colombo as 'locals', western 'indigenes' and monoglots. My inversion of objectifying terminology is not a mere exaggeration, however. This image emerged only after I compared Colombo-based members of the western humanitarian community with the inhabitants of Sinhala Buddhist rural communities.

In southern Sri Lanka, heterodox religious practices parallel the rural poor's multicultural and pluri-local existence as a people living in a social environment that has for centuries been open to the flow of people, goods and knowledge, and has consequently been plural, multicultural, multilingual and syncretising. Periodic invasions by Muslim traders and peoples from the Indian mainland, followed by colonialisation by the Portuguese, Dutch and British have influenced both the language as well as the practices of rural, Sinhala Buddhist communities. This curiosity and openness towards other cultural forms is simply not paralleled by the monolingual, Anglophone members of the international humanitarian community based in Colombo. Western mental health professionals commonly take up the identity of experts and choose an essentially inward looking position rather than an openness towards cultural and intellectual alternatives. This goes hand in hand with monolingualism, a common unintended consequence of the modernist's experience of cultural supremacy. Monolingualism however has indigenising effects on western professionals. Those who seemed trans-local and multicultural could in fact better be qualified as well-travelled locals, while their targeted 'locals', seem to achieve a higher degree of global citizenship.

Once it reaches Sri Lanka, the discourse on war trauma undergoes a culture-specific translation process that is orchestrated not by the international humanitarian community, but by the bilingual members of the Sri Lankan intellectual elite. Precisely because of this type of translation from English into Colombo-style Sinhala and 'high' Sinhala, a language belonging to the cultural context of state-sponsored nationalist orthodox Buddhism, the humanitarian discourse on war trauma paradoxically plays a key role in the propagation of religious extremism. While the propagation of religious extremism sometimes boosts the US and Europe's trade in military hardware[19] – and it certainly does in Sri Lanka – its long-term effects might not be beneficial for Euro-American indigenes and their plans for the world-wide implementation of a free-market economy. The Anglophone international elite is potentially hindered by translation problems and vulnerable to the unintended consequences of the implementation of trauma counselling services world-wide that such translation problems bring about. In line with Noam Chomsky's caustic analysis of the Euro-American attempt at global capitalist expansion by means of 'humanitarian' interventions (1999b), my research points at the limitations of the monolingual Anglophones' indigenous linguistic strategies and their concomitantly ineffectual forms of 'resistance' to non-western, elite forms of religious fundamentalism.

ACKNOWLEDGEMENTS

This chapter is based on a doctoral research project funded by a University College London Graduate School Scholarship and a Harry Frank Guggenheim Foundation Research Fellowship.

I would like to express my sincere gratitude to my research assistant Akkā who accompanied me on numerous visits to Colombo and taught me to see the cultural specificity of the 'Cinnamon Garden culture'.

NOTES

1. In 1998 these included: Association for Health and Counselling, Centre for Family Services, Communication Centre for Mental Health (CCMH), Family Planning Association, Family Rehabilitation Centre, Family Studies and Services Institute, Institute of Human Rights, Life, Muslim Women's Conference, The National Council of YMCAs of Sri Lanka, The National Christian Counsel Counselling Centre, NEST, Sahan Sevana Psycho Therapy Centre, Salvation Army, Family Counselling Centre Sarvodaya Movement, Survivors Associated, Tamil Women's Union, Women's Development Centre, Women for Peace, Women in Need (WIN), Young Women's Christian Organisation, National Council for Mental Health 'Sahanaya', Sri Lanka Sumithrayo (Branch of Befrienders International),

Alokaya Youth Counselling Centre, SEDEC Relief and Rehabilitation, Sri Lanka National Association of Counsellors. All of which are members of the Federation of NGOs on Mental Health and Well-Being.

2. To use Hannerz's (1987) words, such NGOs are the 'bridgeheads for the penetration of metropolitan cultural influences' (549) or channels for the international cultural flow (552).

3. Here I am indebted to Hobart's advice to anthropologists of development: 'Development is effectively a synonym for more or less planned social and economic change. So, defining development as a problem susceptible of a solution, or pathologically as a condition requiring a cure, may well be misplaced' (1993: 1).

4. This involves combining different disciplinary perspectives to understand and interpret other cultures (Sillitoe 1998: 229). Sillitoe (1998: 231) argued that interdisciplinary work is central to methodological advances in facilitatory anthropological research oriented towards agricultural development, which may be carried out by natural-resource scientists aware of the anthropological perspective or social scientists with some technological background.

5. This war was fought amongst the Sinhalese themselves and is distinct from the much more publicised conflict between the Sinhalese majority and Tamil minority.

6. Some detailed data, based on the personal history of 10,192 suspects summoned before the Commission of Inquiry dealing with the 1971 insurgency reveal that: the average age of the insurgents was 20 years, *92 per cent were from the Sinhala Buddhist rural sector*, 20 per cent from elite classes (administrative positions, security services, professions), 6 per cent with parents in middle administrative positions (Ayurvedic physicians, middle grade in government services, clerks and teachers), 40 per cent from the lower middle class, 17 per cent were unemployed and under-employed, 12 per cent were students, and 10 per cent were from the age category between 15 and 19 (students from secondary schools) (Obeyesekere 1971, emphasis added).

7. It is within this context that the role played by my multidisciplinary background I described earlier should be understood. Taking on the role of an anthropologist or social scientist amongst the elite, even the identity of a *foreign* social scientist, did not seem advantageous.

8. Also see article in the Sri Lankan national press (*Daily News*, 17 August 1996) on 'US military cooperation with Sri Lanka'.

9. From the type anthropologists are familiar with.

10. I used the system of transliteration recommended by Gombrich (1971: xiii–xiv) as a guideline. I however made a number of simplifications to make word processing and typesetting easier. I have not made a distinction between the retroflex and dental pronunciations of *d* and *t*, or the short and long pronunciation of *ä*, *i*, and *u*, nor have I marked the palatal or nasalised *n*.

11. In a similar vein Roy (1997) provides a reverse ethnographic description when she alludes to counselling as 'a cheap brand of exorcism' (1997: 191).

Here, however, she does not resort to the vocabulary of high religion but uses a standard objectifying translation of popular religious practices such as 'exorcism' (see below for discussion).

12. See Scott (1994) for a historical deconstruction of some of the standard anthropological translations.

13. Here I would like to borrow an image from Rafael's description (1995) of the linguistic hierarchy in the Philippines. He argues that the 'mediators of modernity' (1995: 105) are 'stranded between aesthetic sensibilities and, by extension, between linguistic registers without, however, the means with which to represent this predicament' (1995: 112). He describes one of the effects of Taglish as 'that of moving between languages without fully surrendering to any of them' (1995: 112). I would be inclined to describe the position of Sri Lankan mental health professionals as similar, except for the fact that during their movement between languages and linguistics registers they found a way to fill the linguistic gap or emptiness: the use of 'high' Sinhala as well as standard English translations of low-status Sinhala words.

14. The attitude of the Sri Lankan elite mirrors the traditional development discourses of western indigenes described by Hobart (1993): 'Remarkably, it seems to have largely slipped notice that the postulated growth of knowledge concomitantly entails the possibility of increasing ignorance. In development this is manifested practically in local knowledges being devalued or ignored, in favour of Western scientific, technical and managerial knowledge' (1993: 10). In other words, the 'growth of ignorance' (Hobart 1993) is continuously reinforced by the Sri Lankan semi-westernised, modernising elite.

15. In the speech he delivered in Sinhalese the message for the NGOs was even made clearer: 'Bohovita antar djātikava bohoma honda ripot hadanavā. Pitarataval valagihillā laksha gananakata e vagema evā gäna katā karanavā namut djanatāvata vädak nä. E nisā eväni sangvidāna valin apita vädak nä!. Apata avashā venne game pungchirāla langata, Hemavatthii langata, Ruupavatthi langata, vatte Ramanādan langata Lechchami langat a gihillā eyālāge mānasika tattvaya gäna hoyalā, e gäna yam adahasak denna puluvan, gamenma soyāgatta svechshā sevakayin dālā, gamata gihillā ingrisiyen katākaralā, kädicha sinhalen katā karalā, mānasika roga handunāganne nätuva, gamenma torāgatta swechshā sevayakin lavā hondin kriyākara ape sangskruttin pasubimata, ape āgamak pasubimata hariyan ākārayata gamata gihillā väda karana sandvidāna āvashayi ... Ape deshiya pasubimata, ape deshiya sangskatatiyata, deshiya avahyatā vayanta hariyana akāriyata boho sangvidāna pratisangvidānaya viya yutuyi. Me nisā ne kāryaya pilibandava me sangvidāna tamange sangvidā na prativyuhagata kiriima itāma vädagat venavā. Me nisā apit radjayat me sandahā denna puluvan siyaluma sahayogaya labādiimata suudānamin sitina bava prakāsha karanna kämati, prakāshakaramin mama ingrisiyen vachana svalpayak katā karanna kämati.' I paraphrase: 'The NGOs write very good reports to present at international seminars but it does not help people in the villages. Therefore we don't need those organisations here!

They go to see ordinary village people, the *Heemavatthi*s, the *Ruupavatthi*s [typical (Sinhala) names of village women], or the *Ramanaadan*s or *Lechchami*s [typical (Tamil) names of village women] and they look for mental illnesses, just to give you an idea, they go to such villages and speak English!, or they speak broken Sinhala!, they don't identify mental illnesses!, the work in the villages should be done by people who know our cultural background, our religion, our local culture, therefore we have to re-organise and restructure the NGOs, our government will support such organisations to restructure themselves, after having made this promise I will now speak some English ...'

16. It can, of course, be debated to which degree the international humanitarian community is aware of such translation problems. As Appadurai (1993) remarked, meticulous and 'correct' translations belong to a system of *beliefs* of the international Anglophone elite: 'When Americans see transformations and cultural complications of their democratic vocabulary, *if they notice them at all*, they are annoyed and dismayed ... *In the migration of our words, we see the victory of our myths. We are believers* in terminal conversion' (1993: 41, my emphasis).

17. For an overview of the historic link between humanitarian interventions and US-led capitalist expansionism and domination, see Chomsky (1999b).

18. I am inspired by Hobart's argument that 'to speak of strategies of "resistance" or "denial" on the part of those designated as inferior is to assume that they recognize and submit to the hegemonic representation of them' (1993: 16).

19. One could thus have reasons to call the international humanitarian agencies' linguistic helplessness and ignorance of the politics involved in the translation of the discourse on war trauma '*criminal*' (see Pottier's chapter), much like the lack of any significant area expertise within the UN and the UN's dependence on the discourse of the Rwandan political elites who suppress local political knowledges.

REFERENCES

Alles, A.C. (1990) *The J.V.P. 1969–1989* (Colombo: Lake House)

Amnesty International (1993) 'Sri-Lanka: "Disappearance" and Murder as Techniques of Counter-insurgency', in *'Disappearances' and Political Killings: Human Rights Crisis of the 1990's. A Manual for Action* (London: Pre-Publication Version)

Appadurai, A. (1993) 'Patriotism and its Futures', *Public Culture*, 5: 411–29

Arce, A. and N. Long (1992) 'The Dynamics of Knowledge: Interfaces between bureaucrats and peasants', in N. Long and A. Long (eds), *Battlefields of Knowledge: The Interlocking of Theory and Practice in Social Research and Development* (London and New York: Routledge), pp. 211–46

Argenti-Pillen, A. (2000) 'The Discourse on Trauma in Non-Western Cultural Contexts', in A. Shalev, R. Yehuda, and A. McFarlane (eds), *International Handbook of Human Response to Trauma* (New York: Kluwer Academic/Plenum Publishers), pp. 87–102

—— (2003) *Masking Terror. How Women Contain Violence in Southern Sri Lanka* (Philadelphia: Pennsylvania University Press)

Bartholomeusz, T.J. and C.R. De Silva (1998) 'Buddhist Fundamentalism and Identity in Sri Lanka', in T. Bartholomeusz and C.R. De Silva (eds), *Buddhist Fundamentalism and Minority Identities in Sri Lanka* (Albany, NY: State University of New York Press), pp. 1–35

Boehnlein, J.K. and J.D. Kinzie (1992) 'DSM Diagnosis of Posttraumatic Stress Disorder and Cultural Sensitivity: A response', *Journal of Nervous and Mental Diseases*, 180(9): 597–9

Boutros Boutros-Ghali (1996) 'Foreword', in Y. Danieli, N.S. Rodley and L. Weisaeth (eds), *International Responses to Traumatic Stress* (New York: Baywood Publishing Company), pp. iii–iv

Bracken, P.J., J.E. Giller and D. Summerfield (1995) 'Psychological Responses to War and Atrocity: The limitations of current concepts', *Social Science and Medicine*, 40(8): 1073–82

Chomsky, N. (1999a) 'East Timor, Horror and Amnesia. Hypocrisy of the West', *Le Monde Diplomatique*, October

—— (1999b) 'NATO, Master of the World', *Le Monde Diplomatique*, May

Daniel, V.E. (1993) 'Tea Talk: Violent measures in the discursive practices of Sri Lanka's estate Tamils', *Comparative Studies in Society and History*, 35: 568–600

Demartino, R., R. Mollica and M. Petevi (1994) 'Evaluation and Care of Victims of Trauma and Violence: Draft guidelines', *Internal Document United Nations High Commissioner for Refugees*

de Sardan, J.P.O. (1992) 'Occultism and the Ethnographic "I". The exoticizing of magic from Durkheim to "postmodern" anthropology', *Critique of Anthropology*, 12(1): 5–25

Desjarlais, R., L. Eisenberg, B. Good and A. Kleinman (1995) *World Mental Health: Problems and Priorities in Low Income Countries* (New York and Oxford: Oxford University Press)

Eisenbruch, M. (1990) 'The Cultural Bereavement Interview: A clinical approach for refugees', *Psychiatric Clinics of North America*, 13(4): 715–35

—— (1991) 'From Post-Traumatic Stress Disorder to Cultural Bereavement: Diagnosis of Southeast Asian refugees', *Social Science and Medicine*, 33(6): 673–80

—— (1992) 'Toward a Culturally Sensitive DSM: Cultural bereavement in Cambodian refugees and the traditional healer as taxonomist', *Journal of Nervous and Mental Diseases*, 180(1): 8–10

Hannerz, U. (1987) 'The World in Creolization', *Africa*, 57(4): 546–59

Hinton, W.L., Y.J. Chen, N. Du, C.G. Tran, F.G. Lu, J. Miranda and S. Faust (1993) 'DSM-III-R Disorders in Vietnamese Refugees: Prevalence and correlates', *Journal of Nervous and Mental Diseases*, 181(2), 113–22

Hobart, M. (1993) 'Introduction: The growth of ignorance?', in M. Hobart (ed.), *An Anthropological Critique of Development. The Growth of Ignorance* (London and New York: Routledge), pp. 1–30

Holt, J.C. (1998) 'The Persistence of Political Buddhism', in T.J. Bartholomeusz and C.R. De Silva (eds), *Buddhist Fundamentalism and Minority Identities in Sri Lanka* (Albany, NY: State University of New York Press), pp. 186–95

ISTSS – Second world conference of the International Society for Traumatic Stress Studies (1996) Abstracts

Kapferer, B. (1997) *The Feast of the Sorcerer: Practices of Consciousness and Power in Sri-Lanka* (Chicago: Chicago University Press)

Kroll, J., M. Habenicht, T. Mackenzie, M. Yang, S. Chan, T. Vang, T. Nguyen, M. Ly, B. Phommasouvanh, H. Nguyen, Y. Vang, L. Souvannasoth and R. Cabugao (1989) 'Depression and Posttraumatic Stress Disorder in Southeast Asian Refugees', *American Journal of Psychiatry*, 146: 1592–7

Mollica, R.F. (1992) 'The Harvard Trauma Questionnaire. Validating a cross-cultural instrument for measuring torture, trauma, and post-traumatic stress disorder in Indochinese refugees', *Journal of Nervous and Mental Diseases*, 180: 111–16

Mollica, R.F., G. Wyshak and J. Lavelle (1987) 'The Psychosocial Impact of War Trauma and Torture on Southeast Asian Refugees', *American Journal of Psychiatry*, 144(12): 1567–72

Obeyesekere, G. (1971) 'Some Comments on the Social Background of the April Insurgency in Sri Lanka (Ceylon)', *Journal of Asian Studies*, 33(3): 367–84

Perera, S. (1996) 'Sri Lanka's South Still Smoulders', *HIMAL South Asia*, 46–8

Pottier, J. (1993a) 'Introduction: Development in practice. Assessing social science perspectives', in J. Pottier (ed.), *Practising Development. Social Science Perspectives* (London, New York: Routledge), pp. 1–12

—— (1993b) 'The Role of Ethnography in Project Appraisal', in J. Pottier (ed.), *Practicing Development: Social Science Perspectives* (London and New York: Routledge), pp. 13–33

Rafael, V.L. (1995) 'Taglish, or the Phantom Power of the Lingua Franca', *Public Culture*, 8: 101–26

Roy, A. (1997) *The God of Small Things* (London: Flamingo)

Scott, D. (1994) *Formations of Ritual. Colonial and Anthropological Discourses on the Sinhala Yaktovi* (Minneapolis and London: University of Minnesota Press)

Sillitoe, P. (1998) 'The Development of Indigenous Knowledge. A new applied anthropology', *Current Anthropology*, 39(2): 223–52

Sluka, J.A. (2000) *Death Squad. The Anthropology of State Terror* (Philadelphia: University of Pennsylvania Press)

Summerfield, D. (1993) *Addressing Human Response to War and Atrocity: Major Themes for Health Workers* (Medical Foundation for the Care of Victims of Torture)

—— (1996) 'The Impact of War and Atrocity on Civilian Populations: Basic principles for NGO interventions and a critique of psychosocial trauma projects', *Relief and Rehabilitation Network, Overseas Development Institute, London, Network Paper*, 14: 1–41

—— (1999) 'A Critique of Seven Assumptions behind Psychological Trauma Programmes in War-Affected Areas', *Social Science and Medicine*, 48: 1449–62

Westermeyer, J., M. Bouafuely, J. Neider and A. Callies (1989) 'Somatization among Refugees: An epidemiological study', *Psychosomatics*, 30(1): 34–43

Young, A. (1996) *The Harmony of Illusions. Inventing Post-Traumatic Stress Disorder* (Princeton, NJ: Princeton University Press)

10 MODERN INFORMATION WARFARE VERSUS EMPIRICAL KNOWLEDGE: FRAMING 'THE CRISIS' IN EASTERN ZAIRE, 1996

Johan Pottier

In late 1996, Rwanda invaded eastern Zaire with the tacit approval of the UN. The invasion ended the refugee crisis, or so it seemed to some at the time, and culminated in the removal of president Joseph-Désiré Mobutu Sese Seko. The UN applauded the end of 'the crisis' as an African solution and congratulated itself on not intervening. Rwanda's vice-president and defence minister, Paul Kagame, now president, later congratulated the Clinton Administration, the driving force behind the UN stance against intervention, for 'taking the right decisions to let it proceed'.[1]

This chapter contrasts the dominant narrative on 'the crisis' in eastern Zaire (and 'the solution' implied) with what historically informed research tells us about *local* politics and discourses. By dominant narrative I mean the perspective which the Government of Rwanda (GOR) and the Rwandese Patriotic Front (RPF) had formulated on 'the crisis', and which the UN accepted as the basis for its decision not to intervene. Bearing the hallmark of an environmental disaster narrative, this dominant perspective portrayed 'the crisis' in eastern Zaire as a security crisis triggered by *a single cause*: the presence of extremist Hutu refugees from Rwanda. The same narrative also insisted that a Rwandan moral community straddled the Rwanda–Zaire border. From *within* this moral community a unique, *single solution* to the crisis had emerged. The solution existed in the readiness of 'the Banyamulenge', a newly created ethnic group, to take up arms in self-defence. This group, the narrative claimed, had been joined by other local anti-Mobutu forces, all of them merging into the strongly cohesive *Alliance of the Democratic Forces for the Liberation of Congo-Zaire* (ADFL). Conspicuously, the narrative made no reference to the region's complex – and well-documented – political history. Empirical knowledge about the past, which exists at local and international (academic) levels, was discarded from the authoritative version of events, according to which it all began in 1994.

Reacting against this dominant, GOR/RPF-functional version of 'the crisis' in eastern Zaire, the present chapter explores a _more local_ narrative, articulated within Kivu and through research by social scientists. Drawing on academic research and local people's recollections of some 30 years of political history, the chapter demonstrates how local and scholarly interpretations of 'the crisis' of 1996 were markedly at odds with the authoritative version promoted by the GOR/RPF and embraced by the UN. On this occasion, local knowledge and empirical research failed to impact on what emerged as international consensus.

THE POWER OF INFORMATION WARFARE: RWANDA INVADES ZAIRE, 1996

With its focus on international opposition to the right to 'local knowledge' in the context of politics (rather than agriculture or health, the conventional domains for discussing local knowledge), this chapter warns against exaggerated optimism when assessing how hegemonic forces impact. While I am not turning my back on the 1993 ASA conference (see Chapter 1) – since my case study confirms that so-called local perspectives can indeed be hybrid products[2] – it is equally important to highlight that other local perspectives, in this case views on the conflict in Kivu by Kivu's own inhabitants, are being denied expression when international interests demand that such views be suppressed. In this case, the UN Security Council, under pressure from the US and Britain, tacitly agreed that many in eastern Zaire, the majority perhaps, should have no voice in formulating what constituted Zaire's 'problem' and 'solution'. Instead, as with global science and some of its applications, a simplistic, decontextualised perspective came to be substituted.

The unique circumstances under which Rwanda invaded eastern Zaire with tacit UN approval require explanation. Three points must be noted. First, the world, that is, mainly the Anglophone diplomatic world, fell for a reductionist narrative regarding 'the crisis'. Second, non-intervention by the UN came to be heralded, within UN and Rwandan political circles, as a moral victory, a breakthrough in North–South relations, a new dawn 'for the residents of Central Africa' (de Waal 1997: 212). Third, in July 1997, Paul Kagame revealed that he, not Kabila, had orchestrated the so-called Banyamulenge (local) rebellion. The world had been misled, but misled for a good cause.

Against the backdrop of Kagame's testimony, which came as not too great a surprise to anyone familiar with the Great Lakes, this chapter begins by asking how Kagame imposed his interpretation of the build-up to the Kivu crisis. Kagame himself once gave the short answer:

We used communication and information warfare better than anyone. We have found a new way of doing things. (Paul Kagame, 8 April 1998, interviewed by Nick Gowing)[3]

Part of Kagame's 'new way of doing things' existed in the construction of a narrative on 'the events' in eastern Zaire, and in the successful adoption of that narrative by many journalists, some academics, many aid workers and (most importantly) those diplomats able to influence the UN Security Council.

There is no space here to detail the defining moments which have helped to shape and consolidate the intellectual climate that led to the adoption of Kagame's perspective on Zaire, but the following stages are noted in summary fashion:

Stage 1. Following the UN decision not to reinforce its troops in Rwanda in April 1994, a decision which made the genocide possible, the RPF intensified its campaign to re-educate the world regarding the 'true' nature of ethnicity in Rwanda. This campaign enlisted the services of western journalists and academics sympathetic to the RPF but unfamiliar with Rwanda. At a stroke, these 'instant experts' deleted (or attempted to do so) three decades of empirical research on society and ethnicity in pre-colonial and early colonial Rwanda (Pottier 1995, 2002). In the process, they resuscitated the colonial, functionalist model of a 'feudal society' in harmony.

Stage 2. One year on, following the massacre of thousands of internally displaced persons (IDPs) at Kibeho, a series of diplomatic victories by President Bizimungu brought home to the (again mainly Anglophone) international community that the outside world was morally so corrupt it had lost the right to understand and judge Rwandan politics. From now on, relevant knowledge about Rwanda would be knowledge the GOR/RPF, that is, the increasingly hard-line voices among them, deemed useful for public consumption. The US and Britain, and many within the UN system, accepted it was now immoral that outsiders should contradict, or even scrutinise, Rwanda's RPF-led government (Pottier 1999b).

Stage 3. The Rwandan government's monopoly on knowledge production was successfully exercised when officials convinced diplomats and journalists (again, mainly Anglophone) that their interpretation of the crisis in Kivu was the only correct one. The present chapter concerns this third stage.

'THE PROBLEM' IN EASTERN ZAIRE: THE POLITICALLY CORRECT VERSION

Bearing the hallmark of an environmental disaster narrative, the Rwandan Government's interpretation of 'the crisis' in Kivu was that it was a security crisis threatening Zaire's ethnic Tutsi, as well as Rwanda's own security, and that the overriding cause of the tensions was the presence of extremist Hutu refugees from Rwanda. The narrative also evoked the existence of a Rwandan moral community which straddled the Rwanda–Zaire border, and from within which a 'purely local' solution to the crisis had emerged. This local solution existed in the preparedness of 'the Banyamulenge' to take up arms in self-defence. This ethnic group, the narrative claimed, had then been joined by other local anti-Mobutu forces under the banner of the (presumed) cohesive ADFL. Strikingly though, this interpretation, which appealed to those unfamiliar with eastern Zaire, made no reference to the region's complex – and documented – social and political history of the past 30 years. Empirical knowledge about the recent past was better deleted from memory.

Like every true narrative (see Hoben 1995), the dominant gloss on eastern Zaire focused on a single cause – aggression by an external force (refugees) – and had an attractive, simple solution: 'the Banyamulenge'. As found in the American press, the dominant version of why Kivu had become 'a problem' stressed the work of Hutu refugee militias:

Hutu militias have launched cross-border raids into Rwanda and have killed refugees who want to return to their homeland. In the last six months, Hutu from the camps joined Zairian soldiers and local vigilantes in attacks on ethnic Tutsi living in Zaire, igniting the current revolt.[4]

The violence of the last six months against Tutsi, and the local solution to this violence, were to be explained solely with reference to a single causal factor.

In *The Times*, Sam Kiley toed the same 'politically correct' line, lashing out at aid workers who failed to understand that a western intervention 'could protect the killers and prolong the agony'.[5] The Kivu crisis, again, was refugee-centred, there was no space, nor indeed any need, to highlight the experiences and thoughts of eastern Zaire's *diverse* population. Following the GOR/RPF-functional narrative, Kiley took

1994 to be the starting point and claimed it was the Rwandan refugees who convinced the local *Zaïrois* that Tutsi must die.

In October this year [1996], at Zaire's frontier post in Bukavu, Zaïrois Tutsis fled, chased by blood-crazed Hutu militiamen. *Unbelievably the Hutus of Rwanda have brainwashed some Zairois into orchestrating a pogrom against the Tutsis.*[6]

These journalistic statements, which can be multiplied, have in common that: a) they omit to situate the build-up of tensions in Kivu within a wider historical framework (1965–96) and b) they overfocus on Zairean Tutsi whilst paying little or no attention to Zaire's 'autochthonous' groups, which had already clashed with Banyarwanda – *Hutu and Tutsi* – in 1993.

The idea of an imported crisis – Kivu's problems being *merely* an extension of the Rwanda genocide – is in evidence, too, in the writings of organisations loyal to the RPF. In an African Rights publication, de Waal writes:

The [Rwandan Hutu] extremists also extended their campaign to eastern Zaire, where Zaireans of Tutsi origin were killed, mutilated or expelled from their land. A series of killings at Masisi, west of Goma, in early 1996 proved a turning point: several hundred Zaireans of Tutsi origin were massacred without international protest. Other Zaireans suffered as well. (de Waal 1997: 205)

That 'other Zaireans suffered as well' is an understatement. While the killing of Tutsi involved unspeakable atrocities, and casualties may have been higher than suggested, the circumstances leading to the massacres were far more complex than the narrow focus on refugees and Tutsi allows for, which will be detailed further down.

The NGO Save the Children (SCF), another strong GOR/RPF ally, also resorted to simplistic narration when formulating its objection to the prospect of a UN-led intervention force. In 'Zaire: Military Intervention Is Not The Answer', a news statement released on 6 November 1996, SCF regarded non-intervention as a prerequisite for ending the regional violence and promoting stability. SCF, too, believed that the outbreak of violence in 1996 had a single cause: the refugees. SCF urged that the priority should be to create stability through a) 'support to the displaced and affected local people, believed to number 400,000', and b) 'support for major and rapid voluntary repatriation of the refugees'. Who exactly these 400,000 were was not spelled out, but SCF did provide a background piece – a statement marked by simplicity and some distortion. It read:

The Banyamulenge in South Kivu and groups such as the Banyarwanda in North Kivu have lived in Zaire for many centuries. Over the past twenty years attempts have been made by the Zaire Government to persecute these groups by trying to deny their rights to citizenship and making various attempts to expropriate property and land. While this situation has persisted for some time, it has been exacerbated in the past two years by the influx of refugees from Rwanda.

The Banyamulenge and Banyarwanda were amongst the relatively better off groups in Kivu province. The Banyamulenge and allied groups lived on the high plateau above the towns of Bukavu and Uvira. The Banyarwanda inhabited the area around Masisi and around Goma. The mass influx of over one million refugees into Kivu has done much to exacerbate economic rivalries and political rivalries and tensions in the region since their arrival two years ago.

As with most interpretations emanating from Kigali (or inspired by the authorities there), this one too says more through its omissions – the spectacular absence of relevant details about history (despite purporting to have historical depth) – than through its actual content. Some of the context, moreover, was blatantly incorrect: Banyarwanda are mostly the sons and daughters of migrants who arrived in Congo-Zaire during or after the 1930s. As for the omissions, the denial of rights to citizenship and property is not the one-sided story it appears to be: in particular, SCF's background piece says nothing about Mobutu's patronage from which some Banyamulenge and Banyarwanda (mainly Tutsi) profited so handsomely throughout the 1970s. And where is the non-Rwandaphone population in SCF's reconstruction of the past? The sketch did provide insight into several important aspects of *regional* instability (for example, military incursions into Rwanda, unrest in Burundi, UNHCR's failures, Mobutu's exploiting the 1994–96 crisis to save his political skin), but then fell flat when analysing the dynamics of the local political situation. Nonetheless, SCF claimed that its strategy for action was 'based on a number of assumptions as to how the crisis [would] develop, recognising both the regional, *as well as the local*, dynamics of the situation' (Save the Children Fund 1996: 3, emphasis added).

If the narrative the GOR/RPF helped to popularise via the press and concerned organisations omitted vital information regarding local modern history, it compensated by zealously wanting to take international observers back to times long gone. For a start, the dominant narrative insisted that Europe had inflicted lasting damage on the Great Lakes region starting in Berlin in 1885, when the colonial powers had assembled to decide on the shape of Central Africa's borders. Anastase Gasana, Rwanda's then Foreign Affairs Minister, spun an interesting yarn about Rwanda's border with Zaire, arguing in effect that the decision of 1885 – when an irresponsible international community had split Rwanda – still had consequences for achieving responsible government today. Gasana:

[The] Berlin conference ... resulted in the [European] powers artificially parti-
tioning Africa. The rights of the populations of Rwandan origin living in Kivu
must be protected.[7]

By acting irresponsibly in Berlin in 1885, and later in 1910, when the
Mwami (King) of Rwanda lost control over certain chiefdoms in North
Kivu, the international community had ensured that Kivu's 'Rwandan
populations' would be at risk a century later. Especially at risk in 1996
would be the Tutsi component of those severed from Rwanda's central
political power, but note how Gasana politely refers to 'the populations'
(plural).

Despite its simplifications, or perhaps because of them, Gasana's
message came through loud, clear and convincingly: since Rwanda's
original/real borders had included large tracts of Kivu, which Rwandan
President Bizimungu confirmed on a map he paraded in front of the
world's cameras,[8] Rwanda now had a duty to protect those at risk. Away
from the attention of the world press, however, Bizimungu's speeches in
Kinyarwanda turned 'the need to protect' into 'the right to exterminate'.
In a muscle-flexing speech in Cyangugu on 10 October 1996, the
president did not conceal his conviction that only Tutsi, that is, Zairean
Banyamulenge and the Rwandan Tutsi exiled in or after 1959 (so-called
59-ers), needed protection (Willame 1997: 93–4).[9] By now, the
Rwandan authorities were more than prepared to come to the rescue of
'the Banyamulenge', that small community (of Mulenge Tutsi) suddenly
elevated to an ethnic group. Bizimungu had made this clear in an earlier
part of the speech when he too challenged the artificiality of the
Zaire–Rwanda border. Bizimungu evoked a 'Greater Rwanda', which
included the highlands where Banyamulenge lived and where, he
claimed, they had lived for several hundred years. Importantly, this
Greater Rwanda, according to Bizimungu, had enjoyed excellent
relations with its Bahunde neighbours until the western colonial powers
arrived on the scene (see Willame 1997: 97).

But the 'Greater Rwanda' Bizimungu evoked was more of an 'imagined
community' (Anderson 1991), since historical research had never found
proof of any close links between the Kinyarwanda-speaking pockets in
South Kivu and the Tutsi court in central Rwanda, which had expanded
its administration westward in the second half of the nineteenth century
(Willame 1997: 97). The original Banyamulenge probably came from
Kinyaga, south-western Rwanda, from where they had fled Rwabugiri's
advancing army (Newbury 1988: 48–9), or they may have arrived at a
later date following a dispute with Mwami Musinga (see Depelchin
1974). These findings from field research, which speak of political fission,

cast doubt on the idea of a moral community severed by external (European) intervention. Pre-colonial Rwanda, moreover, had been made up of several Tutsi dynasties (Rwanda, Ndorwa, Gisaka, Bugesera, Burundi), which regularly fought one another.

The fiction of a fully unified '*Greater Rwanda*', which Bizimungu promoted map-in-hand also at other times, was the president's way of saying that if Rwandan troops were now fighting in Zaire (although this was still officially denied), they were in fact fighting on home soil (Willame 1997: 97). Knowing the world to be mostly ignorant about eastern Zaire's complex past, and by now (late 1996) more than willing to accept the intellectual authority of the GOR/RPF, Bizimungu made it easy for his beginners' class.

Also of interest is that Bizimungu's speech of 10 October 1996 obscured the situation in Masisi, North Kivu, at the end of the 1990–94 war by suggesting the RPF could have gone all the way to take Masisi, but had refrained from doing so because it respected Zaire's sovereignty. The claim requires comment. First, in July 1994, Masisi was relatively calm. Second, the question arises as to who exactly needed saving. During the 1993 'ethnic clashes' in North Kivu, there had been a roughly equal number of IDPs and fatalities on either side of the conflict – that is, among 'autochthones' (Hunde, Nyanga, Nande, Tembo ...) and Banyarwanda – while aggression by autochthones had not differentiated between Banyarwanda Hutu and Tutsi. Although Banyarwanda Hutu had begun to set themselves off from Banyarwanda Tutsi in the early 1990s, notably with the RPF invasion of Rwanda, the 1993 aggression in North Kivu had targeted Banyarwanda irrespective of ethnicity along Hutu–Tutsi lines. Anti-Banyamulenge sentiment only raised its ugly head in August 1996 with the return to Zaire of Banyamulenge (and Tutsi refugees from 1959–63) who had fought in the RPF's Rwanda campaign. According to Willame (1997: 90), there is no evidence of pogroms against Banyamulenge before August 1996.

The dominant narrative on 'the crisis' of eastern Zaire and its 'solution' also portrayed Banyamulenge as fighting within a strongly cohesive alliance. Kagame's propaganda machine dictated that the ADFL be understood as having originated in the *rapid* offensive of 'the Banyamulenge', whose 'armed struggle quickly spread to encompass a coalition of *other anti-government forces* in the region' (de Waal 1997: 206). To the uninformed, this part of the narrative may once again have sounded plausible, but people willing to ask questions about the pre-1994 situation will have seen through this portrayal of solidarity.[10] Of course, all who joined the ADFL had an immense dislike for the Mobutu of the 1990s, but the groups involved also came with their own 'mandates' and histories of internal conflict. Indeed, it would not be too long before the first signs of a cut-throat struggle within the victorious ADFL came to light (details in Pottier 1999a: 168). From the point of view of the GOR/RPF, however, such attention to detailed local knowledge could not be tolerated, since it might result in 'the world' understanding that the ADFL was a desperate fantasy.

Particularly intriguing to those informed about local history was Kabila's teaming up with Banyamulenge (the group that had helped Mobutu to stamp out the mid-1960s rebellion in which Kabila had featured as a second-rank officer) and Banyamulenge being joined by Mayi-Mayi, whose basic agenda is to rid eastern Zaire of every trace of 'Rwandan' influence. Moreover, many Babembe (Kabila's comrades from the 1960s) had refused to join the ADFL as they disapproved of the partnership with Banyamulenge; some went on to fight the ADFL in the early stages of the uprising.[11] All this provided clear signals that spoke of a disaster being inflicted on Kivu. The bottom line was that the various groups that made up the ADFL were not so much joined by their hatred for Mobutu (the official, RPF-functional line) than torn asunder by competing agendas and claims over land. As the GOR and RPF could ill afford such 'revelations', Kagame's propaganda machine made sure that the 'politically correct' line on the crisis would dispense with large chunks of local history.

LOCAL AND ACADEMIC KNOWLEDGE DEBUNKED: THE 'STIFLED' VERSION

Rwanda's leaders and their international backers approached the tension in Kivu purely in terms of the 1994 Rwandan genocide: *Tutsi in Kivu were persecuted because of their ethnicity by Rwandan Hutu who continued the genocide.*

Such an approach is too narrow. Regarding the violence in eastern Zaire in 1996–97, there is a need to broaden the picture, a need to ask questions about Kivu politics in some historical depth. What happened in Kivu following the arrival of the Hutu refugees resulted not just from the latter's presence but also from a chain of political events preceding their arrival. At the very least, any claim to knowledge regarding 'the crisis' in eastern Zaire needs to take account of the events of 1993. For indeed, when Rwandan Hutu extremists pushed into Masisi between November 1995 and May 1996, which they did, they joined forces with Zairean paracommando *and Zairean Hutu*. Among the latter were many who had lost their lands and property in 1993 as a result of the assault by 'autochthonous' groups; an assault in which *all Banyarwanda* had been targeted. The joint push into Masisi purged the area of its Tutsi and of a significant number of 'autochthonous' Hunde and Nyanga. Thousands died, among them ten Hunde chiefs, while some 15,000 Tutsi fled to Rwanda (Pottier 1999a: 156). The pattern of the fighting, however, had been exceptionally complex in that Mayi-Mayi, too, had participated in the killing and expulsion of Tutsi.[12] But whatever it was, the slaughter and the expulsions could not have been *simply an extension* of the Rwanda genocide. While the presence of Rwandan Hutu extremists was the single most important factor in explaining anti-Tutsi sentiment in Zaire in 1996, the violence was also fed in important ways by conditions that preceded the refugees' arrival.

To understand better Kivu's 'battlefield of political knowledge', to re-coin a celebrated phrase (see Long and Long 1992), we need to return to the early part of the twentieth century when Belgian colonists privatised vast tracts of land to create coffee plantations and national parks. Following expropriation, the pressure on land increased steadily, especially with the arrival of wave upon wave of migrants from Rwanda. These 'people from Rwanda' (*Banyarwanda*) had either fled economic hardship (periodic drought and famine, land scarcity) or been picked by the colonial administration to work in eastern Congo (Newbury 1988; Fairhead 1990; Pottier and Fairhead 1991). In North Kivu, Rutshuru received a great many immigrants in the 1930s, but the bulk ended up in Masisi, then a sparsely populated region. Significantly, Belgium pursued a kind of apartheid by having separate settlements for Banyarwanda and so-called 'autochthones', and by appointing Hutu chiefs. The latter strategy created a contrast with Ruanda-Urundi, but resulted in deep frustration for educated autochthones.[13]

To obtain land for Banyarwanda, the colonial authorities made autochthonous chiefs sign 'cessation acts' in return for financial recompense (Pabenel 1991: 33). However, with in-migration from Rwanda continuing unabated in the 1940s and 1950s, the potential for conflict over land was destined to erupt in the deregulatory aftermath of Congo's independence. At this point, autochthones voted with their feet and entered areas previously reserved for Banyarwanda. It was the beginning of a protracted struggle for local and regional power (and resources) in which Banyarwanda and autochthones would find themselves in opposing camps. Increasingly, Banyarwanda became 'potential targets for confrontation because of their allochtony', their foreignness (Willame 1997: 44). Still, despite needing to keep a low profile, several Banyarwanda, notably from Rutshuru, rose to prominence in commerce and politics.

In the first half of the 1960s, Banyarwanda saw their sense of vulnerability increased, first by the 1959–61 wave of Tutsi refugees from Rwanda, some 60,000, who fled the pogroms there as independence was declared, and then again following Rwanda's 'mini-genocide' of 1963–64, which caused a further Tutsi exodus into Congo.[14] The combination of fast-increasing demographic pressures and the general affluence of Banyarwanda triggered the first 'nationality crisis'. Until then, Banyarwanda had had voting rights in the young (pre-Mobutu) *République Démocratique du Congo*, and the nationality question had not arisen. But land scarcity and the economic success of Banyarwanda made 'nationality' an issue. The more Banyarwanda and autochthones jostled for political positions, the more strongly the theme of *l'étranger*, the foreigner, emerged in political discourse. Kivu's autochthones now accused Banyarwanda of large-scale infiltration, an accusation resulting in the 1964 Constitution restricting the Congolese nationality to those residents who could prove they had 'an ancestor who belongs or belonged to a tribe, or part of a tribe, established within the Congolese territory before 18 October 1908' (cited in Willame 1997: 46). The clause excluded, at least in principle, the several hundred thousand Banyarwanda who had arrived in Congo since the 1930s, which was virtually the entire Banyarwanda population.

Following the 1964 change in legislation, Masisi's Hutu administrators, appointed under colonial rule, were replaced by Hunde. It was a blow to the general prosperity of Banyarwanda, who now began to lose land, houses, shops, cattle and plantations. Banyarwanda did fight back to reclaim their civil and political rights, sometimes through determined acts of resilience, but their vulnerability remained. Particularly harmful was the accusation in 1964–65 that Banyarwanda had become *mulélistes*, that they colluded with the anti-government rebels in eastern Congo (Uvira-Fizi region). The accusation was unfounded, even though a sizeable group of Rwandan Tutsi refugees from 1959–63 had joined the rebellion (Young 1970: 996), and resulted in scores of Banyarwanda – *Hutu and Tutsi* – being tortured, expelled or killed.

Rwandan Tutsi exiled around independence had joined the *Armée Populaire de Libération* on the principle of 'reciprocal assistance in the course of military engagements' (Lemarchand 1970: 213). Back in 1970, Lemarchand had specified this all-important principle:

There was a common awareness of the advantages that either party would draw from the realisation of the other's objectives: if the Congolese ['rebels'] were to gain permanent control over the [eastern] border areas, the refugees would then enjoy the benefit of a 'privileged sanctuary' for organising border raids into Rwanda; likewise, if Rwanda's republican [Hutu] regime should fall before the completion of their task, the Congolese could expect similar advantages for themselves. (Lemarchand 1970: 213)

This remarkable passage explains in the most lucid terms why some 30 years later, in 1996, a Congolese rebellion could be launched from within a Tutsi-ruled Rwanda.

The anti-government rebellion in Uvira-Fizi, however, would bring a welcome change of fortune for some Banyamulenge and Banyarwanda, since Mobutu's army crushed it with the help of mercenaries and local groups opposed to Babembe – including Shi from Kabare and Tutsi from Mulenge (later renamed Banyamulenge). The contribution of Banyamulenge in crushing the rebellion lives on in people's memory. After a visit to South Kivu, Willame wrote:

People in South Kivu easily remember that the Banyamulenge helped the national army with its bloody repression of local rebellions during the 1960s. This also applies to Maniema, where entire villages still accuse one another of participation in the clean-up campaign.[15]

When in 1967 Kabila re-entered Fizi to set up his own base at Kibamba, 'where he was welcomed by the inhabitants of the *collectivité* of Mulenge' (Cosma 1997: 15), Congo's president-to-be pursued his utopian socialist dream. On 24 December 1967, he launched the *Parti de la Révolution Populaire* (PRP). Kabila's followers, however, were mainly Babembe from the *secteurs* of Mulenge, Ngandja and Itombwe; followers who had remained faithful (1997: 43). Importantly, these followers did not include Banyamulenge. An obvious fact at the time, but phenomenally important three decades later and not understood by the 'international community' when it developed its opinion on the crisis, Babembe from Mulenge had arch enemies in their Banyarwanda Tutsi neighbours, the Banyamulenge-to-be. While relations between these Tutsi pastoralists and South Kivu's autochthonous groups (Babembe, Bavira, Bafulero) had remained peaceful until the mid-1960s, when contact was restricted to trading in cattle and cattle products, relations had soured after Mulenge's ethnic Tutsi had fought *on Mobutu's side*.

On quashing the *muléliste* rebellion, Banyamulenge support for Mobutu turned into concrete economic advantage for some. Besides being empowered to levy taxes on autochthones in local markets, certain Banyamulenge now also had the power to acquire extra land.

According to B. Muchukiwa [n.d.], Banyamulenge notably augment their economic powers: these old 'volontaires' recruited by the Congolese army to track down the [*muléliste*] rebels 'now have the means to impose themselves on the local populations and begin to claim lands, as well as tribute and taxes in a number of markets within Itombwe'. (Willame 1997: 83)[16]

Equally important, however, not just certain Banyamulenge but the *entire* Banyarwanda community, though Tutsi more than Hutu, came to benefit from Mobutu's strategic plan for the region. This plan encouraged the political ascendancy of leaders whose ethnic groups could never be a threat to central government – either because they were numerically insignificant at the national level or because of their ambiguous status. Fulfilling both these conditions, Banyarwanda, and within this group Tutsi more than Hutu, were ideal candidates for political promotion.

The chief promoter of Banyarwanda success was Barthélémy Bisengimana, who in 1969 came to direct the *Bureau de la Présidence de la République*, a post he held for eight years. Termed 'the godfather' of all Banyarwanda, but 'particularly of Tutsi', Bisengimana made the *Bureau Politique du MPR* adopt a law in 1972 through which all who originated from Ruanda-Urundi but had lived in Zaire permanently since 1 January 1950, were granted the Zairean nationality (Willame 1997: 53). This new law did not solve the problem of the Tutsi '59-ers', but their presence in Zaire ceased to be a point of public debate and confrontation.

For Kivu's autochthonous groups, however, the 1972 law was a crushing political defeat: Nyanga, Hunde, Nande and others turned 'minority groups' overnight. And worse was to come. One year later, with the passing of the Bakajika law, another blow followed: prosperous Banyarwanda not only clawed back the property and lands they had lost in 1964, but they also acquired important new tracts of land. Protected *and zaïrois*, the Banyarwanda elite, mostly Tutsi, bought into the economy, their prosperity now seemingly unstoppable. When foreigners (non-Africans mainly) had their properties seized by the state later that year, as part of Mobutu's drive for *authenticité*, the Banyarwanda elite acquired up to 90 per cent of the European plantations in Masisi and Rutshuru (see Mafikiri 1996).

But the luck of the Banyarwanda/Banyamulenge elite would run out. When 'godfather' Bisengimana lost his position in 1977, dispossessed Hunde and Nyanga smallholders began to recoup, often through violent means, the properties they had lost earlier in the decade (Willame 1997: 55). Coinciding with the discourse of *authenticité*, now gathering momentum, Bisengimana's dismissal saw the ex-*Rwandais* turn *Rwandais* once again. The discourse also drove a firm wedge, possibly for the first time, into the Banyarwanda community: Hutu began to take their distance from Tutsi, declaring they were Hutu and *zaïrois*.

Fearing the process of colonisation by Banyarwanda had gone too far, autochthones did not buy this Hutu declaration. In June 1981, four years after Bisengimana's dismissal, the government of Zaire annulled the

1972 law. This hit Banyarwanda hard and triggered a progressive decline in their ability to exercise political authority. The decline occurred on two fronts: within the region vis-à-vis autochthones, and internally in terms of lineage and community organisation. The decline was not that sudden, however, but accelerated a process begun in colonial times (Fairhead 1990, for lowland Bwisha; Pottier and Fairhead 1991, for highland Bwisha).

In South Kivu, too, the situation had grown tense by the late 1980s. When in 1987 Wilungula Cosma, who originates from Fizi, researched the organisation of Kabila's maquis (1967–86), relations between Babembe and Banyarwanda Tutsi of Mulenge had dropped to an all time low. In July of that year, the relationship was marred by accusations, skirmishes, poisonings and the boycott by Banyarwanda of the legislative elections (Cosma 1997: 24). The boycott stemmed from anger at the fact that none of the Banyarwanda candidates had made it on to the ballot papers. The boycott also reminded how the results of a previous municipal and local election had been annulled after a 'Rwandan' candidate was elected.

By the late 1980s, ethnic prejudice by Babembe against their Tutsi neighbours, now calling themselves Banyamulenge, was rampant. Cosma:

Babembe consider the Tutsi as good-for-nothing, incapable, without physical force, uncircumcised weaklings, an inferior people, people who spend the entire day drinking milk, who weep not for their dead but for their cows. For their part, Tutsi consider Babembe to be turbulent, barbaric, excessively proud, and only fit to do heavy [farm] work in exchange for a calf close to death. (Cosma 1997: 24, referring to Kimona Kicha 1982)

Stereotypes these may have been, but they reflected a tense undercurrent caused partly by the political ambitions of certain prominent Tutsi, including '59-ers', and partly by the memory of how Banyamulenge had fought on Mobutu's side to quash the Uvira-Fizi rebellion.

For Banyarwanda in Kivu, the crisis deepened in 1991 when the *Conférence nationale souveraine* (CNS) excluded their representatives. At the CNS, there were many diatribes against 'the province's exploitation by "foreign Rwandans"' (Willame 1997: 63), *the target being all Banyarwanda, not just Tutsi*. The exclusion was triggered in part because of the past pro-Mobutu stance of Banyarwanda (autochthones were now exceedingly anti-Mobutu), and in part because of the strong support and sympathy Banyamulenge and Banyarwanda Tutsi had shown for the Rwandese Patriotic Front (RPF) when it invaded Rwanda in October 1990. Sympathy and support were interpreted to mean that

Banyarwanda – all Banyarwanda, but Tutsi more than Hutu – identified with Rwanda and should be denied the right to Zairean citizenship. North Kivu's deputy governor expressed popular sentiment when he declared:

History has shown that the Tutsi, ever hungry for power, are innate destabilisers. By every possible means they seek to dislodge law and order ... The people of Walikale zone have elected me to ensure the zone does not become overrun by Tutsi ... (quoted in Vlassenroot 1997: 53)

To their exclusion from the CNS, Banyarwanda Hutu reacted in self-defence, just as they had done in the late 1970s, proclaiming strongly and openly to be *zaïrois*. Taking their distance from 'the Tutsi', Hutu now ran their own voluntary organisation, the *Mutuelle agricole des Virunga* (MAGRIVI), and prepared for confrontation with autochthonous leaders, which they did initially through a campaign of civil disobedience. Tensions escalated in March 1993 after the replacement in Walikale and Masisi of all

gendarmes from outside the region by officers of Nande, Hunde and Nyanga origin ... According to the bishop of Goma, there would have existed a plan for the systematic liquidation of Banyarwanda living in 'red zones' [Ngabu 1993: 38ff]. (Willame 1997: 65)[17]

Banyarwanda Hutu were massacred in Walikale market and in several churches. This happened also in Masisi, where Hutu fought back. Casualties were high *on both sides*, among Banyarwanda and autochthones, as was the number of internally displaced persons (IDPs) that resulted from the fighting (Willame 1997: 66). Importantly, of the estimated 350,000 displaced (UNICEF/OXFAM estimate), roughly 100,000 had yet to return home by the time the Rwandan refugees arrived in July 1994 (Simmance, Page and Guindo 1994: 15). This suggests that a significant number of displaced Banyarwanda Hutu were likely to be found prepared to fight for the right to return to Masisi when Rwandan Hutu refugees poured across the border. These displaced Zaireans did not need to be 'brainwashed' (see Kiley, above) before joining the assault on Masisi.

The pre-1994 history of North Kivu, but also of South Kivu, warns that it is analytically incorrect to isolate 'the Tutsi' as a long-term target for persecution by autochthonous groups. Before 1994, Tutsi *were* targeted, but as members of the larger Banyarwanda group, a group known to have benefited substantially from close collaboration with Mobutu. Within Kivu, autochthones perceived these benefits as threatening both their livelihoods and the region's political stability. The details of Kivu's pre-1994 history, however, were conveniently ignored in the GOR/RPF's portrayal of the 'Kivu crisis'; a portrayal cast in simplistic, essentialist ethnic terms, that is, all aspects of the conflict being linked to the 1994 refugee exodus. We should now take a closer look at how the refugee crisis made its mark on the struggle for land and resources within Kivu.

IMPACT OF THE RWANDAN REFUGEE CRISIS

Predictably, the Rwandan Hutu refugee influx resulted in Zairean Hutu (many still displaced) joining forces with *interahamwe* to attack Zairean Tutsi. This happened in Rutshuru first, then in Masisi. The attacks in Rutshuru may have been an extension of the Rwanda genocide, but they also came in the wake of an attack on Bunagana by members of the Uganda People's Defence Forces (UPDF) in collaboration with elements of the Tutsi-dominated Rwandese Patriotic Army (RPA) (Pottier 1999a: 157). *The violence in Masisi, however, was aimed not just at Tutsi but also at autochthones*, for the attackers included many displaced Banyarwanda Hutu bent on retaking the lands they had lost to autochthones after 1981 (often in 1992). Those with whom they attacked, Rwandan Hutu refugees moving into Masisi for the first time, also felt they had a rightful claim to land, for they pursued a logic very similar to that with which the Government of Rwanda operated: Masisi was part of Rwanda.[18]

Between November 1995 and May 1996, the assault on Masisi drove some 250,000 autochthones (Hunde and Nyanga mainly) from their homes, while tens of thousands of Tutsi fled to Rwanda.[19] Several hundred Tutsi were killed. Casualties among autochthones are not so well documented, but it is known that over 400 Hunde and Nyanga were killed in December 1995 alone.[20]

Given the massive displacement of autochthones, it was no surprise that Mayi-Mayi guerrilla soldiers reappeared on the scene in North Kivu.[21] They had a history, a recent history, of wanting to rid Kivu of every form of 'Rwandan' influence and a somewhat older history of guerrilla warfare. These Mayi-Mayi targeted especially the Zairean army (FAZ), the cause of their dispersal in 1988 (Willame 1997: 71–2), but Banyarwanda were their second favourite target. This explains why in May 1996, Mayi-Mayi simultaneously terrorised villages in Rutshuru, where Banyarwanda were numerous, and waged battle also with the FAZ (Pottier 1999a: 157 for details).

Once the events of 1995–96 are situated historically, that is, understood as they revolved around a 30-year-long struggle over resources/land in a politically charged setting in which Banyarwanda, often Tutsi, had at times had the upper hand, it becomes clear that the explosive situation in North Kivu in 1996 was too complex to be explained through short-hands such as 'ethnic cleansing' or 'genocidal virus'. Detailed, contextualised knowledge of Kivu's 'problem' warns us not to fall for the simplistic crisis narrative which reduces 'the crisis' in eastern Zaire to a mere extension of the 1994 Rwanda genocide – the narrative the GOR/RPF and their sympathisers have popularised so very successfully.

What about South Kivu? As with North Kivu, one must guard against the temptation to see the 1996 troubles of 'the Banyamulenge' as caused exclusively by Rwandan Hutu *génocidaires*. When it came, anti-Banya-mulenge sentiment was whipped up by *autochthonous* politicians and elites (Vlassenroot 1997: 56), whose grievances appeared anchored in well-remembered acts of opportunism. The close relationship between Banyamulenge/Banyarwanda and Mobutu, and the spoils their elites enjoyed after they helped crush the 1960s rebellion, were still fresh in people's minds in the early 1990s (see above). What also facilitated the relabelling of genuine Banyamulenge *Zaïrois* into *Rwandais* was that many young Banyamulenge had fought with the RPF in Rwanda from 1990 onwards. It is against this background of memories old and new that Mwami Lenghe III, *chef coutumier* of the Bavira, issued a letter in late October 1995 in which he spelled out that 'within his territory, the so-called Banyamulenge [are] like strangers' (Willame 1997: 90). Up to then, and until the middle of 1996, the question of their identity had been fought only through memoranda and verbal provocations; 'no pogrom had been undertaken' (Willame 1997: 90). While extremist Rwandan Hutu are the main reason why Banyamulenge came to be persecuted in 1996, the deadly links they forged with certain autochthonous leaders and Zairean Hutu must also be understood as grounded in the area's complex modern history.

It must be stressed, though, that the 'well remembered acts of opportunism' might not have been so well remembered had local politicians not been under pressure to prove themselves at a time of imposed change and uncertainty: that is, imposed democratisation, uncertainty about Mobutu's reward system for political allegiance, and the unsettling arrival of new refugees from Burundi. It was a time also when vast wealth was being created locally because of the inter-national humanitarian effort. Faced with these uncertainties (and opportunities), influential politicians in South Kivu tried to maintain their power base by crafting new alliances, which invariably involved a selective but forceful remembering of Kivu's complex past. (Vlassenroot 2002: 198)

Anti-Banyamulenge (and anti-'59-er') sentiment flared up in August 1996 when news broke that Banyamulenge who had fought with the RPF in Rwanda had returned to Zaire. Numbering between 800 and 3,000, these returnees, however, had been joined by soldiers from Uganda and Rwanda (Willame 1997: 93). Tension peaked instantly.

Willame, though, also refers to the presence of an enlarged FAZ force in Kivu, a source of tension equal to that of the returned Banyamulenge fighters. Following a shoot-out between Banyamulenge and the FAZ on the last day of August 1996, which left several FAZ soldiers dead, the authorities in Uvira declared that only 14 Banyamulenge families could now be called *zaïrois*, which led to officials calling for the expulsion and return to Rwanda of all other Banyamulenge. In the mayhem that ensued, many innocent, genuine Banyamulenge families were harassed and forced to flee to Rwanda, and sometimes killed.

In early October 1996, the FAZ–Banyamulenge skirmishes – with 'Banyamulenge' now a generic term referring to all Tutsi living in Kivu – developed into war. Armed Banyamulenge groups clashed not only with the FAZ, but also with Babembe, the old enemy from the 1960s, Kabila's one-time supporters. Seeing their former chief join the arch enemy, many Babembe chose to oppose the ADFL campaign.[22]

HOW MUCH DID KEY UN PERSONNEL UNDERSTAND? HOW DID THE UN RESPOND?

When in late 1996 'the Banyamulenge' burst on to the scene as a heavily armed force, people in Kivu knew that these 'ethnic fighters' were not on a good footing with Kabila and his followers. If the outside world did not see it that way, it was mostly because it had not shown any interest in eastern Zaire before the arrival of the 1994 Rwandan refugees. That 'the Banyamulenge' to whom the world was introduced were a creation, a hold-all category, the world did not seem to know either. And as few international players had ever heard of Banyamulenge, that relatively small community of Mulenge, it was easy to turn that community into a large ethnic group. Paul Kagame, though, must have known he was taking a risk: if Kabila had any supporters left in Mulenge, they were Babembe, not Banyamulenge. A lasting alliance between Banyamulenge and Kabila? Not very likely.

Having previously ignored the 'ethnic tensions' in eastern Zaire, especially in 1993, it was unsurprising that the 'international community' also failed to notice how the wheels of the (dis)information machine began to turn faster as the troubles spread. Being surrounded mostly by 'beginners' – journalists, diplomats, aid workers and newcomer academics – the GOR/RPF leadership spelled out what background knowledge the world needed to have to read the events 'correctly'. Its easy-to-grasp line would be bought and, in stark contrast to the 'shame of non-intervention' in Rwanda in April 1994, would culminate in the 'honourable' decision by the UN/US to stay away from the fighting.

Buying the GOR/RPF-functional version of 'the crisis' implied accepting that eastern Zaire was a place which spoke with one voice, that of the threatened Banyamulenge, now reconstituted as a *large* ethnic group. Other groups in Kivu remained unknown entities, one did not need to know or worry about them. More than that: ignorance about local political complexities could be turned into virtue. Those who accepted the GOR/RPF-functional perspective on eastern Zaire were now seeing the correct political light, which brought salvation for some of the old humanitarian sinners. Thus, African Rights congratulated Save the Children (SCF) on its level-headed decision not to call for intervention (de Waal 1997: 208) and hailed the *laissez-faire* stance at the UN, which effectively endorsed the so-called Zairean rebel offensive, not just as 'an imminent solution to the problem of the *interahamwe*', but as 'the beginnings of a solution for the residents of Central Africa' (1997: 212).

The GOR/RPF/African Rights' approach reduced complex events and history to a case of straightforward ethnic persecution induced by humanitarian naiveté: a 'fundraisers' catastrophe' which began and ended with the humanitarians' lack of political awareness. While there is much of value in the broad critique of humanitarian aid (see especially African Rights 1994), it is an insult to the majority of people in eastern Zaire (or any population in the world) when their complex – and well analysed – political universes are shrunk to a mere comment on humanitarian aid. Such reductionist reasoning, however, was part of the GOR/RPF's intellectual propaganda, part of that massive smokescreen with which to hide, and later justify, the invasion of Zaire by the Rwandese Patriotic Army.

The smokescreen worked. The day some 700,000 refugees were marched back to Rwanda, incidentally also the day the UN Security Council gave the all-clear for a scaled-down and strictly humanitarian intervention, 'interested' international parties found reason to backtrack quickly. Even before Mugunga camp was attacked and destroyed, Raymond Chrétien, the UN special envoy in the Great Lakes, had already bought the GOR/RPF line on the Banyamulenge persecution and uprising, and made it clear that the UN needed to respect Kigali's wishes. A week before the exodus in reverse got under way, Chrétien accepted that

two years after the genocide, Rwanda had 'the right to impose conditions' and that one needed 'to take [Kigali's] preoccupations into account at the very highest level' within the UN.[23]

The RPF, which stopped the genocide and conquered Rwanda, had been elevated to a morally superior force; the UN, in contrast, had become (and accepted it had become) a morally inferior player. Kigali was in full *military and intellectual* command. The GOR/RPF brand of 'local political knowledge' now counted for much more than the 'local knowledge' of the inhabitants of Kivu whom the front had come to colonise. It never occurred to political leaders in the US or Britain to ask in public whether the 'local perspective' and 'local solution' promoted in Kigali were representative of views within Kivu. It was the beginning of a killing spree off-camera (United Nations 1998).

It was not that alternative, more local perspectives were never articulated, but they failed to make an impact. In mid-November 1996, speaking in Brussels, Emmanuel Nashi, journalist and president of the NGO Sima-Kivu (*Soutien aux initiatives des mouvements actifs au Kivu*), argued that the war in Kivu could not be a liberation war. The region, which does not produce weapons, is now awash with armoury, he pointed out, and that can only mean two things: death and slavery; the people of Kivu had become the slaves of those who really profit from war, the international arms dealers. Other Sima-Kivu representatives pleaded for a speedy international intervention:

'Time presses,' says Marcellin Cishambo, 'for hundreds of Rwandans and Zaireans die every day. Why this ongoing palaver about UN neutrality? Nobody is neutral. A certain balance between the countries participating [in the UN force] ought to suffice.'[24]

Other voices from Zaire also reached Europe via the Belgian press. They, too, stressed that globalisation and slavery were issues ignored by those who argued against a UN-led intervention. In a joint statement, Thierry Nlandu (Amos) and Jac De Bruyn (Broederlijk Delen) expressed the thoughts of many in Kivu when they wrote:

every day we learn, with hard feelings, that we no longer control our own destiny, that the metaphor of 'globalisation' has brought us a new kind of 'slavery' ...

Allow us to ask this of the rulers of both Zaire and Rwanda: do you need the blood of so many powerless to maintain or consolidate your own power position? Does the president of Zaire need this civil war to emerge as the nation's saviour? Must Rwanda's rulers repeat the genocide blamed upon the former dictator [Habyarimana]? Is all this needed to keep the peace in Rwanda? ...

And what do we make of the Western passion for humanitarian relief, with all its publicity and living off prêt-à-porter catastrophes? Is it true that Westerners do not sleep in peace unless they can give to lighten the suffering of the wretched ones in Black Africa, whose misery was created by an unfair economic system?[25]

Before the arrival of the Rwandan Hutu refugees, and without any support from the Mobutu Government, with whom all collaboration had ceased by the beginning of the 1990s, Kivu's infrastructure, including the basic provision of health and education, had been ensured through self-help organisations, and international and local NGOs. In an interview (Goma, 29 April 1995), Dr Mugisho Soran'gave (CEMUBAC) told me that Kivu's health system had functioned reasonably well until the arrival of the Rwandan refugees. Until that time, a medical consultation had cost the equivalent of a bottle of beer (not cheap but affordable), and Kivu's hospitals had been well stocked in comparison with the rest of Zaire. All this changed when the refugee crisis drained the province of its medical personnel (now offered high salaries by humanitarian agencies) and of its supplies for preventative medicine. UNICEF, a major supplier in the past, was reportedly 'diverting from locals to refugees' (Soran'gave, 1995, Goma). Little wonder then that Kivu voices on the conflict, and on the prospect of domination by the authorities in Kigali with UN/US support, regularly spoke of globalisation and slavery. Regularly, but without impacting on the world powers which pulled the political, military and humanitarian strings.

UN diplomats who backed the no-intervention stance were not concerned about the shallow historical depth of the GOR/RPF-functional narrative. Such diplomats rather accepted a) that the crisis in Kivu could be explained solely in terms of an external presence, that is, Rwandan Hutu refugees whose actions Mobutu condoned; and b) that the military campaign 'the Banyamulenge' seemed to spearhead was a truly local uprising. These diplomats should have known better, they could have consulted a few academic works on the politics and history of eastern Zaire (for example, Verhaegen 1966, 1969; Lemarchand 1970; Young 1970; Coquery-Vidrovitch et al. 1987), but they chose not to. Empirically derived understandings were not considered. An empirically grounded approach to the Kivu crisis would have damaged the GOR/RPF, for insights would have resulted in the outside world understanding that the ADFL was a marriage of convenience doomed to be short-lived. As Kigali could not afford this projection, Kagame's propaganda machine made sure that the politically correct line would leave recent modern history out of the picture. It was better not to know, not to have area expertise, as the lives of UN troops would then be spared. Choosing not to know might also be lucrative in the long run, should western mining corporations secure concessions. The absence of any significant area expertise within the UN (see Barnett 1997) must have been a great help in this respect.

By late 1996, the international community accepted, through the UN Security Council, to approach 'the problem' of Kivu exclusively in terms of the danger posed by the 1994 refugees, whilst assuming that the people of Kivu were happy that the West should 'let it proceed'. The international community was found unwilling to use empirical knowledge to question the correctness of one particular, so-called 'local' narrative.

CONCLUSION: HEGEMONY AND DOMINANCE IN A CONTRACTING WORLD

The events in eastern Zaire, 1996, illustrate the danger – already well understood in debates on technology – that 'local knowledge' is still mostly treated as homogeneous, incontestable and applicable over fairly extensive areas. If the GOR/RPF version of 'the problem' of Kivu and 'its solution' managed to pass as a 'local solution' about which further questions did not need to be asked, it was in part because 'the world' assumed that an African perspective, *any African perspective*, was by definition local, complete and consensual. That some perspectives dominate while others are marginalised, that some perspectives are unrepresentative and locally challenged, was not considered. This happened, of course, not just because of the tendency to regard 'local knowledge' as bounded, but also because the post-genocide regime in Rwanda had effectively persuaded key members in the diplomatic world – ultimately the US and Britain, permanent members of the UN Security Council – that they had lost their right to understand Rwanda in terms other than those dictated by Kigali (see Pottier 2002). Some human rights groups and NGO workers also obliged. The GOR's 'local perspective', however, was just one version of 'the problem' and 'the solution', and only partially representative of views inside Kivu, but it was a perspective powerful enough to smother alternative interpretations. As a hegemonic force, the discourse crafted by the GOR/RPF, and internalised by the Clinton Administration and the UN Security Council, killed off not only the possibility of taking more local readings of politics seriously, but with it a vast number of people.

In this situation, it is still valid to consider, as Foucault did for different contexts, that dominant (outsider) representations of local knowledge have more to do with the exercise of power than with the search for 'objective' realities (Foucault 1970, Gardner and Lewis 1996: 71; also several chapters in this volume). The core issue here is that someone has the power to determine 'what constitutes knowledge, what is to be excluded and who is designated as qualified to know' (Hobart 1993: 2). In the case of eastern Zaire, the power in question was a power derived initially from victimisation in genocide and, later, cultivated by the GOR/RPF through the skilful manipulation of international guilt.[26] Anthropologists may have developed an optimistic view on hegemony in the context of 'normal' development, seeing the local in the global and the global in the local (Moore 1996; Long 1996), but it is a view difficult to extend to the realm of local political knowledge in Central Africa's Great Lakes region.

ACKNOWLEDGEMENTS

I wish to thank the Leverhulme Trust for funding the sabbatical year (1997–98), which enabled me to undertake a comprehensive overview of the international press coverage of the Rwanda and Great Lakes crisis. I also thank all who commented on the draft for this chapter, presented at the AS 2000 Conference, and in particular Professor Ralph Grillo (University of Sussex), who chaired the session during which the draft chapter was discussed.

NOTES

1. *The Washington Post*, 9 July 1997.
2. What masqueraded within the UN as a 'local solution' to Kivu's 'problem' was an exogenous solution prepared in Rwanda and buttressed by the 'international community'.
3. See Gowing (1998: 4).
4. *International Herald Tribune*, 8 November 1996.
5. *The Times*, 8 November 1996.
6. *The Times*, 8 November 1996; emphasis added.
7. *Le Vif/L'Express*, 8 November 1996. (All translations from French or Dutch are my own.)
8. See, for example, *Le Vif/L'Express*, 8 November 1996.
9. A copy of the speech, translated from Kinyarwanda, has been deposited in the *Archives de l'Institut Africain-CEDAF (Brussels)*, III-2985.
10. Willame, in *Le Vif/L'Express*, 8 November 1996; for details see Cosma (1997). Exaggerated claims of solidarity had also been part and parcel of the propaganda surrounding the 1964 rebellion in eastern Congo (Young 1970: 968).
11. *La Libre Belgique*, 20 October 1996.
12. *La Libre Belgique*, 3 December 1996.
13. While 'autochthone' is invariably a construct, its phenomenal emotive and political power must be recognised.
14. These killings were prompted by the failed invasion of Bugesera by armed Tutsi *exiles* from Burundi.
15. Jean-Claude Willame, *Le Vif/L'Express*, 8 November 1996.
16. It is important to stress that not all Banyamulenge benefited. While some did, the majority continued to live in poverty (see Depelchin 1974).
17. 'Red zones' are areas that were occupied by the rebels in the mid-1960s; 'white zones' had remained under the control of central government.
18. These events illustrate Malkki's argument that refugees are not 'uprooted' but move within established conceptual-spacial universes (Malkki 1992).

19. *La Libre Belgique,* 15 May 1996.
20. *Le Soir,* 14 December 1995.
21. New aggressors also appeared on the scene, mainly groups of local bandits willing 'to work' for the highest bidder. Opportunistic banditry explains the clashes between Nyanga and Hunde youngsters in early 1995.
22. Reported in *La Libre Belgique,* 28 December 1996. The exceptions were Babembe from the *secteurs* of Mulenge, Ngandja and Itombwe (see above).
23. *Libération,* 7 November 1996.
24. *De Standaard,* 14 November 1996.
25. *De Standaard,* 15 November 1996.
26. Rwanda's first post-genocide prime minister, Faustin Twagiramungu, openly acknowledged this manipulation, following his departure from government in August 1995, see *De Standaard,* 14 September 1995.

REFERENCES

African Rights (1994) *Humanitarianism Unbound* (London: Discussion Paper)
Anderson, Benedict (1991) *Imagined Communities: Reflections on the Origin and Spread of Nationalism* (London: Verso)
Barnett, Michael N. (1997) 'The UN Security Council, Indifference, and Genocide in Rwanda', *Cultural Anthropology,* 12(4): 551–78
Coquery-Vidrovitch, C. et al. (1987) *Rébellions-Révolution au Zaïre, 1963–1965* (Paris: l'Harmattan)
Cosma, Wilungula B. (1997) *Fizi 1967–1986. Le Maquis Kabila* (Bruxelles: Institut Africain – CEDAF; Paris: l'Harmattan)
Depelchin, Jacques (1974) 'From Pre-Capitalism to Imperialism: A history of social and economic formations in western Zaire', PhD Dissertation, Stanford University
de Waal, Alex (1997) *Famine Crimes: Politics and the Disaster Relief Industry in Africa* (London: African Rights and the International African Institute)
Fairhead, James (1990) 'Fields of Struggle: Towards a social history of farming knowledge and practice in a Bwisha community, Kivu, Zaire', PhD Thesis, SOAS, University of London
Foucault, Michel (1970) *The Order of Things: An Archaeology of the Human Sciences* (New York: Random House)
Gardner, Katy and David Lewis (1996) *Anthropology, Development and the Post-Modern Challenge* (London: Pluto)
Gowing, Nick (1998) 'New Challenges and Problems for Information Management in Complex Emergencies: Ominous lessons learnt from the Great Lakes and Eastern Zaire'. Background paper to the 'Dispatches from Disaster Zones' Conference, London, 28 May
Hobart, Mark (ed.) (1993) *An Anthropological Critique of Development: The Growth of Ignorance* (London: Routledge)
Hoben, Allan (1995) 'Paradigms and Politics: The cultural construction of environmental policy in Ethiopia', *World Development,* 23(6): 1007–22
Kimona Kicha, A. (1982) 'Evolution du Système Matrimonial Bembe'. Unpublished dissertation (Lubumbashi: UNILU)

Lemarchand, René (1970) *Rwanda and Burundi* (New York: Praeger)

Long, Norman (1996) 'Globalization and Localization: New challenges to rural research', in H. Moore (ed.), *The Future of Anthropological Knowledge* (London: Routledge), pp. 37–59

Long, Norman and Ann Long (eds) (1992) *Battlefields of Knowledge: The Interweaving of Theory and Practice in Social Research and Development* (London: Routledge)

Mafikiri, Tsongo (1996) 'Mouvements de la population, accès à la terre et question de la nationalité au Kivu', in Paul Mathieu, Pierre-Joseph Laurent and Jean-Claude Willame (eds), *Démocratie, Enjeux Fonciers et Pratiques Locales en Afrique* (Bruxelles: Cahiers Africains/Afrika-Studies 23; Paris: l'Harmattan)

Malkki, Liisa (1992) 'National Geographic: The rooting of peoples and the territorialization of national identity among scholars and refugees', *Cultural Anthropology*, 1: 24–44

Moore, Henrietta (1996) 'The Changing Nature of Anthropological Knowledge: An introduction', in H. Moore (ed.), *The Future of Anthropological Knowledge* (London: Routledge), pp. 1–15

Newbury, M. Catharine (1988) *The Cohesion of Oppression: Clientship and Ethnicity in Rwanda, 1860–1960* (New York: Columbia University Press)

Ngabu, Mgr. (1996) 'Massacres de 1993 dans les zones de Walikale et de Masisi', *Dialogue*, 192, août–septembre

Pabanel, Jean-Pierre (1991) 'La Question de la Nationalité au Kivu', *Politique Africaine*, 41: 32–40

Pottier, Johan (1995) 'Representations of Ethnicity in Post-Genocide Writings on Rwanda', in Obi Igwara (ed.), *Ethnic Hatred: Genocide in Rwanda* (London: ASEN Publication), pp. 29–53

—— (1999a) 'The "Self" in Self-Repatriation: Closing down Mugunga Camp, Eastern Zaire', in Richard Black and Khalid Koser (eds), *The End of the Refugee Cycle? Refugee Repatriation and Reconstruction* (Oxford: Berghahn Books), pp. 142–70

—— (1999b) 'Reporting the New Rwanda: The rise and cost of political correctness, with reference to Kibeho', in Ruddy Doom and Jan Gorus (eds), *Politics of Identity and Economics of Conflict in the Great Lakes Region* (Brussels: VUB University Press)

—— (2002) *Re-Imagining Rwanda: Conflict, Survival and Disinformation in the Late Twentieth Century* (Cambridge: Cambridge University Press)

Pottier, Johan and James Fairhead (1991) 'Post-Famine Recovery in Highland Bwisha, Zaire: 1984 and its Context', *Africa* 61(4): 537–70

Save the Children Fund, SCF (1996) *Zaire: Military Intervention is not the Answer*. News statement on 6 November

Simmance, Alan, Trevor Page and Adama Guindo (1994) *Zaire: Reassessment Report* (Geneva: Department of Humanitarian Affairs), June

United Nations (1998) Report on the Situation of Human Rights in the Democratic Republic of the Congo, submitted by the Special Rapporteur, Mr Roberto Garreton, pursuant to Economic and Social Council decision 1998/260 of 30 July 1998

Verhaegen, Benoît (1966, 1969) *Rébellions au Congo. Tomes 1 et 2* (Bruxelles: CRISP; Kinshaha: IRES)

Vlassenroot, Koen (1997) '"Des Serpents Déloyaux": De Positie van de Banyarwanda in Oost-Zaire/DRC', *Noord-Zuid Cahier*, 22(4): 45–58

—— (2002) 'The Making of a New Order: Dynamics of conflict and dialectics of war in South Kivu, Democratic Republic of Congo', PhD Dissertation, Ghent University

Willame, Jean-Claude (1997) *Banyarwanda et Banyamulenge: Violences Ethniques et Gestion de l'identitaire au Kivu* (Bruxelles: Institut Africain-CEDAF; Paris: l'Harmattan)

Young, Crawford (1970) 'Rebellion and the Congo', in Robert Rotberg and Ali Mazrui (eds), *Protest and Power in Black Africa* (New York: Oxford University Press), pp. 968–1011

11 PLAYING ON THE PACIFIC RING OF FIRE: NEGOTIATION AND KNOWLEDGE IN MINING IN PAPUA NEW GUINEA

Paul Sillitoe and Robin A. Wilson

The island of New Guinea is adjacent to the 'Ring of Fire', the active plate margin that encompasses the Pacific basin, so-called for its active volcanoes and earthquakes. The tectonic activity results in the formation of valuable ores such as gold and copper associated with igneous rocks and tropical laterite weathering produces nickel and cobalt ores. In recent decades mining companies have increasingly sought to extract these, having developed the technology necessary to work in the island's remote mountains. In other parts of the island, where sedimentary geology predominates, exploration has revealed large petroleum and gas reservoirs which oil companies are seeking to exploit.

The impact of these primary extractive industries on the local tribal populations has predictably been considerable, but their response has been unpredictable from the mining companies' perspective. Companies have found themselves 'playing with fire' in their negotiations with local communities. It has taken them by surprise and cost them dearly, both financially and in damage to their reputations. Instead of behaving like the weaker party and submitting to the dominance of the economically more powerful company, local people resist uninvited incursions into their lives and prove themselves surprisingly effective negotiators adept at securing considerable compensation.

The tragic events on Bougainville made mining companies realise that local communities are not passive and revealed the dangers of ignoring their grievances. Rio Tinto, the company operating the Panguna mine, lost control of it when a popular rebellion occurred, resulting in several years of nasty civil war and the destruction of all capital investments.[1] In Indonesian-administered Irian Jaya there are repeated minor rebellions and clashes as indigenous Papuans protest at their treatment by the large

241

Tembagapura mine. People have resorted to desperate measures, with the Indonesian military ruthlessly repressing any protest, including the kidnap of foreign visitors, one such event in 1996 involving some Cambridge students on a field trip hitting the international headlines and advertising the Papuans' plight widely. The palpable tension between the mine and local community strikes anyone visiting the Porgera gold mine in the highlands of Papua New Guinea. The suppressed conflict is evident in the physical arrangements with fortified compounds and armed persons on both sides, company employees patrolling inside the mine site and local men cruising around outside in pick-up trucks.

It is not all doom and gloom. While local people in Papua New Guinea face problems with a mine's arrival, at the same time they have opportunities. Change is inevitable, as large-scale mineral extraction looks set to dominate the country's economy for the foreseeable future. All parties agree that there is a need to review negotiation strategies with a view to improving relations.

CORPORATE CITIZENSHIP AGENDA

Multinational companies in Papua New Guinea are increasingly reviewing their relations with local communities. They are under increasing pressure to deal more equitably with people and operate in environmentally sustainable ways. They find both their corporate culture and their operational procedures at mines challenged. Companies increasingly have to give a public account of their actions to employees, customers, investors, business partners and governments. Pressure to act more responsibly is coming, for example, from increasing numbers of ethical investors who wish to know how their share dividend is earned, and NGOs, some operating in Papua New Guinea, advertising negative impacts with campaigns overseas and boycotts at home. The response of multinational companies is the corporate citizenship agenda, at the core of which is the idea that companies are not only accountable formally for their actions to their owners, but also in less well-defined ways to other stakeholders and wider society.

Companies are recognising the rights of increasing numbers of stakeholders. These include: 'shareholders; employees; local community groups; existent and aspirant landowners; indigenous peoples; local, regional and national governments and policy makers; local, national and international non-government organisations (NGOs); academics and research organisations' (Placer Pacific Ltd 1997). Mining company staffs are increasingly aware of social responsibility issues. These are central to management. The larger multinationals are attempting to record and value their social contributions as they do the processing of minerals to create wealth. The idea of promoting better 'partnerships' with local people and furthering participation is implicit. This poses problems for both companies and communities. What is the meaning of 'participatory development' to a high-technology, capital-intensive industry? Managers demonstrate a good theoretical understanding of, and sympathy for, the idea of participatory development, it being part of their duty to implement corporate citizenship manifestos adopted by their mines' shareholding parent companies.

Furthermore mining companies wish to improve relations with local people to increase the efficiency and profitability of mining operations. But corporate citizenship reflects the values and aspirations of progressive western business to fulfil obligations beyond the financial bottom line. Yet, however well intentioned, it is not leading to noticeable improvements in company–community relations. Current approaches rely heavily on refining and improving existing strategies with respect to the corporate citizenship agenda but to what extent does good citizenship in the developed world apply to Melanesia? Companies are aware that they must promote methods and approaches that better encourage local stakeholders having a say over priority-setting, policy-making, resource allocation and access to public goods and services. The point is that the corporate climate is favourable to a radical review of company–community relations, and without this, without the powerful mining party on side, change would be unlikely.

INDIGENOUS KNOWLEDGE AND MINING

What is the relevance of indigenous knowledge to primary industry developments in Papua New Guinea? Answering this question illustrates well that indigenous knowledge in development extends well beyond issues relating to technical knowledge, which are the current focus of much work in this field (Sillitoe 1998a). When we talk about introducing indigenous knowledge to the mining and oil industry, this clearly has nothing to do with the technological exploitation of these resources. The societies of New Guinea traditionally had no use for metal ores, being until recently stone tool-using cultures, nor any use for petroleum products, lacking combustion engines. What local knowledge there is of these resources is of scant relevance to primary extraction industry. According to people in the Southern Highlands, for instance, the region's oil and gas deposits are the urine and excreta of an enormous seven-headed snake living underground, which has fled to their region from the Middle East to escape the fighting there (Ungutip, Wabis and Sillitoe

1999; see also Ballard 1998; Biersack 1999). These ideas derive partly from local cosmology, which features subterranean snakes that demand periodic appeasement rituals at certain sites. People say that companies use computers to fix the position of the snake, having seen sophisticated electronic equipment at drill heads, and then fire arrows into it. Other traditional lore associates the oil seeps found across the region with the tormented flight of a mythical white-skinned woman who had a hot stone thrust into her vagina, wherever she rested bleeding oil emerged from the ground (Sillitoe 1996; see also Stewart and Strathern 1999). Yet others talk of a subterranean, land-owning giant and attribute problems companies have drilling through certain strata to the activity of this spirit being wounded by drill bits (Stewart and Strathern 2002).

When we talk about indigenous knowledge in the context of Papua New Guinea mineral extraction we are referring largely to the need for a better understanding of, and accommodation to, people's knowledge of their rights to land, their tenure arrangements and their approach to payments such as compensation. The company's understanding of these determines in large part the distribution of royalties and other benefits from a mine, disputes over which are frequently at the root of mining disputes. It is inappropriate for companies to think that they can somehow deal with local communities as if they are companies too, by constituting landowning companies, when communities comprise conglomerations of sovereign individuals each with their own equal rights and recognising obligations to kin and others, but not recognising anyone as their leader who can represent their interests. The membership of these communities is also ever-changing and flexibly defined, subject to negotiation.

Regarding payments, the societies of New Guinea esteem highly the exchange of things between people, such behaviour is central to their social orders. Exchange for these people is central to social relationships. Exchange institutions comprise chains of transactions between persons standing in certain relationships to one another who recognise reciprocal moral obligations and not one-off payments. People view social life as a continual round of negotiation, it is on this that their exchange founded polities stand. The exchanges that morally constitute and validate relations are subject to constant negotiation. Local people predictably approach negotiations with mining companies in the same attitude. They have no idea of entering into a final and binding contract for 20 or more years. They approach relations with mines as if these should feature continual negotiations, and companies need to adopt their strategies to accommodate to this local expectation. Failure to do so promotes conflict as local people become increasingly frustrated and relations with the company deteriorate. But how is it possible to balance such opposing notions as presenting gifts to people with getting full return on investment?

COMMUNITY RELATIONS NOT COMMUNITY MANAGEMENT

It is widely agreed that local people and companies can effectively improve the outcomes of mining by modifying the ways they negotiate with one another. The interaction of mining companies with local communities is set within a wider series of relationships involving community, company, state and others, which affect negotiations, as parties interact with one another, each seeking to maximise its benefits from agreements (Figure 11.1).

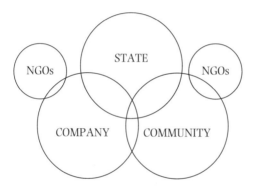

Figure 11.1   Community–State–Company (and NGOs) Relationships

A cultural gulf persists between mines and communities despite physical proximity and daily interaction. The conflict of values is apparent when visiting any of the large mines in Papua New Guinea. The policies of companies towards local people do not meet their aspirations. Current approaches to community affairs fail to appreciate the changing expectations and sentiments of local stakeholders. Mines wish to be in control, and understandably local people do not wish to be controlled. The challenge is to find ways to change the mines' conventional understanding of their relationship with local people and the conflicts this promotes between stakeholders without threatening their interests. It is necessary to devise ways that allow the tribal order to work out its own relationship with the corporate one, to avoid telling local people what they need. This is taking place, although largely not thought out but through unintentional impacts of mining and with unacceptable conflict.

The balance of power between companies and local people informs how mines see their role and communities react. While this chapter asks how the apparently weaker local community might achieve parity in negotiations, it queries the scope of mining company power. The literature portrays multinational companies and traditional communities on opposite sides, pitting the global economic resources of one against the local resources of the other, rendering communities powerless victims of capitalism. Mining companies often take this view, regarding themselves as the dominant partner, which maleficently shapes responses to community issues. But events indicate that their current attempts to manage and control relations with local communities are counterproductive. They question the extent of mining company power. Management's major concern with local communities is the risk of disruption to mine operations through violent confrontation that could put shareholders' investment in jeopardy. The Bougainville tragedy reinforces this view, as do continuing disruptions at all mines. Companies have learnt that they are 'playing with fire' in dealing with local communities.

Commercial aims – shaped primarily by responsibilities to shareholders to ensure good returns on investments – inevitably inform company compliance with legal socio-economic and environmental obligations. Corporate headquarters formulates policy accordingly and disseminates it via company vision statements, social and sustainable development plans and rehabilitation and closure plans. The making of policy in the boardroom largely excludes local communities – indeed casts them as enemies not partners. There is no structural mechanism currently for communities and companies to come together on equal terms outside of conflicts. Nonetheless, community affairs information is largely passed upwards from the bottom of the hierarchy to inform policy-makers in management, unlike technical mining directives that pass downwards. This is significant for incorporating local agendas into corporate policies and warrants further attention. It is also noteworthy that mine managers are aware of the complex issues in company–community relations and are trying to do something to address problems. 'Higher up in the company there is good dialogue but this fails to be passed down through the company and into the community' (Porgera Joint Venture Mine General Manager, 2001).

Local people need to be more involved in resource extraction developments, but it is unclear what will benefit them best and whether their understanding of what is in their long term interests has improved as a result of community relations policies. Information flow between stakeholders affects the size, nature and distribution of benefits accruing to local communities through negotiations. We have to improve cross-cultural communication. Satisfactory results for local people can only be obtained by increasing dialogue between parties so that each has a better idea of the others' view of what any developments entail. There is a need to improve local people's usually partial understanding of mining operations, promoting more realistic expectations of mines. They need better knowledge and understanding of the corporate partner and its aims, and the corporations need to seek to include local people in new ways that more closely reflect Melanesian understandings and expectations.

Again this is occurring in part. Cultural change is not one of uni-directional impacts upon communities. It is widely overlooked that their interaction changes both community and company. The relationship between them is increasingly complex. We find that companies have adjusted culturally to their encounters with local people, more effectively to negotiate with them, attempting to include them more efficiently in decision-making and reducing conflict. A process of 'Melanesianisation' of mining companies is occurring as they take steps, sometimes inadvertently, to facilitate the cross-cultural negotiations necessary for the everyday functioning of mines. It is an environment favourable to participatory methods and greater communication between company and community to facilitate fairer negotiations over benefits.

MINES AND DEVELOPMENT

We can see the cultural conflict of values between mine and community in company aspirations to bringing what it thinks is 'development' to the local region. Mine managers generally believe that the large sums of money invested in the country must benefit it. Yet regardless of the massive increase in revenue flow that has resulted post-independence, largely through the exploitation of mineral resources by foreign-owned mining and petroleum companies, the lives of the majority of Papua New Guineans have not significantly improved as measured by the provision of basic services such as health care, housing or education. Indeed for many, levels of social well-being have declined. The problem is urgent and there is need for further research as local communities come under increasing pressure to become 'partners' in the economic exploitation of their natural environment. The impression that development has stalled presents major problems for encouraging future investment in the country.

There is vigorous discussion in the mining industry about complying with legislation designed to protect the welfare of communities and it is common for companies to go well beyond mandatory compliance. Mines find themselves forced to perform quasi-governmental roles that are not expected of them in developed countries. They routinely fulfil many governmental functions that go beyond basic provision of services necessary to run the mine, which the state would not otherwise supply. They commonly provide facilities such as hospitals and medical services, schools, roads, housing, power generation, clean drinking water, sewage treatment, telecommunications, shops and supermarkets. This serves to reinforce the perception that the company, rather than the elected government, is responsible for decision-making, benefits and change. Both academics and company officials question whether mines should take on provincial and national government functions where these are absent. They undermine further already weak government. What role should a mining company take in regions where government is perceived as weak, corrupt and ineffective? The paradox is that a company providing infrastructure support usurps legitimate government, promotes social fragmentation and undermines some customary practices, while any company that did not provide these services would be criticised as exploitative, unconcerned with local peoples' socio-economic well-being and ignoring corporate citizenship agendas.

We see here the clash between tribal orders and those of state and corporation. Mining companies are increasingly obliged to adopt quasi-governmental roles but without any real understanding of Melanesian society and its struggles to adjust. As a result, development and change often reflect and reinforce a western ethos of 'development' which may frustrate local people as they apparently attempt to conform to it, when it conflicts with their own aspirations. The apparent lack of success of many projects intended to benefit communities, not only mining company projects but also those of multinational agencies (for example, World Bank) and the Papua New Guinea Government, suggests either that the projects are improperly implemented or that local people have a different set of priorities and aspirations to those who seek to help them. The evidence indicates that neither side really understands what the other wants. The appropriateness of developments is rarely questioned. Is it possible for Papua New Guineans to have the benefits mines bring without having to adopt some aspects of the foreign social system that goes with them?

COMPANY RESEARCH AND CONSULTANCY CULTURE

The mines commission social research largely for monitoring purposes, to meet statutory obligations to make social and environmental impact assessments (Filer 1998, 1999), such as those contained in the Papua New Guinea Oil and Gas Bill (1998 Part 111, Div. 5, Sect. 47), which states that 'the licensee shall conduct – (a) a full-scale social mapping study; and (b) full-scale landowner identification study, of the customary landowners and the occupants of the land which will be comprised in the license area of the development'. Social impact assessment involves gathering data to monitor, predict and ameliorate the effects of proposed development projects. It is policy-oriented research that seeks to understand the local social environment to help forecast changes expected when a developer undertakes certain action (Burton 1996). The aim is to mitigate the impacts of large-scale industrial development and head off conflict (Oliver 1991). The companies submit reports to the national government, and often make some provision for them to be available to local communities. It is unclear how useful they are to communities or how many persons see them. Companies rarely publish the research. Reports focus largely on the mines that commission them and infrequently adopt a comparative view. The indications are that reports do little to improve the quality of communication or reduce the risk of conflict between community and company.

The widespread assumption is that problems can be overcome largely by monitoring of impacts and by increasing the efficiency of traditional corporate approaches to external relations. Mines seek to fit what monitoring they undertake to existing company endorsed strategies, and to distil from reports working guidelines for employees. These approaches at best lengthen periods of uninterrupted mine operation. Solutions that genuinely help local people require new research strategies that go beyond refining monitoring methodologies and data collection. The mining industry needs to do more than collect data if it is to approach community relations in radically different ways. For example, companies currently carry out too little research to implement research-driven community-oriented projects. They are coming to realise the shortcomings of over-reliance on social monitoring, reducing such work but with no adequate replacement. While the Bougainville tragedy initiated closer attention to socio-economic monitoring programmes (Carruthers 1990; Filer 1990; Brooks 1991; Quodling 1991; Thompson 1991; Moody 1992; Banks 1993; Imbun 1995), there is evidence that companies today carry out only minimal social impact analysis and monitoring work, necessary to comply with preliminary reporting demands at the beginning of a mining project (Banks 1999b).

Academic research is largely a by-product of consultancy work for the mining industry. Many researchers who work in the Papua New Guinea mining sector are academics who serve as consultants to the industry.

The multiple roles played by some actors is noteworthy. The commissioning of research by mining companies serves to illustrate the problems that arise when an interested commercial body funds research. They compromise the impartiality that should characterise research. They threaten to distort research by applying pressure for certain results and possibly suppressing findings that they do not wish to be known. The close involvement of companies in commissioning work inhibits criticism and research often overlooks problems or limitations in the corporate perspective. Anthropologists employed in consultancy work may receive terms of reference with which they are unhappy, such as to map the descent groups that own land in a certain region and conduct a census to establish their membership. These requirements have more to do with multinationals' capitalist informed expectations than they do with local social arrangements, which are more flexible than such demands allow. The consultants are afforded no opportunity to question in a fundamental fashion such terms of reference and are often obliged by personal necessity – that is, a need to earn a living – to go along with them and produce reports to order. Meanwhile it is not unusual to hear those who have engaged in this work informally complaining, for example, making quips about obliging local people to invent descent group theory. The variable recommendations of authors illustrate the conflicting pressures that they experience working as consultants for the mining industry; for example one author who has contributed greatly to our understanding of the social impacts of mining, advocates landowner compensation strategies at the earliest stages of exploration (Filer, Henton and Jackson 2000) of a kind that he asserts elsewhere lead to social disintegration (Filer 1990).

The majority of corporate-driven academic publications concern benefit distribution (Filer, Henton and Jackson 2000), community affairs functions (Power 2000) and documentation of monitoring data, which are not research. The commissioning of social monitoring exercises and use of data to advise on national legislative change avoids research into fundamental issues. They do not challenge nor offer alternatives to the western model of 'development'. Social monitoring and social impact assessment ignore the inappropriateness or otherwise of western-style business solutions and focus on practical data-gathering to inform companies of impacts. Recommendations focus on inadequate understanding of local communities by companies, and suggest that social monitoring and data collection can provide answers. Although it has the potential to promote participation in decision-making by affected communities (Goldman and Baum 2000), social mapping is not concerned with community involvement.

THREE ANALYSES

The mining literature covers four main topics: geology, economics, environmental impacts and socio-cultural issues. It comprises academic work, technical reports (commissioned by mining companies, NGOs, Papua New Guinea government departments and multinational agencies such as the World Bank) and media reports. Research at mines throughout Papua New Guinea has resulted in an extensive literature: for example, on the Porgera Mine (Banks 1999b; Filer 1999; Imbun 2000; Hyndman 2001; Townsend 2001), the Ok Tedi Mine (Jackson 1991, 1992, 1994, 1998, 2001; Banks 1993; Townsend and Townsend 1997; Low and Gleeson 1998; Imbun 2000; Hyndman 2001) and the Lihir Mine (Filer and Jackson 1989; Filer 1996; Cochrane 2000). The literature presents us with three interpretations of the outcome of mining on local communities. Each reflects to some extent the situation at particular mines where the authors worked as consultants. All agree that as currently constituted large-scale mining in Papua New Guinea promotes social conflict with the local population. They all reflect on the likelihood of community breakdown and conflict.

Social Disintegration Analysis

The first assessment (Filer 1990) claims that the arrival of a mining operation sets off a cycle of self-destruction in communities with Melanesian social structures. It likens the establishment of a mine to priming a 'time-bomb'. It takes the Bougainville tragedy as a type case and predicts similar events elsewhere, for example at the Lihir and Porgera mines, where the scenario is elaborated to include conflict-ridden community-state relations and the evolution of a 'handout culture' dependent on compensation (Filer 1992, 1996; Filer, Henton and Jackson 2000). The Bougainville events challenged the idea that local communities will passively endure whatever changes come with a mine. Violence and premature mine closure result from mistaken reliance on kinship to redistribute rent payments through customary networks (Filer 1990). The demand by companies that communities define land ownership in fixed terms to facilitate the distribution of benefits by local representatives to families with rights to the affected area leads to problems in communities. Such attempts to apply non-local definitions to local people promote social conflict. The actions of persons the company designates as community representatives, who receive and distribute royalty and other payments, inevitably leads to entrenched grievances and promotes disputes within land-owning groups (Filer

1990; see also Local Gatekeepers and Land Management, below). The model predicts detonation of the landowner 'time-bomb' after one to two decades of mining operations (Filer 1990). During this period people experience increasing difficulties with customary inheritance mechanisms in passing responsibility for negotiating with the company from one generation to the next. Events at the Mount Kare prospect (Biersack 1992) suggest that the disintegration 'time-bomb' may have a more erratic, perhaps far shorter fuse than thought, depending on cultural and historical factors that vary between communities affected by mine operations.

The social impact and assessment work commissioned by companies may contribute in part to the problems identified in this analysis, particularly that involving social mapping, which seeks to record the distribution of resources between social groups and hence their 'ownership' for royalty payment and other purposes (Burton 1996; Filer 2000; Goldman 2000; Goldman and Baum 2000). The compilation of base-line surveys primes the 'time bomb'. The reports give social data, evaluating kinship structures and descent to help companies see how local people relate to their land and each other (for example, Filer 1992, 1994). They seek to document essentially fluid and ever negotiated social arrangements once and for all on paper and as such are ethnocentric exercises (while the same criticism can be levelled at ethnographic reporting, this is not nearly so dangerous as it does not seek to inform actions to intervene in people's lives). The value-for-money calculations that inform decisions to cut back on monitoring surveys may paradoxically worsen matters and prove flawed even on their own terms (leaving social responsibility and moral issues to one side), costing companies dear in the longer term. While social assessment surveys provide distorted data, they at least supply some information on which to base predictions of impacts on population, land-use and so on. Moreover, they may inform decision-makers in formulating mining company policies towards local communities and give some background intelligence to mine community affairs departments. On the other hand, such surveys date fairly quickly with changes in the community and without continued monitoring of the effects of its operations the company becomes increasingly ignorant of any shifts in local attitudes and practices, particularly build up of local tensions.

Capital Logic Analysis

The second assessment argues that the predestined financial lifecycle of mines results progressively in community disillusionment and mounting tension (Gerritsen and Macintyre 1991; Biersack 1992). It draws on socio-economic studies at the Misima gold mine. It has parallels with the disintegration model, but stresses growing disenchantment with the mine rather than community failure to deal effectively with compensation and royalty payments. The term 'capital logic' refers to the international financial imperatives that constrain operational decisions at mines that vary at different stages of the operation. The model focuses on declining economic benefits to the local community from mine construction to closure. At the outset, a prospecting company raises expectations in the local community but has no resources to mine the ore. When a mining company arrives to invest in the prospect it may initially meet local demands. During the mine's construction phase, resources are available for investment and time is at a premium, and companies tend to pay out money more freely to solve problems with communities, for example, meeting compensation claims for damage to property. The company will pay out large sums for land occupied by the mine site. Employment of local labour will also be at a maximum. Benefits from the mine are at their greatest for local communities. When the mine enters production, the company focuses increasingly on profitability, with creditors and shareholders to repay, and less readily concedes to local demands, seeking to resolve problems by negotiating settlements. Although it will distribute royalty payments as a share of production and continue to make some compensation payments, the company will find itself increasingly unable to meet the expectations and demands of local communities, which tend to increase during mining. Discontent in the community grows proportionately as benefits fail. Towards the end of a mine's life profitability decreases, until the cost of recovering the ore is no longer offset by its value (as the ore body is depleted, pre-mined stockpiles of lower-grade ore may be milled if metal prices allow). Returns to the local population decline too, until finally – assuming that the social disintegration 'time-bomb' has not detonated – mining ceases and with it wages, compensation and royalties to local people stop.

The model, like the previous one, has an air of inevitability about it, suggesting that the cycle of capital investment inexorably forces company and state to act as they do towards local communities, leading to dissatisfaction, apathy, hostility and even revolt. The implied inevitability is questionable. If it is simply the case that the flow of finance at different stages of a mining project is at the root of problems with local communities, then it should be within the power of companies to control. They should be able to offset the build up of disenchantment if they adopt a policy of level payments throughout a project, rather than high payouts at the start, which inflate local expectations, followed by declining returns. Indeed it should be possible for accountants to devise a scheme that gradually increases the level of payments over the lifetime of a mine, so keeping up with possible inflation in people's expectations, perhaps with investments to fund large pay-outs as the mine closes to boost the local economy at this difficult time. There is evidence that some companies are moving in this direction with the establishment of foundations to channel resources to local regions after mining ceases. Many problems remain with mine company–local community relations, indicating that while the flow of returns to the community is doubtless an important issue, it is not the only one.

Rules and Resources Analysis

The third assessment stresses the complexity of the interactions that characterise local community and mine relations, and seeks to analyse and evaluate events (Banks 1999a). It does not think that local community and mining company relations follow some inevitable trajectory. The word 'rules' refers to norms of responsibility and obligation imposed through individuals' social networks and 'resources' to the capital, knowledge, influence and power available to individuals. This model focuses on the distribution of power in the community–company–state relationship (Biersack 1992; Banks 1993, 1994, 1996, 1999a, 1999b; Burton 1996; Filer 1996, 1999). Early work refers to 'impacts' and exploitation of local communities, and portrays communities as uniform in their dealings with, and relations to mines (Hyndman 1987a, 1987b, 1994, 1995), whereas ethnographic evidence shows them to be internally factionalised, politically fragmented and varying in financial resources, education and access to information (Jackson 1991). The depiction of the mining company is equally misleading, portraying it as distant, homogeneous and rational (Kirsch 1989, 1993, 1996), with a unified corporate 'ethos' based on western business culture. Although company understanding of the relationship derives primarily from western corporate behaviour, the varied interests of its employees, several of whom are local, have a significant influence on relations. This approach questions the assumption that companies have the information necessary competently to manage 'impacts' on local communities, even if it were desirable for them to do so.

This interpretation reaffirms the complexity encompassed in such terms as 'community' and 'company' and points to the need to work closely with companies, as well as communities to understand fully problems with the negotiation process. Individuals in mining companies act in many ways as a community, parallel to the local one. Indeed mine staff include many members of the local community, which is particularly significant regarding company–community relations. The ratio of expatriate and Papua New Guinea national to local staff is important because it directly affects the ability of the company to negotiate with local people. The most recent employment data for the Porgera Gold Mine are typical (Table 11.1). The multilingual and multinational make-up of the Porgera workforce is characteristic of mines in Papua New Guinea (Banks 1999a). Many local people from the mine-affected area find employment with the Community Affairs Departments and represent an important connection between local communities and companies. The ethnic and gender make-up of the Community Affairs Departments partly reflects that of the mine affected region and, while the workforce is overwhelmingly male, females are usually better represented in them than in other departments.

Table 11.1   Direct Employment by Porgera Mine, 1990–2000
(Data supplied by PJV, 2001)

Year	% of Total Workforce from PNG	% of PNG Workforce Porgeran	% of PNG Workforce Engans (less Porgerans)	% of PNG Workforce Other PNG	% of Total Workforce Expatriate
1990	77.3	33.4	19.9	24.0	22.7
1991	75.2	39.1	15.0	21.1	24.8
1992	74.2	30.3	18.5	25.3	25.8
1993	77.9	32.9	18.8	26.2	22.1
1994	82.9	34.8	16.7	31.4	17.1
1995	83.7	36.8	13.5	33.3	16.3
1996	85.4	38.9	12.3	34.2	14.6
1997	85.8	38.9	11.2	35.7	14.2
1998	85.4	48.3	10.3	26.9	14.6
1999	86.6	51.5	9.8	25.3	13.4
2000	87.4	53.0	9.2	25.2	12.6

COMMUNITY AFFAIRS DEPARTMENTS

Mining companies act to promote and protect their operations through policies and projects that interface with the local population. Community Affairs Departments comprise the interface, managing company relations with local communities. They disseminate company information to local communities and implement policy relating to communities. They are also the source of socio-economic information used to guide company policy formulation. The daily tasks of

Departments reflect company attitude towards the community. They vary with the mining cycle. In the exploration and construction phases, Community Affairs Departments seek to convince local people of the benefits they will receive from the mine (Gerritsen and Macintyre 1991), promoting future expectations and allaying fears. During the operational phases their interests shift to long-term social monitoring largely to protect the interests of the mine.

Community Affairs Departments have taken some steps towards appreciating the community perspective during negotiations. There is scope to build on these positive, albeit unplanned, developments. The structure of these departments differs from that of operational departments at most mines. Typically, they are flatter – the Ramu Nickel Community Affairs Department is highlighted grey in Figure 11.2 – with large numbers of locally recruited employees at lower levels, nationally recruited Papua New Guineans in supervisory roles and fewer expatriates than technical departments. This reduces somewhat the difference between mine and community, although the senior supervisory levels act as important gatekeepers controlling flow of information between

Figure 11.2   Ramu Nickel Corporate Hierarchy, March 2001

company and community. Community Affairs Departments facilitate negotiation and communication by incorporating people in the company who have local obligations as landowners and kinsmen. This is positive for the mines because negotiations are conducted on a day-to-day basis with more common cause and better chance of success.

Not enough is known about the role of local people in mining companies. The degree to which research informs community projects varies widely from mine to mine but Community Affairs Departments do not have the time to research and reflect on problems because of the demands of the daily running of the mines. They are hampered in their aims because they are not able radically to rethink what should be done to improve company relations with the community. Some of the problems are probably beyond company commissioned research because their Community Affairs Departments are party to them. In advancing communication between company and community, for example, Community Affairs Departments materially benefit and advance certain individuals above others, promoting social stratification alien to the local community. These are potentially explosive changes.

MANAGEMENT AND HIERARCHIES

While the nature of the relationship between community–company shapes local responses to mining, it is not clear that ensuing socio-economic change inevitably results in social disintegration (Filer 1990). Cultural conflict seems more likely if it produces local hierarchies where none previously existed.

The formal information and decision-making channels of companies reflect the hierarchical organisation of western business. The Ramu Nickel corporate structure (see Figure 11.2) is a typical example of the hierarchical organisation common to most western multinational mining companies. It strongly contrasts with the local communities surrounding the mine site and refinery. The higher levels in the management structure are located furthest from the local community in secure office compounds, headquarters buildings in Port Moresby, or corporate head offices outside of Papua New Guinea. The Community Affairs Departments, fitting into the company structure, are themselves hierarchically organised. The organisation at Ok Tedi is typical of the larger mines in Papua New Guinea and follows the usual western industrial pattern (see Figure 11.3).

Is it possible that the above organisational structure is flawed at the outset simply because it follows the usual business pattern of the developed world? Ethnographic comparisons with local communities surrounding Ramu, Ok Tedi or any of the Papua New Guinea mines are informative. These have never traditionally structured themselves hierarchically. Companies organised in this way expect to negotiate with community 'leaders' whom they take to represent the community in the same way that senior Community Affairs Department staff see themselves as representatives of the company.

While there are good grounds for mines to continue to deal with communities through local employees, it would profit them to reconsider both their employment policy and that of negotiating through nominated local leaders. Usually these people have some experience of work in Port Moresby, Hagen, Lae or Australia and seek to distance themselves from their tribal roots in order to better themselves at the expense of others. This process is further fuelled by the imposition of landowner companies, incorporated landowner groups, and landowner associations designed with the best intentions of distributing benefits but instead serving to generate resentment and tension. Currently, as will be shown in the next section, what happens is that the few persons who are able and willing to adapt closest to the western ethos benefit inordinately.

We know that in Papua New Guinea there are no true authority figures as conceived in western business culture. Demands for community representatives to channel opinions, knowledge and information amounts to a demand for the community to constitute itself in the same hierarchical way as a company. So long as this ethnocentric approach persists it will thwart genuinely informed interaction. It is as likely to succeed as demands by communities that companies constitute themselves as tribes! A consequence of imposing a hierarchy is to differentiate members of local communities along lines that were previously unknown. The companies recruit the most adaptable and opportunistic local people with damaging effects on communities.

By pursuing current policies, mines are promoting differentiation that characterises western society but affronts the egalitarian principles that structure Melanesian societies (Sillitoe 1998b). In providing income to certain members of a community, the mines are doing nothing new in Papua New Guinea. The problem is that the mines may provide such large incomes that they promote the breakdown of traditional levelling mechanisms. Kin obligations tend to level the incomes Papua New Guineans earn working in urban centres and they would have to cast these aside for marked social differentiation to occur in the absence of mines. At the moment, their attachment to land and natal place is very strong and kin driven social levelling continues (Sillitoe 2000).

Furthermore, mines may advance certain clan groups – the 'landowners' – such that they overcome any regional levelling process,

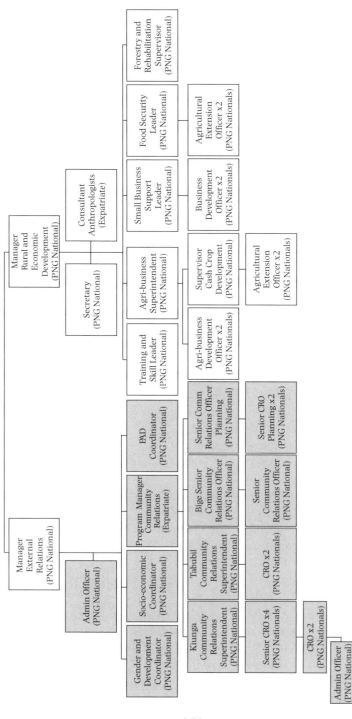

Figure 11.3   Ok Tedi Community Affairs Department Structure, 2001

259

enabling real lasting social differentiation to occur. This primes the 'time-bomb' referred to in the social disintegration model (Filer 1990). The localised nature of mines is promoting regional inequality and the emergence of a hierarchy of those who have and those who do not, by benefiting the landowners in the immediate areas of the mine. While companies invest in community affairs and development projects, they cannot (even with help of Australian aid) realistically provide national infrastructure and services to the entire country. Mines also provide substantial revenue to national government but they are too weak, as mentioned previously, to supply comparable developments elsewhere.

LOCAL GATEKEEPERS AND LAND MANAGEMENT: THE PORGERA CASE

Events have obliged mines to incorporate participatory approaches to resource development (sometimes unawares) into their everyday institutional and bureaucratic practices leading to changes in company behaviour. Villagers respond, rather than passively accept the positive and negative impacts of mining. They predictably seek to maximise the benefits they receive from resource development and minimise the costs. The mechanisms and processes by which local people react to mines reflect existing indigenous political ways and one outcome of local participation in the mining process is to challenge, directly or indirectly, existing power relations. The Porgera Gold Mine situated in the highlands' Enga Province illustrates aspects of community land negotiation strategy when faced by mine induced change. The exploration history has profoundly influenced how local representatives apparently exhibit new types of understanding that are often old types of understanding in new contexts.

Compared to earlier mine developments at Bougainville, Ok Tedi, Misima or Tolokuma, the scope for 'landowner' participation in the new gold mine was widened for the Ipili people who inhabit the Porgera Valley. While compensation and relocation agreements existed at the earlier mines, as they do at Porgera, between the mine and the local people, those signed at Porgera making provision for royalties, equity and infrastructure development go well beyond the legal minimum set out in the 1977 Mining Act. A tripartite agreement was negotiated involving the Enga Provincial Government, the National Government and the Porgera Landowners setting out favourable clauses for the local population in the Mineral Development Contract signed between the state and company. The post-independence continuation of the colonial Australian administration's policy that customarily owned land is inalienably strengthened the local parties' hand in these negotiations, making the favourable agreement possible.

Under the 1962 Land Act traditional landowners not the state hold unregistered land. The entire Porgera Valley was unregistered at the time of the proposed mine development and so under traditional usufruct. By definition, the state held no record of customary ownership, but before the State would sign the Mineral Development Contract it was necessary for the company to sign compensation and relocation agreements with the 'landowners'. It needed urgently to define membership of the 'landowning' group and identify representatives to act as signatories to such agreements. Government Patrol Officers carried out a land study to do so. Unfortunately they mistakenly assumed that they had to document the Ipili population as comprising defined clans and sub clans, each with a representative leader or 'big man'. The presumption of these virtual clan structures had profound implications, effectively disenfranchising many people and preventing them from claiming their fair share of the mine's dues, planting seeds of resentment that have been steadily growing since mine establishment.

The land tenure system of highlanders is misleadingly simple in principle but very complex in practice. People express and act on their kinship relations in activating rights to land, kin-defined obligations controlling access. Claiming rights to land features centrally in the constitution of local groups (the so-called 'clans'), which result from the coming together of a range of kin on territories to which all residents can claim cultivation rights by virtue of recognised consanguineal and affinal links to the land holding corporation. Tenure rights define who may belong to which territorially constituted local group. Many more persons have rights of usufruct than actually activate them at any time, only a fraction of those with rights may reside on a territory. Both land rights and use have transient aspects to them. Families may come and go, communities are socially in flux. The relativity of land rights is an integral aspect of the social order, and to attempt to freeze them at one instance in time, as in mine negotiations, is to do them violence.

The mining company decided where to locate the mine and applied for a Special Mining Lease (SML) and sought to define the 'landowning clans' and their 'agents'. The resulting 200 'leaders' who emerged to represent the estimated SML area population of 3,000 people was too many for the company. It required them to nominate a smaller group of 23 from their number to form a manageable forum for decision-making called the Landowner Negotiating Committee (LNC). The nominees of nominees from a 'clan' thus purport to represent local people in negotiations with the mine. The mine sought corporate representatives whereas for the

Ipili, like other highlanders, society is kin founded. Day-to-day interaction features kin, affines and acquaintances not contractual relations with business partners, company employees and political associates. The LNC reflects the need of the company to gain consent quickly through signatories in order to make decisions where delays may effect the productivity or safety of the mine. Thus, in a seemingly reasonable step to the company, it introduced the western legal concept of 'representative agents' and effectively stratified the previously non-hierarchical local community. Some power also resides in other outside imposed, non-mine institutions, with Provincial politicians and Local Government councillors.[2]

Leadership is a difficult concept in the Porgera Valley where the 'big-man' institution is weak, as in some other parts of the highlands (such as the Was Valley; Sillitoe 1979). Individuals with extensive social networks of reciprocal obligations and responsibilities may exert influence in certain situations, for example, help to resolve disputes by drawing on connections with both conflicting parties, in contrast to conceptions of disinterested arbitration by neutral parties with nothing or little to gain. It does not promote long-lived dominance by a single individual and certainly not hereditary succession. The mine, located in the upper valley, has further upset the local power balance geographically, communities in the lower valley previously dominating the Porgera Valley, leading to further dangerous resentment.

The early history of mines produces a local leadership in the traditional mould where those who manage to incorporate the company most effectively into their web of personal interactions emerge as representatives. The negotiation of the Porgera agreements between 1986 and 1990 created the potential for foreign forms of leadership to emerge in conflict with deeply held local values of equality. When the mine discusses with local people issues concerning the SML area, it meets LNC members. They enjoy the power to sign and negotiate agreements, receive money and distribute it. As prominent agents of the local community they claim rights to large amounts of land in the gold mountain, further legitimating their positions. They comprise a powerful new elite in the Porgera Valley but their positions are unstable, they hold power tenuously backed up with guns, bullet-proof clothing and armed kin. But the hierarchical arrangements concentrating power in the hands of a few are even more serious with a Development Forum above the LNC on which only three LNC members sit.

It is necessary to know how these powerful gatekeeper positions have been filled and by whom. Most of the 23 LNC members have at some stage worked for the mine company in the Community Affairs

From: Golub (2001).

Department. The three members of the Development Forum have occupied the widest range of roles. One of them was a pupil in Porgera primary school's first ever class and went on to become a junior Patrol Officer at Porgera government station, in charge at the mine site government post and closely involved in the land study. This prominent Porgeran has served as a district administrator, company Community Relations Officer and Mining Liaison Officer for the District Government, and was one of the three local negotiators of the Porgera mine agreement. Another Development Forum member, who has gained some notoriety in tribal fighting, was the first Porgeran to be a policeman and later became a Provincial Government minister. After financial success in the nearby Mt. Kare gold prospect, he was made president of the local landowners association (PLA), acts as the unofficial leader of LNC and is head of Ipili Porgera Investments (IPI). The third member of the Forum was President of the Local Government Council at the time of the negotiation of the mining agreements, has worked for the company as a former Community Relations Superintendent for Sustainable Development and was one of the main players in the creation of IPI. This complex picture of interconnected and overlapping roles occupied by a few persons typifies Porgera. They drive Land Cruisers, own houses in the new mining town of Paiam, watch DVDs, and have heavily armed bodyguards escort them.

Shared contacts and multiple institutional personas tie the actors into a tight web of obligation and responsibility that closely resembles the traditional social order hidden by superficial compliance with corporate structures. These local leaders largely interact with the mine as negotiators in dispute resolution. While the mine sees them within its imposed corporate frameworks, as LNC and Forum agents and councillors, they work locally through entirely Porgeran structures. They use traditional processes that feature in the settlement of disputes in communities to resolve mining disputes with large financial stakes.

They call on connections and obligations through kinship, friendship and marriage. They maintain complex networks of relations locally, and act to suppress, politically co-opt or otherwise neutralise rivals to retain their positions on corporate boards, and so on. The current leaders rely on their personal networks in interfacing between mine and community, their success depends on their personalities rather than any authority invested in their positions. They have created their roles rather than the roles conferring authority on them. This is dangerous for the community and the mine.

The typical development and production lifecycle of 20–30 years for the large mines in Papua New Guinea militates against the same leadership being present at mine opening and closure. Local leaders are replaced, overthrown or pass away, and mining company personnel change over time. The incoming generation of new leaders played a decisive role in the Bougainville tragedy. It is almost certain that the local leadership at Porgera will change before the mine closes. No new leaders have yet emerged to challenge the supremacy of the existing elite. Some of the leaders made it clear in interviews that they think that it is time for younger people to take over some of their roles. They see themselves retiring Australian fashion and living on the considerable wealth they have invested in Queensland. It is uncertain how a new leadership will emerge. Like wider highland society, as far as it is possible to generalise, there is no formal mechanism for passing leadership to a new generation. If the current leaders who were involved with the development and production stages of the mine represent the adaptation of Ipili society to western ways, the future is likely to reflect traditional Ipili strategies reasserting themselves.

The change in leadership will occur in less auspicious circumstances than those that marked the emergence of the original leaders. The new leaders will take over at a time of diminishing income locally, not of growing wealth as when the current leadership arrived. Monetary benefits that pass to the local leadership and communities will decrease and eventually cease. In the stages leading to the mine closure, the remaining ore will decrease in grade until it is no longer viable to extract and the company will turn to milling its stockpiles. At this point, the wages of the majority of local Porgerans who are employed in the open cast pit will cease. No more tailings will be produced and waste dumps will cease to expand. Land will revert to the 'owners' and compensation will cease along with the loss of wages and royalties. After a generation of wealth dividends, irrespective of their disputed distribution, the expectation is of continued growth. New leaders will require capital from somewhere if their influence is to depend on manipulation of the same traditional distribution networks. They will have to convince Porgerans that mining is unsustainable and that future growth will depend on themselves, when up until now the wealth has arrived through no initiative on their part. A superficially stable, ageing local 'leadership' deeply rooted in traditional social structures handing over to others at a time when their hold on power is weakening is ominous. It questions the ability of leaders, new or old, to control events. The failure of leadership will be borne by those they nominally represent. The recent crisis at Gold Ridge in the Solomons and the ever-present spectre of Bougainville illustrate the seriousness of loss of control by negotiators and leaders. Yet the mine has to stay open if it is to mill its stockpiles and fulfil environment and social sustainability commitments before closure.

The looming 'leadership' crisis is worsened by the unsatisfactory relations between the majority of the population and the mine that the imposed management structures have resulted in, which are an affront to local egalitarian ways. 'Landowners' do not pool resources and knowledge as the company does and very small numbers of people have made decisions since the mine's inception that have greatly affected the course of mine developments. While a knowledge interface may exist between mine and community – represented by company personnel and local leaders respectively – the spread of knowledge into the local community is attenuated. While high up there is seemingly good dialogue at Porgera, this has failed to extend to the grassroots either in the company or beyond in the valley. There is a dangerous gulf that different perceptions of mine–community relations widens further. Compensation is one of the key aspects of the company and community relationship. The egalitarian ethos that informs land rights should influence the process by which a mine recompenses local people for damages and disruption of lifestyle. People equate mining company compensation payments with traditional indemnity payments such as those given in reparation for kin killed in tribal fights. Both involve negotiated recompense for loss. The corporate view of transactions is single cash payments made to settle claims for loss or damage. In contrast, the traditional view embraces long-term reciprocity, consolidation and reconciliation involving a web of associated persons. Local communities find their attempts to enter into reciprocal compensatory arrangements rebuffed, distanced from the company with their 'leaders' negotiating for them, acting as buffers with whom they do have such enduring relations but whom they have come to suspect of double-dealing, if not corruption. It is fuelling ever-mounting resentment and the mine at Porgera may be running out of time.

FUTURE NEGOTIATIONS

Strategies that mines should explore ought to involve negotiations involving the entire community, not just the 'leaders' or local employees of the mine. The difficulty that companies face is that local communities are true democracies in which everyone has a voice and opportunity to express opinions and that no leaders are ever truly representative. People's expectations that negotiations will parallel those of the exchanges that characterise their social lives further compounds these communication problems, challenging the notion of a finally agreed contract. They expect companies to negotiate continuously. How can we devise a methodology that allows all persons from local communities to have a say without resulting in a confused cacophony that the company will not be able to understand or act upon?

At Lihir, Porgera and Ok Tedi, Community Affairs Departments have been deliberately located at the mine site to maximise accessibility to large numbers of people. At Lihir, for example, the Community Affairs Department is located next to the Landowner Association's and the Mining Department representative's office in an unguarded area adjacent to the supermarket and small port that are the focus of the mining settlement. But accessibility is not enough. Offices, however open and unguarded, still represent a world apart for many local people. No schemes are currently proposed that consider the process of consensus building in the local population in a way intelligible to the company view but honest to the values of the people. Schemes proposed by mining companies for 'capacity-building' involve the slow shifting of responsibility for governing the mining areas and provinces from the company back to the state. These are generally seen as good because they are a step towards promoting responsible government in Papua New Guinea but they do not promote mass local participation. The real challenge is to devise ways in which the tribal order is able to work out its relationship with the corporate one without the latter imposing its western hierarchical ideology and elevating a limited number of individuals, at the expense of their local identity.

Many of the current Community Affairs Department strategies merit further investigation. For example, how effective are Pidgin and English newsletters produced by mines that are largely intended for employees but circulate in the wider local community? How are these newsletters received in communities and what function do they serve in mines? How does passage of information via rumour affect the community understanding of mining companies and vice versa? To what extent do local people recast what they hear and read into their own local idioms? By addressing such questions we should further our understanding of how the tribal orders relate to mining companies. Furthermore employees from different language groups develop separate informal social networks within companies that run across departmental and skills boundaries channelling informal communication and rumour that often 'subverts the more formal means of company communication' (Banks 1999a). These informal channels reflect the employees' very diverse interests and backgrounds such that people working in the organisations often have different agendas and understandings to the 'organisation' itself. Individuals sometimes see problems differently according to their roles within the organisation. The Community Affairs Departments evidence the same crosscutting ethnic lines of communication, rumour and compartmentalisation. Counter-information in these departments is unwelcome to companies as the point of contact with the local community. It results in the unmanaged dissemination of some information that is not necessarily in the company interest and not always linked to reliable sources of information or corporate policy.

There is a need to undertake research independently of companies and yet in close association with them. At the same time, it is necessary to work closely with local communities without alienating companies. Any association in the minds of local people between researchers and mining company will immediately arouse distrust, just as a partiality towards local people will make mining companies suspicious. In other words, research is necessary without taking sides, transparent and with the trust of both. We have to resolve questions of responsibility to both sides and carefully consider all information so as not to compromise either by our actions. Transparency is itself an issue that demands further research. There is a profound difference between the academic approach to research and the company approach, which seeks to exploit knowledge commercially. Unlike companies, academics believe that with greater understanding on both sides, which implies open transfer of knowledge, local communities will better adjust and come to terms with events. There are ways in which research might further communication of information with less distortion and misunderstanding on both sides, which we see as being at the root of some of the conflict. One promising strategy is the innovative use of information technology, such as satellite imagery, modelling presentations, opinion canvassing, and so on.

CONCLUSION

The mining industry faces many dilemmas as it attempts to comply with ambiguous policy directives originating from the confrontation of western multinationals with local communities. Companies have begun to look for new solutions to meet their corporate citizenship agenda objectives. The time is right for research into alternatives, the industry is in a receptive mood. It has burnt itself in its dealings with local communities that are far from defenceless tribal groups. There is a broad-based commitment by management to finding solutions to community–company relations and willingness to encourage new directions for future research. One of the main features of such research has to be how both sides, communities and companies, can remain true to themselves yet better understand one another.

There are more questions here than answers. Indeed from this chapter's perspective it could hardly be otherwise, as it does not see research providing solutions but rather facilitating the parties' search for them. There is a need to involve all local people more in the process. Only participatory approaches involving all are likely to prove fruitful. It is for local communities to work out their relations with mines, not companies nor academics to research for an answer that may be imposed on them, even if this was possible, which we doubt in the current political climate. We should not advocate outsiders sorting out these issues because we believe that it is for local people to reach their own decisions about how to participate, but we think that companies might do more to make participation possible on local terms and not create conditions likely to promote social conflict. Tribal people must work out their own relationship to corporations. While the aim of any anthropologically informed research is to help local tribal people fend off the imposition of foreign arrangements that promote conflict, this does not imply fending off foreign mining operations, whose contribution to Papua New Guinea's national growth is undoubted to continue. The broad aim is to facilitate greater knowledge by each party of the other in order that they can reach better-negotiated agreements having a more reasonable understanding of the true position of the other. The intention should be to contribute to the negotiation process as a catalyst, not to take on the role of brokers. We need to investigate ways to inform all local people of the consequences of mining operations, in particular the environmental ones and potential social problems, and involve them in decision-making. The aim is to facilitate sounder decision-making and negotiation through greater transparency and free flow of information, to create the environment and space for profoundly different socio-cultural traditions to interact on equal terms in mutual respect, and so reduce misunderstanding and conflict.

NOTES

1. This occurred in the 1990s when, after two decades of environmental destruction and social disruption, the mining company and PNG Government dismissed Bougainvillian claims for compensation and part-ownership of the mine, sparking a rebellion and sabotage of the mine, closing down the operation to this day (Sillitoe 2000: 136–41).
2. There is also a wide variety of service institutions that support the mining process in which local people find themselves in positions of increasing responsibility. In Porgera, some of the royalties from the mine fund the Porgera Landowner Association (PLA) and its executive. Acronyms abound in Porgera. In addition to the PLA and LNC, there are the Porgera Development Authority (PDA), the Community Issues Committee (CIC) composed of the members of the LNC and also of 18 councillors from the Porgera Valley, the Paiam Development Corporation (PDC), the Paiam Management Corporation (PMC), the Paiam Accommodation Development Corporation (PADC), Mountain Steel Builders (MSB), the Paiam Women's Association (PWA), Ipili Porgera Investments (IPI) and the Porgera Joint Venture (PJV) itself. There is scope for many Porgerans to fill a broad range of positions, and they have created and found places for themselves on all of these bodies. Membership of any one does not preclude membership of any of the others. It is possible to be a councillor, LNC agent and to work for the PJV simultaneously.

REFERENCES

Ballard, C. (1998) 'Roles for the State and Mining Communities in Indonesia and Papua New Guinea', in J. Strongman (ed.) *Mining and the Community for Asia and Pacific Nations* (Washington: World Bank – CD-Rom)

Banks, G. (1993) 'Mining Multinationals and Developing Countries: Theory and practice in Papua New Guinea', *Applied Geography*, 13(4): 313–27

—— (1994) *Porgera Business Study*. Canberra and Port Moresby, Unisearch PNG Pty Ltd for PJV

—— (1996) 'Compensation for Mining: Benefit or time-bomb? The Porgera Gold Mine', in R. Howitt, J. Connell and P. Hirsch (eds), *Resources, Nations and Indigenous Peoples* (Melbourne: Oxford University Press)

—— (1999a) 'Historical Vines: Enga networks of exchange, ritual and warfare in Papua New Guinea', *Journal of Pacific History*, 34(2): 235–6

—— (1999b) *Mountain of Desire: Mining Company and Indigenous Community at the Porgera Gold Mine, Papua New Guinea* (Canberra: The Australian National University, Department of Anthropology)

Biersack, A. (1992) 'Short-fuse Mining Politics in the Jet Age: From stone to gold at Mount Kare and Porgera'. Annual Meeting of the American Anthropological Association, San Francisco, 5 December

—— (1999) 'The Mount Kare Python and his Gold: Totemism and ecology in the Papua New Guinea Highlands', *American Anthropologist*, 101(1): 68–87

Brooks, C.K. (1991) 'Killing the Goose that Laid the Golden Eggs: The story of the Panguna Mine, Bougainville Island, Papua New Guinea', *Terra Nova*, 3(1): 98–107

Burton, J. (1996) 'What is Best Practice? Social issues and the culture of the corporation in Papua New Guinea' (Canberra: Mining and Mineral Resource Policy Issues in Asia-Pacific, Research School of Pacific and Asian Studies, The Australian National University)

Carruthers, D.S. (1990) 'Some Implications for Papua New Guinea of the Closure of the Bougainville Copper Mine', in M. Spriggs and R.J. May (eds), *The Bougainville Crisis* (Bathurst, NSW: Crawford House Press), pp. 38–44

Cochrane, G. (2000) *Short-Term PNG Requirements (Lihir)* (London: Rio Tinto HQ)

Filer, C. (1990) 'The Bougainville Rebellion, the Mining Industry and the Process of Social Disintegration in Papua New Guinea', *Canberra Journal of Anthropology*, 13(1): 1–39

—— (1992) *Lihir Project Social Impact Mitigation: Issues and Approaches* (Port Moresby: University of Papua New Guinea), Department of Anthropology and Sociology

—— (1994) 'Socio-economic Impact Assessment of the Tolukuma Gold Mine, Central Province', *Research in Melanesia*, 18: 1–84

—— (1996) 'Participation, Governance and Social Impact Mitigation: The planning of the Lihir gold mine' (Canberra: Mining and Mineral Resource Policy Issues in Asia-Pacific, Research School of Pacific and Asian Studies, The Australian National University)

—— (1998) *Social Monitoring Programs and the Management of Social Risk in PNG*. Paper presented to the 'Mining and the Community' conference in Madang

—— (1999) *Dilemmas of Development: The Social Impact of the Porgera Gold Mine 1989–1994* (Boroko: National Research Institute)

—— (2000) 'Governance and Reform in the South Pacific', *Oceania*, 71(2): 164–5

Filer, C., D. Henton and R. Jackson (2000) *Landowner Compensation in Papua New Guinea's Mining and Petroleum Sectors* (Port Moresby: PNG Chamber of Mines and Petroleum)

Filer, C. and R. Jackson (1989) *The Social and Economic Impact of a Gold Mine on Lihir: Revised and Expanded* (Port Moresby: Lihir Liaison Committee, Department of Minerals and Energy)

Gerritsen, R. and M. Macintyre (1991) 'Dilemmas of Distribution: The Misima Gold Mine, Papua New Guinea', in J. Connell and R. Howitt (eds), *Mining and Indigenous Peoples in Australasia* (Sydney: Sydney University Press in association with Oxford University Press)

Goldman, L. (2000) 'Social Mapping', in L. Goldman (ed.), *Social Impact Analysis: An Applied Anthropology Manual* (Oxford and New York: Berg), pp. 152–90

Goldman, L. and S. Baum (2000) 'Introduction', in L. Goldman (ed.), *Social Impact Analysis: An Applied Anthropology Manual* (Oxford and New York: Berg), pp. 1–34

Golub, A. (2001) *Gold +ve (Positive): A Brief History of Porgera 1930–1990* (Madang: Kristen Press)

Hyndman, D. (1987a) 'Native Power: The quest for autonomy and nationhood of indigenous peoples', *Mankind*, 17(1): 58–9

—— (1987b) 'Mining, Modernization and Movements of Social Protest in Papua New Guinea', *Social Analysis*, 21: 20–38

—— (1994) 'A Sacred Mountain of Gold: The creation of a mining resource frontier in Papua New Guinea', *Journal of Pacific History*, XXIX(2): 203–21

—— (1995) 'Afek and Rebaibal: Ideologies of social protest and the Ok Tedi mining project in Papua New Guinea', *Journal of the Polynesian Society*, 104(1): 75–88

—— (2001) 'Academic Responsiblities and Representation of the Ok Tedi crisis in Postcolonial Papua New Guinea', *Contemporary Pacific*, 13(1): 33–54

Imbun, B.Y. (1995) 'Enga Social Life and Identity in a Papua New Guinea Mining Town', *Oceania*, 66(1): 51–61

—— (2000) 'Mining Workers or "opportunist" tribesmen? A tribal workforce in a Papua New Guinea mine', *Oceania*, 71(2): 129–49

Jackson, R. (1991) 'Not Without Influence: Villages, mining companies, and governments in Papua New Guinea', in J. Connell and R. Howitt (eds), *Mining and Indigenous Peoples in Australasia* (Sydney: Sydney University Press), pp. 18–34

—— (1992) 'New Mines for Old Gold: Ghana changing mining industry', *Geography*, 77(335): 175–8

—— (1994) 'One Full Circle: BCL to PJV', *Taim Lain*, 2(1): 18–26

—— (1998) 'The Ok Tedi Settlement: Issues, outcomes and implications', *Journal of Pacific History*, 33(3): 307–11

—— (2001) 'The State and Internal Conflict', *Australian Journal of International Affairs*, 55(1): 65–81

Kirsch, S. (1989) 'The Yonggom, the Refugee Camps along the Border, and the Impact of the Ok Tedi Mine', *Research in Melanesia*, 13: 30–61

—— (1993) *The Yonggom People of the Ok Tedi and Moian Census Divisions: An Area Study* (Unisearch PNG Pty Ltd for Ok Tedi Mining Limited)

—— (1996) 'Return to Ok Tedi', *Meanjin*, 55(4): 657–66

Low, N. and B. Gleeson (1998) 'Situating Justice in the Environment: The case of BHP at the Ok Tedi copper mine', *Antipode*, 30(3): 201

Moody, R. (1992) 'Bougainville and Mining: "breaking all five fingers"', in D. Robie (ed.), *Tu Galala: Social Change in the Pacific* (Aotearoa/New Zealand: Bridget Williams Books), pp. 92–102

Oliver, D. (1991) *Black Islanders: A Personal Perspective of Bougainville 1937–1991* (Honolulu: University of Hawaii Press)

Placer Pacific Limited (1997) *Towards Sustainability*. Progress Report

Power, T. (2000) *Community Relations Manual: Resource Industries* (Port Moresby: PNG Chamber of Mines and Petroleum)

Quodling, P. (1991) *Bougainville: The Mine and the People* (St Leonards, NSW: The Centre for Independent Studies Limited), Pacific Papers 3

Sillitoe, P. (1979) *Give and Take: Exchange in Wola Society* (New York: St. Martin's, Canberra: ANV Press)

—— (1996) *A Place Against Time: Land and Environment in the Papua New Guinea Highlands* (Amsterdam: Harwood Academic Publishers)

—— (1998a) 'The Development of Indigenous Knowledge: A new applied anthropology', *Current Anthropology*, 39(2): 223–52

—— (1998b) *An Introduction to the Anthropology of Melanesia: Culture and Tradition* (Cambridge: Cambridge University Press)

—— (1999) 'Beating the Boundaries: Land tenure and identity in the Papua New Guinea Highlands', *Journal of Anthropological Research*, 55(3): 331–60

—— (2000) *Social Change in Melanesia: Development and History* (Cambridge: Cambridge University Press)

Stewart, P.J. and A. Strathern (1999) 'Feasting on my Enemy: Images of violence and change in the New Guinea Highlands', *Ethnohistory*, 46(4): 645–69

—— (2002) *Remaking the World: Myth, mining and ritual change among the Duna people of Papua New Guinea* (London: Smithsonian Institute Press)

Thompson, H. (1991) 'The Economic Causes and Consequences of the Bougainville Crisis', *Resources Policy*, 17(1): 69–85

Townsend, P.K. (2001) 'Dilemmas of Development: The social and economic impact of the Porgera gold mine, 1989–1994', *Pacific Affairs*, 74(1): 144–5

Townsend, P.K. and W.H. Townsend (1997) 'Papua New Guinea and the Environmental Impact of the Ok Tedi Mine', *Indigenous Affairs*, (1): 27–31

Ungutip, W., B. Wabis and P. Sillitoe (1999) 'Some Wola Thoughts on the Year 2000', in C. Kocher-Schmid (ed.) *Expecting the Day of Wrath: Versions of the Millennium in Papua New Guinea* (Boroko: Papua New Guinea National Research Institute Monograph No. 36), pp. 57–69

12 FROM SEDUCTION TO MISCOMMUNICATION: THE CONFESSION AND PRESENTATION OF LOCAL KNOWLEDGE IN 'PARTICIPATORY DEVELOPMENT'

Dario Novellino

While the involvement of local communities in developing projects is today recognised as a necessity, there is still a tendency to underestimate the role of the factors that jeopardise successful communication between development workers and local people. The conditions under which people may decide to 'disclose' their 'knowledge', and make their needs explicit, are very difficult to create. Interaction between community members and project workers (for example, developers or conservationists) seldom leads to mutual comprehension. Frequently, negotiation builds upon a number of misunderstandings that may be fostered intentionally or spontaneously due to differences in cognition, expectation, background knowledge, language and attitudes.

One key objective of this chapter is to identify some of the dynamics under which knowledge is shared or hidden in the course of negotiations between 'project planners' and clients. Specifically, I am interested in the question of who holds what knowledge for which purpose, which knowledge is used to seduce the 'other' into confessing, and which is used to protect oneself against discursive forms of deception. As this chapter attempts to show, local viewpoints are vulnerable to misrepresentation in countless ways. This is mainly because people's presentation of their own knowledge, and the representation of the latter by external agents, is always rooted in the attitudes and stereotypes that the two parties have of each other, and in the stigmatisation that may follow from these perceptions.

In keeping with the ethnographic focus of this chapter, my primary objective is to explore the psycho-cultural dynamics and moral values underlying communication between project planners and the members of a specific indigenous society: the Batak of Pälawan (Philippines). The Batak population is estimated at around 380 individuals (Eder 1987), and continues to decline. They have a varied mode of food procurement, which centres on swidden cultivation integrated with hunting, gathering and the commercial collection of non-timber forest products (NTFPs). During the past decade, Batak have become increasingly involved in conservation-development projects, which the communities neither understand nor control. One project ends and another one starts, but each one continues to propose more of the same (see Novellino 1998). When projects fail, as they do, Batak are blamed for being opportunistic, unreliable, 'lazy', incapable of standing up for their own rights, being uncooperative. When 'participatory meetings' take place, silence on the part of the 'beneficiaries' of development (the Batak participants) is often interpreted as a form of consent or, even worse, as apathy.

I shall argue in this chapter that failure to make Batak 'participate'[1] in conservation-development projects (CDPs) cannot be attributed to any of the attributed Batak characteristics. In reality, the relationship between Batak and development workers (government, NGOs, representatives, etc.) 'falls far short of equality, either perceived or actual' (Gewertz and Errington 1991: 56),[2] and this is one of the causes inhibiting 'communicatively achieved agreements' (Habermas 1998) between the people and various categories of outsider. In this respect, I shall identify Batak moral values and norms of conduct that determine whether Batak share information with 'outsiders' or withhold it. A look at Batak ethics, and specifically at notions[3] of 'fear', 'anger', 'individual will', 'withdrawal' and 'refusal', will yield insight into the local counter-strategy for dealing with externally imposed discourses of development.

BATAK MORAL CATEGORIES

A number of closely related psycho-cultural notions determine the ways in which Batak respond to outsider-led conservation-development projects (CDPs). These notions (for example, fear, anger, individual will and refusal) constitute central components of the motivational context of Batak social life (see Gibson 1989; Howell 1989; Robarchek 1989) and inform Batak relationships with new categories of outsiders, such as developers and conservationists. As we shall see, the themes of anger and fear are closely intertwined with refusal and withdrawal, and can be expressed physically, verbally or through a combination of both. In day-to-day interaction, Batak always avoid causing anger, or being involved in situations that may lead to fear. Such precautions, and maintaining a desire for independence, are among the most important moral imperatives in Batak society. As a result, the intrusion of non-Batak members in Batak territory is always a cause of preoccupation. This is mainly because the intentions of 'new' categories of outsiders cannot be predicted in advance. When the motives of outsider intrusion are not clear, Batak tend to avoid face-to-face contact and ultimately withdraw, either physically or verbally.

'Fleeing' (*lukbu*) has always been the standard Batak response to intrusion; it is a way of avoiding direct contact with those having a 'different custom' (*aget a ugalin*). Most of the Batak I have known share the view that it is of 'no worth' (*da'ay balì ya*) to confront a 'bad person' (*makawat a taw*). Unless direct contact is absolutely unavoidable, answering back (physically or verbally) does not constitute an adequate response. 'Looking hard' (*biribiri*) or 'to be brave' (*matapan*) is undesirable, because such conditions can add (*magdugang*) anger (*iseg*). To be 'afraid' (*takut*) and to avoid confrontation are not perceived as defiance or as something to be ashamed of; indeed, one should do everything possible to placate an angry person (*amùamu*). In addition, one should avoid 'quarrelling' (*magsuay*), 'to be jealous' (*mainggit*), 'to say bad things about others' (*raway*), 'to talk behind somebody's back' (*dimat*), 'to provoke others to be jealous by bragging about possession' (*sirisiri*), and 'to refuse to give something even when he/she has it' (*magaruk*). 'Giving' (*magbegay*) and 'sharing' (*magparti parti*) are principal ingredients of self-perceived 'Batakness'. Those who comply with such norms are said to have 'a good custom' (*magayeng ugali*). As much as possible, one should not 'complain' (*baribariwat*) about one's own situation, but instead 'suffer in silence' (*aguanta*). Explicit complaints should be made by 'talking nicely' (*matilnu arampangan*), since it is possible 'to hate without anger' (*lasay*) or 'to argue without being angry' (*barisbaris*). 'Angry speech' (*basul*) 'is not good to hear' (*dagway sayud a bati'en*) and it 'contravenes customs' (*damangen*). Generally, anger is detected by the changing tone of the voice, but it seldom leads to an 'emotional outburst'. On certain occasions, thoughts are 'reflected upon, without being revealed' (*nakemnakem*). More importantly, 'following along' (*usuy*) with one's own 'custom' (*ugali*) is the only guarantee to 'avoid troubles' (*andam*). In spite of all such good norms of behaviour, 'being disappointed' (*sungun*) is still a commonly experienced feeling among Batak. This is generally expressed by withdrawing, not taking part in something and, at the worst, by 'separating' (*magbelagbelag*) from one's own group. There are many Batak words expressing disappointment and refusal, for instance, the words *natigam* and *singga* denote 'refusal to work having been denied payment', and *se'ked* indicates that something has been given up because of discouragement.

This brief account of Batak moral concepts, and the motivational context within which they are articulated, will prove useful in the second part of the chapter which deals with how Batak respond to top-down projects.

Today, reduction of the traditional territory (due to logging, encroachment by migrants, establishment of a national park, etc.) and increasing contacts with outsiders have put Batak in a situation where physical withdrawal is increasingly difficult or impossible. Pawat, a Batak from Tanabag, describes the situation in his community:

> Wherever we go, far in the mountains or close to the coast, it is exactly the same. Those who want to contact us will reach us anyhow. When election time comes, candidates send their representatives even to our summer camps. Missionaries have followed us from one settlement to another. The Haribon [a local NGO] has sent field staff to live in our village. No matter how far we go, outsiders will show up unexpectedly and say they want to help us.

Prima facie, it seems that Batak are left with no alternative other than to come to terms with different categories of outsiders. They must attend meetings, reply to questions, sign documents and take a stand over a number of new and increasingly complex issues. As acculturation increases, Batak feel more helpless and vulnerable to intrusions that are largely beyond their control. The people often describe this condition as feeling 'pressed between things' (*ipit*) and experiencing 'fear/anxiety inside' (*kebkeba tu seled*). There is nothing more distressing for a Batak than being forced 'to obey because of fear' (*magsuku* or *magampu*), especially when orders and instructions are coming from an influential politician, and hence cannot be easily dismissed. In fact, Batak place great value on the will of the individual to refuse and to withdraw if he/she 'does not like' (*da'gwa magkeliag* or *da'gwa gustu*) to take part in or comply with something. No one can be forced to do anything if he or she does not wish to do so. Hence, it is virtually impossible to persuade (*agak'*) or push someone to do something, unless the person involved 'is in accord' (*magpauyun*). To coerce a person into doing something he or she does not want to do is to make the person debilitated (*malubay*), and thus to weaken his mental and physical strength.

It does not come as a surprise, then, that certain conservation-development projects (for example, tree planting) may be accepted by certain members of the community, while being refused by others. As we shall see, the desire for personal autonomy contrasts starkly with the 'communal' ethos outsiders assume, and because of which Batak are encouraged to form co-operatives (Novellino in press) and manage communal plots of cultivated land. In fact, people's desire for individual autonomy may constrain collective actions[4] and make it difficult for Batak to mount an effective challenge against the external pressures confronting them. The difficulty has contributed to the stereotype that Batak are uncooperative, unable to reach consensus and incapable of managing their own affairs. As the ethnography (below) tells us, in attempting to cope with external pressure, Batak still rely on customary forms of denial (for example, silence) and have developed new counter-strategies in pursuing particular purposes and goals (for example, fostering miscommunication, omitting or offering partial accounts of their 'knowledge').

MEETING THE 'EXPERTS': THE COMING INTO BEING OF MISCOMMUNICATION

The extent to which Batak use a customary moral code and norms of behaviour to counter various forms of external pressure can now be examined. I will draw on two events I personally witnessed in 1993 and 1999.

'Filling in Questionnaires and Constructing Identities'

In April 1993, the Batak community of Tanabag was visited by a team of government departments and NGO personnel. This mixed team gave an introductory presentation to inform community members of the objectives of their mission. The primary aim, officials explained, was to alleviate poverty; in order to take the right measures, people's problems and aspirations needed to be identified. The mission relied on a question-naire[5] which covered the respondents' occupation, their preference for technological innovation(s) and the type of education they desired for their children. Respondents were told to choose from a block of items and options, none of which adequately reflected local cultural precepts. As a result, community members had no choice but to reply to wrong questions with wrong answers. For instance, people were asked about their occupation and had to choose from the following: farmer, fisherman, hunter, contract labourer, other. None applied. Batak have a very het-erogeneous economy; they prioritise specific food procurement activities depending on the season, but often carry out tasks simultaneously. Furthermore, the Batak vocabulary has no specific words for farmer, fisherman, etc., but only generic terms referring to the various food-seeking activities (for example, *magsagiap* – searching for; *maglugitem* – getting edible things from the forest). Specific food-seeking practices are also named individually (for example, *ga'aret* – hunting for wild pigs; *magbila'* – fishing with hook and line; *maglugu* – fishing with poisonous *magarrawa* vine; *maglebet* – honey gathering; etc.). More importantly in Batak livelihood practices, gathering with tools is not distinguished from foraging for plants and predation without tools (Tanner 1994); animals are hunted as well as domesticated, seeds are collected from the wild and also planted in swiddens. In sum, hunting-gathering and horticulture are inseparable components within a single logic of procurement.

The narrow questionnaire employed by the visiting team ignored the complexity of circumstances that surround people's practices. It introduced 'needs' and 'identities' that did not reflect people's aspirations and self-image. Batak were also requested to reveal their most urgent needs by choosing from just three options: irrigation, potable water, electrification. These were not recognised needs. Batak therefore needed to play the game. Thus, when asked more explicitly about their environmental knowledge and how they utilised it, Batak stressed the importance of gathering NTFPs (which fitted into the official development rhetoric), but omitted crucial details regarding their swidden practices and other food procurement activities such as the extraction of palm cabbage.[6] These reflected the nationwide prohibition of slash-and-burn cultivation following the Forestry Act no. 1148 of 1904 and the Revised Forestry Code (Presidential Decree no. 705 of 1975). Since then, indigenous swidden cultivators in the Philippines have been classified as squatters on public land, regardless of length of occupancy (Novellino 1998). As Batak are aware of the ban and the negative stereotyping of the practitioners, they refrain from providing information on their agricultural practices in their dealing with government representatives and conservationists. Similar omissions can be observed when Batak engage in participatory mapping. Such maps, made through the direct contribution of community members, lack historical references and do not give information on places of symbolic value. The names of mountains and rivers may appear, but without cultural elaborations.

When Batak 'present' their 'local knowledge'[7] to outsiders, they omit relevant details for a number of reasons, for example, sensing that outsiders have a practical reason for showing an interest or wanting to avoid being labelled as illegal *kaingineros* (shifting cultivators). As a result, when verbally disclosing their 'local knowledge' to outsiders, Batak will share selectively or omit important cultural information. Typically, people's accounts of their 'local knowledge' are simplified through excessive emphasis on one activity (for example, gathering of NTFPs) at the expense of others (for example, swidden cultivation). This has the effect of confirming rather than contradicting the common stereotype according to which Batak possess a poor knowledge of agriculture.[8]

It is no wonder that generic assumptions regarding the Batak foraging economy and their approach towards nature can be easily detected in reports by NGOs and international organisations. For instance, in the final Haribon-IUCN project report, we learn that 'the Batak are among the Philippines' last remaining aboriginal forest hunter-gatherers. They are nearly wholly dependent for their livelihoods upon the collection and sale of non-timber forest products (NTFPs), primarily rattan, almaciga [Manila copal, a tree resin], and honey' (Haribon-IUCN 1996: 2). The same report informs that 'Batak began practising shifting cultivation one hundred years ago after becoming accustomed to eating rice received from barter of NTFPs with lowland merchants ... [The] Batak prefer a life in the forest which precludes investing time required to attend to intensive *kaingin* (swidden cultivation)' (1996: 6). Surprisingly, Batak dependency on agriculture and the antiquity of their swidden cultivation practices are not mentioned. No mention is made, for instance, of the very complex and detailed Batak mythology dealing with rice. Numerous legends trace the origin of rice to people's mythological past, and people can list more than 50 local varieties of upland rice that are regarded as '*Batak tunay*' (truly Batak) (Novellino in press). If such information had been revealed to international conservationists, they might have found much less grist for their mills. Batak 'slash-and-burn' agriculture is often deliberately kept 'hidden' by local conservationists to avoid ruining the idealised version of the 'last surviving hunters and gatherers' (Novellino 1998).

At stake here is the persistence of construed descriptions of what Batak and their society are thought to be about. Batak, I argue, present themselves to outsiders in a way which is 'miscommunicative', since the presentation strategically omits important details of their culture and thus leads to an incomplete version of their 'local knowledge'. But Batak are not irredeemably trapped in the 'Procrustean bed' of stereotypes; they also use stigmatisation and stereotypes in a 'profitable' way. For instance, perceived as 'people in need' and 'last survivors', Batak have acquired the status of being one of the most disadvantaged people in the Philippines. Recently, this stereotype has encouraged Batak to seek help and donations from local politicians, organisations, tourists, etc. It would thus appear that, after long-term exposure to stereotypes and stigmas, Batak are less susceptible to derogatory judgements and more adept at adopting stereotypes, ethnic categories and labels as roles (Nadel 1956; Goffman 1958). Ultimately, Batak may perceive compliance with externally imposed stereotypes more as a means of achieving specific ends (for example, obtaining financial or food assistance) than as a loss of self-esteem.

THE BEGINNING OF CBFM: BATAK MEET WITH MR MACABIHAG

Presently in the Philippines there is a resurgence of repressive forest policies (see Novellino 1998) reintroduced under apparently benevolent rubrics and acronyms such as CBFM (Community Based Forest Management) agreements. CBFM is a DENR (Department of Environment and Natural Resources) policy that allows local communities to manage forests that have been converted to non-timber uses. Its ultimate objective is to develop self-sustaining production systems in the uplands by substituting indigenous swidden practices with permanent forms of agriculture.

A closer look at CBFM, however, reveals that this policy strengthens government control over indigenous people's lives. Through the implementation of such policies, indigenous peoples' role in their own territory is reduced to that of stewards of the public land. For instance, in one agreement entered between PENRO (Provincial Environmental and Natural Resources Office) and the Association of Batak of Tina, it is specified that the indigenous beneficiaries should

immediately assume responsibility for the protection of the entire forest-land within the CBFM area against illegal logging and other unauthorised extraction of forest products, slash and burn agriculture (*kaingin*), forest and grassland fires, and other forms of forest destruction, and assist DENR in the prosecution of violators of forestry and environmental laws.

Clearly, the contract mandates that Batak themselves must guard their area from their own practices, such as swidden cultivation. In brief, it places under governmental control indigenous forest management practices, and uses Batak as subcontractors of DENR.

But how do government authorities attempt to convince local communities to accept and comply with CBFM schemes? I will base my discussion on a video-recorded meeting which took place in Kalakuasan settlement on 21 August 1999 between Mr Bonifacio Macabihag, a forester from the Department of Environment and Natural Resources (DENR), and a group of Batak from the settlement of Kalakuasan, and will make use of relevant passages and quotes from the video. In this context, I should specify that, before the meeting took place, I informed the Batak of the content of the CBFM agreement, which had been written up only in English. I told my Batak friends that by accepting the CBFM scheme, they would obtain a licence to sell and collect forest products in their own areas, yet at the same time, be forbidden to practise swidden cultivation. The Batak agreed that it was proper for me to explain the problem *before* the public meeting, rather than during it. Subsequently, they seemed determined to obtain the licence at all costs, and agreed not to be explicit about sensitive issues (that is, swidden cultivation) which, they thought, might thwart the final objective of getting the permit. On my part, I encouraged the Batak not to take any immediate decision regarding the CBFM scheme, whether in favour or against.

Summarised below, the case study sequence has particular relevance for the purpose of this chapter, since it shows how miscommunication can be interactionally constituted between 'clients' and project proponents, or speakers and hearers, in order to construct messages and ideas of 'local knowledge' that are intentionally ambiguous, that omit as much as they reveal (see Giles and Wiemann 1987). Often, this ensures the achievement of specific ends desirable to each party engaged in the miscommunication. This is particularly true of so-called 'participatory meetings' and consultations where project proponents and indigenous participants are not always willing to declare their real intentions and objectives. Agreements, in other words, are based on the understanding of the partial information that has been communicated in the course of the meeting.

Unavoidably, when 'background knowledge is only shared to some degree, but is not fully mutual' (Sperber and Wilson 1982: 67), a significant degree of misunderstanding is bound to come about. As Sperber and Wilson argue, 'we all take risks, whenever we engage in verbal communication. At this moment we are taking the risk of being misunderstood, you are taking the risk of misunderstanding us, and yet we proceed' (1982: 68–9). What is striking about misunderstanding is that it is not simply a problem of communication but rather a process which can be consciously fostered (Benda-Beckmann 1993) by both 'clients' and 'project proponents'. Hence, we are dealing not only with misunderstanding but with devices, such as omission, silence, apparent agreement, use of jargon and foreign terminology, and even rhetorical use of ideas such as 'cultural preservation'. Under these conditions, assessing mutual comprehension and the 'truthfulness' of people's statements about their local knowledge is almost impossible or better, perhaps, not necessary. As Sperber and Wilson[9] suggest, communication is a matter of degrees of relevance. An act of comprehension – in order to be successful for both the hearer and the speaker – must 'allow the hearer to go beyond comprehension proper'. Specifically, 'the hearer, by recognising the speaker's intentions, should be made capable of going beyond them and establishing the relevance of the utterance for himself'

(1982: 78). Going beyond the speaker's intentions, I will now attempt to show, may include understanding people's capacity to detect strategies of deception employed by the speaker, as well as their ability to counter-attack in non-confrontational ways that use local forms of refusal (silence, apparent agreement, verbal omission, etc).

SUMMARY OF 60 MINUTES' DISCUSSION BETWEEN MR MACABIHAG AND THE BATAK

1. Speaking in Tagalog, the Philippines national language, Mr Macabihag opens the discussion by stressing the importance of retaining one's own culture. Culture, he emphasises, represents people's richness and should never be abandoned. He draws a distinction between two ways of approaching culture. The first, he claims, involves the documentation of somebody else's culture (for example, taking photographs and filming), which brings economic benefits to the researcher, but not the people concerned. The second approach is to preserve a people's culture by improving livelihoods, which is the exact purpose of his mission. Attempting to show his 'good' intentions to the Batak, Macabihag waves a folder filled with sheets of paper in front of the audience, saying, 'This is your legal instrument, here it is. This is the evidence ... As you can see, I have kept my word!' While doing this, Macabihag mentions the name of the government institutions endorsing the scheme, and claims to be the person responsible for the achievement. To emphasise that this 'legal instrument' stems from the Batak's own desires, he shows them a few pages from the folder and says, 'This is your socio-economic analysis' (using the English terminology). He refers to the information on land and resources provided by the Batak on previous consultations, and later included in the CBFM application as supporting evidence.

2. The Batak do not comment during Macabihag's introductory talk, with the exception of Padaw, a respected community elder, who talks in the local language and encourages the young men to express their opinions. Stressing that young Batak are in charge of gathering resin and rattan, he urges that they, rather than the elders, should be the ones to talk. Batak participants listen and remain in silence.

3. Mr Macabihag explains that with the implementation of CBFM, outsiders will be prevented from gathering NTFPs in Batak territory. To safeguard their rights, Batak will receive the support of government agencies, and any complaint should be forwarded to them. He also informs the Batak that the CBFM document, before it can be finalised, requires the signatures of other government members. At this point, Macabihag tentatively calculates the monthly amount Batak will make

from the sale of NTFPs. He writes his computations on a blackboard, and often pronounces the numbers in English. Macabihag proposes to organise Batak men into a co-operative. He asks the participants to suggest a monitoring mechanism to ensure that each member will be informed about the proceedings of each sale and be paid according to his specific contribution.

4. The Batak do not reply directly to Macabihag. Some remain silent, others discuss the matter among themselves in the local language.

5. Macabihag says he has received information that a fund of 20,000 pesos is available to the Batak. Then he continues to estimate the quantity of NTFPs that each Batak gatherer could collect in one year, as well as the amount to be earned. He urges that Batak participate actively in this project.

6. Some 20 minutes into the meeting, Ubad, the community's oldest member, raises the question of whether the new CBFM scheme will imply abandoning swidden practices. He uses (local language) indirect speech, as he would when addressing his Batak fellows, but also uses the Tagalog word *kaingin* (shifting cultivation) rather than the equivalent Batak term, *uma*. His intention, I suspect, is to allow Macabihag to grasp the content of the question, while giving the impression that the question is not directly addressed at him.

7. Ubad may have achieved the desired effect. Macabihag explains that the prohibition on *kaingin* is a national law, which applies not exclusively to indigenous people but to all citizens. Then he suggests that Batak should make a compromise and choose agroforestry as the most desirable alternative to swidden cultivation.

8. Macabihag's statement is immediately followed by a gutteral mumbling on Padaw's part – a sound expressing disappointment upon discovering the speaker's real intentions. The majority of Batak participants remain silent, however, while some whisper customary expressions of assent (for example, *tamayan*, which can be translated as 'this is right'). The term *tamayan* is here simply employed as a form of apparent agreement. It serves not to contradict openly what the speaker says, thus hiding the listener's real feelings.

9. To support his statement in favour of agroforestry, Macabihag asks, 'How many hectares of forest do you have to cut to obtain just five sacks of rice? For an amount of about 5,000 pesos in rice you have to give up something that is valued much more ... It is really a big waste! Your source of livelihood is destroyed ... That's why the DENR wants to give you this project, to overcome food shortage, this is the purpose of agroforestry and aquaculture. Why do you have to come down to the coast to buy fish? Let the people from the coast come here and buy your tilapia.

This is a possibility. One kilogram of tilapia is worth 60 pesos in Puerto [the capital city]. Combining rattan, almaciga, agroforestry and aquaculture you can have a good life.'

10. It is only at this point that Ubad decides to ask Macabihag how he intends to implement agroforestry in his community.

11. Macabihag replies, 'We will select one area where the people can engage in agriculture. We will put a fence around it so that the wild pigs cannot enter. Inside that area, the people can plant cassava, sweet potatoes and other crops. They can make swidden agriculture there!'

12. Ubad asks whether the people will be allowed to open areas covered by small trees; he is referring to the possibility of opening new swiddens outside of the fenced area.

13. Macabihag replies that small trees may include young specimens of valuable timber, which would be destroyed in the process of clearing new areas. People, he repeats, will be allowed to keep swidden fields inside the proposed fenced areas. He adds, 'You can sell honey, every product from the mountains. *Kaingin* also goes together with the other rights you have, but it is limited ... We will give you all the rights, from the surface to what is below the land, the fruits, the wild animals ... all you need to live will be given to you ...'

14. Elisio, a Batak participant, timidly approaches Macabihag to explain how Batak cultivate their land.

15. Macabihag responds in a very accommodating way. He encourages Elisio to draw a sketch on the board and share his knowledge with all participants.

16. Elisio draws four parallel lines, representing a swidden field, and explains how on each strip of land a different crop is cultivated, with trees planted around the edges ...

17. After listening to Elisio's explanation, Macabihag replies, 'This is exactly what I mean, this is agroforestry!'

18. Elisio: 'OK then, [agroforestry] is the same as how we do it [agriculture]'.

19. Macabihag: 'Yes, but agroforestry is done only in one area [meaning that the fields are not shifted]. You may ask why this is so. This is to prevent too much land being cleared. If everyone opens their own plot there will not be enough land for future generations. With agroforestry, on the other hand, the people work together for the same land, there is no need of membership, they all contribute equally with their labour, and future generations will continue to work as partners to keep the same land productive.'

20. In the background, Batak participants remain silent, some whisper apparent assent.

21. Macabihag continues: 'With this system [agroforestry] everyone gives his own contribution and the benefits are shared equally. There are no officials, no members. Your system [Batak agriculture] is good only in the short term, but when the population increases it is no longer sustainable.'

22. Again, Batak express apparent assent, but now try to divert the conversation towards other topics. Ubad urges the young participants to ask questions on resin collection.

23. Unexpectedly two French tourists guided by a Filipino guide reach the house where the meeting is taking place. A conversation begins between one of the tourists and Mr Macabihag; Batak participants remain silent.

24. After the tourists leave, Ubad tells Macabihag that it will be difficult for his people to produce and sell resin and rattan, since outsiders are already involved in this activity; they are harvesting NTFPs in the Batak territory. The legal authorisation for the collection of NTFPs should therefore be endorsed as soon as possible.

25. Macabihag reminds the participants that, once in possession of the legal document, they will have the authority to apprehend illegal gatherers. They need only show their permit to the illegal gatherers, not hand it over. He reassures Ubad that his people will receive full support from the local authorities in Puerto.

26. Ubad explains that his people should be supported with food while engaging in the collection of NTFPs. Food will be needed for the family members who are left in the village, and for the gatherers collecting resin in the forest. Then Catalino, another Batak participant, asks Macabihag to explain how to apprehend the illegal gatherers and seize their products without risking retaliation.

27. Macabihag suggests that in the event of an encounter with illegal gatherers, Batak should clarify that they are the sole authorised collectors. They should request them to abandon the harvested NTFPs.

28. One Batak explains how community members have contracted debts[10] with certain outsiders whom they cannot stop from gathering NTFPs in the area. Now more Batak become involved in the conversation. Most of them seem very keen to discuss issues related to the price and marketing of the NTFPs. No one brings the issue of agroforestry and swidden cultivation back into the discussion. Ernesto suggests that *balktik* resin should be delivered only when a fair price has been agreed with the buyers. Alternatively, the resin should be stored until the price goes up. Other issues relate to the utilisation of large fallen trees.

29. Macabihag ends the meeting by showing again a copy of the CBFM document. 'I am not hiding these documents from you,' he says. 'You

keep a copy of this, your rights are all mentioned here ... So do you understand now? ... You have your own land ...' Macabihag ends by asking Batak to repair the roof of the hut where the meeting has taken place, the hut will be converted into a store house for NTFPs.

UNDERSTANDING THE CASE STUDIES

A number of conclusions can be drawn. First of all, it was not the number of inquiries made during the team survey (case study 1) which bothered the Batak respondents, rather they were frustrated by the fact that there seemed to be no way they could express their real problems and aspirations. Rather, they were forced 'to confess' their needs using the standardised vocabulary the visiting team imposed. Similarly, in the second case study, Macabihag welcomes Elisio's disclosure of certain aspects of Batak agricultural practices (paragraphs 14–16). Elisio knows that the issue of shifting cultivation is a sensitive one, but he is again encouraged by Macabihag 'to confess' aspects of his knowledge.

It is appropriate here to recall Foucault's argument that 'confession' is a strategic disciplinary tool not only for the control of bodies and population, but of society itself. Writing on 'confessional technology', Foucault argues that,

the confession has spread its effects far and wide. It plays a part in justice, medicine, education, family relationships and love relationships, in the most ordinary affairs of everyday life, and in the most solemn rites; one confesses one's crimes, one's sins, one's thoughts and desires, one's illnesses and troubles. One admits to oneself, in pleasure and in pain, things it would be impossible to tell anyone else ... (quoted in Dreyfus and Rabinow 1982: 1)

For Foucault, 'the key to the technology of the self is the belief that one can, with the help of experts, tell the truth about oneself' (1982: 175).

Developers, NGOs and conservationists also exercise a special form of power, a form Foucault defines as 'pastoral power'. This power 'cannot be exercised without knowing the inside of people's minds, without exploring their souls, without making them reveal their innermost secrets' (1982: 214). Similarly, in the practice of development, through participatory meetings and consultations, indigenous people are often lured into the belief that their own knowledge can finally be disclosed to them and made 'useful' *if it is confessed in front of a body of experts* (Novellino 1997). This technique, however, also represents a central component in the art of 'seduction'. According to Baudrillard (1988: 160), 'to seduce is to divert the other from his truth' and to draw him or her 'within your area of weakness, which will also be his or hers'

(1988: 162). It follows that to seduce[11] is to weaken, that is, to convince the other to withdraw his knowledge after confessing it.

To explain how this strategy works in relation to development projects, a few more words are needed. Several times during fieldwork in the Philippines, I have witnessed participatory consultations where project planners, before an audience of indigenous participants, claimed their ignorance about indigenous local knowledge. So they asked indigenous participants to reveal and explain (like Macabihag does with Elisio). I would argue that this specific form of 'seduction' is close to dissimulation in that it pretends 'not to have what one has' (Baudrillard 1988: 167). Often, 'simulation' and 'dissimulation' are common attitudes displayed by project planners when dealing with indigenous informants. As Baudrillard puts it, 'to dissimulate is to feign not to have what one has. To simulate is to feign to have what one hasn't. One implies a presence, the other an absence' (Baudrillard 1988: 167). As often seen, development workers have the ability to display both attitudes at different times, depending on the circumstances. For instance, they may assert that they possess the sustainable technologies and technical expertise that indigenous people do not have. On other occasions, when 'seduction' takes place, they may resort to the alternative strategy of pretending to be genuinely interested in indigenous practices and local knowledge, thus feigning ignorance. By exhibiting their lack of understanding about 'traditional' practices, developers often succeed in persuading the other 'to confess' their local knowledge.

But there is a twist to the tale. After indigenous explanations of local practices have been provided to the 'experts', these practices are no longer regarded as a 'confession of wisdom' but rather as a 'confession of ignorance'[12] (Hobart 1993). This is quite evident in the second case study (paragraphs 19–21). After listening to Elisio and apparently agreeing with him, Macabihag suggests that Batak agricultural practices are not sustainable, and hence should be changed with imported agroforestry models. By confessing their 'local knowledge', indigenous participants become 'weaker and weaker'. The more they talk (or are forced to talk), 'the more science knows [and] the one who listens and interprets becomes a master of the truth' (Dreyfus and Rabinow 1982: 179). What we are witnessing in the case studies is a spectacular manipulation which aims to control the knowledge 'others' possess. The final and most pernicious stage of this 'seduction' is to convince the 'others' to accept their ignorance, in this case, their inability to manage forest resources in a proper and ecologically sustainable way. Perhaps this is why after listening to the account of Elisio, Macabihag attempts to convince Batak that their agricultural practices are not compatible with population increase (paragraphs 19–21). At first, Macabihag pretends that Batak agriculture is almost like his proposed model of agroforestry (paragraph 17), which Elisio appears to accept (paragraph 18), but he then adds that the former still needs to be improved to resemble the latter (paragraph 19). As Dreyfus and Rabinow note, according to Foucault, 'not only confession of madness, but also the patient's own recognition of madness, were the essential dimension of the cure' proposed by mid-nineteenth century psychiatrists. The corollary of this is that development 'experts' routinely redefine traditional practices according to conventional criteria of sustainability and 'ecological soundness'. In so doing, 'experts' extract, select and readjust meanings from indigenous 'local knowledge', which is 'not diverted from its truth but towards it and so it is made to say what it did not wish to say' (Baudrillard 1988: 149). Significantly therefore, when Batak realise that Macabihag's objective contradicts their own desire, they prefer to move the discussion towards other issues (see paragraphs 24, 26, 28), rather than attempt to defend the point of view Elisio expressed.

By way of a further reflection, it is fair to suggest that misunderstanding between 'clients' and 'project proponents' can be intentionally fostered by the latter to the extent that deception becomes a salient, even desirable, ingredient, which steers the conversation towards a specific end. For instance, Macabihag wants Batak to think that there is a fund available (paragraph 5); he estimates the quantity of NTFPs to be harvested and sold in one year, drawing big numbers on the blackboard to impress on Batak that fortunes await (paragraph 3). He also shows the 'legal document' as proof that Batak rights are recognised, that they are the 'owners' of their land (paragraphs 13, 29) while, in reality, the document still needs additional signatures before it can be finalised (paragraph 3). Macabihag uses deception instrumentally to seduce the clients to 'participate'. In addition, Macabihag computes the expected yearly income from NTFPs without taking into account significant yield fluctuations, nor does he consider that this Batak population has decreased since the original census. His computations are far too optimistic. Macabihag also uses deception at the very beginning of the conversation (paragraph 1), when stressing the importance of protecting one's culture. In doing so, he tries to induce (and seduce) the hearers to form positive opinions and to adopt a positive stand towards the proposed activities. Macabihag thus attempts to induce indigenous participants 'to behave in a desired way by manipulatively employing linguistic means, thereby instrumentalizing' (Habermas 1998: 121) Batak for their own success. Borrowing from Habermas (1998), I propose that Macabihag's talk be regarded as an example of 'strategic' action oriented toward success 'following rules of rational choice' (1998: 118). This precludes that Batak engage in communicative actions, 'co-ordinated not through egocentric calculations of success but through acts of reaching understanding' (1998: 118). In this respect, it is significant that Macabihag uses English words (for example, report, socio-economic assessment, minutes, agenda, agroforestry, livelihood, aquaculture, instrument, etc.) and acronyms (CENRO, PENRO, etc.) that are not readily identifiable by the participants. This enhances the likelihood that misunderstanding will occur.

But Batak are not passive objects of verbal deception and manipulation. On the contrary, both Batak and Macabihag appear to co-operate in constructing messages that are ambiguous, that omit as much as they reveal (see Giles and Wiemann 1987). The two parties are careful not to reveal their real intentions to each other. Macabihag avoids showing or translating for the Batak the portion of the CBFM document where the prohibition to open swidden fields is clearly stated. He only talks about the national law forbidding shifting cultivation, and he asks the Batak to 'make a compromise' about their own agricultural activities in favour of agroforestry (paragraph 7). He does not clarify that the prohibition on swidden fields is a prerequisite for implementing the CBFM scheme. In other words, he does not reveal that DENR endorsement of exclusive rights to NTFPs is conditional on Batak giving up their agricultural practices. For their part, Batak are well aware that an honest expression of disappointment or disagreement towards Macabihag's 'agroforestry' proposal would jeopardise the possibility of obtaining the endorsement. So they refrain from stating their unwillingness to abandon swidden practices, and either express apparent assent for Macabihag's proposed solutions or remain silent. Macabihag probably interprets the latter as tacit assent.

Through silence and the expression of apparent agreement however, Batak enact important features of their moral categories, outlined at the beginning of this chapter. Batak avoid the risk of generating 'anger', they keep the 'conversation nice' (*matilnu arampangan*) since it is possible 'to hate without anger' (*lasay*) and 'to argue without being angry' (*barisbaris*). They avoid antagonism (which could delay the approval of the licence) and, by not replying back, they safeguard their individual will; the will to refuse in silence an agreement which has not been achieved in a communicative way. Whereas communicatively achieved agreements have a rational basis, and truthful agreements rest on common convictions

(Habermas 1988), Batak 'agreement' with DENR meets neither of these. Batak prefer to remain intentionally vague, aware that ambiguity may carry multiple potential benefits (Redding 1972). Ambiguous communication enables certain goals to be achieved, for example, the endorsement of the licence on NTFPs, but not others. It may also result in stereotyping. As we have seen, 'remaining silent' and 'omitting important details' may induce 'others' (developers, conservationists, etc.) to develop 'false' or 'partial' perceptions of Batak local knowledge.

The silence Batak express during meetings and consultations with outsiders, however, is not simply an act of obstinacy or a form of denial. Silence can also be regarded as a valuable space, as it gives one a pause to critically revise one's own 'means of combat' (Foucault 1988, quoted in Best and Kellner 1991) and to compare one's own view with that of others. For Batak, silence carries moral and emotional connotations (see Novellino 1997). Batak possess a rich vocabulary to express emotions, with some terms manifesting simultaneously anger (or dissent) and intentionality. In Batak epistemology, the emotional state of being angry is often related to an intended refusal to talk. The term *mu'uk* can be translated as 'being angry and so not answering back to persons speaking to you'. *Silag*, which refers to anger caused by jealousy, also conveys a double meaning: 'to refuse to speak because of anger'. The term *sawala* too can take a range of glosses, from 'feeling strong dislike for somebody' to 'not wanting to talk', and 'revolting against'. Other terms are also worth mentioning: *batuk* has to do with 'refusing or disobeying so as to defeat the opposition' while *dukut* is associated with feelings of anger or hate, and with the act of refusing to answer or fight when meeting the object of one's own anger. Lastly, the word *balala*, derived from Tagalog, may convey the following: 'not answering when called or when told to do something, which signifies that you are not going to comply with a request'.

Batak 'silence' in participatory meetings may also represent a local strategy to counterattack the dominant discourse (for example, silence neutralises in a peculiar way Macabihag's attempt to master the situation). Silence thus gives the impression that consensus has been achieved, and leads the speaker to reveal more and more of his real intentions (see paragraph 21). Thus, not only seduction fostered by 'experts' may lead to the confession of 'one's own knowledge' but also prolonged silence on the part of the listeners can induce the 'experts' to 'open up'. Even when playing the role of listeners, Batak are seldom objects that the speaker can influence; they are silent subjects and strategic actors in their own right.

CONCLUSION

The increasing engagement of Batak with representatives of dominant society, each with their own agenda and objectives, has imposed 'communicative constraints' as Batak have become aware that 'outsiders' is a category more diverse and heterogeneous than it used to be. While for centuries they have been considered as a set of 'heathens', 'negritos', 'jungle people', etc., Batak do not seem to apply the same degree of generalisation when referring to non-Batak. For Batak, a Filipino is never just a Filipino, but someone who also needs to be defined according to place of origin (Tagalog, Bisaya, Bicolano, etc.). Similarly, a westerner is never just the stereotyped 'white man', but rather defined according to his or her specific role or achievement. Indeed, it would appear that Batak have the capacity to operate an accurate and non-standardised distinction between 'similar others', something most developers and even anthropologists have been unable to achieve. Therefore, in dealing with outsiders interested in 'local knowledge', Batak provide 'strategically adjusted' versions of that knowledge, depending on the category in which they fit the interlocutor (see Novellino 1997). In short, not only Batak practices but also their verbal accounts are 'improvisational capacities called forth by the needs of the moment' (Richards 1993: 62). Now that physical flight from intruding outsiders is no longer possible, verbal responses have come into place. Many Batak I interviewed claim that if they flee back into the mountains, government will regard them as *'rebelde'* (members of the guerrilla). So they are left with no alternative but to learn how to deal with different categories of outsiders. Traditional moral values and culturally specific ways of dealing with fear, distress, disappointment and anxiety are all relied upon to face the new external pressures.

On a parallel level, this chapter has shed light on how 'local knowledge' may be appropriated by foreign 'experts' though 'seduction', showing how seduction becomes coterminous with 'confession'. Confession of one's own knowledge, however, is not the only possible outcome of participatory meetings and consultations. In fact, to reduce Batak or other indigenous communities to passive victims of seduction would mean to deprive them of their 'power of defiance' (Foucault 1988, quoted in Best and Kellner 1991), which is very pervasive and often effective. Thus, during participatory meetings, Batak may employ an indirect speech to express a difference of opinion without risking retaliation (see Brenneis 1987). Perhaps the most effective form of people's counter-strategy[13] to 'seduction' is to refuse to reply or take part in the conversation, but ultimately remaining silent.

Miscommunication[14] between Batak and project proponents is common and stems from attitudes, stereotypes and stigmatisation. However, miscommunication must not be interpreted as always synonymous with 'failed' communication or 'a deviation from some underspecified ideal' (Coupland, Giles and Wiemann 1991). Miscommunication, rather, is a 'creative' form of conversation in which ambiguity, omission, deception and seduction are mastered with competence and '*savoir faire*' to avoid direct conflicts or 'to conduct encounters and relationships in a manner that is adequate or merely 'good enough' rather than excellent or perfect' (Wiemann and Kelly 1981). From this perspective, miscommunication is interactionally constituted between clients and project proponents, speakers and hearers, to construct messages and ideas about 'local knowledge' that are intentionally ambiguous, that omit as much as they reveal (see Giles and Wiemann 1987). Often, this ensures the achievement of specific ends which are desirable to each party engaged in the miscommunication, although adverse consequences (for example, the way CDPs are implemented) may also result.

To recapitulate, local knowledge and viewpoints are liable to misrepresentation in countless ways,[15] mainly because Batak, when talking to outsiders about themselves, tend to exclude from their statements, *ab initio*, aspects of their knowledge which they do not wish to disclose. These 'truncated presentations' of local knowledge, distorted and rehearsed, may have the effect of reinforcing old stereotypes, with the obvious outcome that the search for local knowledge becomes an integral component in a new system of power and domination. To put it bluntly, what is incorporated in CDPs today is not 'local knowledge', but very often the experts' interpretation of people's strategic accounts about their knowledge. This misappropriation (and manipulation) of someone else's knowledge to fit and legitimise one's own agenda and objectives is not only a fraud but also a scandal, a conscious act of epistemological terrorism. Drawing on Foucault (1982), it would appear that 'the will to knowledge' (or possibly the will to possess and master the knowledge of someone else) is intrinsically linked to the 'will of power' or to the hegemonic aim of imposing one's own 'regime of truth'. The challenge is to ask: What can we do to improve our own 'receiving' capacity of peoples' accounts? How can we create the conditions for communicative negotiation and mutual understanding?[16] The answer still lies ahead, while evidence also suggests that there is still insufficient communication between developers and anthropologists. Perhaps this is because anthropology is wound up by the same mechanism of power and knowledge it so nobly tries to unpack.

ACKNOWLEDGEMENT

This chapter is based on fieldwork carried out intermittently from 1 February to 31 July 1993, 1 March to 31 May 1994, 12 February to 30 May 1998, and 1 July to 27 August 1999, while I was a Visiting Research Associate of the Institute of Philippine Culture (IPC) of the Ateneo de Manila University. I owe a special debt to my Batak relatives of Kalakuasan, especially to my *sandugo* (blood brother) Timbay for his warm hospitality and brotherly support.

NOTES

1. To be effective, participation requires a good degree of communication. It is very unlikely that two parties can participate in the same activity without having a mutual understanding of what they are doing. Sadly, 'participation' as it is being promoted among Batak communities is still based on what Hobart calls the 'myth of mutual comprehension', that is, the belief that 'if people exchange words, they understand each other' (Hobart 1993: 14).

2. Working among the Chambri of Papua New Guinea, Gewertz and Errington have described the confusion and frustration local people experience when dealing with outsiders. In their relation with tourists, for instance, the Chambri are said to be 'troubled by the fact that there seemed to be no way in which they could establish even the basis of negotiation, entailment and potential social equality. The differences remained painfully incommensurate' (Gewertz and Errington 1991: 172).

3. For the translation of Batak terms, I have relied on the excellent work by Mayer and Rodda (1965) of the Summer Institute of Linguistics.

4. It would be wrong to assume that desire for individual autonomy is the cause of Batak social fragmentation. The causes instead must be sought in people's increasing participation in the cash economy. Cash obtained through selling NTFPs has contributed to destabilise Batak cultural limits on material wealth and appears to cause social unrest and internal conflict. Increasing pressures from the outside and enduring uncertainty about land rights are also encouraging Batak to be more independent and 'opportunistic'. As a result, customary 'institutional' arrangements and conflict-solving mechanisms are crumbling.

5. In 1993, I witnessed a similar case in the Pälawan settlement of Kadulan (see Novellino 1997), where a 'visiting expert' used a questionnaire very similar to the one used in Tanabag.

6. The gathering of 1–2 kg of palm edible cabbage is made possible through the felling of a 10-year-old Oncosperma palm tree. Local conservationists regard the practice as 'environmentally unfriendly'.

7. With 'local knowledge', I refer not only to its most obvious meaning (empirical knowledge of plants, animals and of the environment in general), but also to people's ideologies, moral values, norms of conduct,

and to that knowledge on which people rely in the course of socio-ecological adaptation.

8. There exist different and often contrasting stereotypes associated with Batak. In the environmentalists' imagery, Batak become the archetypal primitives who do not modify the environment in any substantial way; they incarnate the 'noble savage'. Conversely, the foresters of the DENR may regard them as destroyers of forest resources.

9. Sperber and Wilson criticise Clark and Marshall's approach according to which mutual knowledge is determined by three possible items of evidence: physical co-presence, linguistic co-presence, and community membership. This approach has its drawbacks, they argue, since 'one might need quite lengthy chains of evidence to connect a particular item of mutual knowledge to the physical evidence which supports it, and, in a largely inductive framework, each step in the chain may go well beyond the data' (Sperber and Wilson 1982: 65). They further argue that assessing mutual knowledge with absolute certainty is almost impossible, or at least not necessary.

10. Batak are trapped in a vicious spiral of indebtedness as they often borrow more than they can pay back. They regularly buy food on credit to take with them on trips into the forest, for example, when harvesting resin or rattan canes. When harvests are poor, often because outsiders harvested before them, Batak see their debts increase.

11. For a detailed discussion on seduction, see Baudrillard (1988). Of interest is one of his descriptions of seduction: 'The secret of seduction is in this evocation and re-evocation of the other, in movements whose slowness and suspense are poetic, like a slow motion film of a fall or an explosion, because something has had, before fulfilling itself, the time to be missed, and this is, if there is such a thing, the perfection of desire' (Baudrillard 1988: 163).

12. In a similar vein, Vitebsky has argued that 'the very essence of "development" is to declare an essence in someone else, in order to end their previous state of knowledge by transmuting it into ignorance, a sort of reverse alchemy. If local traditions are allowed to survive, they do so only as "beliefs" and are encapsulated as "folk" or "little tradition" and put into quotation marks' (Vitebsky 1993: 108). See also chapters by Argenti-Pillen and Frankland, this volume.

13. The term counter-strategy is here preferred to resistance. Hobart (1993) cautions us to be aware that talking about resistance is a way of assuming that the people concerned have accepted and submitted to the hegemonic representations that others have created for them.

14. The study of how 'miscommunication' operates in applied development is a vast and relatively virgin research field. I have only touched one corner of it. My argument must thus be regarded as tentative and subject to validation by other scholars.

15. The primary fallacy is that 'local knowledge' can be simply extracted from discussions with local informants, without considering the complex factors underlying the context of communication (see also Marchand, this volume). The second fallacy is that 'local knowledge' can be understood by being

there, visiting an area, taking notes, documenting and memorising all that the eyes can grasp. In both approaches, local knowledge either slips from view completely, or is interpreted too narrowly and imprecisely to be of any use at all. Often the tendency among development workers is that of equating 'seeing' with 'knowing'. For instance, to see a Batak field under fallow is sufficient reason for the 'forester' to 'know' that the area has been depleted and thus that it needs restoration. But, as Ingold has argued, 'seeing is qualitatively distinct from knowing, for whereas the former consists in the receipt, by the private human subject, of transitory and meaningless sense data, the latter consists of the ordering of these data into commonly held and enduring conceptual categories. Only then do we know what we see' (Ingold 1986: 44).

16. The reader may be disappointed because I have not offered any remedial prescription on how to enhance mutual understanding and communicative agreements between development workers and local communities. Any attempt in that direction, however, would require consideration of certain fundamental theoretical themes: the debate on rationality and relativism (Wilson 1974; Horton and Finnegan 1973; Goodman 1978; Hollis and Lukes 1982), and specifically the debates on metaphor (Salmond 1982; Fernandez 1991), and on communication and commensurability (Overing 1985). This cannot be done within the space allowed.

REFERENCES

Baudrillard, J. (1988) *Jean Baudrillard – Selected Writings*, ed. M. Poster (Cambridge: Polity Press)

Benda-Beckmann, F. von (1993) 'Scapegoat and Magic Charm: Law in development theory and practice', in Hobart, M. (ed.), *An Anthropological Critique of Development: the Growth of Ignorance* (London: Routledge)

Best, S. and D. Kellner (1991) *Post-Modern Theory. Critical Interrogations* (London: Macmillan)

Brenneis, D. (1987) 'Talk and Transformation', *Man*, 22(3): 499–510

Coupland, N., H. Giles and J.M. Wiemann (1991) *'Miscommunication' and Problematic Talk* (Newbury Park: Sage Publications)

Dreyfus, H. and P. Rabinow (1982) *Michel Foucault: Beyond Structuralism and Hermeneutics* (Chicago: University of Chicago Press)

Eder, J.F. (1987) *On the Road to Tribal Extinction. Depopulation, Deculturation and Maladaption among the Batak of the Philippines* (Berkeley: University of California Press)

Fernandez, J.W. (ed.) (1991) *Beyond Metaphor. The Theory of Tropes in Anthropology* (Stanford: Stanford University Press)

Foucault, M. (1982) *The Archeology of Knowledge and the Discourse of Language* (New York: Pantheon Books)

Gewertz, D. and F. Errington (1991) *Twisted Histories, Altered Contexts: Representing the Chambri in a World System* (Cambridge: Cambridge University Press)

Gibson, T. (1989) 'Symbolic Representations of Tranquillity and Aggression among the Buid', in S. Howell and R. Willis (eds), *Societies at Peace* (London: Routledge)

Giles, H. and J.M. Wiemann (1987) 'Language, Social Comparison and Power', in C. Berger and S. Chaffee (eds), *The Handbook of Communication Science* (Newbury Park: Sage), pp. 350–84

Goodman, N. (1978) *Ways of Worldmaking* (Brighton: Harvester Press)

Goffman, I. (1958) *The Presentation of the Self in Everyday Life* (New York: Doubleday)

Habermas, J. (1998) *On the Pragmatic of Communication*, ed. Maeve Cooke (Cambridge, Mass.: The MIT Press)

Haribon-Pälawan and IUCN (1996) *Sustainable Utilization of Non-timber Forest Products, Phase I: Final Report* (Pälawan, Philippines)

Hobart, M. (1993) 'The Growth of Ignorance?', in M. Hobart (ed.), *An Anthropological Critique of Development: The Growth of Ignorance* (London: Routledge)

Hollis, M. and S. Lukes (eds) (1982) *Rationality and Relativism* (Oxford: Basil Blackwell)

Horton, R. and R. Finnegan (eds) (1973) *Modes of Thought* (London: Faber & Faber)

Howell, S. (1989) 'To be Angry is not to be Human, but to be Fearful is', in S. Howell and R. Willis (eds), *Societies at Peace* (London: Routledge)

Ingold, T. (1986) *The Appropriation of Nature – Essays on Human Ecology and Social Relations* (Manchester: Manchester University Press)

Mayer, A. and R. Rodda (1965) *Batak-English Dictionary* (Manila: Summer Institute of Linguistics, Philippine branch)

Nadel, S.F. (1956) *The Theory of Social Structure* (London: Cohen and West)

Novellino, D. (1997) *Social Capital in Theory and Practice: the Case of Palawan* (Rome: Food and Agriculture Organization (FAO) of the United Nations)

—— (1998) '"Sacrificing People for the Trees": The cultural cost of forest conservation on Palawan Island (Philippines)', *Indigenous Affairs*, No. 4: 4–14

—— (in press) 'The Ominous Switch: from Indigenous Forest Management to Conservation. The Case of the Batak of Palawan Island, Philippines'. Paper presented to the Asian Conference on Indigenous Rights & Protected Areas, Kundasang, 14–17 December 1998, Sabah, Malaysia

Overing, J. (ed.) (1985) *Reason and Morality* (ASA Monograph 24) (London: Tavistock)

Redding, M.J. (1972) *Communication with the Organization* (New York: Industrial Communication Council)

Richards, P. (1993) 'Cultivation: Knowledge or performance?', in M. Hobart (ed.), *An Anthropological Critique of Development: the Growth of Ignorance* (London: Routledge)

Robarchek, C.A. (1989) 'Hobbesian and Rousseauan Images of Man: Autonomy and individualism in a peaceful society', in S. Howell and R. Willis (eds), *Societies at Peace* (London: Routledge)

Salmond, A. (1982) 'Theoretical Landscapes – On a cross-cultural conception of knowledge', in D.J. Parkin (ed.), *Semantic Anthropology* (London: Academic Press)

Sperber, D. and D. Wilson (1982) 'Mutual Knowledge and Relevance in Theories of Comprehension', in N.V. Smith (ed.), *Mutual Knowledge* (London: Academic Press)

Tanner, N.M. (1994) 'Becoming Human: Our links with our past', in T. Ingold (ed.), *What is an Animal?* (London: Routledge)

Vitebsky, P. (1993) 'Is Death the Same Everywhere? Context of knowing and doubting', in M. Hobart (ed.), *An Anthropological Critique of Development: The Growth of Ignorance* (London: Routledge)

Wiemann, J.M. and C.W. Kelly (1981) 'Pragmatics of Interpersonal Competence', in C. Wilder-Mott and J.H. Weakland (eds), *Rigor and Imagination: Essays from the Legacy of Gregory Bateson* (New York: Praeger), pp. 183–297

Wilson, B.R. (ed.) (1974) *Rationality* (New York: Harper and Row)

13   THE STILL WATERS OF THE NILE

Stan Frankland[1]

WHOSE UGANDA?

As with the rest of Africa, Uganda makes the world headlines only when it lives up to the myth of the heart of darkness; when an act of brutality evokes an image of (re)primitivisation strong enough to meet the expectations of media consumers and producers. Floods, starvation, massacres and military coups: these are the thematic signs that make up the populist image of modern Africa. Post-independence Uganda has proved to be a fertile source for such grisly images of human suffering, its bloodthirsty history encapsulated by and in the ridiculed figure of Idi Amin. He stands alongside Mobutu, Bokassa and the current *bête-noire* of the western world, Robert Mugabe, as a prime exemplar of the failure of Africa to rise above its 'primitive' past. More recently, Uganda has burst back into the global headlines with the murder of eight tourists and a Ugandan Park Warden at the gorilla trekking centre of Bwindi on 1 March 1999. The world's media descended upon this 'remote' place, locating an example of 'new African barbarism' (Hoyweghen and Vlassenroot 2000: 114), wrapping it up with images of near-naked *interahamwe*. Just over a year on from the horror of Bwindi, more Ugandan gore coloured the headlines red when, on 17 March 2000, up to 1,000 members of The Movement of The Restoration of The Ten Commandments of God were murdered by their own leaders. CNN reported at the time that this was a new world record for mass murder exceeding the previous best set at Jonestown. Truly, Uganda had made its mark on the world again.

However, the Conradian (1973) myth of the heart of darkness is not the only phantasm attributed to Uganda. Among the movers and shakers of the development business and among the political masters of the western world another equally bogus and pernicious fallacy clouds the mind. This is the myth of Uganda as one of Africa's great hopes for the future, as an 'aspiring lion' (Gordon et al. 1998: 62–4)[2] governed by one of the 'new' breed of leaders[3] and heralding the much touted 'African Renaissance'. This undoubtedly positive image of Africa feeds off the history of failure encapsulated within the first myth. Out of the chaos caused by colonial intrusion and the failures of post-independence leaders, hope is reborn.

In this optimistic scenario, Uganda 'has been brought back from economic, political, and social collapse, and has emerged as a key diplomatic player both in the Horn of Africa and the Great Lakes region, as well as a staging point for vital emergency and humanitarian operations' (1998: 64). This current geopolitical significance of Uganda comes after a long period in the political wilderness. The country that Museveni took over on 26 January 1986 had been ravaged by the successive misrules of Amin and Obote. The social, economic and political infrastructures of the country had been quite literally blown away. Museveni's National Resistance Movement Government was faced with the task of rehabilitating and developing a shattered economy and it has been these twin policies of rehabilitation and development that have characterised economic policy since the president took office. With the end of the Cold War, there was no longer the chance of playing the Communist bloc off against the capitalist coalition. Only the West remained as a viable source of developmental income, leaving Museveni the alternatives of co-operation with the West or to opt for a self-imposed exclusion.[4] Museveni plumped for co-operation and adopted a Structural Adjustment Programme in 1987. Since this agreement to follow World Bank and International Monetary Fund guidelines, the World Bank alone has provided 'an estimated US$790 million in adjustment support, in addition to an estimated US$1 billion in project support in agriculture, infrastructure and social sectors'.[5]

United Nations Development Programme statistics indicate that Uganda's economy grew between 1991 and 1995, with an average annual growth in Gross Domestic Product of 6.4 per cent (Hauser 1999: 633). While elsewhere in Africa many economies were in decline, the success of Uganda took on great importance to foreign donors. Uganda became a success story to tell the taxpayers back home, an example of the efficacy of economic liberalisation and provided a role model for politico-economic development elsewhere in Africa (1999: 632–3). Uganda has been celebrated for its economic rebirth, presented as a picture of progress to the outside world and this has been an image that the political world of development has been happy to accept and foster. With the rehabilitation of and belief in Uganda's global image, foreign investment, from both state and private sectors, has poured into the country. Since the early 1990s, the extent of such support has transformed Uganda into an 'aid-dependent country' with most of the government budget financed by donors. As one US official is quoted as saying: 'If you're serious about democracy in Africa, if you're serious about development in Africa, [your programme] should work in Uganda. If it can't work in Uganda, it can't work' (1999: 623).

In essence, as our ideas of how Uganda should progress are seen to be fulfilled or at least not to fail, then further aid is injected to continue that progress. That foreign aid comes in four basic interlocking shapes that combine as the form of development: global institutions; world governments; NGOs; and private corporations. It is the last of these categories that I want to look at in this chapter to see to what extent such private sector developments can be said to conform to the current discourses of development and, in particular, the discourse of indigenous knowledge. In doing this, I will focus on the ethnographic example of the proposed Bujagali dam, a project being carried out by the AES Corporation, the largest independent power producer in the world, with the strong support of the International Finance Corporation (IFC), the private arm of the World Bank. The intended site for this dam is 8 km downstream from the Owen Falls dam, completed by the British in 1954, which is, in turn, a further kilometre or so on from Ripon Falls, the source of the Nile discovered by John Hanning Speke in 1862.

THE RHETORIC OF PROTECTION

While the economic success of Uganda can be seen as a success of development practices, the whole notion of development itself has long been called into question. The Brundtland Report (1987) first acknowledged the direct linkages between development and environmental degradation and brought the term 'sustainability' into popular currency. The Report did not simply reject the idea of economic growth but advocates that development should be 'based on policies that sustain and expand the environmental resource base' (Croll and Parkin 1992: 6). This idea of harmony between economic development and the environment has itself spawned a large body of critiques. The principle of progress has come under fire because it presupposes a 'unidirectional evolutionary account of social change' based in western scientific knowledge; ignorance among those being developed is assumed by those developing by dint of the technological superiority of the West (Hobart 1993: 6). The top-down character of development with the incumbent belief in trickle-down economics was understood as an imposition of one way of thought onto many. From this critical standpoint emerged an awareness of the silenced voice of those being developed and a realisation that 'outside knowledge can no longer be so singularly privileged or knowledge and ignorance so singularly defined' (Croll 1993: 177). As such, the ethnocentric faith of the community of donors in the progressive influence of western management and technology was challenged (Bell 1994: 193).

An alternative paradigm for development began to solidify in which the idea of local knowledge became fundamental. 'Humans create and exercise understanding and agency on their world around them, yet operate within a web of perceptions, beliefs and myths which portray persons and their environments as constituted in each other'; cosmology and environment entwine into a sense of ecosmological holism (Croll and Parkin 1992: 3). Ignorance should not be presupposed and for any project to be sustainable there should be a reversal from a top-down to a bottom-up approach that took full account of the beliefs and practices, the local knowledge, of the intended recipients. This change in ethos was not only among academic critics of development, it has also filtered into the mainstream of the industry. For example, James Wolfensohn, the President of the World Bank, has written: 'We are realising that building development on local forms of social interchange, values, traditions and knowledge reinforces the social fabric. We are starting to understand that development effectiveness depends in part on "solutions" that resonate with a community's sense of who it is.'[6] Out of such realisations, the language of 'alternative development' sprung forth, and with it a vocabulary of certain keywords. Among this litany are the chants of sustainability, environment, community participation and locally based knowledge. These keywords and their multiple synonyms, the rhetoric of the alternative, have spread through the development world, becoming the intended norm for practice and being used as incantations of hope and almost as guarantors of success.

Particularly under the spotlight during this time of reappraisal was the 'ecological imperialism' behind large-scale development projects, such as hydroelectric schemes, that were perceived as a short-term exploitation of natural resources at the cost of a sempiternal degradation of the human and natural environment (Adams 1990). Large dams became notorious for their many adverse effects particularly on the people relocated from the immediate vicinity of the site. The African Energy Policy Research Network have analysed four such projects in Africa to conclude that 'the impact on the environment and the local communities should be given careful attention in all phases of the project, from the design right up to its management after it becomes operational'

(Roggeri 1985: 48). Arising out of these concerns, such mechanisms as national and international safeguards and guidelines, as well as Environmental Impact Assessments (EIAs), have been institutionally incorporated into most development projects. Within these operational frameworks, the notion of environment has been expanded to incorporate the idea of the human environment and the rhetoric of the alternative. Uganda's EIA regulations,[7] for example, call for issues such as 'biological diversity', 'sustainable use', 'ecosystem maintenance' and the 'effects on culture and objects of cultural value' to be considered. Local knowledge is now centre stage.

However, along with the codification of operational procedure there exists scope for semantic confusion. How is the new language of development interpreted by the practitioners themselves? Just which guideline comes into operation during a particular project? Such questions are particularly pertinent in the Bujagali hydropower project, especially since the project's architects and promoters can choose between World Bank operation manuals pertaining to culture[8] and indigeneity.[9] As with elsewhere in Africa, the idea of indigenous is hard to specify in Uganda. Multiple definitions of this word exist (see Colchester 1994: 5–9) that tend to incorporate what can be called the three main principles of indigeneity. First, there must be a strong association with land through a close attachment to ancestral lands or, at the very least, long-term residence; second, there must be a definable socio-cultural difference from the dominant/national society, for example an indigenous language; and third, there is the self-identification by the people themselves as to their being 'indigenous'. The World Bank operational directive[10] on indigenous peoples adds on to these three core features the presence of customary social and political institutions and also that production should be primarily subsistence-oriented. Such principles could be said to apply to almost all of the peoples of Uganda, diffusing the meaning of indigenous into a generalised concept that refers mainly to marginalised societies that exist on the economic periphery of the country. Those peoples that cannot be bounded by a perceived lifestyle or enclosed within a specific environment fall outside of the meaning of indigenous and into the more nebulous categorisation of the local.

This is particularly true for the inhabitants of the area to be affected by the Bujagali project along the banks of the Victoria Nile. The building of the Owen Falls dam during the late 1940s had enabled the river valley to be opened up for habitation and agriculture because of the eradication of the *mbwa* fly and the onochocerciasis (river blindness) it caused. This colonial action resulted in an influx of migrants from all over the country, attracted by the available land in the cotton-growing centre of Uganda

(Robertson 1986: 48). The Baganda make up the majority on the west bank, while on the east bank the Basoga do likewise, yet the general population is 'the most heterogeneous population in the whole of Uganda'.[11] In a report from the 'panel of experts' hired by AES to oversee the project, one of the enumerators who carried out the EIA is quoted as saying: 'Every ethnic group in Uganda lives there. They speak all the different languages and move back and forth between them in the same sentence. They all marry each other and live side by side without any problem. It is a lesson for the rest of Uganda.'[12]

In this pluralist scenario, there would appear to be no easily definable sense of indigeneity. As such, national and international guidelines pertaining to the indigenous have not been understood as necessary in relation to the Bujagali hydropower project. Instead, the more nebulous concept of 'culture' comes into play and with it a less demanding set of guidelines to follow. In the World Bank's *Framework for Action* on culture and sustainable development, culture is described as possessing 'creative expression, community practices, and material or built forms'.[13] Another World Bank document,[14] however, introduces the terms 'cultural property' and 'cultural heritage', defining them as 'the present manifestations of the human past'. It is this diminished view of culture as a museum piece as opposed to the idea of it as an ongoing creative process that has made it into the World Bank's operational policy.[15] Ultimately, however, the responsibility towards culture lies with the government of the country in which the project is located. Central to this self-responsibility are Uganda's own guidelines and the practice of Environmental Impact Assessments. A project cannot go ahead until the National Environment Management Authority (NEMA) has approved the EIA prepared by the proponents. In NEMA's *Guidelines for Environmental Impact Assessment in Uganda*[16] cultural impacts are perceived in the same material sense as put forward by the World Bank. All of the seven examples given by NEMA of possible cultural impacts refer to physically locatable manifestations of culture: historic and prehistoric sites; sites of public and scientific interest; the oldest or best example of an historic resource; graves, shrines and current ceremonial sites; and lastly, sites that are 'important in preserving unique ethnic cultural values'.[17] In the same way that indigeneity has to be a bounded entity, so does culture have to be a discrete resource, identifiable by three particular elements. First, it has to be site specific, a property in the strictest sense of the word. Second, there has to be an historic attachment to that place. And third, culture must be religious.

The EIA carried out for the Bujagali hydropower project was conducted within this narrow framework of meaning in relation to culture as property. As such, W.S. Atkins, the consultants employed by AES to carry out this work, identified graves and shrines, the markers of the past in the present, throughout the area to be affected by the construction of the dam. For example, they found that 37 per cent of the plots within this area contained shrines.[18] Despite this proliferation of cultural properties, only one site was deemed to be of significance in the terms of impact on cultural heritage. This site was the Bujagali Falls themselves, the natural resource from which the project derives its name.[19] This location has become the centre point, the key issue, surrounding the pros and cons of the construction of the dam.

DAMMING THE NILE

By selecting which set of guidelines pertains to the affected area, AES have circumscribed what counts as local knowledge within the confines of cultural property. This limitation on what is deemed relevant is further compounded by the two methodologies employed in producing the project EIA. First, there was the quantitative process of surveying and identification and, second, there was the heavy reliance on previous studies of the area. The first method revolved mainly around the application of a questionnaire among the residents of the affected area, which produced the statistic that the Bujagali shrines were considered important in 117 households or 17 per cent of those asked.[20] To say one way or another whether this constitutes significance is problematic not only because it relies on value judgement but also because it relies on a questionable notion of the local. As I mentioned above, the population along both banks of the river is made up from a conglomeration of peoples from all over Uganda. Within this mix, however, the west bank (Mukono district) is associated historically with the people of Buganda whilst the east bank (Jinja District) is associated with the Basoga. On their respective sides of the Nile, these peoples continue to be the majority; in Mukono, the Baganda are 56 per cent of the total population; in Jinja, the Basoga make up 65 per cent of the total. Within this multi-ethnic population the EIA states: 'whilst they ("the shrines") are clearly of some cultural significance, it is understood that generally the population of the area do not attach particular importance to the sites or the myths associated with them.'[21] However, in relying on statistics derived from both banks in determining cultural significance, the fact that Bujagali is a Basoga cultural site is ignored. To assume that the general population might place significance upon an alien cultural attribute homogenises the concept of culture into an undifferentiated conceptualisation of the idea of the local. A generic form of culture that excludes difference subsumes the hotchpotch of locals within locals that exists on the ground and the many cultures present among them.

This meltdown of meaning becomes more apparent when the second means to knowledge is analysed. In the context of culture, only one text was utilised in the production of the EIA[22] with the information given being purely descriptive:

He ("Karatunga") stated that the Bujagali area derives its cultural significance from a hereditary clan leader called Baise Waguma of the Ntembe clan who had his headquarters at the present tourist site. This site housed offices of the most powerful spiritual governors of the clan. Consequently all the clan leaders came to be known as Bujagali. Since the Ntembe clan was the most powerful clan in Jinja, its headquarters gained more recognition than that of other clans. What makes the area even more popular is the myth that the Bujagali have supernatural powers, thus enabling them to cross the rapids at Bujagali using a bark cloth from a fig tree. Due to the existence of the rapids and the proximity of the source of the Nile, the area became a popular place for tourists ... Karatunga concluded that apart from being an ancestral burial ground for the Ntembe clan, there is little cultural historical significance at the site.[23]

Within this account of Bujagali, the paucity of the understanding of both the local and culture as exhibited in the EIA is further revealed. Stressing the importance of the site to the Ntembe clan, and placing that clan within the panoply of other Basoga clans of the region underline the relativity of significance and the partiality of its interpretation. It again renders the simplification of cultural impact to the site area more than questionable. On one level, significance is reduced to that of a specific clan, the Ntembe, while, on another level, it expands it outwards to include other Basoga clans within the wider area of Jinja. In the first instance, the shrinkage of cultural property to one site and one clan reinforces the futility of searching for significance among the diverse population of the affected area. In the second instance, the inclusion of other clans from outside that same area renders that site specificity intellectually bankrupt. The limit imposed by the EIA on where and for whom there should be significance dissolves both inwards and outwards; inwards towards an even less inclusive understanding that focuses only on the Ntembe; and outwards to a far broader understanding that draws in the whole of Busoga.

Although the EIA does not pursue this line, preferring to exclude the implications of the information it actually gives, the reference to other Basoga clans draws attention to a wider conceptualisation of cultural practices that includes the ideal of the Basoga as a unified people. This is not simply a return to the outmoded anthropological noumenon of tribe, but a realisation of the current cultural politics of Uganda. In 1994, the

Museveni regime reinstated the kingdoms that were dissolved in 1966 by Milton Obote. Although more a colonial creation than an indigenous institution,[24] the kingdom of Busoga has its *Kyabizinga* (King) and its own *Lukiiko* (Parliament) and within this autonomous structure is engaged in an ongoing process of defining a cohesive and distinct Soga identity. As such, the Basoga can be understood as a self-identified whole with an identifiable history and range of beliefs that are unique to these particular people. Despite the wide variety in means and method of subsistence, the Basoga can be said to fit the category of indigenous as put forward in the Operation Manual. Within this new connotation of culture the fashionable notion of indigenous knowledge (IK) enters the scene, accompanied by another batch of World Bank documents and guidelines as well as constitutional rights within Uganda.

The intention behind the World Bank's 'Indigenous Knowledge for Development Initiative'[25] is to acknowledge 'a growing consensus that knowledge exchange must be a two way street'.[26] In this thoroughfare of sharing, IK is defined by several traits that distinguish it from other forms of knowledge: 'IK is unique to a particular culture and society. It is the basis for local decision-making in agriculture, health, natural resource management and other activities. IK is embedded in community practices, institutions, relationships and rituals. It is essentially tacit knowledge that is not easily codifiable.'[27] Again, this re-emphasises the paradigm shift within the rhetoric of the development business from the mass to the alternative. But as with other keywords in this mind switch, a blurring of definitions occurs. As the quote above demonstrates, there is a coalescence with the more nebulous idea of the local. Indeed, in the same paper, 'local knowledge' is used coterminously alongside IK with the site of practice being among 'local communities'.[28]

The problem with these mixed meanings again remains the definition of the boundaries that mark out the local/indigenous from other knowledges. In the EIA produced for them, AES stick with the rigid boundaries of the affected area. This enables them to limit culture to the conditions of cultural property rather than expand it to include IK. And, by ignoring the broader context of Basoga culture in the EIA, AES can narrow the focus of information required to the site specific and exclude knowledge extraneous to this confined space. This is particularly relevant in the context of 'natural resource management' and the Bujagali Falls. Through expanding the frame of reference to the Basoga people a more complex picture of the cultural significance of Bujagali emerges. An elderly Musoga has been quoted as saying 'we Basoga believe that everything on earth; man, animals, trees, stones, water and such natural objects undoubtedly possess natural life' (Balikoowa 1993: 15). This belief in natural life forms a continuum between the world of the living and the world of the ancestors:

Water bodies like rivers, lakes and wells, waterfalls and springs are believed not to exist without spirits in them. They are regarded as dwelling places for spirits of the living dead. It is because of this understanding that near them are places consecrated to traditional prayer. A waterfall like Budhagali[29] on the River Nile at Jinja is said to contain a spirit called Budhagali. (1993: 9)

The *Misambwa* (spirits of the dead) that inhabit natural resources like Bujagali Falls are tutelary deities in the sense that they guard and protect the place in which they dwell. The belief behind these spirits dwelling in specific environments is 'because all Basoga believed that everything on earth was created by God; therefore it is He who gives life to such so that they do not perish; that makes the Basoga call such life of lives "spirits"' (Lubogo 1960: 259–60). In the context of IK, this cosmological harmony can be seen as a form of indigenous environmentalism, as a means of ensuring the continued existence of certain valued resources such as forests, lakes, rivers and waterfalls. Matovu (1995: 138–58) has identified strategies of environmental conservation, manifested through cultural practices and language use, among the Baganda that are very close if not equivalent to those of the Basoga. The Baganda also believe in *Emisambwa* as the guardians of all created matter, both animate and inanimate, and as the conduits through which *Katonda* (God) revealed his plans. 'The implication of this is that traditionally, one never simply cut trees or started fires, or tampered with rivers, lakes or hills, and the like, because one's religious beliefs controlled one's interaction with nature' (1995: 145).

While the EIA may acknowledge the presence of spirits at Bujagali,[30] this deeper understanding of just what the existence of those spirits implies is excluded in favour of simple references to the supernatural powers of the living Bujagali in being able to move across the rapids on bark cloth. This is knowledge that can be gained by any of the thousands of tourists that visit Bujagali each year and in no way can it be considered indicative of quality research. Instead, by regurgitating this myth stripped of symbolic context, the EIA trivialises cultural practice by reducing it to the realm of the fantastic. This poor calibre of research is shown again in the total lack of any reference to what can be termed indigenous hydrology. Lake Victoria is more than just a lake for both the Baganda and the Basoga. The name for the lake in Luganda is *Nnalubaale*, 'which means that this lake is the mother or source of all other spirits' (1995: 146); it is the giver of life. The same reverence exists among the Basoga, who call the lake *Lwitamakoli* and the River Nile *Kiira*. The lake and river are conjoined with *Lwitamakoli* being the husband to the Basoga people and *Kiira* being his 'stick', his penis, and the tool through which *Kibumba* (God) gives life by penetrating deeper and deeper into the river valley (Igaga 1996: 1–10). These sexual metaphors extend further in reflecting a consciousness of the importance of water levels in both river and lake; 'after every swelling of the stick of life, all the people of Busoga witness a hope of life' (1996: 3). The variations in level and flow were cyclical, changing with the wet and dry seasons. Before the construction of the Owen Falls Dam altered the nature of discharge, 'the rise of these lakes[31] and the consequent rise of the Nile begins in January, becomes marked in June, thence dropping rapidly to the end of November' (Johnston 1902: 302). However, the potency of the river could not simply be relied on and changes could also be extraordinary. In the latter part of the nineteenth century, Busoga was subjected to a series of famines due to a number of unusual droughts (1902: 720). The waters of the Nile were not only the source of life, the loss of their power also brought death.

The fear and reverence accorded to *Lwitamakoli* and *Kiira* are also evident in the naming of the two major rapids at Bujagali Falls. They are called after the vernacular terms for the parents of twins, *Salongo* (the father) and *Nalongo* (the mother). Twins are highly ambivalent cosmological figures for both the Baganda and the Basoga. 'The mass of custom and belief surrounding the birth and life of twins made the attitude of parents to whom they were born rather a mixed one' (Kagwa 1969: 108). This ambiguity shows again in the beliefs associated with Bujagali. When *Salongo* roars there will be rain, there will be life, and when *Nalongo* roars it will be dry and there will be hunger. It was for this reason that the spiritual leaders of Busoga came to Bujagali to appease the spirits of the Falls. In describing the history of Busoga, Lubogo has written, 'no Musoga would rebel or refuse to comply with the orders of these spirits or *Misambwa* until such time that the European religion was brought into the country' (Lubogo 1960: 260). The change in religious practices, with the spread of not only Christianity but also of Islam, has indeed resulted in a decline in importance of this fusion between hydrology and cosmology. However, there are still people within the area to be affected by the dam who remember Iseja, the spiritual leader of Busoga, performing sacrificial rituals at Bujagali. Such knowledge may well be passing, overwhelmed and transformed by the products of colonisation, but it has not yet gone. Close by to the waterfall is the compound of Nabamba Budhagali,[32] widely perceived within Uganda and throughout the local community as the guardian and medium of the spirit of Bujagali Falls.

THE ILLUSION OF TRANSPARENCY

Nabamba Budhagali has said that he is the thirty-ninth ancestral head of the clan that owns Bujagali Falls and the spiritual leader of that cultural property (Maloba 1997: 4). Unlike other clan heads in Busoga, his position is not hereditary. Rather, he is appointed by the Bujagali spirit through dreams and by 'outright self confession backed or demonstrated by systematic possession of spiritual portion [*sic*]' (1997: 5). There is more to these powers than simply floating across the rapids on a magic carpet of bark cloth. They also include the power to heal and the power to solve social problems such as impotence, barrenness, famine and food production (1997: 4). In a sense, these spiritual powers are further evidence of the IK of the Nile's hydrology and also of efforts to try and manage the forces of nature.

That the powers of the Bujagali spirit are ongoing cannot be contested. This is testified by AES's acceptance of and dealings with Nabamba Budhagali. Not only does the EIA refer to him as the living Bujagali but it is also through the man himself that AES have been attempting to negotiate the relocation of the Bujagali spirit. It is by this act of relocation that AES hope to mitigate the cultural loss of Bujagali Falls. If one was being generous, it could be said that this is a way to preserve a cultural practice that corresponds with the intentions of the World Bank's *A Framework for Action*.[33] That this is by accident rather than design is apparent when the actual processes of development already underway in the hydropower project are analysed. The negotiations connected with the relocation are part of a broader consultative process that encompasses the idea of compensation in general. AES are proud of this procedure, posting the *Public Consultation and Disclosure Plan*[34] on their official project website and proclaiming that 'the report provides a transparent paper trail of consultations held with stakeholders'.[35]

However, by following this trail, we are not led into the open space of honest practice. We are led instead into a hall of mirrors where the appearance of rhetoric is distorted by the substance of practice. AES went directly from government negotiating rooms to the villages in the affected area. They did this without first approaching the local political and cultural leaders of both Jinja and Mukono districts, the two areas directly affected by the dam's construction. When I asked[36] the then leading AES representative at their Jinja office why they had not followed standard protocol she replied that, while negotiating with the Government, the Minister of Natural Resources had suggested that AES should 'start from the bottom' in order to find out whether the project was desired. When I put the same question to the country director in Uganda for AES,[37] he explained to me that it was the tendency of this multinational corporation 'to begin at grass roots because we're most concerned with the local residents and less concerned with upper levels'. He went on to say that it was a 'mistake' not to follow the hierarchy of political de-centralisation and that 'we're trying to make amends' by talking to local leaders but for 'a few years when we started out we didn't'.

Perhaps this 'mistake' would not matter so much if it were not for the actions of AES during that time. By not involving local leaders in open meetings and by excluding the broader segment of Ugandan society, AES created a situation whereby the local population on the river's banks was told only of the great benefits the dam would bring. On my first visits to the affected area, I was struck by the constant repetition of positive impacts the people told me the dam would bring. There was little awareness of any negative factors associated with any dam nor was there any cognition of the arguments against the dam. Time and again, I was told that the project would bring 'free power, new schools and health clinics, and jobs for the young'. Although AES claim that they have never promised anything concrete to the population in the affected area, interviews with the people themselves do not corroborate that claim. A number of the residents of Namizi Trading Centre, the closest to the construction site at Dumbbell Island, told me that 'investors are telling us that we will get new schools and hospitals, and that we will get jobs and free power'.[38] At Bujagali Trading Centre,[39] I was informed that AES employees specifically had told the people there that they would benefit through employment opportunities and that they were also promised free power. During a public meeting on the pros and cons of the dam,[40] the Mayor of Jinja stated categorically 'AES made promises that they will not keep.' The making of false promises by AES has acted as a muting technique, silencing the danger of opposition voices within the affected area. The widely repeated mantra, 'free power, new schools and health clinics, and jobs for the young', bears witness to the efficacy of this technique and the way in which it has supplied the vocabulary for support.

The Uganda country director of AES denies that this was the case. When I said to him that people believe they will receive 'free power', he replied, 'Well, yeah, I'm told that by everyone it's true, but go to the residents and ask them if it's true.' When I informed the country director that this was exactly what I had done and that it was they who had told me of the promises, he continued that it was true that many people had the impression that they would get free electricity but that this was a false impression. He went on to blame 'the LC1 guys' (elected village leaders) who 'were running for re-election last year and were basically saying I'll get you free electricity from NIP (AES)'.[41] Having acknowledged AES's 'mistake' by claiming that it was a misguided attempt to get to the very people who matter most in the project, the country director then turns round to blame those same 'grassroots' for the consequences of that mistake. The rhetoric of the alternative is replaced by a denial of responsibility as word is separated from deed. AES have continually used the rhetoric of the alternative throughout their promotion of the proposed Bujagali dam, but in their manner of so doing they have twisted the logic behind the alternative and corrupted the intentions of it. This is not transparency; it is the illusion of transparency.

By raising expectations to an unrealistic level through false promises, AES stimulated an atmosphere of greed among the local community, feeding in to a pre-existing attitude towards wealth accumulation. Despite the best intentions of President Museveni in rehabilitating the formal economy of Uganda, the *magendo* economy – 'parallel' (Jamal 1987: 127), 'illicit' (Kasozi 1994: 119) or 'regressive' (Banugire 1987: 137) – still flourishes as legitimate incomes fail to keep pace with rising expenses.[42] An example of this type of economy, that began as a consequence of the Economic War declared in 1972 by Idi Amin against the Asians, would be the street traders of Kampala, 80 per cent of whom operate without a licence, and who 'have managed to get a source of income, however meagre, which has helped them not only to maintain themselves, but those with families have supplemented the family earnings' (Nyakana 1995: 215). However, the *magendo* economy is more than just a method of survival beyond the bounds of legality. It is also a means of opportunism, of extracting maximum financial benefit from a given situation. Such economic Darwinism grew top-down through 'the factors of ethnicity, exploitative and closed cliques of politicians and the rich, the vast system of clientelism, and the "politics of the belly"' (Waliggo 1999: 44) to the extent that the vice president describes corruption as being 'deeply embedded in Uganda's culture' (Kazibwe 1998: v). Following the example of the corruption among the social elite, an attitude has grown among the general population in which unethical economic practices have become normalised and 'to steal it, loot it, or destroy it does not seem to effect the consciences of many' (1998: 52). It is within this 'culture of *okuliira mu kavuyo* (literally "eating in the confusion")' (Mutibwa 1992: 117) that the actions of AES must be understood.

The combustible mix of the confusion wrought by AES and the illegitimate expectations of the local community have blown up over the compensation process.[43] Bribery and corruption tainted the whole procedure and involved a great many of the residents of the affected area. These criminal practices are also a symptom of AES's bottom-up approach to development and their desire to be alternative. The problem for the corporation is that having been responsible for fostering unrealistic desires within a relatively undeveloped area they now have to deal with the ramifications of that action. Rather than sensitise people to the complex issue of compensation, the initial enticements of future gain scattered by AES staff among the local population have enhanced the growing sense of dependency displayed towards the project. This attitude can be summed up by a phrase continually repeated by the local residents during the public hearing on the EIA, a phrase that demonstrates a degree of dependency most normally associated with the type of development that operational guidelines were meant to prevent: '*Twenda damu, mutuwe akaife*' (Lusoga for 'We want the dam, give us our money').[44] What could be more transparent? What could be further from the alternative?

RELOCATING CULTURE

The prevalence of this attitude shows up in the events concerning the relocation of the shrines and spirits of Bujagali Falls. As with all other aspects of the compensation process, the relocation plan has been confused by claim and counterclaim over rightful ownership. At the time of writing, the spiritual shrines at the water's edge of Bujagali Falls have become the cause for such an argument. There are now two further claims of ownership put forward for the shrines by local politicians. This is not surprising when one realises that in the EIA,[45] AES estimated that these very shrines could be relocated with an estimated one-off payment to the living Bujagali of US$20,000. In the context of Uganda this is a huge sum of money and the current wrangles over rightful ownership reflect a growing 'gold rush' mentality of local people towards the dam in which culture has been reduced to the level of commodity.

The World Bank's *A Framework for Action*[46] recognises the fragility of IK in the wake of global capitalism and recommends that care should 'be taken not to undermine *effective* indigenous practices'. Unfortunately, this is exactly what AES has done in two differing ways. The first way is through the lack of understanding, the epistemological ignorance, demonstrated in the EIA towards IK. This limited knowledge is also reflected in the second way that AES has undermined indigenous practices by reducing them to the more manageable idea of cultural property. With this reduction, they have installed a western notion of property into an alien cosmology, with culture being transmogrified into something that can be bought and sold, built up and then relocated. Even AES's own panel of experts balk at this: 'The EIA mentions that cash compensation is payable for graves and shrines. This is inappropriate. Compensation should cover the costs of relocating graves and shrines. Individuals should not receive cash compensation.'[47] In Uganda, however, there are no legal restrictions that prohibit cash compensation and for many previous projects in the country this has already been the preferred method of imbursement. And this is what AES have already done as far as relocation is concerned. On 3 September 1999, Nabamba Budhagali initiated a function to ascertain whether or not the spirits of the Falls supported the project. This event was carried out immediately upon the receipt of £1,000 paid to him by AES in order for Budhagali to facilitate the proceedings. At this meeting, the spirits agreed to support the project in principle, but further consultations would be required.[48] As with the rest of the population of the affected area, Budhagali recognises an opportunity to make money, especially when it is served up to him on a silver salver.

There would appear to be no cognition on AES's behalf that the concept of relocation gets sucked back into the murk of corruption precisely because of the whorl of confusion engendered by the actions of AES themselves. However, trust is relative in the case of the Bujagali project. The lack of trust shown towards Nabamba Budhagali concerning financial aspects of the relocation evaporates in relation to the cultural feasibility of such an action. The EIA states 'we are assured from discussions with relevant parties that relocation is possible'.[49] As could be expected, this is supported by the panel of experts who write, 'all parties consulted to date indicate that the spirits of the falls can be moved, but there are specific rituals that must be undertaken to satisfy them'.[50] Quite who these relevant parties are is not revealed to the reader but, as the EIA makes clear, in the end it comes down to the word of Nabamba Budhagali himself: 'Ceremonies are involved and extensive consultation will need to be undertaken by Bujagali Namamba [*sic*] before the ceremonies can be performed.'[51] The fact that one of these ceremonies has already gone ahead indicates that AES believe the word of Budhagali when it suits them to do so but question that same word when it stands to cost them more than they are prepared to pay.

The indigenous hydrology that I have outlined does not in itself preclude the idea of change. Forests, rivers, waterfalls and other natural resources can be considered as sacred places but this does not prevent their utilisation. 'Instead they are utilised conscientiously as a divine endowment for the survival of all the earth's species' (Ezatirale 1995: 93). In a sense, this was conservation rather than preservation with a practical use of nature a key element in ecosmological harmony. For example, Roscoe (1911: 10–13) describes that before a large tree which was considered the abode of a spirit could be cut down, the gods had to be consulted and offerings made to the tree-spirit. The same practice continues at Bujagali Falls. Budhagali is quoted as saying, 'culture dictates that nobody should not cut down trees anyhow or destroy certain types of trees and grasses as everything was preserved' (in Maloba 1997: 4). 'Thus, on each mountain, in each tree, stone, river, lake and similar things, there is the overall owner who usually does not prohibit people from meaningful use of his charge, but would get extremely annoyed when his or her property is handled without care, love and respect' (Matovu 1995: 142).[52]

On the surface this may appear to support the idea that relocation is possible as a pragmatic solution. However, the power that Budhagali has as the guardian of the spirits is derived from both the long-standing historic associations with and intrinsic qualities of the Falls. The name of the place itself changed from Ivunamba to Bujagali in honour of the like-named spirit and the overwhelming powers manifested through the ancestral heads. The ability of the Budhagali clan leaders to heal and to solve social problems is directly associated with the properties of the water of the Falls (Maloba 1997: 4). The fact that a specific set of beliefs is bound to a specific location raises a number of questions. How and where does one relocate such beliefs? To another set of Falls with its own spirits, waters and traditions? Ezatirale writes, 'It is impossible to conserve the environment of say the Madi, Acholi, etc., in a foreign culture' (Ezatirale 1995: 95). The same is true of culture and, in the context of Bujagali, relocation has the appearance of being a western solution based on the premise of culture as property that fails to understand a non-western system of belief. Despite his assertions that it will be possible to relocate the spirits, Budhagali seems aware of the con-sequences of such an act. He has said that 'development is to modify but not to destroy' (in Maloba 1997: 5) and is even more direct in a letter to AES in which he refers to the corporation as 'the one who wants to destroy us'.[53] Suitably, AES have proposed that a Bujagali Museum should be built and that there should be an annual day of remembrance and that this will 'heighten awareness of the spirits in the future much more than they are now or have been in the recent past'.[54] They too seem to be saying that relocation will turn culture into a museum piece and transform living practice into an act of memory. Quite how the fos-silisation of IK enhances cultural awareness is unexplained. What is certain, however, is that the cultural issues surrounding Bujagali Falls are considerably more complex than is evident in the project EIA and it was a simplified form of knowledge, bereft of context and content that was presented to the Ugandan people.

SILENCING THE NILE

Despite the many problems with the Bujagali hydropower project raised by opposition voices within Uganda, such as the National Association of Professional Environmentalists and the Save Bujagali Crusade,[55] NEMA accepted the EIA on 1 November 1999. Uganda had made its decision in favour of the dam. But ultimately the decision does not lie in Uganda. In the end, responsibility returns to the World Bank. Unlike NEMA, neither the IFC nor the World Bank was prepared to accept the EIA in the form in which it was presented to the Ugandan people. The original EIA has had to undergo extensive revision so as to comply with the World Bank Group's Safeguard Policies and environmental and social guidelines.[56] This is standard practice as most EIAs are, in the words of Dr Clay, one of AES's panel of experts, 'usually inadequate'.[57] One of the main areas that had to undergo a major overhaul was cultural property. To this extent, AES have had to hire a new set of consultants in order to 'ascertain the spiritual significance of the water, and Bujagali Falls, to local communities and the possibilities of providing mitigating measures that are consistent with the way of life of the local communities'.[58]

The revised edition of the EIA is expected to be presented to the World Bank at the end of 2000, at which time it will also be made available in Uganda and through the Internet. This will give Ugandans the chance of a further 120 days in which to deliver comments through the World Bank on the new information provided. Only then will a decision, with further conditions attached, be taken; a decision made with the input of many Ugandans but by the World Bank. It could be said that this decision is an endorsement of that already made by Ugandans. However, the EIA presented to Uganda was so inadequate in numerous different aspects that it provided partial and substandard information on which to base that initial decision. The inadequacy of the original EIA's understanding of culture is not only an example of this simple fact; it also reveals the malleability of national and international guidelines for procedure. Uganda's EIA guidelines call upon the ethic of the alternative, writing, 'public participation has the double benefit of producing better projects and a better-informed public'.[59] However, what counts as knowledge is controlled and limited by AES through the self-selection of guidelines and by hiring the consultants who follow them in preparing the EIA. By restricting the concept of culture to site specificity, the broader context of the ecosmological associations with Bujagali Falls that link in with

Basoga IK is excluded. This impacts on both the range of knowledge included and the mitigation measures suggested in the EIA, a process of inclusion further delimited by methodological weaknesses in research. The consequence of this has been an ill-informed public at best and a misinformed public at worst. But by being seen to follow a set of guidelines, however deficient they may be in this case, AES can wrap themselves in the security of language and the rhetoric of the alternative. As such, all the guidelines laid down do not appear to be set in place for the benefit of the people on the receiving end of the project. Rather, they would seem to be in place to safeguard the project proponents, national governments and international financiers by acting as a defence mechanism against the possibility of criticism.

So here we have it, the Bujagali hydropower project, a project intended to eradicate backwardness while at the same time being committed to protecting traditional practices. On the one hand there is the doubly mimetic development of trying to industrialise the country through hydropower. Not only does this replicate the idealised path of western progress but it also repeats the colonial policy that saw the building of the Owen Falls dam. On the other hand, there is the concern of the alternative with other forms of knowledge as laid down within national and international guidelines for development practice. And it is here that the fundamental contradiction between the two intentions is made clear as top-down collides with bottom-up. When John Hanning Speke first looked down on what he believed to be the source of the Nile, in 1862, he witnessed a truly pastoral scene. Baganda and Basoga fishermen stood on rocks in the river while a ferry crossed over above the falls. Cattle drank at the river's edge and thousands of silver fish leapt, gleaming, through the turbulent waters (Maitland 1973: 170). Colonial policies of industrialisation flooded this scene, stilling the waters of the Nile and silencing the voice of the local communities. The mimetic development behind the Bujagali hydropower project continues this process, transforming the source of the Victoria Nile into one long reservoir, inundating local knowledge with ill-chosen guidelines and drowning out the local voice with a deluge of rhetoric. Words used in the discourse of development may change to reflect more enlightened times, political contexts may transform into the illusion of more peaceful and self-defining times. However, the overuse of words such as 'transparency' dilute the intentional meaning behind such words into a normalised world of sound bite and sloganeering in which the appearance of the alternative is used to cloak the spectre of dependency. For the fishermen and their families along the banks of the mythical source of the Nile, whatever changes may occur, the practice remains very much the same. Decisions are made elsewhere, by others, and for them. In the words of Elias Canetti: 'Progress is made on crutches; we rely on the past rather than push its failed ideas away and proceed at our own pace' (1998: 118).

NOTES

1. I would like to thank the Economic and Social Research Council, James A. Swan and the Emslie Horniman Scholarship Fund for their financial support of my research, carried out in Uganda between November 1997 and June 1999.

2. Gordon and Wolpe (1998) classify African states into three categories that dictate their usefulness to US foreign policy. First and most important, the 'emerging lions' such as South Africa and Ghana which are characterised by 'relatively well-developed economies and infrastructures, increasingly stable political institutions, well-trained militaries, and high governmental capacities' (1998: 52). Second, the 'aspiring lions' like Uganda, Eritrea and Mali, countries that still face significant problems but about which there are reasons 'to be optimistic about their economic progress' (1998: 62). Third, 'the giants in crisis', counties like Nigeria and the DRC that are too big to ignore yet too destabilised to engage co-operatively with. These categories are of course fluid, dependent on changing politico-economic climates.

3. More detail on these new leaders can be found in P. Buchaert, Z. Freeman et al., 'The Movement System and Political Repression in Uganda 1998–99', Africa Division, Human Rights Watch. This can be reached via their website (www.hrw.org/hrw/reports/1999/Uganda). Recent members of this club of new leaders have been Eritrea, Ethiopia, Rwanda and, for a very brief period, the Democratic Republic of Congo. The latest country to have been blessed with this myth was Mozambique.

4. As Museveni made clear in his speech to the Commonwealth Business Forum, London, October 1997, these remain his options. In the speech, he said that the economic transformation of Uganda can be achieved through 'international partnerships by pooling our markets and getting assistance from our friends', but 'if that is not possible, we will have to build our own block in Africa for long enough until we are strong within' (www.tcol.co.uk).

5. Buchaert et al. (1999: 5).

6. Foreword by the President, *Culture and Sustainable Development. A Framework for Action*, World Bank – Idbang.org

7. The Environmental Impact Assessment Regulations, 1998. First Schedule – Issues to be considered in making EIA. Statutory Instruments Supplement, *The Uganda Gazette*, No. 28, Vol. XCI, 8 May 1998, pp. 68–9. UPPC, Entebbe.

8. World Bank Operational Policy Note No. 11.03 – Management of Cultural Property in Bank Financed Projects.

9. World Bank Operational Manual OD 4.20.

10. World Bank Operational Manual OD 4.20, para. 3.

11. Bujagali Hydroelectric Power Project Environmental Impact Statement, Final Report, March 1999, Vol. 1, 4–27.

12. Second Report of the International Environmental and Social Panel of Experts, 22 August 1998, 4.6.

13. *Culture and Sustainable Development. A Framework for Action*, World Bank – Idbang.org

14. Environmental Assessment Sourcebook Update, No. 8. Cultural Heritage in Environment Assessment – wb1n0018.worldbank.org

15. World Bank Operational Policy Note No. 11.03 – Management of Cultural Property in Bank Financed Projects.

16. National Environment Management Authority, 1997, 'Guidelines for Environmental Impact Assessment in Uganda', Kampala, p. 57.

17. National Environment Management Authority, 1997, 'Guidelines for Environmental Impact Assessment in Uganda', Kampala, p. 57.

18. EIA, Vol. 3, 3–12.

19. The actual location for the dam's construction is not at Bujagali but is a further 2½ km downstream at a place called Dumbbell Island.

20. EIA, Vol. 3, 3–12.

21. EIA, Vol. 3, 4.40, 4–9.

22. The work referred to in the EIA is: Karatunga Ali Mohammed, April 1997, Evaluation of Environmental Impacts at Bujagali and Kalagala as potential hydropower sites in Uganda. I have never seen this paper myself so I do not know the full depth of his cultural analysis of Bujagali. The comments I make relate directly to use of Karatunga in the EIA and nothing else.

23. EIA, Vol. 1, 4.236 – 4.238, 4–51– 4–52.

24. In this sense, the Busoga Kingdom is different from the other restored kingdoms of Toro, Bunyoro and Buganda. Those three kingdoms all existed before the arrival of the British, whereas the Busoga kingdom emerged, in part, as a product of the colonial formation of the nation that became Uganda.

25. *Indigenous Knowledge for Development. A framework for action.* Knowledge and Learning Center, Africa Region, World Bank, 4 November 1998.

26. *Indigenous Knowledge for Development*, p. 3.

27. *Indigenous Knowledge for Development*, p. 1.

28. *Indigenous Knowledge for Development*, p. iii.

29. Budhagali is the Lusoga spelling for the waterfall, while Bujagali is the Luganda spelling. Both AES and the media in Uganda use the Luganda spelling so, as to avoid confusion, I have done the same in this paper except when referring directly to the living Bujagali, Nabamba Budhagali. The fact that it is the Luganda version and not the Lusoga that is used by AES can be taken as yet another example of the corporation's confusion over ideas of culture and indigeneity.

30. The original spirit of the Falls, Budhagali, is believed to have come from Sumba island, in Lake Victoria. Connected to this dominant spirit are a number of sub-spirits, each with their own living guardian. These guardians act as spiritual bodyguards to Nabamba Budhagali, the current 'living Bujagali'.

31. Johnston is referring to Lakes Victoria, Kyoga and Albert, all on the Ugandan sections of the Nile.
32. Any information about Nabamba Budhagali not directly referenced is a product of my own research.
33. *Culture and Sustainable Development. A Framework for Action*, World Bank – Idbang.org, p. 7.
34. It is an IFC requirement that a PCDP is produced.
35. www.bujagali.com
36. Interview with Desnei Leaf-Camp, 2 June 1998.
37. Interview with Christian Wright, 14 September 1998. This interview was taped with the full knowledge of Mr. Wright and at no point during the conversation does he mention that any information is off the record.
38. Group interview, 23 July 1998.
39. Group interview, 21 August 1998.
40. The Sheraton, Kampala, 3 March 1999.
41. Interview 14 September 1998.
42. Banugire (1987: 137–51) provides a thorough economic analysis of the deterioration and structural regression that led to the magendo economy. His basic definition is of 'an economy in which the basic needs basket for the majority of the population is several times greater than their formal wage incomes' (1987: 137 n1).
43. For greater information on the corruption of the compensation process see the Fifth Report of the International Environmental and Social Panel of Experts, 26 February 1999, 2.1.
44. Public hearing for the proposed AES Nile Power Bujagali Hydro-Electric Power Project held at Jinja Senior Secondary School, Jinja 6 August 1999.
45. EIA, Vol.1: 7.15.
46. *Culture and Sustainable Development. A Framework for Action*, World Bank – Idbang.org, p. 7.
47. Third Report by the International Environmental and Social Panel of Experts, 21 December 1998, 4.3.10.
48. Nabamba Budhagali gave this information to me during an interview, 28 June 2000. I have not been able to confirm the figure of £1,000 with AES.
49. Third Report by the International Environmental and Social Panel of Experts, 21 December 1998, 4.3.10.
50. Second Report of the International Environmental and Social Panel of Experts, 22 August 1998, 4.11.
51. EIA, Vol.3, 6.15.
52. That this is the case at Bujagali is clear from a recent incident in which the owners of the tourist picnic site at the Falls cut down a tree close to the shrines of the spirits to make the counter for a bar. This resulted in the owners having to pay for a ceremony to appease the spirits at which Budhagali and his followers invoked the spirits through the sexual imagery connected to Kiira with explicit references to the sexual relations between Nalongo and Salongo.
53. Letter from Nabamba Budhagali to Corrie Bell, compensation and resettlement co-ordinator for AES, dated 1 June 2000. A copy of this letter was shown to me by Nabamba Budhagali.

54. www.bujagali.com
55. www.uganda.co.ug/bujagali/
56. World Bank Project Information Document – www.worldbank.org
57. Seventh Report of the International Environmental and Social Panel of Experts, 15 October 2000.
58. World Bank Project Information Document – www.worldbank.org
59. National Environment Management Authority, 1997, *Guidelines for Environmental Impact Assessment in Uganda*, Kampala, p. 25.

REFERENCES

Adams, W.M. (1990) *Green Development. Environment and Sustainability in the Third World* (London: Routledge)

Balikoowa, A. (1993) *Ancestral Veneration among the Basoga*. As partial fulfilment of Diploma in Philosophical and Religious Studies, Katigondo National Major Seminary, Masaka (unpublished)

Banugire, F.R. (1987) 'The Impact of the Economic Crisis on Fixed-income Earners', in P.W. Wiebe and C.P. Dodge (eds), *Beyond Crisis. Development Issues in Uganda* (Kampala: Makerere Institute of Social Research and African Studies Association), pp. 137–51

Bell. M. (1994) 'Images, Myths and Alternative Geographies of the Third World', in D. Gregory et al. (eds), *Human Geography: Society, Space and Social Science* (London: Macmillan), pp. 174–99

Brundtland, G. et al. (1987) *Our Common Future: World Commission on Environment and Development* (Oxford: Oxford University Press)

Canetti, E. (1998) *Notes from Hampstead. The Writer's Notes: 1954–1971*, trans. J. Hargraves (New York: Farrar, Straus and Giroux)

Colchester, M. (1994) *Salvaging Nature. Indigenous Peoples, Protected Areas and Biodiversity Conservation*, Discussion Paper No. 55 (Geneva United Nations Research Institute for Social Development)

Conrad, J. (1973) *Heart of Darkness* (London: Penguin)

Croll, E. (1993) 'The Negotiation of Knowledge and Ignorance in China's Development Strategy', in M. Hobart (ed.), *An Anthropological Critique of Development: The Growth of Ignorance* (London: Routledge)

Croll, E. and D. Parkin (1992) 'Anthropology, the Environment and Development', in E. Croll. and D. Parkin (eds), *Bush Base: Forest Farm* (London: Routledge), pp. 3–10

Ezatirale, G. (1995) 'Approaches to Environmental Problems in Uganda', in P.G. Okoth et al. (eds), *Uganda: A Century of Existence* (Kampala: Fountain Publishers), pp. 84–96

Gordon, D.F., D.C. Miller Jr and H. Wolpe (1998) *The United States and Africa. A Post-Cold War Perspective* (New York and London: W.W. Norton)

Hauser, E. (1999) 'Ugandan Relations with Western Donors in the 1990s: What impact on democratisation?', *The Journal of Modern African Studies*, 37(4): 621–41

Hobart, M. (1993) 'Introduction: The growth of ignorance', in M. Hobart (ed.), *An Anthropological Critique of Development: The Growth of Ignorance* (London: Routledge)

Hoyweghen, S. Van and K.Vlassenroot (2000) 'Ethnic Ideology and Conflict in Sub-Saharan Africa. The Culture Clash Revisited', in R. Doom and J. Gorus (eds), *Politics of Identity and Economics of Conflict in the Great Lakes Region* (Brussels: VUB University Press), pp. 93–118

Igaga, J.M.N. (1996) *Walugerempongo's Thoughts on Kiira (Nile)* (Jinja: Kwala Educational Publishers)

Jamal, V. (1987) 'Ugandan Economic Crisis: Dimensions and cure', in P.W. Wiebe and C.P. Dodge (eds), *Beyond Crisis: Development Issues in Uganda* (Kampala: Makerere Institute of Social Research and African Studies Association), pp. 121–36

Johnston, Sir H. (1902) *The Uganda Protectorate*, Volumes 1 and 2 (London: Hutchinson and Co.)

Kagwa, Sir A. (1969) *The Customs of the Baganda*, ed. M. Mandelbaum, trans. E.B. Kalibala (New York: AMS Press)

Kasozi, A.B.K. (1994) *The Social Origins of Violence in Uganda, 1964–1985* (London: McGill-Queen's University Press)

Kazibwe, Dr S.W. (1998) 'Foreword', in A. Ruzindana et al. (eds), *Fighting Corruption in Uganda: The Process of Building a National Integrity System* (Kampala: Fountain Publishers Ltd), pp. v–viii

Lubogo, Y.K. (1960) *A History of Busoga*, a translation from the Luganda undertaken by the Eastern Province (Bantu Language) Literature Committee, Uganda (East African Literature Bureau)

Maitland, A. (1973) *Speke and the Discovery of the Source of the Nile* (Newton Abbot: Victorian (and Modern History) Book Club)

Maloba, O. (1997) 'Bujjagali the Man Talks about Bujjagali the Falls', in *The Events*, 1(1): 4–5

Matovu, K.B.N. (1995) 'Environmental Conservation through Cultural Practices and Language Use', in P.G. Okoth et al. (eds), *Uganda: A Century of Existence* (Kampala: Fountain Publishers), pp. 138–58

Mutibwa, P. (1992) *Uganda since Independence. A Story of Unfulfilled Hopes* (London: Hurst and Co.)

Nyakana, J.B. (1995) 'Youth in Development: Street traders of Kampala City, Uganda', in P.G. Okoth et al. (eds), *Uganda: A Century of Existence* (Kampala: Fountain Publishers), pp. 207–19

Robertson, A.F. (1986) *Community of Strangers. A Journal of Discovery in Uganda* (London: Scholar Press)

Roggeri, H. (1985) *African Dams. Impacts in the Environment. The social and environmental impact of dams at the local level: A case study of five man-made lakes in Eastern Africa* (Nairobi: Environment Liaison Centre)

Roscoe, J. (1911) *The Baganda* (London: Macmillan and Co.)

Waliggo, J.M. (1999) 'The Historical Roots of Unethical Economic Practices in Africa', in G.J. Rossouw and D. Carabine (eds), *Fraud and the African Renaissance* (Nzoki: Uganda Martyrs University Press), pp. 43–53

LIST OF CONTRIBUTORS

ALBERTO ARCE is a Senior Lecturer in the Department of Sociology of Rural Development, University of Wageningen, The Netherlands. He recently co-edited with Norman Long the volume *Anthropology, Development and Modernities: Exploring Discourses, Inter-Tendencies and Violence* (Routledge, 2000).

ALEX ARGENTI-PILLEN is a Research Fellow in the Department of Social Anthropology, University College London, University of London. She is the author of *Masking Terror: How Women Contain Violence in Southern Sri Lanka* (University of Pennsylvania Press, 2002).

ALAN BICKER is a Research Fellow in the Anthropology Department, Eliot College, University of Kent. With Paul Sillitoe and Johan Pottier, he edited *Participating in Development: Approaches to Indigenous Knowledge* (Routledge, 2002). Other publications include the edited volume *Indigenous Environmental Knowledge and its Transformation: Critical Anthropological Approaches* (Harwood, 2000, with R. Ellen and P. Parkes) and '"We are all French here": A case study of the dynamics of appropriation, incorporation and exclusion in contemporary France', in A. Krynski and M. Szcerbinski (eds) *"Prace Naukowe" swiatowej Rady Badan nad Polonia tom 6. Ze studiow nad Polskim dziedzictwem w swiecie* (Czestochowa, World Council on Poles Abroad, 2002).

ELEANOR FISHER researches at the Centre for Development Studies, University of Wales, Swansea. She is Guest Editor for *Whose Livelihoods?: Community Development and Sustainable Livelihood Approaches* (special issue, Community Development Journal, 2003) and for a forthcoming issue in the *Journal of International Development* (vol.15, no.3, 2003).

STAN FRANKLAND is a Teaching Fellow in the Anthropology Department, University of St Andrews, Scotland. His publications include 'Turnbull's Syndrome: Romantic fascination in the rainforest', in *Central*

African Hunter-Gatherers in a Multidisciplinary Perspective: Challenging Elusiveness (CNWS, Leiden, 1999).

RAMINDER KAUR is a Lecturer in the Department of Social Anthropology, University of Manchester. She co-edited *Travel Worlds: Journeys in Contemporary Cultural Politics* (Zed Press, 1999) and is the author of *Performative Politics and Cultures of Hinduism: Public Uses of Religion in Western India* (Permanent Black, 2003).

TREVOR H. J. MARCHAND is a Lecturer in the Anthropology Department, School of Oriental and African Studies, University of London. His publications include *Minaret Building & Apprenticeship in Yemen* (Curzon Press, 2001) and 'The Lore of the Master Builder: Working with local materials and local knowledge in Sana'a', in *IASTE Working Paper Series*, volume 137, *Traditional Knowledge: Learning from Experience* (University of California, Berkeley, 2000).

ANTÓNIO MEDEIROS teaches in Department of Anthropology, Instituto Superior de Ciencias do Trabalho e Empresa (ISCTE), Lisbon, Portugal. He has undertaken extensive fieldwork in Minho (NW of Portugal) and Galicia (NW of Spain). Publications include 'Estados e Tráficos nas Representações da Cultura no Noroeste Ibérico', in Maria Cátedra (ed.) *La Mirada Cruzada en la Península Ibérica: Perspectivas desde la Antropología Social en España y Portugal* (Madrid, Catarata, 2001) and 'The Minho: A nineteenth-century portrait of a selected Portuguese landscape', *Journal of The Society for the Anthropology of Europe* (December, 2002).

DARIO NOVELLINO is a PhD student in the Department of Anthropology, Eliot College, University of Kent, Canterbury. His longitudinal fieldwork in the Philippines and other parts of South East Asia began in 1986. Publications include 'The Relevance of Myths and Worldviews in Pälawan Classification, Perceptions and Management of Honey Bees' in R. Stepp and F. Wyndham (eds), *Ethnobiology and Biocultural Diversity* (University of Georgia Press, 2002) and 'Contrasting Landscapes, Conflicting Ontologies' in D. Anderson and E. Berglund (eds) *Ethnographies of Conservation: Environmentalism and the Distribution of Privilege* (Berghahn, 2003).

JOHAN POTTIER is Professor of Anthropology in the Department of Anthropology and Sociology, School of Oriental and African Studies (SOAS), University of London. His publications include *Re-Imagining Rwanda: Conflict, Survival and Disinformation in the late 20th Century*

(Cambridge University Press, 2002), *Anthropology of Food: The Social Dynamics of Food Security* (Polity Press, 1999) and *Migrants No More: Settlement and Survival in Mambwe Villages, Zambia* (Manchester University Press, for the International African Institute, 1988). He edited *Practising Development: Social Science Perspectives* (Routledge, 1991).

GONÇALO PRAÇA is a researcher at the Centro de Estudos de Antropologia Social (CEAS) in Lisbon, Portugal. His publications include 'O que faz a "experiência"? – colectivos híbridos no Instituto de Meteorologia' ('What makes "experience"? – the hybrid collective at the Portuguese Meteorological Office'), in *Fórum Sociológico* (May 2003). He is completing a science-in-action ethnography entitled *O Tempo: uma etnografia no Instituto de Meteorologia* (*The Weather: an ethnography of the Meteorological Office*).

MARY RACK is a freelance anthropologist and consultant, affiliated to the Anthropology Department, University of Durham. Publications include 'Bandits and Heroes: the past and the present in Central China' in W. James and D. Mills (eds) *The Qualities of Time: Critical Moments in Experience and History* (Routledge, in press).

MANUEL JOÃO RAMOS is Professor of Anthropology in the Department of Anthropology, Instituto Superior de Ciencias do Trabalho e Empresa (ISCTE), Lisbon, Portugal. His publications include *Histórias Etiopes: Diário de Viagem* (Assírio & Alvim, Lisbon, 2000).

PEDRO SENA is a researcher at the Centro de Estudos de Antropologia Social (CEAS), Lisbon, Portugal, as well as a freelance researcher. His publications on agricultural development and identity in Portugal include 'A Figura do Campino: A Feira do Ribatejo. Feira nacional da Agricultura de santarem como lugar de reflexão antropologica (1936–1993)', in *3a Edição do Programa Nacional de Bolsas de Investigação para Jovens Historiadores e Antropólogos – Beira Litoral, Estramadura e Ribatejo*, Vol 3: 121–81.

PAUL SILLITOE is Professor of Anthropology in the Anthropology Department, University of Durham. His publications include *Social Change in Melanesia: Development and History* (Cambridge University Press, 2000), *An Introduction to the Anthropology of Melanesia* (Cambridge University Press, 1998), *A Place Against Time: Land and Environment in the Papua New Guinea Highlands* (Harwood Academic, 1996) and *The Bogaia of the Muller Ranges, Papua New Guinea: Land Use, Agriculture and Society* *of a Vulnerable Population* (Oceania Publications Monograph 44, Sydney, 1994). With Alan Bicker and Johan Pottier, he co-edited *Participating in Development: Approaches to Indigenous Knowledge* (Routledge, 2002).

JONATHAN SKINNER is a Research Fellow at the Refugee Studies Centre, Queen Elizabeth House, University of Oxford. He co-edited *Scotland's Boundaries and Identities in the New Millennium* (University of Abertay Dundee Press, 2001); articles include 'Licence Revoked: when calypso goes too far', in B. Watson and J. Hendry (eds) *Indirection, Intention and Diplomacy* (Routledge, 2001) and 'The Eruption of Chances Peak, Montserrat, and the Narrative Containment of Risk', in P. Caplan (ed.) *Risk Revisited* (Pluto Press, 2000).

BENJAMIN RICHARD SMITH is a Postdoctoral Fellow at the Centre for Aboriginal Economic Policy Research, The Australian National University, Canberra, Australia and Adjunct Lecturer at the School of Australian Environmental Studies, Griffith University. His publications include *Local and Diaspora Connections to Country and Kin in Central Cape York Peninsula* (Native Title Research Unit Issues Paper vol.2, no.6, Canberra, 2000), and 'Contemporary Aboriginal Population Mobility in Central Cape York Peninsula: the social underpinnings of an "outstation" movement', in J. Taylor and M. Bell (eds) *Population Mobility and Indigenous Peoples in Australasia and North America* (Routledge, 2003).

ROBIN A. WILSON is a Research Fellow in the Anthropology Department, University of Durham. A geo-chemist by training, he holds a Nuffield Career Development Fellowship that introduces researchers trained as natural scientists to social science research.

INDEX

326